Moscow Performances

Russian Theatre Archive

A series of books edited by John Freedman (Moscow), Leon Gitelman (St Petersburg) and Anatoly Smeliansky (Moscow)

This book is part of a series. The publisher will accept continuation orders which may be cancelled at any time and which provide for automatic billing and shipping of each title in the series upon publication. Please write for details.

Moscow Performances

The New Russian Theater 1991–1996

by John Freedman

 harwood academic publishers
Australia • Canada • China • France • Germany • India
Japan • Luxembourg • Malaysia • The Netherlands • Russia
Singapore • Switzerland • Thailand • United Kingdom

Amsteldijk 166
1st Floor
1079 LH Amsterdam
The Netherlands

British Library Cataloguing in Publication Data

Freedman, John
  Moscow performances: the new Russian theatre, 1991–1996. –
  (Russian theatre archive; v. 12)
  1. Theater – Russia (Federation) – History – 20th century
  I. Title
  792'.0947'09049

  ISBN 90-5702-181-1

Cover illustration: Vasily Bochkaryov in A. K. Tolstoy's *Tsar Boris* at the Maly Theater, directed by Vladimir Beilis. Photo: Alexander Ivanishin.

To Alma Law

CONTENTS

INTRODUCTION TO THE SERIES

The Russian Theatre Archive makes available in English the best avant-garde plays from the pre-Revolutionary period to the present day. It features monographs on major playwrights and theatre directors, introductions to previously unknown works, and studies of the main artistic groups and periods.

Plays are presented in performing edition translations, including (where appropriate) musical scores, and instructions for music and dance. Whenever possible the translated texts will be accompanied by videotapes of performances of plays in the original language.

LIST OF PLATES

PREFACE

This book records my impressions of some of the five hundred or so theatrical performances I have seen in Moscow between 1991 and 1996. In addition to the main "genre" of the book—reviews written for various publications—there are a number of feature or news articles which go behind the scenes of some of the most important events of the period.

In the five years I have been writing regularly about theater in Moscow, I have had the unique opportunity to gain insight into the trends and developments that characterize not only Moscow, but Russia as a whole. I have seen numerous productions by theaters from Chelyabinsk to Voronezh, and have been able to compare them to touring shows by many of the top theaters and directors of the world. In all, during the half-decade covered in this book, I have observed the work of about 250 directors for 150 theaters from 35 cities in 20 countries.

As Russia's theatrical capital, Moscow naturally draws ideas and inspiration from the hinterlands as well as sending them outward. Even such a unique vision as that of Lev Dodin, the artistic director of St Petersburg's Maly Drama Theater, is clearly a development of ideas and forms that originated with Yury Lyubimov at the Taganka Theater. Also, even after the collapse of the Soviet Union, Moscow remains a common ground for several non-Russian traditions which have heavily influenced and been influenced by Russian theater. That is why when such brilliant directors as Eimuntas Nekrosius from Lithuania and Robert Sturua from Georgia bring their work to Moscow, the events have an undeniable feeling of homecoming, occasionally tinged with controversy.

Moscow's position as a world theater center has increased manifold with the removal of the old boundaries that once set the Soviet bloc off from the West. Peter Stein's realization in 1994 of his longtime wish to work in Russia was eloquent proof of that.

Russia in the first half of the 1990s changed rapidly, often and radically. Perhaps more than anything, it was a time of collapses—of the Soviet Union, coup attempts, ideals, economic programs, legal revisions, political reforms and even a communist revanche. This had a lot of people singing dirges and, in many cases, understandably so. But another side of disintegration is the ferment and growth which come of it. And it is a fact that, for all the shocking problems of instability, corruption, poverty and war which had gripped Russia by the mid-'90s, the country had taken significant steps toward becoming more open and flexible than it had been since the second decade of the present century.

Naturally, none of these trends failed to find expression in the realm of theater, for over 200 years one of Russia's key cultural and social mirrors. The collapse of Soviet theater—with its encoded, "Aesopian" language telling unspeakable truths, its often virtuosic use of the classics to tackle contemporary problems, and its general focus on social themes as opposed to individual, personal issues—had some observers bewailing the death of Russian theater. What was really going on, of course, was a process of renewal. But like all revitalization processes, this one was chaotic, confusing and often crass.

Many doubted that the directors whose names began cropping up were worthy of replacing such authorities as Anatoly Efros and the Leningrad-based Georgy Tovstonogov, who had died in 1987 and 1989 respectively. Anatoly Vasilyev, after a brilliant start in the 1970s and '80s, disappeared into seclusion at his School of Dramatic Art. Openly admitting that he had no interest in or toleration of the realities of modern life, at least as they were manifested in Moscow, he conducted semi-private experiments with his students while occasionally going abroad to stage shows.

Yury Lyubimov did in 1989 what was always assumed impossible—he returned, sort of, from exile—but it wasn't the same Lyubimov, it wasn't the same Taganka and it wasn't the same Russia. He had his artistic successes and failures in the 1990s, but all were over-shadowed by the bitter breakup of the once-proud Taganka Theater into warring factions.

The biggest crisis concerned playwriting. It was not, as many suggested, that writers had stopped writing plays. That opinion was a superficial misconception caused by the fact that in the late 1980s a few old guard Soviet playwrights did, indeed, fall silent.

Alexander Gelman quit composing industrial potboilers and went into politics for a while. With the demise of the Soviet Union, Mikhail Shatrov no longer had reason to churn out revisionist history plays about Bolshevik leaders. Lyudmila Petrushevskaya, never an officially sanctioned playwright, was able to go back to what she really preferred—prose. She had only begun writing plays because in Soviet times nobody would publish her stories. Edvard Radzinsky found a new career writing bestselling books on Russian and Soviet historical themes for foreign markets.

Thus arose the myth of the collapse of modern dramatic writing. In fact, the problem actually was that the directors raised and educated in the Soviet period did not know what to do with the plays being written and so they did not stage them. Even the younger directors often bore the stamp of their teachers' limitations. In the relatively few instances of contemporary plays being staged in the early '90s, rigid realism, pointed historical parallels and social principles were often forced upon them rudely and with dismal results.

There were a few striking exceptions to this rule, and mixed signs in the 1995–96 season suggested that the situation was on the verge of changing. If that is true, it was thanks in some degree to the journal, *Playwright*, founded in 1993 by the "older" playwrights Alexei Kazantsev and Mikhail Roshchin. That periodical featured the works of Yelena Gremina, Olga Mukhina, Nadezhda Ptushkina, Mikhail Ugarov, Maria Arbatova and many other talented writers still struggling for recognition.

On the whole, however, contemporary playwrights had tough going in the first half of the 1990s.

The reverse side of the coin was the passionate love affair which arose with the classics. The plays of Ostrovsky, Chekhov and Gogol, and adaptations of Dostoevsky's prose were produced in staggering numbers. The approaches ran the gamut from the purely traditional to the distinctly experimental, but there could be no doubt that as the last decade of the 20th century progressed, people were still looking for inspiration and wisdom in the works of the Golden Age of the 19th century.

The late 1980s had seen an explosion of interest in many of the formerly banned plays written in the 1920s and 1930s. Nikolai Erdman, Mikhail Bulgakov, Yury Olesha, Andrei Platonov, Isaak Babel and other forgotten or partially forgotten authors seemed finally to have taken their rightful place in the Russian repertoire. But it was a short-lived phenom-enon. In the first half of the '90s they seemed to die again as quickly as they had been resurrected. The few attempts to interpret the largely poetic drama of the Silver Age of the first decades of the 20th century produced little of lasting interest.

These pages reflect the organizational shifts which occurred with the displacement, but not removal, of a centralized (communist) system. Almost immediately after the dissolution of the Soviet Union, one saw the first appearance of independent production companies and private theaters. They pioneered the search for private funding which federal and municipal theaters soon found themselves scrambling for as well. Inflation, combined with substantial cuts in state sponsorship, hurt most theaters financially in the early '90s. But by mid-decade, state spending on culture was again on the rise, and most venues had found ways to augment their income by renting out space for offices, installing currency exchange windows or opening restaurants or night clubs on their premises.

The Moscow theatrical topography bore several scars left over from the late 1980s, a time when people drunk on the notion of independence often fell into crippling schisms and bickering. Breakups shook the Taganka, the Yermolova, the Nemirovich-Danchenko Musical Theater and others, although the one that set the standard took place in 1987 at the Moscow Art Theater.

This international icon of theater, then approaching its 90th birthday, was the first to let its internal squabbles go public when it split into two independent troupes, both of which retained the right to use the prestigious Art Theater symbols and name. The company which moved into a newly constructed building on Tverskoi Boulevard kept the Soviet-era name of the Gorky Moscow Art Theater. The one which remained in the "house that Stanislavsky built" on Kamergersky Lane soon took the name of the Chekhov Moscow Art Theater.

Several new theaters arose, of which a few survived. The highly touted Learned Monkey, formed from a graduating class at the Shchukin Institute in 1992 hardly got off the ground before disappearing without a whimper. The Sarkisov Theater Group existed for a few years as an independent company playing most often in the Stanislavsky Memorial Museum. In 1996 it dissolved into the new Theater D, headed by the leading actor Armen Dzhigarkhanyan. The Moscow Salon which enjoyed such an impressive start in 1994 never put out a second show.

The unquestioned star of the new venues was the Fomenko Studio, created on the basis of Pyotr Fomenko's 1993 graduating class of actors and directors. The Studio lived through some rocky times, perhaps best exemplified by its 1994 production of *The Puppet Booth*, based on two plays by Alexander Blok. Staged especially for a Paris premiere, it received lukewarm responses in France and flopped when it returned to Moscow where it played only three times before closing. A visually gorgeous but bracingly empty show, it raised questions about the company's readiness for all the attention it was getting. But in time, the young crew proved itself, becoming one of the most successful venues in town.

Meanwhile the physical image of the city itself transformed dramatically. When I wrote about Anatoly Vasilyev's School of Dramatic Art in 1992, I noted the enormous number of abandoned buildings lining Moscow's streets. By 1996 they were not all gone, to be sure, but the city was undergoing an extraordinary wave of reconstruction. In fact, the entire neighborhood around Vasilyev's theater on Sretenka Street was taking on the look of a high-rent district.

Reconstruction of theaters themselves was also in full swing. In 1995 alone, Vasilyev unveiled his spectacular, reconstructed quarters on Povarskaya Street, the Maly Theater reopened its opulent, refurbished affiliate on Ordynka Street, and the Theater na Pokrovke opened a sleek, modern new home.

Readers may note a few discrepancies in street names throughout the course of the book. In this time of upheaval, names and titles seemed to change with the weather, often the result of attempts to restore the original prerevolutionary names. Thus, the Chekhov Art Theater seems to "move" from Art Theater Lane to Kamergersky Lane, Vasilyev's base for the School of Dramatic Art from Vorovsky Street to Povarskaya Street, the Lenkom Theater from Chekhov Street to Malaya Dmitrovka Street. Students who entered the State Institute of Theater Arts (GITIS) in 1991, received their diploma four years later from the Russian Academy of Theater Arts (RATI).

My aim in collecting these articles was to bring the diversity, energy and imagination of the living Moscow theater process—with its beauty spots and warts—to readers who may be drawn to the Russian tradition for any number of reasons. For some, the interest in Russian theater and drama comes from the plays of Anton Chekhov. For others it may be the writings of Konstantin Stanislavsky, Vsevolod Meyerhold and Mikhail Chekhov. In recent times, tours abroad by companies large and small, from the Taganka Theater to the spunky South-West Theater Studio, have brought the "real thing" to audiences who would otherwise never have had a chance to experience it.

Russian directors are increasingly invited to stage shows in the West. Kama Ginkas works more in Finland than in Russia. Sergei Zhenovach has become a frequent guest in Norway. Vladimir Mirzoyev spent several years in Canada and Valery Belyakovich has realized several projects in Japan. Lev Stukalov of Omsk enjoyed success with a dramatization of Dostoevsky's *The Gambler* in Milwaukee, Wisconsin, while Mark Weil of Tashkent (he also occasionally works in Moscow) staged Gogol's *The Inspector General* in Honolulu, Hawaii.

Even actors have found ways to cut across language barriers, sometimes performing (as Oleg Menshikov has in London and Paris), sometimes teaching (as Yevgeny Lazarev has in Atlanta, Georgia, Alexander Feklistov in Toronto, or Alexander Kalyagin in Paris). And yet the atmosphere and the milieu in which these people live and create at home remains little more than an amorphous shadow for most Westerners.

* * *

To describe this time of transition, many observers have latched onto the words "crisis," "decline" or "death"; I generally, though not always, avoid them. At first as an outsider (I have lived in Moscow since 1988), and later as a transplanted "local," I have always been struck by the vitality of the searching going on. For all the pessimism and sarcasm that infiltrates Moscow's impression of itself, I firmly believe that the first half of the 1990s unleashed a variety of styles, directions, approaches and talents which will lead to the innovations of the future. Meanwhile, the best efforts of this short period have already made their mark on history.

Whether by coincidence or unseen design, two of my earliest reviews, and the first entries about Moscow-based shows in this collection, were about productions by a pair of directors who emerged atop the short list of Moscow's best: Kama Ginkas and Pyotr Fomenko.

After nearly two decades of skitting from city to city, creating unorthodox, wrenching and compelling theater in out-of-the-way venues and apartment rooms, Ginkas found something of a home in Moscow in the late 1980s. By the mid-'90s he had gained worldwide recognition for his unique, personal and fine-tuned productions.

But it was Pyotr Fomenko who most universally symbolized the notions of excellence and regeneration in the early post-Soviet years. Born in 1932, and having begun his career in 1960, Fomenko was anything but a new name. He had worked as an assistant with Lyubimov on two shows in 1965, simultaneously staging his own production of Alexander Sukhovo-Kobylin's *The Death of Tarelkin* at the Mayakovsky Theater. But that show ran into censorship trouble, as did his 1967 production of Peter Weiss's *The Investigation* for the Taganka.

During the 1970s Fomenko worked at various venues in Moscow and Leningrad and made several movies of the classics for television. From 1977 to 1981 he was the chief director at the Leningrad Theater of Comedy, but was forced to leave that post for political reasons. He then returned to Moscow to teach at the State Institute of Theater Arts and stage several popular productions for the Mayakovsky and Vakhtangov theaters. But nobody was prepared for what he would seem suddenly to achieve in the early '90s.

Fomenko's 1993 production for the Vakhtangov Theater of *Guilty Without Guilt*, Alexander Ostrovsky's classic backstage melodrama, was a bona fide sensation, the stuff of which legends are made. To a certain extent it had the great fortune of catching people at a point when they were finally getting tired of bemoaning the sorry state of all things theatrical. They wanted to praise something beautiful, touching and exhilarating, and Fomenko gave it to them with a vengeance.

Also by this time, a talented group of students Fomenko was teaching at the Russian Academy of Theater Arts was attracting the kind of attention students rarely do. (They would soon become the Fomenko Studio.) This phenomenon, together with the scintillating *Guilty Without Guilt* and the perceived dearth of quality in Moscow's shows, focused a glaring spotlight on Fomenko as a leader and a savior. When he followed with another dazzling show in 1994, Fernand Crommelynck's *The Magnificent Cuckold* at the Satirikon Theater, his position as Moscow's number one director was confirmed.

It is fascinating now to look back at Fomenko's 1991 production of *Sovereign, Our Father* and at his 1996 production of *The Queen of Spades*, both done for the Vakhtangov Theater. They were similar in that each was meticulously constructed and shot through with subtle detail, although neither expressed everything Fomenko was after. The difference is that *Sovereign* was the work of a respected director, while *The Queen of Spades* was already the product of a "master." That transition is observed in the following pages.

Another name that became a sign of the times is Valery Fokin. After making a reputation for himself in the '70s and '80s at the Sovremennik and the Yermolova Theaters (his 1985 production of *Speak!* at the Yermolova was one of the first to proclaim the arrival of perestroika) he suddenly found himself at the center of a storm.

He was at the helm of the Yermolova when an actors' revolt split the house in two in 1989. That garnered him some bad press, and more of it came with his much ridiculed dramatization of Dostoevsky's *The Idiot* under the title of *The Demoness*. (It was a short-lived show which I did not see.) The howls did not end when he left the Yermolova to found an ambitious international cultural organization called the Meyerhold Center.

It could hardly have been a coincidence that Fokin left Russia for a couple of years in the early '90s to work in Poland, Switzerland, Germany and Japan. The road abroad, of course, was one no Russian artist had taken voluntarily for some 70 years, although it was one that several, including Vladimir Mirzoyev and Roman Kozak, would soon embark on. But they, like Fokin, eventually found themselves longing for the commitment, maybe even fanaticism, of the Russian approach to theater, and they returned.

Fokin made his Moscow comeback with a superb production in 1994 of *A Hotel Room in the Town of N* (based on Nikolai Gogol's novel, *Dead Souls*). It easily turned the critics' former jeers to cheers. His brilliant 1995 dramatization of Kafka's story, "The Metamorphosis," at the Satirikon Theater sealed the critics' renewed acceptance of him and put his reputation more or less on a par with Fomenko and Ginkas.

Other key figures of the period include Mikhail Levitin, the artistic director at the Hermitage Theater, Konstantin Raikin, the leading actor and artistic director at the Satirikon Theater, Sergei Zhenovach, a staff director at the Malaya Bronnaya Theater, and Roman Viktyuk, the flamboyant, prolific and highly uneven director who achieved genuine mass popularity for his open treatment of homosexual themes.

I mention Levitin not so much because of any specific production, but because his theater had a rare consistency of purpose. At a time when almost any theater was capable of putting out a good show, but few were able to create a sense of artistic unity over time, the Hermitage stood out as a house with its own clearly defined aesthetic. Levitin applies to his theatrical extravaganzas the principles of the Russian literary absurdists from the 1920s—the Oberiu.

The name of Raikin is one of Russia's most famous and beloved. Arkady Raikin, Konstantin's father, was probably the greatest Russian comic of the 20th century. When he died in 1987, his son took over his theater and soon indicated that he would not merely be following in his father's footsteps: He invited Roman Viktyuk to stage Jean Genet's *The Maids*, the 1988 premiere of which, starring male actors in all the roles, was a landmark production.

It was not until 1994 and 1995, however, when Raikin brought in first Pyotr Fomenko and then Valery Fokin to create vehicles for himself as an actor, that the Satirikon really hit its stride. By the time Raikin himself produced a sparkling version of *Romeo and Juliet* at the end of 1995, he had proved himself Moscow's shrewdest theater manager and his theater had unquestionably become one of the best in town.

The case of Sergei Zhenovach is rather more complex. Even the casual reader will notice my obsession with him, my repeated efforts to respond adequately to his productions. He has been hailed by some as the heir apparent to Anatoly Efros (one of his teachers) and dismissed by others as a competent craftsman lacking imagination. It is no secret that I am inclined to accept the latter definition. At the same time, I do not believe in absolutes, especially when it comes to judging art. The reader should therefore be forewarned that my skepticism in regards to Zhenovach puts me in the minority among Moscow critics.

Roman Viktyuk, on the other hand, has not been especially well thought of by the critics since he turned from being the premier, semi-underground interpreter of works by Lyudmila Petrushevskaya to being the champion of homoeroticism in theater. There is in that response a heavy dose of homophobia. It seldom makes it into print, but anyone who cares to has heard enough to know the prejudices that weigh against Viktyuk. The quality of the director's work is another story altogether.

As Viktyuk's popularity with audiences—and thus the demand for his services—grew, he began slapping shows together at an alarming rate, often staging a half-dozen or more in a single season, some in Moscow, others in the Russian provinces or abroad. It showed in the final product. While the first offerings of what might be called the liberated Viktyuk had a fresh sense of discovery and daring, the subsequent productions became increasingly superficial and repetitive.

There was a pause in Viktyuk's decline with the heartfelt 1994 production of Nikolai Kolyada's *The Oginski Polonaise*, but it was short-lived. Subsequent outings such as *Love with an Idiot* (1995) and *The Philosophy of the Boudoir* (1996) were so vapid that even Viktyuk's loyal following began abandoning him.

Other directors deserving of special attention are Sergei Artsibashev, Yury Pogrebnichko and Andrei Zhitinkin. The first two, though artists of vastly different styles, both went through apprenticeships in the early 1980s under Yury Lyubimov at the Taganka—Artsibashev as an assistant and staff director, Pogrebnichko as an actor and director.

Artsibashev comes from a small country village, but professionally he is a product of the Moscow milieu, having worked his entire career in the capital. He began making a name for himself after creating his own theater, the Theater na Pokrovke, in 1991. His stated purpose from the outset was to focus on Russian classical drama and, indeed, all of his noteworthy productions have involved interpretations of works written in the 19th century.

Born in Odessa in 1939, Pogrebnichko graduated from the Leningrad State Institute of Theater, Music and Cinema in 1968. While working for Lyubimov in the early '80s, he frequently traveled and staged shows in such Russian cities as Vladimir, Bryansk, Tver, Lysva, Novokuznetsk and Krasnoyarsk. In 1983 he was appointed the chief director of the Kamchatka Regional Drama Theater, where he remained until 1987. At that time he was invited to take over Moscow's once popular Krasnaya Presnya Youth Studio which had entered something of an identity crisis. Pogrebnichko's strange, understated, underplayed and heavily ironic productions immediately gave the theater a new image and new life.

Andrei Zhitinkin is a young director who has parlayed a slick, undeniable talent into a controversial prominence. Often drubbed by the critics, he has had an impressive string of popular hits. In part these shows have been fueled by the presence of famous actors, but it is also obvious that stars want to work with him because they know he will show them off well. The director is also known for happily tweaking the conservative tastes that still reign in Moscow. His treatments of homosexuality and his occasional use of male and female nudity have more than once raised eyebrows and ire both.

As Roman Viktyuk's reputation has declined, Zhitinkin has emerged as perhaps the top author of what are often derisively called "commercial" productions. At his best, as in the moving 1995 revival of Alexei Arbuzov's *My Poor Marat*, he has displayed a fresh, sensitive touch.

* * *

A few words should be said about what has gone into this book and how it appears. The articles are all reprinted from original publications in the *Moscow Guardian*, the *Moscow Times, Slavic and East European Performance* or *Plays International*. Unless noted otherwise, the source is the *Moscow Times*. Dates indicate the time of publication which, in the case of *Slavic and East European Performance* and *Plays International*, leaves a gap between the event and the appearance of my accounts. I have placed the articles to reflect the order in which productions appeared.

Except in a few instances, my editing has been restricted to correcting factual errors, cutting repetitive phrases or removing purely local or temporal information. Because of the nature of newspaper publishing, the *Times* articles were occasionally shortened to fit available space. The versions printed here restore some sentences or paragraphs which did not make the first cut.

A handful of segments differ substantially from the originals. The interview article with Peter Stein is nearly twice as long as what was published, while some of the articles about touring companies and festivals omit non-Russian productions.

The *Times* review of Oleg Antonov's *The Death-Defying Act* has been altered to correspond to what I later wrote for *Slavic and East European Performance* after seeing the playscript. This is an isolated but telling sign of the hazards of writing theater reviews; my original interpretation of some of the play's plot complications (though not its meaning, significance or quality) proved faulty.

In no case have I softened or sharpened my original praise or criticism.

A problem of another kind occasionally arose because my wife, Oksana Mysina, is an actress in Moscow. Consequently, I hasten to point out those instances when our paths crossed professionally. The only show in which she participated and which is reviewed here is the Spartacus Square Theater's *The Joyous Days of Rasplyuyev*. She played a secondary role and I did not write about her. Later, to avoid conflicts of interest and still do my job of covering noteworthy events, I did interviews with her directors, Boris Lvov-Anokhin (*The Aspern Papers*) and Kama Ginkas (*K.I. from "Crime"*). I make passing reference to another show she did with Lvov-Anokhin (*A Heroic Comedy*) in an article about trends in the 1994–95 season.

As for the inevitably clumsy transition which names and titles must make from Russian to English, I always made choices with the interest of the general reader in mind. I tend to translate or anglicize theater names, hoping to walk a fine line between ease of reading and recognition of what is essentially a trademark.

A few venues, such as Theater u Nikitskikh vorot (Theater at Nikitsky Gates), Chelovek ("Human") Theater-Studio and Theater na Pokrovke (Theater on Pokrovka Street) have acquired reputations in the English-speaking world under their Russian names, so I leave them untouched.

Translated names include: Young Spectator Theater for *Teatr yunogo zritelya*, Contemporary Play School for *Shkola sovremennoi pesy*, South-West Theater-Studio for *Teatr-studia na Yugo-Zapade,* Learned Monkey for *Uchyonaya obezyana*, Commonwealth of Taganka Actors for *Sodruzhestvo aktyorov Taganki*.

Anglicized names include: Krasnaya Presnya Theater for *Teatr na Krasnoi Presne*, Malaya Bronnaya Theater for *Teatr na Maloi Bronnoi*, Spartacus Square Theater for *Teatr na Spartakovskoi ploshchadi*, Taganka Theater for *Teatr na Taganke*, ACTors ARTel for *ARTel ARTistov*.

In most cases, I drop the designation of "studio" from theater names since it is usually dropped in general and even official usage. The exceptions are the South-West Theater-Studio and the Chelovek Theater-Studio which proudly hold onto their full names as a statement of sorts.

In most cases, I drop the epithets of "State" and "Academic" from theater names. I anglicize the spelling of some Russian names, such as Maxim, Alexander, Alexei (and their derivatives). I also anglicize a few non-Russian names, such as Heifetz (rather than Kheifets) and Weil (rather than Vail), while others I leave in their Russian form (such as Lia, rather than Leah).

Finally, it is a genuine pleasure for me to thank the people standing behind this book.

Jacqueline Hemmer, whom I met in the summer of 1991 at a performance of the Sibilyov Studio, told me of a new English-language weekly called the *Moscow Guardian* and suggested I write for it.

Betsy McKay, now a Moscow correspondent for the *Wall Street Journal*, was the trusting editor who asked me to hack out an article on the spot and was generous enough to invite me along when the *Guardian* became the *Moscow Times* in 1992.

The *Times*, beginning as a shaky but sincere semi-weekly, soon grew into a strong and popular daily. It has been my good fortune that its publisher, Derk Sauer, and its editors-in-chief, first Michael Hetzer, then Meg Bortin and now Marc Champion, have felt that, in Moscow, theater coverage is crucial even for a foreign-language paper.

I have been blessed to write for talented editors, including Karen Dukess; the delightfully mysterious Daisy Sindelar; Margaret Henry, my friend and soul sister in affairs of the arts; and Frank Brown, a James Brown fanatic, which just about says it all. Others making the *Times* a great paper to write for have been Brenda Gray, Jana Janus, Kelly Leichenko and Katya Turchina.

As the editors of *Slavic and East European Performance*, Daniel Gerould and Alma Law have generously given me access to readers in the United States, while Peter Roberts, the editor of *Plays International*, has kindly given me an outlet in England.

All of these friends and colleagues have made it possible for me to do what for a westerner would have sounded half insane a few years ago: to observe at close hand the evolution of the Russian theater tradition and to make a living writing about it.

Moscow, 1996

PERFORMANCES

1991/1992 SEASON

The Nose, **Lithuanian State Youth Theater**

The appearance of Eimuntas Nekrosius's *The Nose* in Moscow, performed by the Lithuanian State Youth Theater in collaboration with the Moscow Friendship of Nationalities Theater, was timely, indeed. Opening September 21, 1991, exactly a month after the unraveling of the coup and a few weeks after Lithuania regained independence, it created one of Moscow's biggest theatrical sensations since the advent of perestroika. The opening night audience was a genuine who's who of Moscow society while the crowds hoping to find a stray ticket outside the dowdy Pushkin Theater reminded one of the Taganka or Lenkom in the "old days."

Responses broke down predictably. The full houses applauded enthusiastically while critics and "people in the know" whispered quietly that the production was "nothing new": "If he had done this five years ago, it would really have been something," one well-connected person told me, "but now..." Nekrosius himself seemed to anticipate such a reaction in an interview printed in a booklet sold with the program where he called the notion of creating art for the elite "a nice cliché," but "otherwise, nonsense."

Perhaps I was fortunate never to have seen a Nekrosius production, but I couldn't help but feel that—with the removal of one set of political obstacles to art—the dual response was merely a case of politics once again taking precedence over art.

Certainly, Nekrosius himself did not shy from making political allusions. Instead of losing his nose, this Kovalyov (Vladas Bagdonas) attempts to relieve himself of a troublesome attraction to the opposite sex by voluntarily submitting to castration (whimsically achieved by the vicious swing of an ax, followed by the appearance of a dangling pink ribbon to indicate flowing blood). However, shortly after the madcap doctor (played with engaging deviltry by Povilas Budris) tosses Kovalyov's member in a trash

can, the still bloody "nose" emerges in a pink shirt and something resembling a pink yarmulke to pursue its own life and troubles in a new-found state of "freedom." This presents plenty of opportunities for Nekrosius to echo the dismemberment of the Soviet Union, as well as the devastating problems that has engendered.

In one of several such touches, the "nose" attempts to marry a beautiful maiden, eliciting the jealous wrath of Kovalyov who enters in a fascist goose-step and attempts to steal the bride. A comic scuffle ensues, the result being that both of them become her groom. In such ways, Nekrosius teases his audience with the irresolvable paradoxes of a desire for independence and the necessity of interdependence. In any case, Kovalyov's subsequent efforts to coerce the "nose" to return to its proper place are in vain. Standing erect with a new-found sense of potency, and echoing Kovalyov's "fascist" tendencies, the "nose" eventually goes on a rampage and has everyone locked up in trash-bin prisons.

These scenes are far from being programmatic allegories; on one level they may hint at familiar historical and political events, but they neither attempt to represent or resolve them. The "confusing element"—that is, the artistic image that ultimately leads away from politics into the realm of art or philosophy—is the figure of the beautiful maiden who appears in several scenes, perhaps representing a concept similar to "truth," "beauty," or "justice." Naturally, the intent is not to illustrate the complex relationship between Russia and Lithuania, but to grapple with those inherently irreconcilable problems of which the Russia/Lithuania or Kovalyov/ Nose pairings are merely metaphors.

Performed by Kostas Smoriginas with a marvelous sense of naive humor owing much to Harpo Marx, the "nose" triumphantly prances about the stage, humming, squeaking, whistling and spitting water skyward in mock ejaculations (which, thanks to the excellent lighting and a solid black backdrop, form beautiful cascades that gracefully hang in the air). There is never a hint of naturalism in the sexual theme, ever performed in the lightest of farcical tones. And if Harpo served as a starting point for Smoriginas's "nose," the overall atmosphere of a Marx Brothers' film provides the basis for one rowdy café scene replete with fast-paced chases, up-endings and reversals.

Ultimately, *The Nose* is a fantasy that derives only its broadest outline from Gogol's story. Also included are themes faintly reminiscent of other Petersburg stories, excerpts from *Selected Passages from Correspondence with Friends* and quotes from works about Gogol by Dmitry Merezhkovsky and Vasily Rozanov. This provides the basis for one of the play's sub-plots: the role of the artist in society.

The performance begins as Gogol (Remigius Vilkaitis) stands proudly, a statue high on a pedestal in the midst of a wide semi-circle of trash-bins (which, as we see later, are inhabited by socialites, somewhat as in Beckett's *End Game*). A washer-woman bustles around him, cleaning him up to keep him "presentable." When she climbs on a ladder to toss a bucket of water over his head, he pulls out an umbrella just in the nick of time to avoid being drenched. Sub-sequently, he is hounded continually by an elongated barber (Gediminas Girdvainis) who may represent a censor or, perhaps, "good taste": his intent is to make Gogol remain a cold statue on a pedestal. He forces Gogol to lug his pedestal-turned-trunk about on his back and repeatedly clips off the quills that grow on his hands (thereby, both "clipping his wings" of freedom and destroying his ability to write).

From time to time, Gogol breaks loose of his tormentor, seeking release in mad, con-fessional ravings that invariably offend the barber's—and, occasionally, the audience's—civilized sense of propriety. (During inter-mission, one talented Moscow set designer told me with dissatisfaction that Nekrosius had no right to "make" Gogol talk at such length about Russia resembling a bog.) In the finale, the writer is captured in an enor-mous straight-jacket with flowing arms, thus reviving for an instant the motif of Gogol as a bird seeking freedom in flight. Soon enough, however, the arms are wrapped

tightly around him and he is returned, mute, to his pedestal.

With the exception of Gogol's philosophi-cal ravings, language plays an insignificant role in this vividly visual production where the set and the *mises en scene* carry the burden of explication, and the simultaneous translation was nearly superfluous. Nekrosius has clearly found a unique and expressive theatrical language that is readily accessible to all. Whether or not one is prepared to hear or understand what he has to say is a different question altogether.

Whatever the case, I found nothing in *The Nose* that could cast doubt on the sincerity of Nekrosius's statements made on opening night and later carried on Soviet television. He said that he was equally as proud to be the first cultural ambassador of a free Lithuania in Moscow as he was to have the opportunity to interpret one of the greatest writers of Russian literature. "It is a heri-tage," he said, "for which I have an abiding love and affinity."

(*Spring 1992, Slavic and East European Performance*)

We Play "Crime," Young Spectator Theater

We Play "Crime" is the production's title and you can understand it as you like. May-be it means the actors are playing only the "crime" half of Dostoevsky's novel *Crime and Punishment*, or maybe it means they are only "playing" at criminal games. In any case, director Kama Ginkas eventually lets us know what he thinks about Raskolnikov's murderous ideas: They're not worth chopped salad.

This is a production that puts the fifty spectators at the Young Spectator Theater on the hot seat along with the characters. The tiny, converted rehearsal room that serves as stage and hall is just big enough to handle the action. It is also small enough to make you feel that you and your neighbor—like Dostoevsky's notorious flies on the wall—are the only ones witnessing it.

When the frantic Raskolnikov methodi-cally prepares to behead a fluttering, live chicken to prove a point, you don't merely understand an abstract philosophical notion, you feel it and you fear it. When he releases his victim, the tiny hall heaves a sigh of relief in unison. Later, when a murder does take place—cleverly represented by splitting open a head of cabbage with an ax—it evokes laughter in the hall. This is theater doing what it is supposed to do: appealing to our understanding through all the means available to it.

Since language obscures understanding as often as it facilitates it, Ginkas has another effective trick up his sleeve. His Raskolnikov (Marcus Grott) is performed by a Finnish Swede who speaks half his lines in Swedish. There is a good reason, then, why the inspector trying to solve the murder of a pawnbroker and her sister doesn't understand much of what the suspect has to say. What he does understand, like the audience, is what is essential.

The idea for a dual-language production arose when Ginkas staged *We Play "Crime"* in Finland, taking with him the Moscow actress Irina Yuryevich to play the prostitute Sonya (she plays the same role here). She performed in Russian amidst the Finnish actors. Grott played the lead role there as well, and his manic, introspective style was so impressive that Ginkas resolved to attempt something like a mirror-image of that staging in Moscow.

"The result," he says, "was a totally different show. The Finnish production was basically a normal story about a man who overstepped his boundaries. The Russian version, however, took on very different tones, both artistically as well as philosophically."

The shift also owes much to the actor performing the role of the police inspector. Viktor Gvozditsky is sublime as the finicky, effeminate Porfiry Petrovich who clings to Raskolnikov as tightly as his own creme-colored silk suit clings to him. He cajoles and caresses the tormented student with an odd, nervous charm, drawing him ever closer to the fire of confession.

Gvozditsky began working with Ginkas long ago, in another time and another place.

In Leningrad in the 1960s and 1970s, Ginkas was what he himself calls an "unem-ployed dissident." Unable to work in established theaters, he staged plays at home. In 1979, he hooked up with Gvozditsky and they have often been together since.

With no hopes of a future in Leningrad, Ginkas relocated to Moscow in 1984 where, by the end of the decade, he became recognized as one of Russian theater's best directors. Many of his stagings have toured the world, and he is often invited to direct in Europe.

One recent trip, however, may have been sweeter than most. In mid-October, Ginkas traveled to Petersburg to attend a festival entitled "The Productions of Kama Ginkas in Leningrad."

"The word 'Leningrad,'" explains Ginkas, "remained in the title mostly because the literature was printed up long ago. But it only seems natural to me. That town has a long way to go before it can justify calling itself 'Petersburg' again."

The director clearly took pleasure in his triumphant return to the town that once had "kicked him out."

Meanwhile, encouraged by the results of his two experiments with *We Play "Crime,"* Ginkas plans more dual-language productions.

"Russian and Western sources need to be mixed," he says. "Their cultures and mentalities fill each other out."

It is a natural mix for Ginkas. As he puts it, he is a "100% Jew," raised in the Russian culture with a strong affinity for the culture of his Lithuanian homeland, although he also calls himself a "typical 'Sov'."

What he is, by any standard, is a fine director. *We Play "Crime"* is witness to that.

(*Moscow Guardian, October 1991*)

Sovereign, Our Father, Vakhtangov Theater

In *Sovereign, Our Father*, the newest production at the Vakhtangov Theater not counting the most recent revival of *Princess Turandot*, Peter the Great considers his attitude towards Europe.

"Give us 20 or 30 years and we'll catch up with them," he says, before adding to healthy laughter on stage and in the hall: "And then we'll turn our backsides on them!"

Plays about tsars proliferated in Moscow in recent years, but this staging by Pyotr Fomenko stakes out its own niche. The portrayal of an arbitrary and, occasionally, repentant tsar is not what is new. Nor does the picture of a sensitive but spineless heir to the throne add anything unexpected. What is interesting in these days of Russia's most recent turn to the West is Fomenko's and playwright Fridrikh Gorenshtein's interpretation of Russia's first genuine infatuation with Europe.

Following Fomenko's wish to explore the play's theme "theatrically rather than philosophically," Maxim Sukhanov's bawdy Peter the Great stalks the huge stage at the Vakhtangov with a pronounced limp, lugging his throne on his back or sporting a rough-cut bearskin coat. He hardly corresponds to the usual image of Russia's first "European" tsar. Furthermore, the court intrigues, conspiracies and the ruthless manner of quashing them are clearly throwbacks to the medieval Russia of Ivan the Terrible and not harbingers of a modern civilization.

The Christian church, perhaps western society's most prominent manifestation in the production (aside from mannequins dressed in European style and a few other props pushed symbolically to the extreme edges of the stage), is no less atavistic. Priests both encourage assassinating the "anti-Christ" tsar and absolve him of sin when he executes his impetuous son Alexei (performed busily but sincerely by Sergei Makovetsky).

A few select moments clearly, if predictably, indicate that the debunking of the myth of Peter's European principles is not only intended in a historical sense. The first comes immediately in a Taganka Theater-inspired opening where a motley band of jesters stares into the audience calling for reactions from the "people" who, naturally, do not respond. Another comes at performance's end as a "common citizen" plies the troubled tsar with pressing questions. Among them: "Tell us sovereign, our father, where do we obtain oats?"

With its cast of 40 and its frequent changes in place of action, the acting and the multi-layered plot do not always hold one's attention. Indeed, there are times when this three and a half hour marathon seems as long and confusing as Russian history itself.

But, *Sovereign, Our Father* is a grand visual spectacle on a Russian scale. Maria Danilova's expansive set, Pavel Kaplevich's costumes and Fomenko's use of every inch of the stage from the proscenium to the rafters, are a feast for the eyes.

Hanging from the ceiling are several enormous wood tables high above which hang something resembling white cloth stars. From time to time they drop earthward gracefully to form bed linens or, as in the finale, to suggest, perhaps, the souls of executed prisoners and imply the pagan, rather than the Christian, roots of the Russian culture. The dangling tables dance in the air as actors move about them, creating a captivating vision of a world trapped between heaven and earth.

Playwright Gorenshtein has had plenty of opportunity to contemplate the peculiarities of the Russian condition, both as an unpublished Moscow writer who participated in the publication of the scandalous almanac *Metropole* in 1979, and as an emigrant living in Germany since 1980. Director Fomenko himself is no stranger to the Russian enigma. He first made a name for himself in the 1960s, working on several controversial productions at the Taganka Theater.

Said Fomenko, "I long wanted to stage a dramatization of Dmitry Merezhkovsky's novel *Peter and Alexei*. But when I came upon Gorenshtein's play *Infanticide*, I saw that this gave me a more modern source to work with."

Gorenshtein's bulky play, he noted, was written more to be read than staged, and he had to make large cuts in it, while adding snippets from other works of Russian literature to facilitate transitions.

"My main task was to explore the relationship between culture and civilization in Russia," the director said, pointing out that this dichotomy is largely a battle between Russian and European influences.

"The paradoxes and disharmonies of this mix are especially obvious now," he concluded.

Sovereign, Our Father may not be for everyone. But it is an intriguing look at the sources of a culture which prompted Rudyard Kipling to observe acidly, "the Russian is a delightful person till he tucks in his shirt."

(*Moscow Guardian, December 1991*)

From the Life of Rain Worms and Women's Games, Chekhov Art Theater

For many years, the Moscow Art Theater has occupied an odd place in this city of great theaters. On one hand, it maintains the reputation of being the house that Stanislavsky built, Stalin's favorite theater, and the "showcase of the Soviet regime." On the other, it is often the butt of jokes and the most common example of the crisis that, not always justly, many feel has stricken Russian theater.

A few years ago, the theater broke in two. One half, now called the "New" or the Gorky Art Theater, moved to Tverskoi Boulevard. The other half remained in the stylish art nouveau building on Art Theater Lane and is now called the "Old" or the Chekhov Art Theater.

At least the "older" member of the family is showing new signs of life. The recent developments are connected, in part, with the return to the theater of one of its, and the country's, best actresses.

After an absence of several years, Yekaterina Vasilyeva again is working her magic at the Chekhov Art Theater in two new plays, the enigmatically titled *From the Life of Rain Worms*, by the Swede Per Olov Enquist and *Women's Games* by the Poles Krzysztof Zanussi and Edward Zebrowski.

From the Life of Rain Worms is an introspective look at a meeting between Hans Christian Andersen (performed with exquisite psychological exactness by Stanislav Lyubshin) and Johanna Heberg, a famous Danish actress (played by Vasilyeva).

This Andersen is less the celebrated author of fairy tales than he is a frustrated, second rate playwright who has come to the great actress for advice on how to realize his dream of writing a great play. However, as the action inexorably progresses, it is Heberg who comes to rely on the spiritual strength of the "lowly author of children's stories."

Both are of modest, even poor, heritage. But whereas the writer has remained a simple man, even if against his will, the actress has violated her own nature in order to overcome her past and achieve respect. Their marathon meeting is an unexpected revelation for both.

Vasilyeva's Heberg is a suppressed volcano of complexes, anger and lyricism. She does little but sit at her desk, the piano or stand by the window, but one is gripped by her internal drama, which she allows to break surface only rarely. She suppresses within all the tension of her character, transferring to the hall her troubled spiritual aura solely by secondary means of communication, as only an actress of her talent can.

The production, with an elegant set by Boris Messerer, is deceptively quiet and lacking in external action. That is represented by Roza Sirota's captivating performance of the Bald Woman, Heberg's mother-in-law. Excepting some incomprehensible muttering and a few shifts in her chair, she sleeps through the entire performance at center stage.

Director Mikhail Kochetkov noted that he consciously strove for understatement.

"The styles of intrusive directors and political theater have exhausted themselves," says the 35 year-old director. "The time has come for us to deal with affairs of the spirit."

His staging of *From the Life of Rain Worms* is subtle, but powerful, proof that he achieved what he was after.

Women's Games, staged by co-author Krzysztof Zanussi, is a combination of two superficially simple one-act plays. The first, and weakest, tells the story of an aging film actress who outwits a resourceful intruder on her privacy. The second portrays a humorous and uneven game of wits between a bed-ridden French marquise and a young girl hired to sit with her.

Zanussi's direction, like the plays, is transparent and unanalytical. At times, as in the first act, it descends into flatness, although never as a fault of Vasilyeva's performances in the two lead roles.

Glamorous and inaccessible in the first act, Vasilyeva is shrewd and even playfully sadistic in the second as she masterfully befuddles her hapless helper (performed with warmth by Yevgenia Dobrovolskaya). From her static position in the center of a bed in pink sheets, Vasilyeva reigns over her house, France, the world and the stage at the Art Theater.

Comparing a theater's past and present is a dubious undertaking. Still, these new productions at the Chekhov Art Theater hint at the power that once made the venue one of the world's most famous.

(*Moscow Guardian, January 1992*)

Salomé, Alla Sigalova Independent Company

Since its inception in 1989, Alla Sigalova's Independent Company has both offended and delighted audiences with its visually tantalizing dance productions. What some have called pornography, others have taken to their hearts as a celebration of the mystery of human intimacy.

Sigalova herself is a bit baffled by the reactions.

"I am always amazed when people say, 'Oh, how erotic!' I have no desire to create erotic shows and I don't see my work in that light," she says. "For some reason, people constantly try to divide the human experience into elements of spirit and flesh. For me, these things are absolutely indivisible."

Indeed, *A Game of Hide and Seek with Loneliness* is a liberating fantasia in which people search for themselves, sometimes in the reflection of others, sometimes in isolation. From time to time, they are surprised to find what they are looking for already locked in their embraces, but just as often, they don't. And as the episodic scenes progress, it becomes clear that meaning is to be found in the game itself and not in its outcome.

Like all of Sigalova's stagings, *A Game of Hide and Seek* is seldom about sex, although it is charged throughout with sexuality.

Anna Terekhova and Andrei Sergievsky in the Alla Sigalova Independent Company's production of *Salomé*, based on Oscar Wilde, 1992. Photo: Sergei Petrukhin

The company's new production of *Salomé* continues Sigalova's flirtations with the spirit and the flesh. And, as in her earlier staging of *Othello*, she provides in it a free-form mix of dance and traditional drama. Oscar Wilde's sparsely-used text, here, is little more than a pretext for a basic plot on which Sigalova superimposes the theme of Vladimir Nabokov's novel, *Lolita*. As such, the focus is shifted from Salomé's seduction of Iokanaan to Humbert Humbert's unrealizable love for Lolita.

There is little attempt to merge the two stories by means of external signs. Iokanaan (Sergei Shvydky) and Salomé (played by Sigalova's young daughter, Anna Politkovskaya) are outfitted in modern dress and speak their rare lines "realistically." Herod, his wife and their attendants, on the other hand, sport macabre grease-paint masks, black lips and black clothes, and on the rare occasion that they speak, they do so in tense, chanting tones.

But if the characters are divided by their appearance, they are united by the bold movements of Sigalova's expressive choreography. With their sweeping arms and legs and their tense, fanned fingers (which the director calls the "primary conduits of human energy"), the characters seem to be involved in an attempt to master the physical space in which they exist. This is not a "decadent" story of seduction and revenge, but a story of differing individuals seeking to justify their own place in the world.

The centerpiece is the duet of Herod and his wife during which Herod (Andrei Sergievsky) ultimately achieves his demand of seeing Salomé dance. Their tension-packed conversation unfolds slowly as they make love mechanically, but sensually, on the floor. They separate, come together, and separate again. Their terse speech and harsh expressions, adding a second mask to their faces, make it clear that communication between them is being conducted on another plane altogether. Anna Terekhova as Herod's sorceress-like wife is a knot of unearthly strength, power and coercion, but it is not enough. Her weaker, more frivolous husband prevails.

The dance of the seven veils is performed by everyone but Salomé. Echoing the duet of Herod and his wife, the characters occasionally fall into short bursts of unified motion, but, just as quickly, fall apart again, each dancing his own inner vision.

Ultimately, Iokanaan's love is doomed, for it does not have access to the dark mysteries commanded by Herod and his wife. The indifferent Salomé serves up Iokanaan's head in the form of a child's ball that bounces innocently and gaily across the stage.

This brief interpretation of *Salomé* occasionally has the feel of an etude that needs to be filled out in order to bind its parts together. But therein lies its formidable strength as well, for the performance is marked by a striking sense of space and inner freedom. It does not so much illustrate a narrative as it does suggest the feeling and the look of intense emotional states. What is important is not the intentionally vague plot, but the intuitive associations that are bound to arise in the mind of the beholder.

Salomé is a rare and beautiful spectacle whose impression stays with you and continues to grow long after you have left the theater.

(*Moscow Guardian, January 1992*)

I Tap About Moscow, Bat Cabaret

How many theaters in Moscow can boast that their shows *begin* with stormy applause from the audience as the curtain parts?

Of those, how many can make jokes about Anton Chekhov dying from tuberculosis, the consequences of the Doctor's Conspiracy, and KGB recruitment of school boys and do it in a way that elicits warmth, understanding and genuine humor?

And of those, how many can bring on stage a pudgy, somewhat eccentric Vladimir Lenin who wins the spectators' hearts with a sighing glance at a life-size photo of Marilyn Monroe?

Chances are, there is only one. At any rate, you can see all of this and more at the one and only Bat cabaret, located in the heart of Moscow just off Pushkin Square. The theater's newest show is called *I Tap About Moscow* and its author is Grigory Gurvich, the cabaret's artistic director.

Not counting a 69-year hiatus (1920 to 1989), this is the same Bat that gained world-wide fame in Moscow before the revolution and then continued its star-bound trajectory in Paris and New York for many years thereafter. Not only do the shows take place in the very same theater whose walls still emanate the spirit of a glorious past, but, in a contemporary context, naturally, they re-create the intellectual lightheartedness and sophisticated spoofery that made Russian culture the most attractive and influential of all world cultures in the first two decades of the 20th century.

"I build my shows on three principles," Gurvich said recently a half hour before show time, "nostalgia, sentimentalism and musicality."

But don't be fooled. There is nothing weepy in his nostalgia and nothing maudlin in his sentimentality. As for music, there is plenty of it from beginning to end. And in the best tradition of Russian cosmopolitanism, it includes French torch songs, Italian arias, American jazz and English rock. The result is a purely Russian show.

According to its author, *I Tap About Moscow* is a vaguely autobiographical look at life in the Soviet Union from the second World War to modern times. But the atmosphere of the production and the theater alike go much deeper into the past.

Like the Bat's first performance, *The Reading of a New Play*, it is broken into episodes in which each actor plays various characters. Natalya Trikhleb bounds back and forth marvelously among roles including a lovesick girl, an elegant opera singer (what a voice!) and Catherine the Great. Alexander Razalin is, among other things, a warm and rumpled alter ego for the play's author and Inna Ageeva transforms instantaneously from a kind of comic nerd into a French siren.

It all begins as Gurvich himself briefly reminisces about the past under the pretext of responding to a letter from an old friend now living in Detroit. The epistolary structure is what binds together the loosely-connected scenes.

Men lazily play backgammon in an Asian republic during the war, arguing about women and war; school children daydream during ballet class; fantastically wealthy émigrés return to their poverty-stricken home towns; old girlfriends reminisce about a common lover; and a host of celebrities from Hitler to John Lennon gather for a wacky impersonator's contest.

One of the most uproarious scenes portrays the first meeting of a new coalition government chaired by the "first governor ever elected by the people." It doesn't take but two or three words for the new "democrats" to revert to a style of behavior that is much more ingrained in Russian politics than democracy.

Almost everybody tap dances their way through this occasionally wistful, occasionally rollicking tour of Russian life.

"I can't say all my actors are great tap-dancers," comments Gurvich, "but without real training, without a tradition and without the necessary means to give them either of those, I think they do damn well."

Tap-dancing, for Gurvich, is something of a symbol for the Russian intelligentsia's relationship to western culture. Sophisticated Russians have always not only loved western art forms. They have also always been able to assimilate them and create something new on their basis.

"It may be naive," the author/director continues, "but what we are attempting to show on our small stage is that everything a citizen of this country loves can be had right here. You don't have to leave to realize your dreams."

Who would know better than Gurvich? By resurrecting the historic Bat, he is proving his hypothesis by example.

(*Moscow Guardian, January 1992*)

Bald/Brunet, Stanislavsky Drama Theater

Artists often get accused by contemporaries of creating nonsense, while later generations often see revelations in their works. Occasionally, the lag in time between confusion and understanding is foreshortened. That usually happens in periods of major social upheaval when different contemporary generations harbor different expectations.

There could hardly be more fertile grounds for such a classic generation gap than Russia in 1992. And one would be hard-pressed to find a better example of this process at work than the new production of *Bald/Brunet* at the Stanislavsky Theater.

Written by twenty-two year-old Daniil Gink and staged by twenty-five year-old Oleg Babitsky, *Bald/Brunet* stars Pyotr Mamonov, one of the youth idols from the preceding generation. Mamonov, until recently, was the leader of the popular rock group Zvuki Mu.

Their collaboration may be something of a enigma for older generations, but the packed houses of young people haven't the slightest problem understanding this production's language. And there is a good reason for it. This is one of the most exhilarating, challenging pieces of theater playing in Moscow.

As often happens in good theater, the performance that the spectator sees differs from the original idea. Gink noted that his idea was quite simple.

"There is a man," he explained, "who interacts with another man who turns out not to exist. I wrote a play about how a strange man lived alone and had dreams that constantly draw him closer to childhood. He grew old, met a woman and then something happened with him. The performance itself is about something else, although I like it very much because it is independent of me while being a part of me at the same time."

What the performance is about is freedom and transcendence, freedom of spirit, freedom from clichés and transcendence of physical limits. On the surface, Mamonov's eccentric Bald Man may appear to be something of an emotional paralytic. But appearances can be deceiving. In fact, Mamonov plays a beautiful soul struggling to free himself of his earthly body. Echoing Mark Polyakov's bewitching, almost florescent set, Mamonov reveals his character's illuminated state from within.

"This theme exists in my play," Gink continued, "but it was heightened by Mamonov." The playwright then revealed the degree to which generation gaps are at work even among the collaborators on the staging. "After all," he said, "Mamonov has more internal and external limits than I do."

The charismatic Mamonov is a master at finding limits, depicting them physically and breaking through them. His conversations with the enigmatic Woman (Lyudmila Lushina) compel him into a frantic search for a way out of his awkwardness. A few of the play's most revelatory moments come as Mamonov joins with Denis Burgazliev's Brunet in wordless interludes. Freed of language, the duo—which may be merely two elements of a single psyche—interact solely through facial expressions and contorted body movements. They are accompanied by thundering music composed, in part, by Mamonov himself.

For those who are put off by the commonly low level of Russian rock music and by the clumsy manner in which it is usually incorporated into film and stage works, *Bald/Brunet* will be a major surprise. The sparing use of strong rock music is always woven organically into the development of the action.

But more surprising yet is not that the youthful audience responds well to its "own" music or that it worships every move of its rock idol-turned-actor. What is most noteworthy is the way a generation unaccustomed to seeking expression or meaning in theatrical works understands and responds to *Bald/Brunet*. Gink, Babitsky and Mamonov speak a common language with a new generation that is as open and lacking in complexes as they are.

Says Gink, "I am thankful to Mamonov for bringing that kind of spectator into the theater. At times the hall can be a bit uncouth, but it is always alive, theatrical and youthful."

The audience, in this case, reflects brilliantly the spirit of the performance.

(*Moscow Guardian, February 1992*)

Triumphal Square, Theater u Nikitskikh vorot

Any great city is in part a collection of shadows and spirits. And the cataclysmic

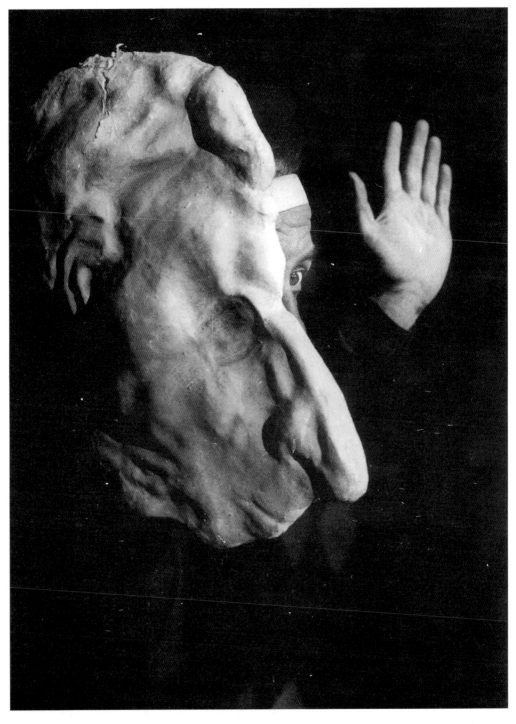

Sergei Desnitsky as Vsevolod Meyerhold in Mark Rozovsky's production of *Triumphal Square*, Theater u Nikitskikh vorot, 1992. Photo: Theater u Nikitskikh vorot

twentieth century probably filled Moscow with more shadows and spirits than any other city. Untold numbers of buildings, streets and people disappeared before their time, leaving behind them powerful traces.

Take, for example, Mayakovsky Square which was once called Triumphal Square. Perched there on the corner is the Tchaikovsky Concert Hall which once housed one of the great theaters of the world, the Vsevolod Meyerhold Theater. The extravagant facade is long gone, and the building was long ago reshaped. But even without plaques or memorials, Meyerhold's spirit still hovers there.

Triumphal Square is also the title of a new production at the Theater u Nikitskikh vorot. Written and directed by Mark Rozovsky, it is a memorial to the director who revolutionized modern theater. Meyerhold's actors called him simply Master, and they didn't stop even after he was shot to death by the secret police in 1940. Rozovsky dares not refer to him differently and it is as the Master that Meyerhold takes center stage in *Triumphal Square*.

Rozovsky was intrigued by the fate of an artist who got mixed up in politics. One of Meyerhold's first theatrical loves was the commedia dell'arte, and Rozovsky surrounds the master with a cast of gay Harlequins, Pierrots and Columbines. Later, Meyerhold would become the director at the tsar's Imperial Theater and, after the revolution, he quickly became the standard-bearer for a new communist art.

Triumphal Square asks, "Who was Meyerhold?" And it gives an answer: He was an artist.

The answer, however, is as complex as the man himself. During the civil war, his communist ties nearly caused him to be shot by the White Army while his former position at the Imperial Theater saved him. During the purges, his friendships with Bukharin and Trotsky caused him to be shot by the NKVD. Meyerhold was an iconoclast and a rebel. That, suggests Rozovsky, mixed with the times in which he lived, made his end inevitable.

The rebel's fate is portrayed in *Triumphal Square* through a composite character bearing the title of Inspector General (from Nikolai Gogol's play of the same name). Performed with chilling and lovable charm by Vladimir Dolinsky, the Inspector is the Master's alter ego. He transforms from a White Army interrogator to an NKVD operative, always opposing the Master, but always working together with him to bring him to that moment history has prepared for him.

This is the tragedy that the Master himself announces at the outset will take place on stage. But this is also theater, and the tragedy is played out as a lively farce filled with cartwheels, water-squirting and circus tricks. This merriment on stage, especially early on, is not always so infectious. But when the Master turns his interrogation in a prison basement into a rehearsal of *The Inspector General*, the performance hits its stride.

At moments, Sergei Desnitsky's Master even acquires an eerie resemblance to Meyerhold himself. His battles with recalcitrant actors, his fount of creative energy and his conviction that he is a medium for the great playwrights of the past create a riveting image of an artist in the spell of his own vision.

Scenes from rehearsals flow into interrogations and back again. Art is confronted by life and the result is not so easy to define. Each triumphs on its own terms. The artist is murdered, but his art transcends his death.

Meyerhold's legacy began to be rehabilitated in the late 1950s. Over the next three decades it slowly returned to the culture that he, as much as anyone, helped create. But, until recently, he still remained too controversial to be incorporated into a prescribed mythology. *Triumphal Square* is an admirable and moving attempt to look past the myth in order to understand the legend.

(March 1992)

The Gamblers—21st Century, ACTors ARTel

Muscovites are apt to complain that Russian theater and film have no stars of the magnitude one finds in the West. It is not a question of talent. The point is the lack of a star-system; recognizability, respect and adulation.

It doesn't take much, however, to create something where nothing was supposed to have existed. A new production by the brilliant actor and director Sergei Yursky should prove that.

First, Yursky created his own company and called it Sergei Yursky's ACTors ARTel. Then he invited a handful of friends—a veritable who's who of Russian theater and entertainment—to help him realize his first project, an adaptation of Nikolai Gogol's *The Gamblers*, renamed *The Gamblers—21st Century*.

Seldom has one stage been graced by so much talent at one time.

The names may be unfamiliar to the uninitiated, but they are all household names, in a word, stars. The list includes Natalya Tenyakova, Leonid Filatov (director of the recent movie *Sons of Bitches*), Alexander Kalyagin (whose starring roles in such movies as *Slave of Love* brought him recognition in the West), Vyacheslav Nevinny, and the popular stand-up comic Gennady Khazanov. Until his sudden death in London on March 4, the cast also included the great Yevgeny Yevstigneev. The set was designed by David Borovsky, Yury Lyubimov's long-time collaborator at the Taganka.

If you don't know them, go see this production and you'll find out why every Russian does.

The setting of *The Gamblers—21st Century* was moved to the present in a seaside resort somewhere in the CIS. However, Russian shysters haven't changed much over the centuries, so the transition was easily made. A modern Russian-style hotel room equipped with a telephone and a tiny refrigerator plus announcements of the next departure of a hydrofoil boat wafting in the window on a breeze are enough to do the trick.

The plot is simple. A card-sharp breezes into town looking for a kill and pays off a hotel maid to provide him some easy pickings. When she brings him a band of likeminded rogues, they join forces and go into business together. Yursky's adaptation may flatten Gogol's clever turn of events somewhat, but only the very hard-hearted will press the point. This is an actor's show created by actors for people who love actors.

The premiere at the Chekhov Art Theater was attended by hordes of just such people who greeted each character's first appearance with cheers and continued to respond to their every move with applause and laughter. One wink from the dissembling Yevstigneev was enough to bring the house down.

The rumpled, obsessed Kalyagin in black shoes with no socks, and the massive Nevinny moaning about the impossibility of dieting, had the audience in the palms of their hands. Khazanov, famed for his comic monologues, makes his dramatic stage debut here and proves that he is not only popular, but that he is a born actor.

In one throw-away scene, Khazanov teams up with Nevinny to act out one of the oldest comic routines in the book. Khazanov stares at Nevinny's feet. Nevinny stares at his own feet. They stare at each other and then at Nevinny's feet. Khazanov goes back to what he was doing and then suddenly whirls around and fires one last stare at Nevinny's feet. Nothing could be simpler, more foolish and, as it's done here, more fun.

In short, *The Gamblers—21st Century* is a showcase. And as a showcase it is unsurpassed by anything playing in Moscow.

But actors aren't the only ones on display. For twenty-five years, David Borovsky's sets have brought him world-wide fame for their simplicity and perfection. They aren't mere decoration, they are a crucial cog in a theatrical machine.

His deceptively common hotel room in the first act is lit from the outside by an extraordinary beach sun that miraculously seems to carry the tantalizing smell of saltwater air with it. And when night falls in the second act, the harsh shadows falling on the balcony are such as one sees only at hotels at the beach. This is the work of a genuine master that exists on a par with the actors who people his created world.

One senses that one of Yursky's tasks in *The Gamblers—21st Century* was to prove there are Russian stars. He did that beautifully. And, in the process, everyone has fun. Most of all, the audience.

(March 1992)

May 32/City of Mice, Shchukin Institute

In 1964 the graduating class at the Shchukin Theatrical Institute made history with their production of *The Good Person of Setzuan.* Together with their pedagogue Yury Lyubimov, the talented students were deemed worthy of having their own theater. The building given them was located on Taganka Square and thus was born the Taganka Theater.

In 1992, many in theatrical Moscow feel that a good idea is worth repeating. This year's graduating class at the Shchukin Institute has caused something of a sensation with its staging of *May 32/City of Mice*, an unusual work that relies almost exclusively on the international language of movement and music. And thanks to guest performances of the short *City of Mice* in Spain and Germany, its fame has spread far beyond Moscow's city limits.

May 32, explained the class's movement teacher Andrei Droznin, was created to compliment *City of Mice*.

"We realized that *City of Mice* was too short to be shown commercially and too good to be abandoned," he said. "So we added a first act structured on the basis of our movement exercises."

The two acts are unified thematically only in that both of them appear to be the product of someone's dreams.

May 32 is a showcase not only for the pedagogical prowess of the well-known Droznin, but for the striking talent of his students as well. In it, a beleaguered young man experiences a series of odd encounters with characters from his imagination. They tumble through windows, fly over walls, walk on champagne bottles and peer back at him enigmatically from the backside of a "mirror."

If the scenes, and the tricks that make them up, are often common vaudeville or circus fare, their execution is not. Even the long and rather tedious slow-motion fight scenes cannot dampen the enthusiasm of the performance. Seeing the confidence and ease with which these young actors and actresses interact leaves no question as to why many hope they will not be scattered among different theaters upon graduation.

Especially noteworthy are an eastern candle dance and an inspired slow-motion Ping-Pong game in which "shadow" characters lift and spin the two players in the air. Their feet seldom touching the ground, they fly over the first row of the audience, dip and dive, tumbling upside down in their mad pursuit of an illusive ball held on the end of a stick by an actor who is determined to make each return more difficult than the last.

City of Mice was created by the students themselves under the direction of their classmate Eduard Radziukevich. It is a haunting fantasia that employs an array of exotic instruments ranging from pipes, bottles and an oversized wrench to the rustling of match boxes.

"When we began composing the music," says Radziukevich, "we started with the bottles and then added pipes. The addition of the match boxes gave us the idea for the title, because the sound they make reminded us of a basement filled with mice."

The act begins as an actor walks out on his hands and the lights come up to reveal a stage littered with bodies covered by black blankets. These are the "mice" who will come to life and act out various scenes. Among them are a fencing match between three men that slides gracefully into a flamenco dance performed by three women, a story of passion and a music-box scene replete with dancing figurines.

The intentionally vague and allusive performance has no concrete plot to speak of. Like the lilting music that occasionally arises unexpectedly from disorganized sounds, the scenes seem to explore the relationship between randomness and order. One easily emerges from the other as a result of a few elemental changes and the addition or removal of rhythm.

There is much about *May 32/City of Mice* that marks it as a student production. In most instances, however, that should be perceived as a compliment. It is a joyous, whimsical performance that is shot through with the promise of talented youth.

There is no telling what history has in store. But if you are interested in catching a glimpse at the direction in which Russian theater may be headed next, this production is an excellent place to start.[1]

(*March 1992*)

What're You Doing in a Tux?, Contemporary Play School

Old icons are falling throughout Russia, so it is hardly surprising that the process has seized the theater world as well.

The most enduring symbol of Russian theater in the 20th century has been the seagull, taken as a trademark by the Moscow Art Theater from Anton Chekhov's play. It stood for the subtlety of psychological veracity and the intricacy of detail that formed the core of the famous Stanislavsky system of acting. During much of the Soviet period, "the system" essentially was imposed upon theaters as the only acceptable dramatic style.

"The system" may have lost its exclusivity some time ago, but directors began taking direct pot shots at it only recently.

Throughout the performance of *What're You Doing in a Tux?* at the Contemporary Play School, a flimsy cardboard cut-out of a seagull hangs above the stage. At play's end, an actor "fires" at it with his cane and it drops to the ground gaily and unceremoniously.

The production is an adaptation of a whimsical early Chekhov one-acter, *The Proposal*, and the choice is hardly coincidental. Many feel that "the system" distorted Chekhov as much as it stunted the growth of Russian theater.

But director Iosif Raikhelgauz doesn't merely brandish a cane at the seagull, he joyously ambushes what it signifies. *What're You Doing in a Tux?* is intentionally frivolous and deliciously wacky. Acted by three of Moscow's finest dramatic actors, it is a mock-opera/mock-ballet performed against an ever-changing cartoon-like set. With a witty libretto by Dmitry Sukharev set to the

quirky music of Sergei Nikitin, it is a delightful and unusual romp.

The story revolves around a marriage proposal. Albert Filozov's meek but proud Ivan Vasilyevich musters his courage, dons a tux and visits his neighbor to ask for his daughter's hand in marriage. There would seem to be no obstacles; the neighbor and his daughter are more than willing. However, an argument arises over who is the rightful owner of the meadows that separate their estates and, when they leave that problem unresolved, they become entangled in a dispute over whose hunting dog is best. The path to "family happiness" is a rocky one, indeed.

Joining the utterly charming Filozov at the play's premiere were the deadly serious Alexei Petrenko as the neighbor Stepan Stepanovich and the sultry Lyubov Polishchuk as his daughter Natalya. (*Tux* will be performed in the future by two revolving casts.)

This performance takes nothing seriously aside from the prodigious talent of the people who created it. The brick-like Petrenko flies heavily from the stage after doing a series of butterfly steps and the gorgeous Polishchuk shines a stiff, broad smile at the audience as she spins in a half-graceful, half-clumsy pirouette. Their antics are performed with such precision that the line between what they are and are not capable of is erased entirely. In his most thoughtful moments, Filozov stares innocently and intimately at the audience and one senses he is as amused by his character as everyone else.

After arias or ballet scenes, the actors not only accept the plaudits of the crowd with exaggerated bows and condescending smiles, but milk them for more if the commotion dies down too quickly to suit them. The result is that the actors join with the audience to pay light-hearted homage to a theatrical style that died out long ago.

During intermission, one could hear enthusiastic conversations about the revival of Russian theatrical parody. Everyone has their own frame of reference. One might also point to a link with the traveling minstrel shows that often formed the basis of W.C. Fields's movies. Whatever the case, the plump, sullen father, the beautiful daughter and the sensitive suitor are a combination

---

[1] The students did stay together as the Learned Monkey theater. See the March 1994 review of *The Beggar, or the Death of Zand* and *Yelizaveta Bam*, and the article on the youth movement in the People, Theaters and Events chapter.

that crosses all cultural barriers. And these stock characters are played with a perfect mix of conviction and irony that make them irresistible.

In a recent interview in *Nezavisimaya gazeta*, Raikhelgauz stated, "I am almost certain that life is not more important than art and that even the most thrilling theatrical ideas mean nothing if [they] don't bring joy."

What're You Doing in a Tux? is the newest among several recent stagings in Moscow that are boldly returning unabashed entertainment to theater. When "entertainment" is offered on a level this high, you can only call it art.

(*March 1992*)

King Lear, Malaya Bronnaya Theater

Moscow may be living through Shakespearean times but theaters have been reluctant to turn to the bard's plays. This season has seen two forays into Shakespearean themes in workmanlike productions of *The Murder of Gonzago* at the Maly Theater and *Fortinbras is Drunk* at the Stanislavsky Drama Theater. Both plays, however, are developments of themes from *Hamlet* written by contemporary playwrights.

The recent premiere of *King Lear* at the Malaya Bronnaya Theater is the first attempt to tackle the real thing head on.

Director Sergei Zhenovach takes care to combat his audience's preconceptions about Shakespeare from the outset. When you walk into the hall, you are directed past the rows of empty seats carelessly covered in white sheets and led through the wings onto the stage. There, with your back to an empty theater, you take a seat in a tiny, makeshift grandstand on the proscenium.

It is an effective device that tangibly affects the spectator's impressions even before the action begins. It shrinks the scope of Shakespeare's grandeur while heightening

A scene from Sergei Zhenovach's production of Shakespeare's *King Lear* at the Malaya Bronnaya Theater, 1992. Design by Yury Galperin. Photo: Mikhail Guterman

the sensation of theater's mystery. After all, you have passed through the "fourth wall" only to find you are still separated from the actors and the play they perform.

In theory, at least, intimacy is the keynote of this *Lear*. There is almost no speech-making and the actors usually deliver their lines in natural, hushed tones. Reduced to a personal, human level, Shakespeare's most famous lines ring at times with new and unexpected power. The theme of Lear's madness, though present, is muted as is his stature as a sovereign. The first act, particularly, seems to hang on a taut wire string between Lear's personal tragedy of betrayal and misunderstanding and the play's larger scope of political chaos and intrigue.

Much of the performance, in fact, is reminiscent of a tight-rope act. Yury Galperin's set consists of a structure of beams on which the actors climb, walk and sit as though eternally hanging over a precipice. On occasion, the structure takes on the form of a corral into which characters are herded or trapped.

That, too, is a metaphor that receives further expression in the costumes. The characters are draped in lush floor-length fur coats that make of them animals or sophisticated beasts of civilization, depending upon an individual scene's context.

Everything is in place for an engaging interpretation of a play capable of saying much to a contemporary audience. But that is just where this "Lear" gets hung up.

Having personalized Lear and his predicament, Zhenovach could not refuse highlighting the social and historical parallels as well. And, just as the actors' constant running around on beams eventually grows tiresome, the desire to balance so much at one time proved to be a heavy burden.

Sergei Kachanov has some excellent moments as a king who is too sympathetic to be scorned. However, this king is too unregal to raise the performance to genuine tragedy, political or otherwise. Indeed, he is a man "more sinn'd against than sinning" for he is bereft of the great passions that make his famous utterance so paradoxical.

Similarly, Vladimir Ivanov is compelling as the betrayed and blinded father of Edgar, but static as the powerful Earl of Gloucester. Lear's daughters are largely reduced to the banal (Cordelia) or to an uneasy mix of bickerers and conspirators (Goneril and Regan).

The play's central idea is best carried by Yevgeny Dvorzhetsky as the homespun, bemused jester, and Sergei Batalov as the irreverently independent and fiercely loyal Earl of Kent. In Batalov's performance one can sense the potential that lies at the heart of this production. He invariably finds the combination that elevates or reduces his role in just the right proportion.

This *King Lear* is ambitious and imaginative. That in itself is enough to make it a welcome addition to the season's listings. If it doesn't always live up to its promise, that is one of the hazards and charms of live theater. Some times you keep your balance, sometimes you don't.

(April 1992)

Lackeys, **Maly Theater**

Tradition is a word that crops up repeatedly in any discussion about Russian theater. There are those who created it, those who sustained it or rebelled against it and, as now happens frequently, those who bemoan its demise. But the sum of a well-grounded tradition is usually stronger than its parts.

One of the charms of the Russian tradition is the concept of the repertory theater. Unlike the western system in which most productions run for several weeks and then disappear forever, here they tend to run for several years, giving a production the limited opportunity to exist in time. So, if you tend to follow only premieres, you risk overlooking some gems.

One staging that easily falls into this category is *Lackeys* at the Maly Theater, an institution whose name is synonymous with the grand tradition of Russian theater. The Maly mounted this old-fashioned, melodramatic family chronicle in 1987, eight decades after it was written by the once-popular Pyotr Gnedich. Today, it understandably continues to draw full houses.

The story revolves around the prim spinster Countess Plavutina-Plavuntsova who is confined to a wheel-chair in her old age. Having spent so many decades observing proprieties and social graces, she doesn't realize she has lost touch with her own life. Those around her willingly play along with her games of etiquette, hierarchy and power, while casually carrying on their own petty and not-so-petty intrigues behind her back.

In this world, being proper is not a manner of behavior, it is a self-serving goal. But the revealing of a sordid secret from the countess's past eventually breaks down the facade of the family's comfortable life, forcing some harsh reevaluations.

The ultra-conservative Maly is frequently reviled for its stubborn refusal to abandon the declamatory theatrical style that died out together with the 19th century. Usually there is ample reason for it. But in *Lackeys* there took place a rare and wonderful confluence of elements that unexpectedly injected a worn-out aesthetic with life.

Director Boris Lvov-Anokhin showed an encyclopedic knowledge of the style's requirements, unfailingly allowing the action to unfold in its own time and manner. He also showed exquisite restraint in his work with a cast of masterful actors, giving them free reign to delve into their characters and reach out to the audience.

Two of the actors, the legendary, 92 year-old Yelena Gogoleva as the countess, and the 90 year-old Nikolai Annenkov as her majordomo, share between them 144 years of experience on the Maly stage. Gogoleva, despite her occasionally faltering voice, is riveting as the focal point of everyone's attention. And Annenkov's famous velvety grace makes him the perfect "lackey." These two survivors from another era bring to the stage an uncommon level of class, nobility and elegance.

Perhaps the finest performance comes from a member of the "younger generation." Afanasy Kochetkov as Pereidyonov, a serf humiliated and banished by the countess long before, is a compelling mix of forces dark and light. Having wandered about "civilized" Europe for years, he returns to Russia and his former mistress seeking revenge. Obsequious and sinister in turn, he ultimately achieves his goal, though at a dubious cost.

The breathtaking set by Andrei Sergeev depicts elegant city palaces and rustic country homes with all the detail and splendor of old Russia.

Lackeys is not without its drawbacks. It has little action to speak of, being built almost entirely on conversations about events in the past. The sub-plots involving a cast of 24 at times make it hard to follow. And perhaps only the very devoted can have the patience to sit through a four-hour performance. However, those who can will be richly rewarded.

This is not a museum-piece or a tired rehash of old forms as are often met with on the Maly Theater stage. It is a living work that gives a rare glimpse into the grandeur of a tradition which spawned so many conflicting new tendencies in the 20th century. Moreover, after five years of performances, it has maintained its freshness. That is a testament to the talent and conviction of everyone involved in it.[2]

(April 1992)

Difficult People, Sovremennik Theater

The Sovremennik Theater was one of the outstanding phenomena of the period in Russian history called the Thaw. Founded shortly after Khrushchev's denunciation of Stalin, the theater opened in 1957 with a play whose title was something of a programmatic statement: *Alive Forever*.

At age 35, the Sovremennik is doing a remarkable job of living up to its promises.

Last week's premiere of *Difficult People* is a bitter-sweet comedy that is a worthy vehicle for the theater that remains young at heart. Translated from the Hebrew of Joseph Bar-Joseph, the play does not so much explore the quirks and beliefs of four different people who have a great deal in common, as it does celebrate them.

These people are united in their misfortune, loneliness, pride and Jewishness, just as

---

[2] The last performance of *Lackeys* took place October 22, 1993, three weeks before Yelena Gogoleva died at age 93.

these facts of their lives invariably stop them from finding common ground.

The 47 year-old Meir-Shimon is a nervous bachelor whose idée fixe is to marry off his 44 year-old spinster sister Rachel-Leah. To arrange a match, he enticed the sincere, but inert Eliezer to travel from Jerusalem to London where Rachel lives. The situation is complicated by Rachel's landlord Benny, whose blind devotion to her irritates everyone, himself included, as it seems.

Director Galina Volchek found the right key in which to play this quartet about broken dreams and the preservation of human dignity. It is at once harsh and heart-warming, eccentric and sentimental. As performed by the brilliant cast, however, the sentimentality is never just served on a platter, but is evoked subtly by the actors' immersion in their characters' personalities.

Lia Akhedzhakova's child-like Rachel, whose answer to any confrontation is to offer another cup of tea, carries her loneliness with a tender respect for the mysteries of the heart. Oft-spurned by lovers, she bears malice to no one, as is witnessed by her gratitude to the annoying Benny (played with a humorous, high-strung sense of dignity by Avangard Leontyev). At first, at least, her deep discontent surfaces only in comical, nervous mannerisms that are always accompanied by a disarming, generous smile.

Igor Kvasha's Meir-Shimon is a swirl of frustrated energy, as tight and threatening as a clenched fist. He initially appears as his sister's antipode, though in time is revealed to be driven by the same forces as she. Tyrannical and cutting, he is ready to resort to anything to ensure her happiness.

Eliezer wants a bride no older than 41? Tell him you're 41. He wants her to be provided for? Tell him you own your apartment. And, no matter what, don't let on you know he spent three months in an insane asylum.

Valentin Gaft as Eliezer appears in Rachel's doorway an imposing giant, a marvelous male specimen who wins the meek spinster's heart instantly. She doesn't care that this "unfortunate truth-seeker," as the acidic Meir-Shimon calls him, turns out to be an insecure pedant who does not con-

verse, but merely poses questions or states facts. A man in desperate search of warmth and stability, he doesn't have the slightest notion of how to find them.

The collision of the enormous Israelite, who thinks only in straight lines, with the tiny Rachel, who is always moving in circles, is a classic mismatch. And when he discovers the trap set for him because of Rachel's inability to dissemble, he wastes no time in rejecting her.

Akhedzhakova is riveting in this scene where her powerlessness before her fate and her brother's machinations come crashing down on her. Like the thin stream of rain drops that fall at the back of Maria Rybasova's set, every nervous detail of the actress's performance builds up imperceptibly before pouring forth in a rushing torrent.

Her outburst prompts Eliezer to reconsider, but after such an emotional purge, the rules of the game are changed.

Difficult People at the Sovremennik exceeds the limits of ethnicity. The situations may be Jewish, but when Meir-Shimon tells his sister quietly, "We are in exile, Rachel," he is talking about the universal human condition of alienation. And what each character finds there is the strength to remain him or herself.

(*May 1992*)

Cathedral Folk, Vakhtangov Theater

Roman Viktyuk belongs to what is occasionally called "the lost generation" of directors. Blessed with talent and originality, he was just what Russian theater "didn't need" in his younger years.

He spent a long time in the provinces, slipping his ideas past sleepy censors in non-traditional stagings. A few respected productions in Moscow added to his underground aura, but no one could have guessed he would flourish as Russia's most controversial director by the beginning of the 'nineties.

His reputation now is built primarily on several teasingly erotic productions that brought homosexual themes to the fore for the first time in this country since the pre-revolutionary years. The best known among them are *The Maids* and *M. Butterfly*.

While his newest offering, *Cathedral Folk* at the Vakhtangov Theater, appears to strike out in a new direction, it actually continues themes long a part of his work. It is Viktyuk's attempt to confront the spiritual and cultural upheaval Russia is embroiled in today.

Nina Sadur wrote the play which is based on a chronicle of the same name by Nikolai Leskov, one of 19th-century Russia's finest writers. But, instead of being a story about the pressures placed on those who answered to a spiritual calling in the last century, this version is reset in the time of the revolution. That heightens the acuteness of the conflicts and makes them more recognizable to a contemporary audience whose experience is similar.

Viktyuk sought to illuminate the contradictory notions of progress and tradition. In his interpretation, the transgressions that each perpetrates on the other must ultimately be atoned for.

The provincial archpriest Savely (performed by Mikhail Ulyanov in his well-worn elevated style) is a wise but simple man who understands that the world must embrace different personalities and forces. The deacon Achilles (Alexander Pavlov) burns with an obsession of righteousness and intolerance of evil. So militant is his faith, one character calls him a warrior, not a priest. But in his friendship with the midget Nikolai (played wonderfully by Vladimir Fyodorov), one espies the conviction of his beliefs.

The primary antagonists of the "cathedral folk" are Darya, a vulgar revolutionary played by Lyudmila Maksakova, and the teacher Varnava, whose commitment to science leads him to violate Christian rites by cutting up the body of a drowned man in order to study his bones for the sake of knowledge. Alexander Filippenko, especially in the second act, finds in the pop-eyed Varnava a subtle mix of tragifarcical traits from Charlie Chaplin and Buster Keaton. Ishmael, a government secret agent, works to foil the lot of them.

Viktyuk's instincts led him to an ultra-contemporary play, but his taste let him

down. Repetitive, superficial and excruciatingly long (it runs for 3 hours and 15 tedious minutes), neither Sadur's play nor Viktyuk's production do more than crudely finger the gamut of problems facing Russian society. Lacking the depth of allegory, metaphor or even symbol, each element in this clash of spirituality and progress is presented as a mere sign that one can only respond to as to a cliché.

Priests step weightily to the edge of the stage to make the sign of the cross over the audience; "freethinkers" undermine tradition; quoting the Bible, Achilles speaks of banning merchants from the Church of God; and several characters bemoan Russia's shame before the West. The play's final scene, with its visual quote from Leonardo da Vinci's "Last Supper," is just the last in a series of moments that "show" meaning rather than developing it.

Instead of being a sincere public confession, as one might find in the works of Dostoevsky, *Cathedral Folk* smacks of hubris. One senses a wicked, out-of-place delight in its treatment of guilt and repentance.

(*May 1992*)

Sorry, a production of the Lenkom Theater and David Smelyansky

She is Inna Rassadina, a typical middle-aged woman almost satisfied with her typical job in a typical Russian morgue. He is Yury Zvonaryov, her college flame who emigrated to Israel 20 years ago, and now has come to "save" her by taking her back with him.

"How come you started drinking so much after you returned?" Inna asks him.

"Wait a minute," Yury cuts her off abruptly. "I didn't return and I never will."

It doesn't take a Russian specialist to see that, in his play, *Sorry*, playwright Alexander Galin isolated a nerve center of contemporary Russian life. It is a complex of problems that has been recurring in various forms ever since Princess Olga first tried, unsuccessfully, to import Christianity in the first century A.D.: Does Russia want to be eastern or western?

Director Gleb Panfilov, the famed film-maker working in the theater for only the second time, teamed up with designer David Borovsky to create a deceptive veneer of normalcy in the setting and in the behavior of the two characters. But he staged the nerve center of age-old Russian problems, not slices of modern life.

That is echoed in Vadim Bibergan's music, whose mellifluous melodies often slide just over the line into discordance.

As is often the case with life in Russia, the tapestry of details in *Sorry* acquires flashes of the surreal.

Yury, who is already married with a child back in Israel, has come back to Russia to marry the only woman he has ever loved. Inna is begrudgingly ready to leave with him, but wants to keep her citizenship so as not to lose her "perfectly good job." The pair get married in an Orthodox Church, but celebrate the wedding at Inna's workplace in the morgue. Inna gets a fake document declaring her pregnant to help with her citizenship problems, while Yury gets a fake document declaring him dead to help with his psychological problems.

Sound over baked? Well, it's not. Even the title warns that nothing is as it seems. Written in English by the playwright, the sounds of the word "sorry" immediately conjure the Russian word for quarrel. And it is this society's time-honored quarrels that emerge predominant.

But don't get the idea that this is just another interesting problem play. One thing alone would make it a must see no matter what it was about: the bewitching Inna Churikova in the role of Inna.

Churikova's morgue-dweller, like every role this actress has played on stage or screen for 25 years, is a rolling sea of emotions filtered through a kaleidoscope of nuances. Only an actress of her stature is capable of making such startling changes in appearance and temperament without the slightest warning.

Meek and pliable at moments, she also can be stubborn or cruel. Plain, even invisible at the beginning, she emerges later as a charming beauty, especially in those rare moments of total accord when the pair slides into a waltz or harmonizes in a Russian folk song. But whatever her moods, she slings her prodigious arsenal at Yury with the skill of a master archer.

The more Nikolai Karachentsov's Yury loses his conviction that his life in the West is ideal, the more the velvety-throated actor fills out the dark recesses of his character. At play's end, he admits bitterly that he has become little more than a merchant, all the while staying one step ahead of the emotions welling in his breast. It is the peak of his performance.

But the play's center is Churikova's Inna. Act I ends as she mutters about going to Israel with a fake child in her womb, accompanied by a legally deceased husband. Suddenly a harsh spot shines from above and she stares into the audience with a mad fire in her eyes. A funny story about real people suddenly takes on the ghastly feel of a horror film.

The line separating the real and the unreal in this production, which requires of its audience more than a superficial feel for the peculiarities of life in Russia, is virtually invisible. Together, they create an indivisible universe where almost anything is possible except finding satisfactory answers to the hardest questions.

What could give a more veritable picture of Russian life?

(September 1992)

1992/1993 SEASON

Far Away ... In Other Lands, Gogol Drama Theater

Personal quarrels are a staple of the Russian literary diet. Most fade into obscurity as quickly as they arise, although on occasion they are given lasting form.

At first blush, there is little in Vladimir Maximov's play *Far Away ... In Other Lands* to indicate that the émigré writer's treatment of the controversial novelist Eduard Limonov will hold much interest in the future. But by a rare, if uneven, confluence of circumstances, the Gogol Drama Theater's new production of it cannot be dismissed so easily.

Maximov was forced out of the Soviet Union in 1974 because his novel, *The Seven Days of Creation*, was too severe in its portrayal of reality and too Christian to suit the Kremlin bureaucrats. Arriving in Paris, he founded the influential journal *Kontinent* and enhanced his reputation as a moralist with more novels.

Limonov managed to head West of his own will in the late 1970s, while still an obscure poet. His first novel, *It's Me, Eddie*, became a cause célèbre for its raunchy language, sexual scenes and its bitter view of destitution in the glass jungle of New York. Later he drifted to Paris, frequenting salons and outraging émigré intellectuals.

By the time he visited Russia in 1991 and joined forces with the ultra-nationalist Vladimir Zhirinovsky, urging Russians "to prepare for blood" and "overthrow the unlawful Yeltsin government," everyone had a fast opinion about him.

Naturally, Maximov did not set out to write a play about Limonov. He sought to illuminate the complexities of émigré life and Limonov merely gave him a rack to hang his hat on.

Rechristened as Varfolomei Ananasov (Bartholomew Pineapple), the struggling writer is a thin-skinned freeloader with a superiority complex who lives in the suburban Paris home of a Georgian friend, Beso Khamelidze (Mr. Fury Boor). Drifting in and out of the picture is Pyotr Govorukha (Peter Talk-a-Lot), a famous poet living out his alcohol-tinged days with his lover Larisa, whose devotion to him borders on sycophancy.

The action is put in motion by a visit from Govorukha's daughter Marianna, whom he abandoned as a baby in Moscow. Govorukha does not want to see her; Ananasov and Khamelidze fall in love with her.

As hinted in the talking names, the play is stiffly schematic. Govorukha represents the established generation and Ananasov represents the ambitious, rootless, young generation. The beautiful, seemingly frivolous Marianna is the pair's tenuous link to modern Russia. Khamelidze, by his condemning name and his violent encounter with Marianna at play's end, seems to form a commentary on problems of nationality, although it's hard to believe a writer of Maximov's stature would be so simplistic, or stoop so low.

A prodigious effort was needed to breathe life into such wooden material. But if director Sergei Yashin wasn't entirely up to the task, he made two shrewd decisions that staved off failure. One was to cast Oleg Gushchin in the role of Ananasov. The other was to pepper the text with excerpts of *It's Me, Eddie*.

Surprisingly, this whiny, self-conscious novel (which some have called "powerful" and "astonishing") provided Gushchin a lyrical footing on which he balances masterfully. Sexually insecure as a result of losing "a great love," bitterly alone in a society that ignores him and consumed by the conviction that he is the "hope of European thought," Gushchin's Ananasov emerges as impotent, bratty, complex and engaging.

One senses that Ananasov charmed even Maximov, for his grating, childish bravado is sketched with much more insight than the other characters.

Irina Smelyova as Marianna creates a believably flighty lure who drives a wedge between Ananasov and Khamelidze (played by Ivan Volkov) and justifies Ananasov's momentary victory over impotence, even if it is only in a sexual sense.

Far Away... In Other Lands is humorless and often plodding. It doesn't say much about the intrigues and tragedies of emigration, but Maximov, Yashin and Gushchin succeeded on one score: They found the soft spot in a character whose primary quality is to irritate.

(October 1992)

Woe From Wit, Chekhov Art Theater

"*Woe from Wit* has been performed—and the soul is plunged into melancholy!"

So begins a lamenting account of the Moscow Art Theater's performance of Alexander Griboyedov's masterpiece in 1906. One can only marvel at how little things change.

Oleg Yefremov, the founder of the famed Sovremennik Theater in 1957 and the artistic director at the Chekhov Art Theater since 1970, intended for his new production of *Woe from Wit* to revive his battered reputation as one of Russian theater's luminaries. Instead, it probably has sealed his fate as an artist whose time has passed.

Griboyedov's sparkling play, written in 1824, is a fount of wit and wisdom. Its catchy verse dialogue, chock full of memorable witticisms, enriched the Russian language with more proverbial sayings than any other single work of literature. But it owes its place in history no less to its wicked insight into the eternal problems of the Russian national character.

The young Alexander Chatsky returns to Moscow after a typically 18th-century "sentimental journey" during which he sharpened his mind with experiences and observations. Hoping to resume his romance with the fair Sofia, he visits the home of her father Pavel Famusov, a portly pillar of society. What he finds is a family mired in banality and intrigue.

Sofia has fallen in love with Molchalin, Famusov's groveling secretary. Famusov, his brain addled by too many years of chasing after the servant Lizanka, quickly pegs the sharp-tongued Chatsky as a pesky intruder into his comfortable life. Neither they, nor any of the Muscovite socialites who attend a ball the night of Chatsky's arrival, are capable of appreciating either wit or wisdom. Sofia's off-hand remark that Chatsky has "gone mad" is overheard by a loose-tongued guest who sees to it that everyone learns the damning news.

The play is a soaring dramatization of an enigma once defined by Pushkin: "The devil deigned for me to be born in Russia with wits and talent." The staging of it at the Chekhov Art Theater is as earthbound as it is empty.

Boris Messerer's set, a palatial interior resembling an architect's drawing or a child's paper cut-out, promises early to lend just the right touch of airiness. But the mass of crisscrossing lines soon comes to resemble prison bars instead.

It's not surprising, as most of the cast performs with the energy of inmates who know they have 20 years left on their 30-year sentences.

Yefremov's staging is so static that one wonders whether the actors eventually will wear holes in the few places on the stage where anyone stands to speak. If the monotonous blocking was intended as a metaphor for the characters' inertia, someone along the way forgot to explain that playing boredom and being bored are two different things.

But that is hardly the only question left us. Can this decidedly unwitty Chatsky (Sergei Koltakov) really have pretensions of regaining Sofia's love? What is it in the nondescript Sofia (Yana Lisovskaya) that attracts him anyway? And one suspects that the only justification for Sofia's infatuation with the pale Molchalin (Sergei Shkalikov) is that the author set it in stone 170 years ago. None of them make plausible the director's alteration of the play's end, where, now, love inexplicably conquers all.

Even an actor the caliber of Oleg Tabakov, despite his warm, round smile and occasionally twinkling eyes, is unable to find motion or life in the usually blustery Famusov.

For connoisseurs there are some spoils worth savoring. Yelena Maiorova fills Lizanka with a vivacious, cat-like playfulness that is so engaging, it stands as a bristling reproach to those around her. She single-handedly staves off disaster in the first act. A similar honor in the second act goes to Andrei Myagkov in the role of Repetilov. This bumbling has-been's drunken tirade, as the guests depart from the ball, is a comic tour de force.

But such moments are too little and too late.

Yefremov has announced that *Woe from Wit* will be performed by three different casts. The only response to that can be, one shouldn't multiply one's woes.

(October 1992)

Don Juan, Hermitage Theater

Don Juan was an infantile womanizer and a rake. Don Juan was a philosopher and an aesthete who challenged the authority of God. Will the real Don Juan please stand up?

With his playful production of *Don Juan*, which opened recently at the Hermitage Theater, Mikhail Levitin gives each Don a chance to have his say. He brings both on stage and lets the audience draw its own conclusions.

The first, a blustery profligate, emerges from *The Trickster of Seville and the Stone Guest* by Tirso de Molina, the Spanish playwright of the Golden Age who was the first to treat the Don Juan legend. Played with light-hearted bravado by Pavel Berdichevsky, he flamenco-dances his way from conquest to conquest.

Don Juan-the-philosopher originates in scenes excerpted from Molière's comic masterpiece, *Don Juan, or the Stone Guest*. Viktor Gvozditsky, who has risen to the top rank of Moscow's actors thanks to scintillating performances in two Kama Ginkas adaptations of Dostoevsky at the Young Spectator Theater, deftly steers away from the cynicism that made Molière's character so controversial in the 17th century. Gvozditsky gives us a thoughtful man of refined sensitivity.

The two Dons never meet, although they live parallel lives. Each haggles with his crusty servant who is appalled by his master's immorality, each encounters pliable peasant girls and each meets a similar end when he confronts the eerie Stone Guest, the tombstone of Commodore Gonsalo whom Don Juan murdered in a duel. But the

similar scenes draw conflicting portraits of the famous lover.

If Don Juan-Berdichevsky literally leaps on the women who cross his path—as he does with a fisherwoman performed with irresistible verve by Yekaterina Galushkina—Don Juan-Gvozditsky is drawn inexorably to the women who become his victims. He is incapable of turning away from beauty of any kind, because for him beauty is life's only enduring truth.

The chasm separating the two opens to its widest during their confrontation with the Stone Guest. Belligerent and terrified, Berdichevsky's philanderer vents his childish fury on the dark visitor who responds in kind, seizing his opponent in a stony grip of vengeance. In contrast, Gvozditsky's Don Juan recognizes with admiration that he is in the presence of a master seducer before whom he has no recourse but to surrender.

But this *Don Juan* has still another thrust which is at least as engaging as the Don Juan story: It is a celebration of the freedom and irreverence that theater makes possible. Levitin himself opens and closes the action in heart-to-heart chats with the audience and the actress (Galina Morachyova) who plays the fateful Don Gonsalo. "The main thing," he reassures her when she doubts she is right for the part, "is to show up on time."

The supporting cast, especially Alexander Pozharov as the harried Sganarelle and Larisa Panchenko as the bubbly peasant girl Charlotte, form a motley crew that usually fits well into Svetlana Kalinina's skewed set depicting something akin to an alchemist's laboratory or a deranged inventor's workshop. During transitions, the stage is overrun with mad apprentices obsessed with creating something. Perhaps they are "making" a play about Don Juan.

Levitin made his name as a director in the 1980s by resurrecting one of the genuine black holes of Russian/Soviet culture: the plays, poems and prose of an eccentric group of writers in the 1920s called Oberiu. The name is partially an acronym for "Association for Real Art" and partially nonsense. The most important part is the nonsense.

But Levitin didn't merely rediscover some forgotten (i.e., banned) works, he used their aesthetics to create a unique theatrical style. Judging by *Don Juan*, at least, the style would appear to be remarkably flexible. This loose, off-the-cuff performance easily makes up in enthusiasm what it lacks in depth.

(*October 1992*)

Electra, Taganka Theater

The Taganka is more than a theater, it is a piece of history. And Yury Lyubimov is more than the Taganka's chief director, he is a legend.

Of course, it is the nature of things that history marches on and legends undergo metamorphosis.

Lyubimov's four years at the Taganka since his return from exile have not been happy. He spent the first reviving some old productions that once had languished under bans. They were received warmly, but whispers that time had passed them by could be heard everywhere.

It took him another year to produce his first new work at the Taganka in a decade. The result was a bold, if somewhat diffuse version of *The Suicide* by Nikolai Erdman, Lyubimov's old friend and a legend in his own right.

Now, two more years down the road, comes the director's abbreviation of Sophocles's *Electra*. Like all of his productions since he founded the Taganka in 1964, this story of treachery, vengeance and cruel justice is presented as an allegory for modern times.

But if, in the past, the Taganka was an insulated world that mocked the political intrigues surrounding it, these days it is embroiled in a power struggle easily as intricate, and certainly more messy, than any that ever took place just across the Yauza River at the former Communist Party headquarters.

Unhappy with Lyubimov's many obligations in the West and his move to privatize the theater last December, three quarters of his troupe mounted a rebellion that peaked in April with the firing of Nikolai Gubenko, the former artistic director at the Taganka, the former Soviet Minister of Culture and a former leading actor at the theater.

As the scandal flared and the public took sides, Lyubimov set to work on *Electra*. During a break in spring rehearsals, a calm Lyubimov stood before a towering, blood-red set on stage and commented on the newest controversy swirling about him.

"All the dirt from the street has been hauled into my theater," he said.

With the premiere of *Electra*, it appears that, for better or worse, the "dirt" of the theater's own problems has entered its work.

Sophocles's tragedy retells the legend of Electra, daughter of Agamemnon and Clytemnestra, sister of Orestes. Together with her lover Aegisthus, Clytemnestra murdered Agamemnon, an act the outraged Electra encourages Orestes to avenge. When news comes that Orestes has perished, she attempts to engage her sister Chrysothemis in her plot of vengeance. Chrysothemis refuses, counseling conciliation. Orestes, however, returns under disguise and carries out the deed.

Perhaps the themes of usurpation and loyalty proved too close to Alla Demidova, the Taganka's leading actress and one of Lyubimov's most vocal supporters. One is willing to overlook the fact that a 55 year-old actress plays the young Electra, but her confusion of mannered hysteria with tragedy cannot be ignored.

Striking poses, slashing the floor with her garments and straining her voice, Demidova looks not into the heart of her tragic character, who is held a prisoner of virginity by Aegisthus for fear of a new heir, but broadcasts her fury outward. The result borders on a parody of the famous Taganka style which always sought to engage the audience with direct appeals. Her assault, which might have carried genuine force were it modulated, leaves no room for dialogue.

Yekaterina Vasilyeva, invited by Lyubimov to play Clytemnestra, delivers a pin-sharp, infernally murderous queen, but the subtleties of this actress, formed in the traditions of the Moscow Art Theater, clash awkwardly with the histrionic Electra and the formulaic Orestes (Oleg Kazancheev) and Chrysothemis (Lyubov Selyutina).

Lyubimov's favorite designer long has been David Borovsky, and *Electra* proves why once again. Echoing the famous sets for *Hamlet* and *The Master and Margarita*, where key props were raised to the level of living beings, the whirling revolving door at center stage delivers or removes people from the stage with the authority of fate.

Electra, frantic as it is, at least captures the upper register of the passions involved in betrayal and vengeance. If it misses its mark as a commentary on the world at large, it provides a glimpse into the agony of a theater divided.

Every artist deserves the courtesy of being judged on his or her own terms. As regards an artist of Lyubimov's stature, that courtesy becomes an obligation. After all, history continues to be written and a legend continues to evolve.

(*October 1992*)

Zangezi, Chyot-Nechet Theater

Avant-garde performances, no matter how intriguing, require more than good intentions and an impressive grasp of the material. They also have to translate intellectual complexity into an intelligible stage language. Failing that, they wander off into the realm of the inside joke. At any rate, that is the conclusion Alexander Ponamaryov's recent staging of *Zangezi* for the Chyot-Nechet Theater leaves us with.

Velemir Khlebnikov, a "poet's poet" associated with the Futurists, wrote the dramatic poem *Zangezi* shortly before he died of malnutrition in 1922. This strange and imaginative work about a poet named Zangezi summed up his ambitious notions about the "language of the stars," the mystical arithmetic of time and the exalted mission of the Poet. Composed in what he called transsense" language, much of it remains gibberish even to those familiar with his theory that sounds are more meaningful than words.

The plotless play, subtitled a "supersaga," consists in this adaptation of 21 scenes which the author called "planes." In them, gods and humans gather to contemplate, imbibe or reject the enigmatic wisdom of the visionary poet. Like a Christ-figure wandering amid skeptics, the lonely Zangezi is the only one who truly understands the truths he speaks.

Aided by Rudolf Duganov, Ponamaryov tried to air out the density of the poem by appending excerpts from other Khlebnikov works, including theoretical treatises. He would have done better to stick to the text or, better yet, to hone it down to the elements best suited to the stage.

The reader who has the luxury of pondering Khlebnikov's curious observations has fun deciphering that Zangezi's status as a visionary is reflected in his name. According to one of the appendixes added to the performance, the letter "z"—which determines the significance of Zangezi's name—"is a ray reflected in a mirror. The angle of incidence is equal to the angle of reflection (vision)." Spectators who are confronted by strings of such riddles in a theater simply drown.

The promise of the production's striking beginning makes the director's over-intellectualizing even more lamentable. There *is* a play here worth staging and Ponamaryov started out on the right track.

The first scene depicts a girl in white against a pitch-black background, speaking to nature in its own language. Anna Torkiani's flowing motions and easy mastery of tongue-twisting bird calls and bee-like buzzing dovetail nicely with the naturalistic sounds of dripping water and chirping birds. It is an impressive and thoroughly accessible introduction to Khlebnikov's deconstruction of man-made language.

After the first girl is replaced by another in white, patterns begin emerging against the black background. They are soon revealed to be the figures of gods who continue the dialogue in an exotic language of their own. Their spectacular costumes and masks, designed by Yaroslava Baranova, reflect the set of abstract Futurist paintings constructed by Yelena Stepanova. In the absence of conventional "meaning," the visuals, combined with the score by Mikhail Korzin and Boris Repetur, give the audience a concrete orientation: We are witnessing something of a pagan mystery play.

But as the performance develops, it drops those secondary modes of communication and relies more and more on words to break the "fetters of words." It is a vicious circle. By the time Zangezi propounds his theory of the meaning of the letters "r" and "l" in the eighth scene, the spellbinding atmosphere of the early scenes has descended into an impenetrable fog that never lifts again.

Dmitry Pisarenko, as Zangezi, makes a valiant effort to breathe life into the poet's significance-laden pronouncements. But, like the rest of the cast, he most often appears to be reciting pointlessly the sounds of an ancient language whose code is long lost.

(November 1992)

The Masquerade, **Russian Army Theater**

It's just a stone's throw from romantic drama to melodrama. And from there, the road to soap opera runs straight and narrow. A new production of Mikhail Lermontov's *The Masquerade* at the Russian Army Theater doesn't go that far, but it doesn't stop far short of it either.

In his brief life—he was killed in a duel at age 26—Lermontov created a body of work, the best of which can be summed up roughly in a line uttered by a character in *The Masquerade:* "The world for me is a deck of cards." Lermontov was the quintessential Russian romantic, a fatalist, hounded by unlucky love and a deep distrust of social conventions.

All of that comes out in *The Masquerade*, where duplicitous intrigues and a case of mistaken identity lead the morbidly passionate Arbenin to murder his beloved young wife, Nina. When she loses her bracelet at a ball, it is found by a masked beauty, Baroness Strail, who gives it to a dashing count as a sign of affection. When the count learns the bracelet is Nina's, he is convinced she is the one pursuing him, while his stubborn wooing of her brings Arbenin to the same conclusion.

If complications like that are common fare for, say, *Santa Barbara*, the American soap opera now running on Russian t.v., they were only window-dressing for Lermontov. He was driving at the tragedy of those whose hubris compels them to demand answers to unanswerable questions. Like most of the people around him, Arbenin was a social rake in

his younger years, and no one was more surprised than he to find genuine love with Nina. So, when his trust in her is shaken, he puts her to the test. On a deeper level, of course, he is testing God: Are love and beauty real or imaginary?

But as always happens with people who challenge the order of God's world, Arbenin doesn't realize he is playing with a stacked deck. A mysterious stranger seeking revenge for old insults orchestrates the course of events and makes their outcome inevitable.

For all its youthful stridency (Lermontov wrote it when he was 21), *The Masquerade* bares the anatomy of emotional pride and spiritual doubt with relentless, almost mathematical precision. What we get at the Army Theater, more often than not, is a common story of jealousy.

Director Leonid Heifetz tried to steer away from that by setting the tone with a prologue. The performance begins as the Stranger (Boris Plotnikov) strolls past the audience and ominously crosses the stage. In principle a good idea, it isn't nearly enough. Before the climactic scenes following the murder of Nina, the Stranger appears only briefly. For his first appearance to have a lasting effect, the other actors needed to echo his presence throughout. Instead, they are invariably buried in the petty details of their libidinous desires. By the time the denouement comes, one wonders what the fuss is about.

Frequently struggling with the terse verse text, Gennady Krynkin's Arbenin comes across as a rather pathetic, waffly old man. He is conquered not by a cruel game with fate, but by his imagined rival, the prosaic Count Zvezdich (Alexander Domogarov). Krynkin trots out an impressive array of tricks to build his character—the cocked eyebrow, the quivering lip, the fiery glare— but it all adds up to little more than a collection of stock mannerisms.

Olga Tolstetskaya gives us a naive, good-hearted Nina who is more apt to illicit a warm smile than a jealous rage. Olga Yegorova, as the Baroness, plays a spirited, if stereotypical femme fatale. Finally, Iosif Sumbatashvili's set shows he did his homework. His series of moving curtains, in which the characters often play hide-and-seek, are a reduced version of the decoration for Vsevolod Meyerhold's famous staging of *The Masquerade* in 1917.

Reduction is the key word, here. This *Masquerade* is a romantic drama with too much "romance" and too little romanticism. (*November 1992*)

The Forest, Malaya Bronnaya Theater

Nobody likes a loose, baggy story better than a Russian. And nobody loves theater better than those who work in it. So what happens when a great Russian playwright writes about the theater? You get Alexander Ostrovsky's 19th-century classic, *The Forest*, a witty, winding tour where the line between who is an actor and who isn't eventually fades to black.

Lev Durov, himself one of Russia's best actors, this time donned his director's cap for the staging of *The Forest* at the Malaya Bronnaya Theater. He gave the performance the ideal traditional twist for it to have that good old-fashioned comfy feel.

Nikolai Epov's set starts things cleverly. Madame Gurmyzhskaya's country estate is painted on rolls of drapes hanging from the flies. But a closer look shows they hang in the shape of tree trunks. Presto! The forest where two itinerant provincial actors, Neschastlivtsev and Schastlivtsev, make their comic entrance. By the performance's end, it's hard to say where civilization ends and the backwoods begin. Svetlana Stavtseva's imaginative, cartoon-like costumes peg the proper socialites as the real actors in this spectacle.

One of Ostrovsky's many fortes was creating blustery matriarchs who tyrannize young female wards aching for freedom. In *The Forest* those slots are filled by Gurmyzhskaya (Anna Antonenko-Lukonina), who patronizes her poor relative with a vengeance, and Aksyusha (Yekaterina Durova), who is hard-pressed not to wither under the attention. The self-satisfied "auntie" plans to marry Aksyusha to the sleazy Bulanov.

The plot expands and the love intrigue thickens with the appearance of Ivan Vosmibratov and his son Pyotr. Ivan

Shabaltas and Alexander Tereshko play them as a pair of bearded twins from a Russian folk tale. Ivan has his eye on a parcel of Gurmyzhskaya's forest, while Pyotr has his eye on Aksyusha.

Meanwhile, a storm of sorts is brewing in the nearby forest, where two old cohorts, a tragedian and a comic actor, unexpectedly meet. Neschastlivtsev (Mr. Unfortunate) suggests visiting his miserly aunt Gurmyzhskaya for a hot bath and a sound meal. What Schastlivtsev (Mr. Fortunate) doesn't realize is that he'll have to play the lackey to his partner's performance of a retired officer. Gurmyzhskaya won't have anything to do with actors.

Oleg Vavilov and Vladimir Yershov are splendid as the tragi-comic team. The long, gangly Vavilov catches the bombast of the provincial Hamlet with just the right mix of irony and solemnity. His flashing eyes, booming voice and expansive gestures are just enough to subdue his skittish and chafing brother-in-profession. The squat Yershov plays the perfect pessimistic clown who expects nothing from life but a boot in the backside.

All hell breaks loose in a wonderful Russian frenzy when Vosmibratov finally consummates his purchase, but cheats Gurmyzhskaya out of 1,000 rubles. Erupting in exquisite outrage, Vavilov's Neschastlivtsev engages the unscrupulous landowner in a war of words that echoes Russian parliamentary debates, street fights and kitchen arguments all in one. Call it "doing business Russian-style." Naturally, it all ends with a begrudgingly friendly handshake and a rousing song.

Gurmyzhskaya still isn't satisfied, though. Now the aging despot sets her own sights on the young Bulanov. That frees the penniless Aksyusha, but it also leaves her without a dowry. Enter Neschastlivtsev, who, by now, has been exposed as a contemptible actor. To his friend's horror, the tragedian gallantly solves the matter at his own expense, while giving all a piece of his mind.

Also featuring sharp, eccentric performances by Viktor Lakirev as Uar, a half-deaf retired soldier, and Tatyana Krechetova as Ulita, a scheming housekeeper, *The Forest*

Vladimir Yershov and Oleg Vavilov in Alexander Ostrovsky's *The Forest*, directed by Lev Durov for the Malaya Bronnaya Theater, 1992. Photo: Mikhail Guterman

runs long. But never in its 3 hours, 40 minutes does it drag. This is one jaunt through the woods that not only promises fun, but delivers it.

(December 1992)

Our Country's Good, Tabakov Theater

Born in America and educated in France, Timberlake Wertenbaker has lately been the toast of British theater. Her plays have been staged by the Royal Shakespeare Company and the Royal Court Theater, some winning prestigious awards. The premiere of her *Our Country's Good* at the Tabakov Theater gives Moscow audiences a chance to see what some consider her best work.

Director Irina Brown, a Russian émigré living in London for 14 years, goes even farther: "I think it's the best play to appear in England in the last 10 years," she said before the opener. If that is true, it probably indicates more about the competition than it does about the merits of this sometimes lively, more often tedious story about an 18th-century Australian penal colony where the inmates are encouraged to put on a play for their own edification.

Our Country's Good puts forth several blatant messages. One is that the line separating executioners and victims is tenuous, at best. Another is that one's sense of cultural belonging (in this case, to England) depends more on the individual than the culture. Finally, it gives rousing support to the idea that theater has the power to ennoble. Much of the actionless play passes in repetitive debates about whether criminal behavior is rectifiable or not, while the rest of it shows us flawed, but sympathetic criminals who ultimately convince us that it is.

There's no doubting that Wertenbaker has a good feel for backstage high jinks, camaraderie and vanities. The scenes involving the convicts' rehearsals are clever and endearing. But the play-within-the-play (George Farquhar's *The Recruiting Officer*, wherein a young woman disguises herself as a man and enlists in the military to be with her fiancé) is only the means to an end. And it is in reaching that illusive end—3 hours and 15 minutes in coming—that *Our Country's Good* does a good bit of clanking and wheezing.

Captain Philip, the Socrates-quoting governor of New South Wales, sees his position as an opportunity to rehabilitate criminals. Played by Mikhail Khomyakov as a colorless, phlegmatic altruist, he holds out against his subordinates who prefer the whip to the word. The withdrawn prisoner Mary Branham, who flowers under the refined influence of art, demonstrates that he is right to do so. Maryana Shults stands out in this stereotyped role which she makes both touching and believable.

Brown's simple staging—she essentially put the characters in their proper places—does well to copy the original 1988 production at the Royal Court. Several actors play officers and convicts simultaneously, forcing us to think twice about an observation made by Gary, the colony's conscience-stricken sheriff: "I would have become a criminal if I hadn't joined the navy in time."

The most impressive of the seven doubles is Andrei Smolyakov, who plays David Collins, the colony judge, and Robert Sideway, a pickpocket with nostalgic memories of visiting the theater at Drury Lane. Penetrating as Collins and impishly quick as Sideway, he imparts to the proceedings a badly-needed sense of pacing. Alexei Seliverstov gives a warm performance of the convict John Wisehammer, a shy Jew with literary pretensions, and plays a functional Captain Tench. Alexander Mokhov is far more subtle as the convict James Freeman, the colony's reluctant but conscientious henchman, than as the odious Major Ross, the governor's most vocal opponent.

Jacqueline Gunn's uninspired set consists of a dirty tarp covering the stage floor, which is split by two trenches, and two piles of even dirtier rags piled along the right wall. Occasionally the opaque back wall becomes transparent and reveals the enigmatic image of an aborigine.

Our Country's Good has its moments, but it would be both more ennobling and entertaining if there were more of them.

(December 1992)

Death and the Maiden, Sovremennik Theater

Death and the Maiden at the Sovremennik Theater poses hard moral questions that touch any society emerging from a totalitarian yoke into a sea of uncertainty. Ariel Dorfman wrote the psychological thriller in response to the fall of the Pinochet regime in Chile, but it doesn't take a lot of imagination to understand why director Galina Volchek saw in it an ideal mirror for the state of the post-communist world.

Therein lie the key strengths and weaknesses of the play and the production both. The harrowing story of a former political prisoner, who takes justice into her own hands by terrorizing the man she suspects was her persecutor, could hardly be more timely for a Russian audience. So much so, that instead of flowering into an independent performance with its own laws, it seldom rises above the level of an effectively theatricalized civics lesson.

Herardo Escobar and his wife Paulina Salas are old dissidents and new democrats. When she learns he has been appointed to a commission that will investigate past political crimes, she asks darkly whether he plans to ferret out "all the truth." His equivocal response that he will unearth "all that is possible" leaves her unsatisfied. An unexpected midnight visit from a doctor, who had given Herardo a ride home after his tires were slashed, is the catalyst that puts everyone to the test.

Herardo amiably chats with Doctor Miranda before insisting he spend the night. But Paulina, who listened in on the conversation from the stairwell, is certain she recognized the voice of the doctor who subjected her to hideous tortures when she was in prison 15 years ago. In the morning, she drags Miranda out of bed, ties him to a chair and begins a cruel interrogation that is aimed at forcing a confession no matter what the cost. The title of *Death and the Maiden* derives from the composition by Schubert, which the doctor used to play while torturing his victims.

The cast is formed by three of the Sovremennik's top actors: Marina Neyolova is Paulina, Boris Dyachenko is Herardo and Valentin Gaft is the unsuspecting doctor. All are handcuffed to differing degrees by a play that is politically rich and theatrically poor. Dyachenko, especially, drew the thankless task of animating a man whose pathetic lack of will makes him totally unbelievable. The most he can do to oppose his wife's mad obsession is to plead with her to apologize and let the poor doctor go. Left alone with the doctor, he sheepishly admits he doesn't condone what is happening, although it never occurs to him to free the prisoner. Eventually, he reluctantly joins forces with Paulina.

Gaft and his character are more effective although one can't help but wonder why he never seriously protests his outrageous treatment. An actor of raw, bullish temperament, he spends the majority of the performance strapped motionless, reduced to filling out his ineffectual lines with facial expressions.

As the woman whose life has been defiled by the experience of mockery and torture, Neyolova has a freer hand. Her 15-year sublimation of the effects of her ordeal make her sudden outburst fully understandable. And in moments such as the first time she ever tells Herardo the grizzly details of the repeated rapes she endured, Neyolova raises the play and the performance to the heights of spine-tingling terror.

Dorfman's play has received wide acclaim throughout the West since its premiere in London and on Broadway a year ago. In these political and politically correct times, that's no surprise. As social criticism and a moral warning, *Death and the Maiden* is unquestionably a powerful work. But its talky didacticism too often slips into overkill, leaving us with a performance that tells too much and shows too little.

(*December 1992*)

The Possible Meeting, Chekhov Art Theater

George Frideric Handel, the fantastically popular author of *Messiah*, never met Johann Sebastian Bach, the modest author of the *St. John Passion* who gained recognition only 80 years after his death. Paul Barz corrected history's little oversight by writing a play

Oleg Yefremov and Innokenty Smoktunovsky in Paul Barz's *The Possible Meeting, or The Four Hand Dinner*, directed by Vycheslav Dolgachyov at the Chekhov Art Theater, 1992. Photo: Mikhail Guterman

called *The Possible Meeting, or the Four Hand Dinner*, in which he brought the two musical geniuses together at last. Fittingly, the production at the Chekhov Art Theater reunites two of Russia's most brilliant actors who seldom perform together anymore: Oleg Yefremov and Innokenty Smoktunovsky. The result is a spectacular duet that is hands down the season's most rewarding performance so far.

The year is 1747 and the occasion is Bach's entrance into the German Society of Musical Sciences. Handel, the society's only other honorary member, bursts into a luxurious room just off the auditorium where Bach can be heard performing for an appreciative crowd. Drunk and irritable, Handel locks horns with his personal secretary, Johann Schmidt. "Listen to that music," coos the fastidious Stanislav Lyubshin as Schmidt, "it's genius!" The grousing Handel corrects him darkly: "It's talent."

From his first moments on stage, Yefremov creates a Handel who is driven from within by his powerful personality, his prodigious talent and his ambiguous attitude towards his legendary fame. Rough as sandpaper, he is consumed with a self-assuredness that hints at an underlying sense of doubt. He denigrates Bach to the dismay of his secretary, grumbling that he should never have agreed to this pointless meeting, but transforming instantly when Bach makes a painfully timid entrance. "My dear man!" he cries a bit too jubilantly, greeting him with open arms.

Innokenty Smoktunovsky is an actor of sublime grace. His understated voice, his softly nervous gestures, his penetrating eyes and his disarming smile have made him the most celebrated Russian actor of the second half of the 20th century. His performance of Bach gently shifts all of that into an unusual key. This Bach is shy, amusingly awkward and certain of only one thing: his own genius.

The young director Vyacheslav Dolgachyov was wise to stand back and let two masters go about their business.

The "meeting" takes an eternity getting underway as the two composers, like two boys playing separate games in the same sand box, stubbornly refuse to engage one another. Bach wants to play the clavichord, Handel wants to down a bottle of wine. Handel reminisces about his father's doubts that anything would ever come of him, as the poverty-stricken Bach, who has never seen such delicacies as are served up by Schmidt, becomes preoccupied eating artichokes.

Slowly, as fat chunks of wax begin dropping from the candles on the chandelier above them, the barriers separating the two giants begin to fall. Handel's jealousy of his guest's genius gives way to grudging respect, while Bach, uncharacteristically seduced by worldly desires, admits he is "burning with envy" at Handel's fame, although he is "the greater genius of the two." Handel is overjoyed. "That's the best compliment of my life," he exclaims. The tipsy, newfound friends even start dreaming of collaborations, and it doesn't matter that it's clearly all for naught.

Margarita Demyanova's elegant old-world set, with its strange, absent back wall created by a curtain of light, positions the characters with one foot in this world and one foot on the road to eternity. And if eternity makes "enemies" of these vastly different artists, as Handel observes with no little delight, it is also the common ground on which they meet.

There's no need underestimating what is at stake in this exhilarating performance. Like the characters they play, two great actors are locked in a sparring match. It is a battle from which everyone emerges a winner. It takes a genius to play one and this performance gives us two at once. Bravo![1]

(December 1992)

Erik, Pushkin Drama Theater

"When I become king!" the Swedish crown prince roars threateningly before taming his emotions and slipping into a whisper, "I will be different." There may be only a handful of human utterances which are as timeless. And at a time when the political waters in

---

[1] Innokenty Smoktunovsky died August 3, 1994. The last performance of *The Possible Meeting* took place February 2, 1994.

Viktor Gvozditsky in the title role of *Erik*, based on plays by August Strindberg, directed by Yury Yeryomin at the Pushkin Drama Theater. Photo: Mikhail Guterman

Moscow have become muddied once again, Yury Yeryomin's staging of *Erik* at the Pushkin Drama Theater does an admirable job of showing that it is timely, as well.

Erik is a collation of *Gustav Vasa* and *Erik XIV*, two plays from August Strindberg's cycle of Shakespearean historical plays written at the tail end of the 19th century. But it doesn't take much to see that this production is not intended as a commentary on ancient Swedish problems.

Upon gaining the throne after his father's death, the impetuous, changeable Erik quickly proves incapable of ruling. Enter his shady friend Joran whom Erik elevates from the rank of commoner to the level of royal prosecutor. At least for awhile, it is a perfect match. Erik represents the semblance of power, while Joran becomes the proverbial gray cardinal.

In many ways, this is a story of bedroom intrigues and doomed marriages, in which the notion of marriage is raised to the level of a metaphor. Queen Elizabeth of England spurns Erik's proposal, forcing him to find solace in the arms of Karin, a Swedish commoner. Karin, in her turn, rejects her fiancé, Max, in order to bear the king two children out of wedlock. Erik's half-brother Juhan travels to Poland on the sly to marry the Polish queen, enraging Erik and giving Joran the grounds on which to arrest him for his "unconstitutional alliance with a foreigner." Finally, Erik's attempt to marry Karin and legitimize his children prompts his brothers Juhan and Karl to unite against him in a coup.

All of these unions, including the most enduring one between Erik and Joran, set the tone for the king's unpredictable reign. "Policy" is formed on the basis of personal pride, fear, offenses and ambition, while personal relationships are a matter of state security.

While the players in this eternal drama are hamstrung by the laws of their unholy alliances, Yeryomin and designer Valery Fomin did everything possible to free the performance from the limits of the stage. A gaping trap in the proscenium allows people to appear from and disappear into the bowls of the earth, while occasionally the action spills over into balcony boxes above the audience. At one point, a huge fire wall is lowered from the flies with a threatening rumble, trapping the actors at the edge of the stage. The basic set is a grandiose construction of towering, riveted walls and a sloped floor with a wide gash down the middle. In turns, it resembles a sea-faring vessel sailing an unknown course and the interior of a dungeon.

This dynamic set, which seems to give a tangible form to the harsh forces of history, requires an equally potent impulse from the people who inhabit it. But the only truly adequate response comes from Viktor Gvozditsky as the troubled Erik.

Gvozditsky, an actor of extraordinary intellectual range, is both the primary reason this production works as well as it does and the measure of its limitations. A master at blending seamlessly the paradoxes of his characters, he sets a standard that leaves his partners groping to keep pace. Alexander Yermakov, as Joran, and Natalya Nikolayeva, as Karin, do their utmost to hold their own, although the remainder of the cast fades imperceptibly into the shadows. Essentially working in isolation, even Gvozditsky occasionally overpowers his own character.

Erik may not be a performance for all times. But it does capture the texture of the times in which it was created.

(*December 1992*)

Joseph and His Brothers, School of Dramatic Art

After getting mixed reviews for his production of Mikhail Lermontov's *The Masquerade* at the Comédie-Française in June 1992, Anatoly Vasilyev moved back to his School of Dramatic Art in Moscow to continue work on a long-term project: his adaptation of Thomas Mann's *Joseph and His Brothers*. In December, Vasilyev gave five semi-public showings, gaining admission to which proved as dramatic as the performances themselves. For days in advance, administrators at the School either denied knowledge of the upcoming showings, claimed the caller had reached a wrong number or merely hung up the phone. At the door, attempts were made to weed out journalists and critics. Those who belonged to Vasilyev's inner circle, or who were especially stubborn, had the opportunity to see six random scenes from *Joseph* as well as the new theater Vasilyev is constructing in the old Uranus movie house on Sretenka Street.[2] Except for a penciled announcement on the exterior that a theater-studio was looking for a doorman, nothing gave any indication that this location was anything but another of Moscow's countless abandoned buildings.

After passing through the future theater's run-down entryway and foyers, spectators enter what begs to be called a clean, well-lighted place. The floor consists of well-lacquered white pine planks, and the walls are covered in canvas painted in off-white. A narrow three-story, U-shaped structure forms the "auditorium" and appears to be something of a light-hearted parody of traditional large theaters. It is essentially a construction of scaffolding consisting of bright red pipes with facings covered in the same off-white canvas that adorns the walls. The top level is reserved for technicians, while the slightly-elevated floor and second levels each have room only for one row of seats. It appears that maximum seating is about 60. Spectators on the floor level are separated from the acting space by a low, stately, white-columned fence. The second level hangs out over the first and there is a narrow slit in the floor which allows spectators to peer straight down to glimpse what is going on below. The acting space, at least for *Joseph*, was the floor area encompassed by the scaffolding. A medium-sized, elevated stage extends from the open end of the scaffolding to the back wall. Financing for the theater is coming exclusively from money Vasilyev has earned while working in the West.

The showing began with an extended prelude. Eleven men and twelve women walked out and formed a circle. They beautifully sang six hymns, after each of which they made the sign of the cross and bowed. Vasilyev himself stood in an aperture in the center of the floor level, where he, too, crossed himself repeatedly and occasionally wept. Carefully, even demonstratively, he removed a handkerchief from his pocket, unfolded it and dried his eyes. Following the singing of the final hymn, the actors took seats positioned in single file in front of the audience. Vasilyev also seated himself in the aperture before a small table on which the only object was a Bible. A spotlight positioned behind him cast his long shadow across the acting space. (It was turned off only after the intermission.) An actress then stepped up to one of three podiums and began reading in a chanting voice from Genesis, the other actors following the text in their own copies of the Bible. As the "cantor" intoned the lines, "Then God said, 'Let us make man in our image,'" the actors began singing another hymn. Upon the completion of the reading, all made the sign of the cross and the actress took her seat. A second actress stepped up to another podium and began reading further. Only then did two actors portraying Joseph and Jacob finally take positions in front of the stage and begin performing the first scene, "At the Well."

The readings from Genesis continued uninterrupted throughout all six scenes and, frequently, a third layer of voices was added as hymns were sung. As each actor finished his or her reading, or as the singing came to an end, all but those performing crossed themselves and bowed.

Besides "At the Well," the other segments performed were "The Unclean One," "The Pursuit," "At the Master's," "Husband and Wife," and "Potiphar." All involved two characters except "The Pursuit," which involved three. The actors did little more than assume positions in front of the stage and deliver their lines. From time to time they sat on one of two chairs, but more often, they stood motionlessly or walked around slowly. Their "gestures" were limited to facial expressions, emotional speech and a few repetitive, stylized motions of the fingers, hands and arms. The text was merely delivered in the form of

---

[2] I attended the first showing on December 24, 1992. The final two were held at the old location on Vorovsky Street.

engaged Socratic dialogues. Some of the actors seemed nervous or unsure of themselves; their hands occasionally trembled and they frequently stumbled over the text. There was no action or interaction to speak of. Only during the scene "Husband and Wife" did the actor and actress embrace once. There were no props aside from the two chairs and some lights depicting stars which hung in a net beneath the ceiling during the performance of "At the Well."

Upon the conclusion of the sixth scene, an actor stepped up to the one podium that was located on the elevated stage. There, as the seated actors sang a hymn, he continued the Bible reading. After he finished, all made the sign of the cross, stood and left silently.

While it would be improper to draw any broad conclusions based on these exercises which were clearly intended for a select audience, it is impossible to avoid making a few general observations. The most obvious is that Vasilyev continues to grow increasingly uncomfortable with the notion of "traditional theater." By having his actors perform exclusively on a space in front of an empty stage—reserving that stage only for the reading of the Bible—he seems to have signaled either that they have already moved off of the traditional stage or, on the contrary, that they are not yet ready to mount it. Moreover, the meticulous conducting of what amounts to a staged religious service throughout the performance implies the director's doubt that theatrical devices alone are capable of expressing satisfactorily what he wishes to say. On the other hand, Vasilyev himself has not yet rejected theatricality altogether. The careful positioning of a spotlight that casts his shadow over his actors and the methodical handling of his handkerchief as he dries his teary eyes while standing at the rim of the acting space are clear signs of that. The clever configuration of his new performing space also implies a healthy dose of "playing at theater."

Perhaps Vasilyev's rancorous break with the masterful actors who helped make his reputation left him more alone than he knows. The new students he is trying to form outside the traditional theatrical educational system are better at imitating their teacher's "terrible,

swift" aura than creating convincing performances. Most of the men sport the same long, black hair, the same flowing beards and the same scowling looks that have made Vasilyev's image famous. Even the women have adopted the "Vasilyev look." What appears to be lacking are strong creative personalities who might enter into a fruitful dialogue with a man of vision and talent. At any rate, Vasilyev's "school" presently resembles a hermetic spiritual sect as much as an environment for developing the dramatic art.

Vasilyev has long been at least one step ahead of his contemporaries. Perhaps he is still out in the lead. Whether that is true or not may become more evident when *Joseph and His Brothers* is completed.[3]

(Summer 1993, Slavic and East European Performance)

When I Wrote, I Saw Before Me Only Pushkin, Krasnaya Presnya Theater

For Nikolai Gogol, a life-long bachelor, the institution of marriage was both esoteric and frightening. In his delightful comedy, *The Marriage*, he poured his discomfort with the idea into his hapless hero, Podkolesin, raising the theme to a strange and quirky hymn to freedom. The new adaptation of the play at the Krasnaya Presnya Theater is all of that and more.

Podkolesin wants to get married, sort of. That's why he engaged a matchmaker to make him a match. Now he can fret comfortably about the tux a tailor is sewing for him, while satisfying himself with abstract fantasies about what married life might be like. His *laissez faire* attitude doesn't suit his friend, Kochkaryov, however.

This good-natured brute doesn't understand the charm of procrastination and he takes his friend's fate into his own hands. Pushing the matchmaker and Podkolesin's three rivals for the fair Agafya's affections out of the way, he ends up pushing Podkolesin to the end of his wits—and out the window of

---

[3] *Joseph and His Brothers* was never completed and many of the actors in it eventually left the School of Dramatic Art.

Agafya's drawing room, where the reluctant suitor drops into a carriage and makes his get-away.

Gogol teasingly subtitled his play "A Completely Improbable Incident." Yury Pogrebnichko staged it less as an incident than as a state of mind, enigmatically renaming it *When I Wrote, I Saw Before Me Only Pushkin*. The shift in focus justifies the improbabilities, giving us a weird, funny and beautiful performance.

A few unnamed characters—one is presumably Gogol—drift in and out, expanding the play's scope. Meanwhile, as if they were crammed into a rush-hour bus, the principles bump and jostle each other on the tiny stage outfitted eclectically by designer Yury Kononenko. More is at stake here than just Podkolesin's future happiness; this is a meditation on dreams of freedom in claustrophobic surroundings. In sum, the Russian way of life.

The key motif sounds as eight actors repeatedly crowd into a corner and raise their voices in a soaring rendition of the Russian folk song, "O, You Spacious Steppe." It creates a poignant, paradoxical image, in which one can readily espy the rift between the myth and reality of Podkolesin's ill-fated fantasy.

Pogrebnichko's troupe can be uneven, but when it's good, it's sublime. Nikolai Alexeev's sad-sack Podkolesin teeters skillfully on the narrow line between naive sincerity and hopeless thick-wittedness. But, the longer the balancing act continues, the more we see that this Podkolesin is no ordinary fool. His fine-tuned instincts for self-preservation only make him appear foolish. In fact, he is an outcast who wants only to march to his own drummer.

Even more than Alexander Starikov's aggressively single-minded Kochkaryov, Yelena Saleikova's virtuoso performance of the matchmaker Fyokla sums up what Podkolesin is up against. Epitomizing the seductive, dual countenance of social convention, her natural state is one of blank indifference. But the instant she launches into her embroidered sales spiels, she transforms into a lively, unrelenting force.

The dead-pan Agafya (Lilia Zagorskaya) and her aunt Arina (Natalya Krupinova) are rather constrained by the skewed form Pogrebnichko gave them, but, in the bit part of the servant Dunyashka, Yelena Slyusareva captures its essence perfectly. Like the performance as a whole, her twinkling eyes and barely-suppressed snickers hint that this world's facade is concealing a fascinating riddle. Nadezhda Bakhvalova's costumes—half prisoner uniforms and half society garb—are a further sign of the performance's dual nature.

Pogrebnichko is a master at creating interplay among language, themes and visual images. *When I Wrote* is further proof that his carefully-wrought, hodgepodge style makes him one of Moscow's most interesting directors.

(*January 1993*)

The Joyous Days of Rasplyuyev, Spartacus Square Theater

It is only natural that the changelings and vampires in the performance of *The Joyous Days of Rasplyuyev* at the Spartacus Square Theater have returned to life in new form. That's the point of this wicked comedy, first staged at this venue a few years ago, but now revised substantially: Old vampires don't die.

Usually known as *The Death of Tarelkin*, it is the final part of a dramatic trilogy by the 19th-century writer, Alexander Sukhovo-Kobylin. He wrote his plays as a cry of despair after a decade of debilitating battles with the Russian bureaucracy. No other work of Russian literature captures so vividly the infernal villainy and the black humor of such an unenviable encounter.

Tarelkin is a petty bureaucrat who seizes the chance to escape the inhuman machine of which he is a part. His neighbor Sila Kopylov has just died, and Tarelkin assumes his identity. Some papers he stole from his superior, Varravin, should provide him the means to begin a new life.

The nefarious Varravin, however, is not so easily fooled. After his suspicions are raised while visiting the "dead man's" apartment, he returns in the guise of the imperious Captain Polutatarinov (Captain Half-Tartar). This time, with the help of the eager policeman Rasplyuyev, he unmasks his underling.

This is neither Tarelkin nor Kopylov, he declares, but a vampire escaped from the grave. The despairing Tarelkin is arrested.

Rasplyuyev and his superintendent, Antiokh Okh, report the shocking news to Varravin, who rewards them by entrusting the investigation of the case to them. Thus begin Rasplyuyev's joyous days, as he methodically grinds down and, ultimately, destroys a series of witnesses summoned to be interrogated. Varravin himself crowns the witches' Sabbath by personally interrogating Tarelkin, and breaking him.

Director Svetlana Vragova's powerful and expressionistic adaptation honed the plot's sociological implications to a razor's edge by couching the action in a mystical, thickly Russian atmosphere that borders on a dream state. The sounds of Orthodox hymns often form a lilting soundscape that tries in vain to cut through the mad goings-on. Characters appear as if out of thin air and disappear just as quickly. Echoing Rasplyuyev's observation that Russia is inhabited by nothing but "snakes and rabbits who turned into people," Vragova gave sub-human characteristics to almost everyone *but* the "vampire" Tarelkin.

The set by Larisa Nagolova and Mikhail Kurchenko literally reflects the performance's keynote with sparkling precision. A sea of shattered mirrors covers the black walls and ceiling, shooting bright rays of light across the dark stage and distorting the images of the actors.

Top-notch acting jobs give the finishing touches of humor and humanity to the nightmarish staging. Yury Rumyantsev's fragile Tarelkin resembles a delicate bird caught in the clutches of a natural predator. He is heartbreaking as he recites his own eulogy to himself, "a man so progressive, he was ahead of progress itself." As Varravin, Oleg Tsaryov is touchingly wicked—as he squeezes out a tear over Tarelkin's demise—and diabolically cruel—as he crushes his opponent. In Antiokh Okh, Alexander Letta draws a textbook caricature of a state functionary: limited, literal and afraid of everything but carrying out orders.

The glue of this performance is the unabashed, folkloric enthusiasm of Sergei Pinegin in the role of Rasplyuyev. With breathtaking energy and unfailing comic instinct, he creates a charming, happy-go-lucky simpleton who "believes no one" and is prepared to "arrest everyone." He is not just a cog in a machine, he is the nuts and bolts that hold it together.

Only those who missed the last Congress of People's Deputies, and didn't hear about Foreign Minister Andrei Kozyrev's recent Geneva speech about Russian wolves in sheep's clothing, could doubt the fundamental truth of this compelling performance.

(January 1993)

As You Desire Me, Novy Drama Theater

Luigi Pirandello wrote most of his plays in the period between the two world wars, and all of them bear the harsh mark of that volatile historical era. No less an influence on him was his wife's losing, 15-year battle with insanity. Pirandello's world is one of uncertainty, hostility and inscrutability. With that in mind, it can be added that a new production of *As You Desire Me*, staged by Vladimir Sedov for the Novy Drama Theater, captures at least the contours of the Italian playwright's style creditably.

The performance is heavily atmospheric and unsparingly obscure, from the first mute appearance of the Poet and the Little Ballerina, to the last cries of "Cia, Cia!"—as the entire cast appeals to the main heroine, who went incognito to create a new identity and escape her tragic past. The characters, most sporting some sort of mask, roam the stage deliberately and speak in portentous tones. Not much happens besides the slow, sporadic unraveling of the past through conversation, although things are livened up at times by a trio of cavorting, demonic "imbeciles."

As we eventually learn with no small difficulty, Cia, or the Unknown Woman (played by Natalya Bespalova with an aloof aura of hardened alienation), was the victim of a gang rape during World War I. Rather than return to her husband Bruno, who had married her for money, she settled in with a lover, Karl Salter (given a devilish twist by Vladimir Levashyov), and made her living as a dancer and "something else even worse." Despite the suspicions of some that she was still alive, no one ever attempted to locate her.

Having declared her dead long ago, Cia's relatives gather to decide who will inherit her villa. The prime candidates are Bruno (Andrei Rudensky), and Cia's conformist sister, Ines (Marina Yakovleva). Her interests are represented by her husband Silvio, an attorney (performed with smiling insidiousness by Sergei Kazakov), while Bruno has the support of Cia's aunt Lena. Marina Nikolayeva's eccentric, hard-edged portrayal of the matron provides the performance's most rewarding moments.

Cia herself attends this convoluted seance in order to "play out the comedy" to the end. But Salter, who does not want to lose his beloved, most aggravates the convoluted intrigues by introducing an insane woman who he claims is the real Cia.

Nothing transpires so sequentially on stage, nor was it intended to. Like Sedov's pointedly unfinished set—which suggests several possible locations at once by means of flowing, pink chiffon drapes, a tree in bloom, a child's swing, some richly embroidered throw pillows and a gold carpet—the play examines Cia's life as she probably perceives it herself: in chaotic snippets of facts and myths that leave everyone groping for the truth.

Cia greets her insane impostor with a kind of wicked pleasure. "This," she says with conviction, "might be Cia too, if that's what you desire." And that is the crux of the play. *As You Desire Me* tackles the disturbing notion that one's destiny and identity are less dependent on reality than on the perceptions of others.

But, Sedov's severely shortened production—with its textures of a psychological holocaust, its satire of bourgeois pettiness and its ambiance of doom—only approximates that Pirandellan precept. Meanwhile, its utter lack of dramatic movement and its fascination with monotonous obscurity leave much to be desired. If you don't know the play, or if you don't have the chance to acquaint yourself with it, don't count on the performance filling in the gaps for you.

(*January 1993*)

The Abyss, Malaya Bronnaya Theater

The young director Sergei Zhenovach has recently seen his star rise with steady, if not lightning, speed. His fifth and latest production, *The Abyss* at the Malaya Bronnaya Theater, provides a fresh opportunity to observe this much talked-about artist.

Like his *King Lear* last season, *The Abyss*, shows the director's penchant for risk-taking and embracing boldly a broad swath of currents and themes. It is a seductive and dangerous combination. If you hit, you hit big. If you miss, you hit bottom, hard and loud. That is what happened with *The Abyss*.

The performance is a two-in-one job that intersperses the four scenes of Alexander Ostrovsky's *The Abyss* with the three acts of Victor Ducange's 19th-century melodrama, *Thirty Years of a Gamester's Life*. The latter segments are performed in reverse.

Ostrovsky's play tells the story of Kiselnikov, an honest and unambitious young man who ultimately falls victim to the greed and vulgarity of his wife, Glafira, and her parents. He leaves school to marry for love, but love is the least of Glafira's interests. As the modest government clerk's family grows larger, he grows poorer. And after his father-in-law, Pud Borovtsov, joins with a friend, Lup Pereyakov, to cheat him of his last money, Kiselnikov is pushed to accept a bribe and take his first step toward ruin.

Zhenovach pasted Ducange's play onto *The Abyss* in order to compare and contrast the various roads to hell. George is an inveterate card-shark whose marriage to the wealthy orphan Amalia will give him means and respectability. With the help of his sleazy cohort, Warner, he succeeds in winning Amalia before his true designs are revealed. But George's union with Warner also seals the inevitability of his doom. Thirty years on, broken and penniless, Warner convinces George to rob and kill a stranger in his home. What George doesn't know is that it is his own son, who has returned to mend fences with his parents. By flipping the play front to back, Zhenovach shows George's squalid end at the outset and tips off what is in store for Kiselnikov.

So much for detail and theory. The reality is that *The Abyss* is convoluted, often flatly acted (there are some exceptions) and—no wonder—interminably long. Zhenovach has a flair for unusual ideas and he has proven in all his stagings that he is capable of creating effective, intimate scenes. The problem is that he appears to lack that crucial inner voice which might help him differentiate between what is and isn't possible.

The almost breakneck speed of the scenes from Ducange begs a reference to the old saying that "almost" only counts in horseshoes. If this was intended as a parody, it needed wild abandon and killing humor. What we get is a moderately hysterical, backwards performance of a play consigned to the dump heap of history for 150 years. Sergei Kachanov's perfectly demonic instincts in the role of the young Warner are lost in the shuffle.

The Ostrovsky scenes fare somewhat better, but the constant interruptions of the French melodrama never let them muster a head of steam. Some well-aimed comic moments from Sergei Batalov, as Pereyakov, and Vladimir Ivanov, as his comrade Turuntayev, fizzle out like sparklers in the general chaos. Most frustrating of all is that Sergei Taramayev's truly stunning performance of Kiselnikov's final, insanity-washed scenes comes after so much chaff and tedium. By then, there has long been little worth saving.

Theater needs stars. But becoming a star before you're ready is a terrible burden. What Sergei Zhenovach really needs is some breathing room to find out what he is truly capable of.

(February 1993)

The Marriage of Figaro, Lenkom Theater

The Marriage of Figaro at the Lenkom Theater starts off with a walloping bang, a rousing song-and-dance number, and does a splendid job of keeping the pace right up to the revealing, happy end.

Forget all the commentary about the role Beaumarchais's 18th-century classic may, or may not, have played in the French Revolution: The biting social satire it once contained has long since lost its teeth. What it has retained is a barrel of wit and a stagefull of impeccably-drawn characters. And the convoluted plot, which now smacks of run-of-the-mill French farce, is half the fun.

The commoner Figaro and his sweetheart Susanne have their penetrating sights set on getting married. But, naturally, they have to wriggle through a maze of imposing obstacles first. Toiling in the service of Count Almaviva and his wife, they get tangled up in a web of real and imagined amours which put all of them, and several others, on a grand collision course.

Marceline wants to force Figaro to marry her, at least until she learns he is her son. The young Cherubin steadfastly courts Countess Almaviva until he winds up in the arms of Fanchette. The Count pursues Susanne until he is tricked into a clandestine nighttime meeting with his own wife—and falls in love with her. At the center of each twist and turn are Figaro and Susanne, whose taste for intrigue is as boundless as their energy.

Credit directors Mark Zakharov and Yury Makhayev for honing the play's blunted edges to a point and buffing up its slightly faded sheen. The action moves forward gaily and briskly, and is punctuated with plenty of musical interludes.

The driving force behind the performance is the delightful young Natalia Shchukina in the role of Susanne. With her sparkling eyes, darting movements and bubbly voice, she is a sight to behold. Shchukina brilliantly captures the lightheartedness and instinctive wisdom of the girl who is always one step ahead of everyone else. As Figaro, Dmitry Pevtsov may lack Shchukina's charisma, but this talented actor moves with extraordinary grace and draws a thoroughly engaging portrait of the commoner weaving his way through the intricacies of an aristocratic world.

Lyudmila Artemyeva, as the witchy Marceline, injects a wonderful note of grotesque comedy into the proceedings. Gruff and peremptory, her eccentric expressions and explosive mannerisms form the perfect counterpoint to Alexandra Zakharova's fearfully timid Countess Almaviva and Alexander Lazarev, Jr.'s dryly dashing Count.

Like a full-scale Broadway musical—which *The Marriage of Figaro* imitates with verve—the success of this production also depended on a large team of behind-the-scenes artists pursuing a common vision.

Valentina Komolova dressed the actors (especially the extras) in a brilliant array of colorful costumes. The snappy dance numbers and actors' movement, choreographed by Alexei Molostov, epitomize the production's carefree, upbeat tone. Designer Oleg Sheintsis's versatile set utilizes well the height and depth of the stage, and, in the final scene, his starry night in the Count's garden is gorgeous. The masterful lighting by Mikhail Babenko (who perished tragically in a fire at the theater shortly before the premiere) gives it all a sparkle that is rare on Moscow stages. Finally, the sound by Valery Andreev and Vladimir Cherepanov crisply carries the actors' voices, and Sergei Rudnitsky's musical arrangements of Mozart and Rossini, to every corner of the theater.

If entertainment is what you're looking for, there is no better place to find it than at *The Marriage of Figaro*.

(February 1993)

Napoleon I, Mayakovsky Theater

Napoleon I at the Mayakovsky Theater is a fascinating example of what used to make first-rate theater in Moscow—and what still does. The late Anatoly Efros, one of Moscow's most innovative directors from the 1950s through the 1980s, staged Ferdinand Brückner's play a decade ago. Now, thanks to the efforts of Efros's leading lady, Olga Yakovleva, and director Tatyana Kazakova, the play has been restaged for a new generation.

The primary focus is on the complex relationship between Napoleon (Mikhail Filippov) and Josephine (Yakovleva), although the performance is hardly a typical love story. We enter the action as Napoleon announces his plans to divorce Josephine and marry a woman who will provide him both a link to European royalty, as well as an heir to the throne.

These two seemingly routine moments are the keys to understanding what rules the

commoner who crowned himself Emperor of France. Napoleon asks: "Who am I? The Emperor? No, I am an impostor." His frank admission makes it all the more clear that the wars he wages and the intrigues he weaves are directed to a common end: to legitimize the personal status of a man who, by all the conventions of politics and society, should not be where he is. Obtaining a noble wife who can bear him a son, will give him a past and a future he does not have on his own.

The earthy Josephine, on the other hand, is Napoleon's sole link to the reality of the present. And, as Napoleon learns, by losing that, he loses everything else with it.

The pairing of Filippov and Yakovleva in the leading roles was especially successful. Aside from bearing a striking resemblance to the stocky Corsican, Filippov portrays deftly the difficult combination of a man who wields absolute power, yet is at the mercy of the people and forces who surround him. He is an elastic knot of passions, sometimes tightening, sometimes loosening, but always on the verge of snapping.

Yakovleva creates a non-traditional Josephine, whose considerable feminine power derives less from external appearances than from her unbending, inner conviction in the power of the love that unites her with Napoleon. Her superficial calm is colored with broad strokes of disgust and resignation that her "little boy," as she calls Napoleon, is not capable of seeing what is so obvious to her.

Sterling performances in supporting roles flesh out the play's details nicely. Galina Belyayeva gives a touchingly fragile portrayal of Napoleon's rejected Polish mistress, Maria Walewska. Tatyana Augshkap is childishly haughty as the young Austrian princess Marie Louise, who can offer Napoleon nothing but respectability and an heir. Nikolai Volkov, with his thin voice and quiet arrogance, creates a treacherous Talleyrand, whose slippery demagoguery shines darkly through a stiffly proper facade.

Aside from being a fine performance in its own right, *Napoleon I* provides a rare opportunity to glimpse two eras of Russian theater. Efros staged it at a time when even his notoriously apolitical productions could not help but acquire unmistakably political tones. And this play about a whimsical and ruthless ruler is filled with potentially explosive moments.

Take, for example, Napoleon's claim that he is prepared to "fight to the bitter end" to unite Europe and the world, or, Josephine's admission that she has lost faith in God and, believes "everything," because "the revolution taught us there is no God." Such moments would have sent tremors through the hall ten years ago. Now, there isn't so much as a cough. It is a strong sign that theater in Russia is shedding the burden of being a soapbox and is reestablishing itself as an art form.

(*February 1993*)

Nijinsky, Bogis Agency

Nijinsky is an inspired and inspiring hymn to Vaslav Nijinsky, the great Russian dancer, whose career ended tragically in 1919 at the age of 30. It was then that he finally lost his five-year battle with schizophrenia. He spent much of the next 30 years in institutions before passing away in a London hotel in 1950. The inaugural production of the fledgling Bogis Agency, *Nijinsky* is one of those exciting moments when a truly great performance not only sums up recent developments in theater, but points forward to the future.

First and foremost, it combines an excellent play by Alexei Burykin, a first-time playwright, with brilliant performances from two of Russia's most respected young actors—Oleg Menshikov and Alexander Feklistov. But the revelations hardly stop there.

Nijinsky was mounted in the Western style. Its creators are not members of a repertory company, but independents who came together specially to realize a project. That in itself, of course, is not necessarily a virtue. There have been several such undertakings in the last two years, although most have been long on hype and short on quality. Only *The Gamblers–21st Century* and *Sorry*, both produced by David Smelyansky's Russian Theater Agency, maintained the

high level of quality that one expects from the best Russian theatrical ventures.

With its first outing, Bogis—an acronym for the agency's founders, Galina Bogolyubova and Larisa Isayeva—has provided convincing proof that the independent movement has taken firm root in Moscow.

Also of note is that *Nijinsky* was essentially staged without a director. Three directors took part in the early stages of rehearsals, but none of them met the approval of the actors or the designer, Pavel Kaplevich. The trio completed the production on their own. Such a step flies in the face of a tradition which—from Konstantin Stanislavsky to Yury Lyubimov—has long perceived the director as theater's primary moving force.

The triumph of this performance certainly does not sound the knell for directors, but it does fuel speculation that we may be on the threshold of some realignments. Several of the season's best offerings have been actor-oriented productions in which directors assumed a reduced role. There have also been a few weak attempts by prominent actors to break the director's hegemony by creating their own theaters or productions. *Nijinsky* is a rare, and unusually successful example of a creative group bypassing the director altogether.

The action takes place in a small, ornate hall that evokes perfectly the spirit of the Nijinsky age. Kaplevich added a series of inflatable "marble" columns which increase the stateliness of the environs, while giving it the fragility of sanity: All that is needed for the columns to collapse in a heap are a few swipes of the hand.

Menshikov and Feklistov divide between themselves the ailing former dancer's two warring personalities. As befits a performance devoted to a great dancer, their movements, interplay and even inner thoughts are choreographed with stunning precision.

The tone of the performance flows from the eerie (when an effigy of Menshikov's character suddenly comes to life), to mock tragedy, to lyrical comedy (a marvelous two-man Chaplin imitation).

Menshikov gained international fame last year by playing the Russian poet Sergei Yesenin opposite Vanessa Redgrave's Isadora

Duncan in the award-winning London production of *When She Danced*, and he brings the same poetic grace to his performance of Nijinsky's intuitive half. Charming, boyish and coy, he refuses to remember his glorious days as the star of Sergei Diaghilev's *Ballets Russes.*

Feklistov, as Nijinsky's cerebral half, comes across early as a rational psychologist, whose task is to draw the impetuous Menshikov out of his sublime estrangement from reality. But, as Menshikov lightly spins away from each attempt to make him define himself, Feklistov slowly loses his confident facade. When he begins imitating Nijinsky's famous movements and poses, we realize that we are witnessing the mystery of an internal process. Feklistov's almost unnoticeable descent into the sometimes disturbing, but, more often, liberating world of the irrational is a stunning achievement.

Illuminated with a wide-eyed sense of wonder, humor and irreverence, *Nijinsky* does not lament the loss of talent to madness, but celebrates the enigma of genius.

On one level, this production is proof that theater, too, can soar in a state of perpetual suspension—as legend has it Nijinsky himself did in *Le Spectre de la Rose*. On another it is proof that the post-Soviet theater is continuing its search for forms and methods—and that, from time to time, it is discovering them.

(*March 1993*)

Uncle Vanya, Theater u Nikitskikh vorot

How many thousands of productions have there been of Anton Chekhov's *Uncle Vanya* since the first, 94 years ago? There are at least five right now in Moscow, two of which premiered within the last month. But the one to see is Mark Rozovsky's new staging at the Theater u Nikitskikh vorot.

This often intense, often humorous portrayal of squandered lives in the 19th-century Russian countryside is blessed with a bushel-full of fine performances. And Rozovsky's subtle direction makes as much room for quirky interpretations of Chekhov's classic text as it does for time-

honored, traditional elements. It casts a new light on a great play which we may think we know too well.

Most surprising is Vladimir Dolinsky's interpretation of Professor Serebryakov as a slightly peevish, slightly impish old man who understands a lot more than others think he does. Dolinsky sidestepped the usual portrayal of a grandiloquent, crotchety man of science, laying the foundation for the performance's comic undercurrents.

Rather than being confounded by Uncle Vanya's deep-seated frustration at having sacrificed his youth in the service of a "famous scholar," this Serebryakov is simply fed-up with what he sees as a whiner: "Don't leave me with him!" he shouts in terror. "He'll talk my head off!" Meanwhile, his suspicions that his beautiful young wife, Yelena, has had a romance with Astrov, the provincial doctor, seem to give him almost as much pleasure as the knowledge that she is leaving her new lover to return home with him to the city.

This twist deepens even further the crisis of the sympathetic, but hapless Uncle Vanya, who loses out in the battle for Yelena's affections to Astrov (played by Andrei Molotkov with equal doses of jaded selfishness and charming gallantry). Sergei Desnitsky's Vanya is a man who believes too sincerely that he is a tragic figure to realize just how foolish he can be.

The one with legitimate claims to a tragic existence is Vanya's niece, Sonya. Hopelessly buried in the tedium of provincial life, the only source of light in her life is the secret love she carries for Astrov. When that dream is dashed, she is left nothing but the prospect of a monotonous future with her embittered uncle. Viktoria Zaslavskaya's brilliant portrayal of this "homely girl" with the "beautiful hair" is pieced together meticulously through alternating turns of touching naiveté, self-parody and indomitable inner strength.

The scene in which Sonya confesses to Yelena her love for Astrov is conducted as a subtle, calculating duel between two unequal enemies playing at being equal friends. The overmatched girl maintains her guard as long as she can against the quietly predatory pledges of sisterhood that Natalya Baronina's Yelena plies her with. Assuring Sonya that knowing an unpleasant truth is better than living with uncertainty, Yelena promises to find out whether Astrov shares Sonya's feelings. But, Sonya instinctively realizes the game is lost. Standing deep in the shadowy stage, her face expressing horror, she silently fends off Yelena's platitudes with short, frightened gestures of the hands. It is a chilling moment in which her fear of rejection in love takes on the aura of an encounter with the devil.

Designer Tatyana Shvets's set of wooden, see-through walls, which are rearranged from act to act, does a fine job of giving the excellent ensemble of actors and the theater's tiny stage the room to embrace the teeming passions, conflicting personalities and broken biographies of Chekhov's expansive play. Performances like this are what remind us that the classics are classics because they have the power to inspire directors, actors and audiences again and again.

(*March 1993*)

La Divina, Alla Sigalova
Independent Company

The newest production of the Alla Sigalova Independent Company, *La Divina: In Memory of Maria Callas*, brings the young choreographer and dancer closer to her classical roots than she has ever been before. Educated at the Kirov school of ballet, Sigalova raised eyebrows in 1989 by creating her own hybrid of modern dance and drama theater. Many of her productions, such as *Othello, Salomé* and *Pugachyov* relied in varying degrees on dramatic texts, while *A Game of Hide-and-Seek with Loneliness* was a composition done to contemporary pop songs.

La Divina is a very personal dance interpretation of various stages in a woman's life, ranging from memories of childhood to the experiences of sexual and motherly love. The entire performance is done to many of the soaring arias that made Maria Callas one of the great opera singers of our time. It bears the same stamp as Sigalova's other

work—the choreography is eclectic, physical, emotional and often humorous—but, under the influence of Callas's truly divine voice, it is also washed in a smooth tone of charged serenity.

Callas's seemingly effortless ability to inspire is apparent from the outset: Sigalova, alone on stage, face upturned, stands in tense motionless profile as the diva's voice fills the hall. There is little doubt that we are watching not only the prologue to the performance, but also that fleeting moment when Sigalova herself is gathering the inspiration which will carry her through to the end.

The cast consists primarily of the dramatic actors-turned-dancers who have been with Sigalova from the start: Anna Terekhova, Nikolai Dobrynin, Andrei Sergievsky and Taras Kolyadov.

But the uncontested star is Sigalova herself, who, previously, has performed only in *A Game of Hide-and-Seek*. It is no coincidence that, until *La Divina*, that was the Independent Troupe's most effective outing. During the performance, the charismatic, lightning-quick Sigalova does not once leave the stage, even for her numerous costume changes, which are conducted upstage during near black-outs between scenes.

Aside from a few brief, but extremely expressive moments during the prologue, in which Sigalova's character has a disconcerting meeting with herself as a child (played by Anna Politkovskaya), the dancer spends most of the first two scenes merely observing the action. In the second of them, Sigalova haughtily plants herself, legs spread, on the forestage and gazes on challengingly as the three men perform an angular, even cantankerous "male dance." Finally, Sigalova stands, waves them aside and takes center stage. The men now stare at her in surprise and admiration. Exuding fiery energy and projecting her powerful stage presence, she virtually conducts a clinic in grace, agility and feminine chutzpa.

The "plots" of the various scenes are as simple as they are timeless—flirtation, sexual attraction, love, unfaithfulness and jealousy—and, at times, they retrace ground covered in earlier productions. The same might be said of the choreography, with its bold, sweeping movements that seem to echo the forms of Egyptian hieroglyphs, 1920s dance halls, and maybe even modern comics.

But, pointing out familiar strains in an artist's work is often the flip side of saying that he or she has achieved a unique, personal signature. That is certainly the case with Sigalova, who has proved time and again that she has the ability to create provocative, amusing and liberating visions of the human experience.

La Divina is a beautiful performance, both as a tribute to a great singer and as a vehicle for a choreographer and dancer who has no lack of star quality herself.

(*April 1993*)

Ivanov, Stanislavsky Drama Theater; and *Le Canotier*, Mossoviet Theater

It can be disconcerting to enter a theater and realize that the performance you are about to see is probably doomed before it starts. But that is the dilemma created by Mikhail Feigin's staging of Anton Chekhov's *Ivanov* at the Stanislavsky Drama Theater. The offender in this case is Alexander Borovsky's strikingly obtrusive set.

The clunky wooden structure, which towers over the edge of the stage, forms the porch of a country home. Its crisscross railings hide most of the action on the porch itself, and turn everything that occurs behind it, on a second white-columned porch, into a kind of theatrical rumor. You may hear voices drifting through the hall, but good luck matching them with the speakers. Ultimately, you spend most of your time watching other spectators bob and weave in hopes of catching a glimpse of what is happening on stage.

Ivanov was one of Chekhov's first plays. It is bloated and diffuse, although its examination of a typical Russian Hamlet in the title character justifies the frequent attempts to stage it.

In this production, however, Ivanov is hamstrung by aimlessness rather than contemplation. His Jew-turned-Orthodox wife, Sarah (Yevgenia Simonova), claims he once was charming and witty, while Ivanov,

calling himself "harsh and ferocious," says he used to do the work of ten men.

Nothing in the performance, however, by Mikhail Filippov—who moves mountains across town at the Mayakovsky Theater in *Napoleon I*—gives us reason to believe either that or the fact that his neighbor's daughter, Sasha (played with spark by Yelena Kravchenko), could fall hopelessly in love with him. This Ivanov drowns in a sea of whimpers and sighs.

Throughout, Feigin highlights Chekhov's leitmotif of the resurrection of Lazarus, seeming to imply there is hope even for the Ivanovs of the world. But, in this production at least, Ivanov—and the evening's offerings—are beyond redemption.

In Nikolai Kolyada's *Le Canotier*, at the Mossoviet Theater, director Boris Shchedrin addressed another facet of the Russian Hamlet syndrome: the generation gap, in which the children traditionally see their parents as the epitome of ineffectuality. The hero here is a liberal intellectual with his roots in the 1960s. Although the performance descends into an evening of topical catch-phrases, it is not without its redeeming moments.

The play focuses on Viktor, a failed artist who is divorced and living in a communal apartment constantly shaken by passing subway trains. It is Viktor's birthday but, aside from his caustically irreverent young neighbor Katya, he isn't expecting guests. A surprise visit from his former wife Viktoria, and her son Alexander, ruffles the relative calm of the day.

Viktoria and Alexander essentially represent their respective generations' mercantile view of life. Nelli Pshennaya and Dmitry Bozin, as mother and son, give workmanlike performances. Viktor and the eccentric Katya are of a more bohemian and spiritual cut, though no less at odds with one another.

Alexander Lenkov's rumpled and quietly charming Viktor has maintained his dignity, as is represented by his *canotier*, or hat, which he proudly dons on festive occasions.

Meanwhile, Larisa Kuznetsova's Katya is delightfully hip, despite being crude and foul mouthed (some say that is Kolyada's main claim to fame). Aside from some maudlin moments when she tries too hard to be sincere, Kuznetsova is the life of this party of misfits.

(*April 1993*)

Tribute, Anton Chekhov Theater

The popularity of snappy, theme-oriented television sitcoms flashes a lure at American playwrights that even a saint probably couldn't resist. Their paint-by-numbers formula promises the closest thing to sure-fire success there is. Take a serious topic that nobody really wants to confront, drain all the poison out of it, recast it in alternating cascades of one-liners and tear-jerking scenes, and—presto!—matinee meditations for the masses.

Bernard Slade's *Tribute*, lushly produced by Leonid Trushkin for the Anton Chekhov Theater, is a perfect case in point. The topic here is untimely death. More specifically, Scottie (Alexander Shirvindt) is a robust fifty-one years old, but he has just been diagnosed with cancer. He doesn't want to talk about it, nor, so it would seem, do most of his friends. The sole exception is Gladys (Larisa Golubkina), a nurse who was once one in a long line of lovers.

But the friends, lovers and family of the fun-loving Scottie want to do something worthy of him and they rent out a theater where they throw him a gala farewell party. Snippets of this celebratory evening, emceed by Scottie's best buddy (Mikhail Derzhavin), are woven in among scenes from the last months of Scottie's life. These flashbacks let us get to know not only Scottie, but his latest, light-headed one-night stand, Sonny (Yekaterina Semyonova), his understanding ex-wife, Maggie (Vera Alentova), his goofy, one true love, Hilary (Tatyana Dogileva) and his estranged teen-age son, Jud (Alexander Strizhenov).

The conflict between the convivial dad and his hung-up son is the fulcrum around which this world turns. Trying to loosen his son up, Dad suggests a trip to the strip bars on 42nd Street. But Jud prefers to take in a new exhibit at the museum and trudges off

alone with his camera dangling around his neck. Undaunted, Scottie gives Sonny a call and sends her to the museum to hit up on his son. It's all in good fun, of course, because the loosey-goosey girl of modern mores is really a true, golden heart. She is the catalyst who, after a lot of frustrating spats, causes the prudish Jud to begin studying Scottie's source of charm and to reconsider his attitude towards himself and his father.

Jud is not the only one visited by revelations. As Scottie stands dwarfed by flashing, neon lights pointing the way to a smoky afterworld, he chokes up and calls for his son. Weeping and shouting, Jud bounds to his side from out of the audience for a last-minute reconciliation.

Trushkin's aim in staging this play coincided neatly with Slade's intention in writing it: He set out first and foremost to entertain. Aided by the fine lyrical talent of Alexander Shirvindt, he succeeded at times. As Scottie, Shirvindt has a suave way of sidestepping the corny elements of his character to create a sympathetic, forgivably irritating man facing his own mortality.

Lacking Shirvindt's cool subtlety, the remainder of the cast gives us clear-cut, one-dimensional performances. Semyonova is energetic, Dogileva is comically vulgar, Alentova is sincere. No more and no less. Strizhenov, as Jud, confuses youthful stridency with nerdiness, and emotional speech with guttural shrieking, injecting a decidedly sour note into the proceedings.

Boris Valuyev's set—the comfy interior of a two-story town house and the neon-lined theater stage—joins with Vladimir Davydenko's softly sentimental score to work at making everyone feel a little better about death.

(*May 1993*)

The Miller Who Was a Wizard, a Cheat and a Matchmaker, Malaya Bronnaya Theater

In 1779, a new comic opera called *The Miller Who Was a Wizard, a Cheat and a Matchmaker* enjoyed unprecedented success when offered to the judgment of the Moscow public. An anonymous author recorded the

Sergei Taramayev, Yelena Matveeva and Nadezhda Markina in Sergei Zhenovach's production of Alexander Ablesimov's *The Miller Who Was a Wizard, a Cheat and a Matchmaker* at the Malaya Bronnaya Theater, 1993. Photo: Alexander Ivanishin

event for posterity: "This opera so excited the public's attention that it was played several times in succession, and the theater was ever full. Not only was it heard with pleasure by nationals, but even foreigners exhibited a healthy curiosity." We might add that a rousing new production of this folk-inspired work at the Malaya Bronnaya Theater leaves little doubt; once a crowd-pleaser, always a crowd-pleaser.

Following his painfully disorganized production of *The Abyss* earlier this season, director Sergei Zhenovach bounced back in spectacular fashion. He took Alexander Ablesimov's charmingly naive tale, about a resourceful miller who arranges a marriage for a lovelorn peasant, and infused it with an exquisite sense of balance. Chock-full of authentic Russian folk songs arranged by Vitaly Galitsky, and set in a starry-skied, winter wonderland designed by Yury

Galperin, *The Miller* is a grandiose celebration of the Russian spirit.

It all begins as Faddei-the-miller laments the lack of wind, without which he cannot earn his keep. Enter Filimon, a farmer from a neighboring village, who has lost his horses. Like everyone else, he believes the superstition that all millers are wizards for their mastery of the winds.

For a fee, the "wizard" locates the wayward horses, and the overjoyed Filimon is encouraged to divulge a secret: He wants to marry the fair Anyuta. But he also knows he'll never get her parents' permission without supernatural help. Faddei quickly recognizes a new source of income when he sees it. Plying his otherworldly "powers" on Anyuta, her mother Fetinya, and her father Anukdin, Faddei convinces them all that Filimon is their chosen suitor. No matter that mama wants a nobleman for a son-in-law, while daddy wants a man of peasant stock. No task is too tall for the quick-witted miller.

Zhenovach lovingly enveloped the performance in a thick, warm blanket of parody. While portraying their well-defined characters with folkloric precision, the actors never lose sight of the fact that they are at play. Their softly stylized gestures and intonations both mock and elevate the story's blissful artlessness. That dual approach gives them the freedom to act out their own affectionate relationships to their characters, drawing us into the fairy-tale world with them.

Nadezhda Markina infuses Fetinya with a radiant, stately dignity, although that doesn't preclude her occasionally taking a step back to look at herself with a knowing, affectionate smile. Yelena Matveeva delights in creating a deadly-serious Anyuta. Even the sparkling smile of this rosy-cheeked, bell-shaped beauty can't hide that she is far more interested in when she will marry than whom. Vladimir Yavorsky's Filimon is hopelessly gullible, while Sergei Perelygin's Anukdin is the proverbial salt-of-the-earth.

Sergei Taramayev plays Faddei as a variation on the theme of Ivanushka-the-fool, that Russian hero who is infinitely smarter than he looks. With his twinkling eyes and funny, bow-legged, hopping gait, he weaves a good-natured, deceptive spell that no one can resist.

All else aside, this performance is a must-see for the music alone. Winding in and out of the action, the Rusachi folk ensemble joins the cast to hit notes and find rhythms most of us didn't know existed. *The Miller* creates a stirring vision not only of the Russia some say has been lost, but of the Russia that is eternal.

(*May 1993*)

Guilty Without Guilt, Vakhtangov Theater

This year marks the 170th anniversary of the birth of Alexander Ostrovsky, Russia's first great man of the theater. Aside from writing 54 plays, nearly half of which are considered masterpieces, Ostrovsky led the movement to protect authors' and actors' rights, and was a co-founder of Russia's first private, commercial theater. The Maly Theater, which produced nearly all of his plays during his lifetime, is known as "the house of Ostrovsky."

Non-Russians are often baffled by the reverence Ostrovsky is afforded by his countrymen. His plays may appear as melodramatic potboilers about money-hungry upstarts and poor young women beset by others' insensitivity, but Ostrovsky's theatrical instincts bordered on the magical. Few have written plays that spring to life so vividly when staged well. There is no better proof than Pyotr Fomenko's brilliant production of *Guilty Without Guilt* at the Vakhtangov Theater.

The story is pure Ostrovsky. A young woman, who bore a child out of wedlock, is cast off by her lover, who sneaks away to marry her wealthy girlfriend. While recuperating from that blow at her grandmother's, she learns that her son has died, and runs away to become an actress. Twenty years on, she returns home a star, having changed her name from Otradina to Kruchinina. As is to be expected, she must suffer the intrigues of the local folk before learning that the news of her son's death was a lie.

In Fomenko's hands, the play's seeming sentimentality is revealed as gripping, human drama, splashed with broad swaths of humor and infused with sophistication. That was achieved, in part, by the director's unusual choice of a "stage."

A short prologue, showing the young Otradina, is performed in a cramped room that reveals a spectacular "aerial" view of the Vakhtangov's foyer when a simple sheet curtain is drawn back. The remainder of the performance takes place in the theater's buffet. (For this reason, seating is limited to 80 and all performances are matinees.) Tatyana Selvinskaya's simple sets, consisting of some antique knickknacks and furniture, suggest the air of elegance through a careful use of detail, space and dark colors.

Proving that even cameos in an Ostrovsky play are an actor's dream, the entire cast turns in what may be the strongest ensemble work Moscow has seen in recent years. In the prologue, Lidia Velezheva is scintillating as Otradina. Her masterful command of

Pyotr Fomenko's production of Alexander Ostrovsky's *Guilty Without Guilt* at the Vakhtangov Theater, 1993, with Marina Yesipenko and Lidia Velezheva. Photo: Mikhail Guterman

nuance, understatement and temperament creates a complex and deeply moving portrait of a character who could otherwise appear to be too good to be true. Displaying an unerring, lightning-quick feel for comedy, Marina Yesipenko is unforgettable in her sole scene as Otradina's attractively unscrupulous girlfriend, Taisa. This taut, half-hour segment could easily stand on its own as a finished performance.

The continuation begins with old-fashioned leisure. Yury Yakovlev, as Dudkin, the impresario who brought Kruchinina home, saunters in singing a tune and blowing kisses to the women in the audience. To the dismay of his leading lady, Korinkina (Lyudmila Maksakova) this selfish, spoiled and charming old man has set his sights on the visiting celebrity. The mercurial Korinkina responds by renewing her affair with the actor Milovzorov (Viktor Zozulin), who is also smitten by Kruchinina's "French" refinement.

The tangle of intrigues is compounded when Kruchinina (performed with grace and warmth by Yulia Borisova) intercedes with the authorities for a hot-headed young actor, Neznamov (Yevgeny Knyazev). He is threatened with banishment for getting into a brawl with Milovzorov. Accompanied by his salty sidekick, Shmaga (Yury Volyntsev), Neznamov takes offense at Kruchinina's uninvited benevolence, but senses in her the mother's tenderness he never knew. The truth of the past slowly emerges as Kruchinina encounters her son's former nanny (a sparkling, comic cameo by Alla Kazanskaya) and her repentant, unfaithful lover (Vyacheslav Shalevich).

The actors use the entire buffet room as a stage, mingling and even interacting with the spectators. That direct contact, together with the constant alternation of the performance's tempo and tone between brash, fast-paced humor and sensitive, lyrical scenes, draws us irresistibly into the fascinating interior of an "improbable" world which is shot-through with the undeniable truth of the human experience. *Guilty Without Guilt* is a rare example of a great playwright being matched by the prodigious talents of the artists who bring him to the stage.

(*May 1993*)

Orison, Chelovek Theater-Studio

Fernando Arrabal's *Orison* is a parable about a man, Fidio, and a woman, Lilbe, who try to abandon their wrongful ways and start anew. One in a series of mini-plays Arrabal has called Panic Theater, *Orison* illustrates the natural human inclination toward sinfulness. Lyudmila Roshkovan's staging of it at the Chelovek Theater-Studio comes across as something of a light-hearted polemic with the author.

Consisting of just a few pages of text, the play is purposefully naive. Fidio buys a Bible and tells his mate that, from this day forth, they will be "good and pure." No more sex, no more killing and no more poking out the eyes of the dead at the cemetery. She is skeptical, and he's not so sure about the idea himself. But that doesn't stop him from trying to convince her anyway.

The performance, which fills in the sparse dialogue with pantomimic movement and the airy, jazzy music of the Homo Ludens trio, is characterized by a warm, ironic humor that has little to do with panic. To be sure, the voracious Lilbe (Tatyana Kulikova) is shocked that she may be deprived of physical pleasure. She spends much of her time wrapping her legs around Fidio in an attempt to snap him out of his illusions. For his part, Fidio (Vladislav Demchenko) is aghast at the task he has set himself. But in his clumsy stab at saintliness, he looks more like a simpleton who has bit off more than he can chew than a man confronting the abyss of evil.

Even the set by Viktor Platonov and Grigory Fomin works to soften the impact of the performance before it begins. The floor of the small hall is covered in a rolling sea of chopped rubber bits. And when you make your way to one of the seats scattered around the perimeter, you can't help but feel that the earth is swaying under your feet. It is an effective and humorous reminder that, while we may usually take the sense of touch for granted, it is probably the most powerful of all the senses. Ultimately, Arrabal's notion that physicality blocks the road to spirituality is turned on end and shown in a different light.

The action begins with a prolonged pantomime. Lilbe is alone on stage and, without a partner to mirror her existence, she seeks various ways to define herself. She counts her hairs (stopping at the Divine number of 33), interacts with a bowler hat and draws chalk outlines of her body on the tiny, oval plexiglas stage.

Fidio's appearance introduces a brief sense of harmony as the two silently imitate each other's movements. But that moment fades quickly when Fidio announces his plans to be "good." Later, he involuntarily erases the drawings of Lilbe's body while writhing on the floor in search of his Bible. That simple metaphor epitomizes the thrust of the performance: In striving to attain an abstract spirituality, one is likely to lose contact with the here and now.

In the early going, Demchenko imparts a mysterious, childlike wonder to the obsessed Fidio, echoing his desire that the couple be "pure as children." He is less effective later on when his emotional outbursts often violate the spell of the performance. Kulikova, who remains the (almost) unwavering link to "reality" from beginning to end, does a nice job of illuminating her character from within.

Orison can tend toward the banal when it slips out of the primitivistic simplicity that marks its best moments. But, in all, it evokes an unadorned immediacy that makes for an engaging performance.

(May 1993)

Uncle Vanya, Maly Theater

The new production of Anton Chekhov's *Uncle Vanya* at the Maly Theater marks the professional theater debut of the well-known film director, Sergei Solovyov. His films, *Assa* (1987), *Black Rose—the Symbol of Sorrow, Red Rose—The Symbol of Love* (1989) and *Home Under a Starry Sky*, (1991) brought him "fame as a frenzied post-modernist," as he writes himself in the program notes. But, his purpose in joining with Russia's oldest theater was to create "a hyper-academic production," he adds.

"Academic" theater usually suggests the arrangement of a profusion of "lifelike" details in an artificial context. It isn't so much a slice of life as it is a conscious simulation of life, a subtle ruse. If that's what Solovyov had in mind, then he accomplished what he was after. One seldom sees tedium, aimlessness and mediocrity reproduced with such veracity.

This *Uncle Vanya* begins with what may be the longest pause of the season, and, from there on, things only get slower. Birds sing, crickets chirp, bells ring, dogs bark, thunder booms, rain starts and silence falls—all at the prescribed moments. Amidst that careful schematic of sounds, the actors whine, sigh, fiddle, fret and, on rare occasion, bluster, as people are wont to do. All to no discernible purpose.

Chekhov wrote a brilliant play that reveals the killing effect of lethargy on talent, intellect and spontaneity. Uncle Vanya and Doctor Astrov are not merely witnesses to their own inexorable decline, they drag down everyone else with them. Their infatuations with the self-important Professor Serebryakov's superficial young wife, Yelena, are little more than cries of despair. Of the principals, only Vanya's niece, Sonya, has maintained her inner dignity, but she is incapable of combating the deadly air around her. Solovyov's production captures none of that, nor does it offer an alternative.

One suspects he failed to grasp the fundamental difference between screen and stage. In film, the roving camera's selective eye creates tension by focusing on fragments of action. We are left to create the rest of the picture by processing those hints in our own imagination. Theater, even at its most experimental, is a more static medium. An actor's every movement is constantly on display, and the setting seldom changes. The dynamics of a performance are built on the subtle interlacing of relations: character to character, actor to actor, and all of them to the director's vision of what the playwright was up to.

But the members of this cast are so obsessed with the figures they cut, they never make contact with one another, to say nothing of the author. Yury Solomin isolates Vanya behind an impenetrable wall of self-pity. Vitaly Solomin, as Astrov, is a crowd-pleaser with his funny noises, screwed-up faces, and affected voice, although one wonders where that all fits into the production. Svetlana Amanova's Yelena strikes a nice, touch-me-not pose, but this is theater, not photography, and one also has to act. The sole oasis in this wasteland is Yelizaveta Solodova's warm interpretation of the old nanny.

As Sonya, Tatyana Drubich is a special case. The leading lady in most of Solovyov's films, she is making her first-ever stage appearance. It shows. She spends most of her time trying to remember the right intonations, and looking for something to do with her hands.

Valery Levental's gorgeous set unites the worlds of cinema and theater. The front half of the stage is cluttered tastefully with antique props and furniture, while the back half, depicting a garden and the woods beyond it, is set off by a transparent drop. Effective lighting gives it the feel of a movie screen.

(*June 1993*)

Pas de Trois, **Pushkin Drama Theater**

The most intriguing thing about the production of *Pas de Trois* at the Pushkin Theater is the play itself. Not because it is very good, but because it smacks teasingly of being a "drama à clef."

Author Nina Berberova was a moderately prominent member of the first wave Russian emigration. She is better known as the first wife of the poet Vladislav Khodasevich and the author of controversial memoirs (*The Italics Are Mine*), than as a novelist, poet or dramatist in her own right. Judging by the opinionated style of her memoirs and the banal transparency of *Pas de Trois* (which Berberova called *Little Girl*), it may well be an encoding of a real-life incident. If not, one wonders why it was written.

The story involves the unorthodox relationship between a well-provided for, middle-aged couple, Sergei and Olga, and a wayward young girl, Doe. The former have most everything but youth, while the latter lacks most everything but spirit and daring.

Sergei starts out thinking he will have a harmless affair to rekindle the energy and spontaneity of his younger days. What he doesn't count on is Olga's understanding and support. After foiling the potential lovers' tryst with well-meaning intervention, Olga invites the girl to be a live-in house guest. Raising eyebrows among others, the troika delights in giving giggly free reign to their newfound lifestyle. But when Sergei begins sensing he is the odd-man-out, he presents his wife with an ultimatum: either the girl goes, or he goes.

As do many plays written by those who are primarily prose writers, *Pas de Trois* gives short shrift to action, internal drama and the other crucial laws of the theater. It abounds in weighty, informative chit-chat, such as in the early-going, when Doe asks Sergei whether he loves her. Sergei's reply: "I love your youth and I'll say nothing else." The Idea—in this case, the illusive lure of Youth—is not only the play's sole reason for being, it is also the only level on which the author attempts to communicate.

The hints at a lesbian connection between Olga and Doe, had they been crafted by a surer hand, might have opened up a window on what makes these people tick. But, like everything else in this play that concerns characterization, the ambiguous relationship is flatly self-reflective. The emphasis is on the ambiguity, rather than on the relationship, and the result is just a faintly titillating question mark in the proceedings.

Following Berberova's lead even while shortening the text, director Yelena Dolgina created a performance that bobs atop the characters' hopelessly submerged passions and complexes like a tinny skiff in stormy seas. Presumably, Andrei Maiorov's Sergei is a paunchy archaeologist suffering a mid-life crisis, although he might just as easily be a good-natured, overmatched masher. Nina Popova's Olga is giddily vivacious until her "game with fate" backfires and she runs the risk of losing her husband. As the rootless Doe, who reportedly poses nude for free and hangs out with suspicious friends, Yekaterina Sibiryakova pouts and squeals her way through from beginning to end.

The choreography by Tatyana Borisova, consisting mostly of repetitive twirling and outstretched arms, was probably intended to evoke a youthful spirit. It all takes place in the recognizable, intellectual's drawing room designed by Tatyana Selvinskaya.

Whether or not *Pas de Trois* is a dramatization of someone's real experience, as drama, it is little more than an exercise in stating the obvious. The natural response to that is, "So what?"

(*June 1993*)

Zhivago, Taganka Theater

The Taganka Theater was looking deceptively like the hub of progressive Russian society this week. The theater's mercurial director staged his own libretto of a banned classic by a great Russian writer "in disgrace" and set it to a score by a "disreputable" composer. The director was Yury Lyubimov, the classic was *Doctor Zhivago*, the writer Boris Pasternak and the composer Alfred Schnittke.

But the 1990s aren't the 1970s. Lyubimov, 75, now jets into Moscow from Israel, where he is a citizen. Pasternak is taught in every school and *Doctor Zhivago* is sold on every street corner. Schnittke lives in Germany, revered as one of the world's great contemporary composers. Meanwhile, this week's premiere of *Zhivago* was only a local first. It actually opened a month ago at Vienna's Festwochen '93.

Little of that mattered to the Who's Who crowd, mostly from the Brezhnev and Gorbachev eras, that packed the Taganka for Wednesday's Moscow opener. After a sluggish response to a chaotic first act, the audience showered Lyubimov and his actors with flowers and cheers at performance's end. But when the euphoria dies down, *Zhivago* will be remembered as an afterthought to an illustrious career.

In addition to including snippets of poetry by Alexander Pushkin, Alexander Blok and Osip Mandelshtam, Lyubimov did his best to include every twist and turn of Pasternak's epic novel in a performance he calls a "musical parable." It's all there if you are quick enough to catch it. The workers' demonstrations. Zhivago's marriage to Tonya. Larisa's humiliation at the hands of the odious Komarovsky and her marriage to the revolutionary, Strelnikov. The love triangle that binds Zhivago, Tonya and Larisa, and the interference of politics and jealousy that eventually separates them. Most of the scenes pass as perfunctorily as they are described here; many last only a matter of seconds.

As is usual for a Lyubimov production, the action is accompanied by a large chorus, representing the "people." Choreographed by Svetlana Voskresenskaya, the actors' rhythmic movements echo the familiar constructivist images of the 1920s. They make an effective visual background, although they do little to further our understanding of what is transpiring.

That is not surprising. The principals are so lacking in personality that they seem little more than extensions of the chorus themselves. Valery Zolotukhin's flat performance of Zhivago suggests a shy bookkeeper more than a sensitive doctor and poet. As Larisa, Anna Agapova has a nice voice and flashes a charming smile, but is bereft of any sense of inner drama. Lyubov Selyutina's Tonya merely reads her part, apparently assuming that the audience can fill in the rest. From the second line of characters, only the towering Alexander Trofimov, as Strelnikov, convincingly portrays the drama of a dedicated revolutionary who is devoured by the machine he helped create.

The performance is not without its compelling moments. But therein lies the chief problem. Like a vehicle with a balky engine, it sputters and hesitates for long periods. Suddenly, it lurches forward at full force for a brief instant before bogging down again in awkward chaos. Lyubimov's cluttered libretto is clearly part of the problem. But it is also evident that the actors are uncomfortable singing the majority of their lines. Schnittke's complex score usually comes across as an alien element, imposed on the material by force.

Andrey von Schlippe's versatile, gray set consists primarily of animated objects. Shovels, a "flying" table, a huge book that pops up out of the floor, street lamps and sheets that create the image of a train when lit from behind—all of them help explain the moments which the libretto itself didn't have the time or space to include. Together with the expressive chorus scenes, the setting contributes to the performance's most effective aspect: its visual impact.

Moscow may not have many chances to see *Zhivago* in the near future. At a press conference Monday, Lyubimov left no doubt that his former hometown is not high on his list of priorities. Frustrated by a lack of respect from the Russian press, and irritated by what he sees as the Russian penchant for disorganization and disorder, he repeatedly spoke of the advantages of working in the West. The irony is that even this world-class artist is not immune to the problems of his native society.

(June 1993)

1993/1994 SEASON

Six Specters of Lenin on a Piano,
Laboratory Theater

For all its riches, the local theater scene lacks one crucial thing: a place for new playwrights to try their hand. Maybe it's just Russian extremism or the impatience brought on by so many years of frustrated hopes, but the critical atmosphere in Moscow tends to hover consistently in the range from hostile to homicidal.

And if you're a nobody with designs of becoming a somebody and you've just written a new play, the last thing you want to do with your baby is feed it to a pack of wolves.

You can't help thinking about that state of affairs after taking in Viktor Denisov's whimsical *Six Specters of Lenin on a Piano* at the Laboratory Theater. Sure it's a bit formulaic, sure it's derivative (of Ionesco, for instance) and sure the theme of Vladimir Lenin's legacy is a tad clichéd.

But wait a minute. Denisov can write clever dialogue and he has a nice flair for situation and characterization. That's no mean feat for starters. And the homespun atmosphere at the Laboratory, buoyed by an energetic cast, provides just the supportive setting to give this fledgling work its first chance at life.

The story is one of those little absurdities that, in the 20th century, seems to make perfect sense. A multi-layered fantasy is given flesh as a young piano student (Olga Pletnyova) and her tutor (Alexander Mazurenko) act out a possible reality lying behind Salvador Dali's painting, "Six Specters of Lenin on a Piano."

She can't learn Chopin, she says, because the notes on the sheet music are really ants that keep crawling off the page. He tells her she's just nuts and a no-talent. Eventually, he falls asleep exhausted by her attempts to seduce him into apologizing for being rude.

Enter six mumbling and bumbling characters whom the young student wants to poison because she thinks they are ants. We recognize them as the six specters of Lenin.

In a series of slapstick and pass-the-punch-line episodes, the six Lenins diligently set about restructuring things. Specifically, their idea of the "process of piano perfection" leads them to break off the piano's pedal box which, they say, can just as easily be attached to the keyboard.

Appalled at the intruders' barbaric ways, the girl valiantly tries to defend her sleeping tutor's world. But the real shock is yet to come. When he finally wakes up, the muddle headed tutor falls right in step with the feverish songs and dances of reconstruction.

Andrei Rossinsky's hands-off direction and Irina Balashevich's simple set, consisting of Dali's painting, an oversized grand piano top and a piano painted on a drop cloth, combine with the unpretentious acting to create a simple, unadorned and engaging performance.

The trick is that no one hits too hard on the obvious metaphors of Lenin-as-insect or the intellectual as his own worst enemy. On the contrary, the most endearing characters are the colorful, indefatigable and, eventually, even sympathetic Lenins who appear under the various guises of "The Leader," "The Prophet," "The Monument" and others.

Credit the whole company with a performance that is greater than the sum of its parts. And if there is a message to be gleaned from it all, it's one of reconciliation. As if author Denisov were saying, "Hey, my heritage may be baffling. But it's mine. All of it!"

(*September 1993*)

The Master and Margarita, **South-West Theater-Studio**

Boiled down to its basics, the prevailing method at the feisty little South-West Theater-Studio is to swarm the tiny, dark stage with a raging, Mongol horde of actors intent on attacking the senses as quickly, as loudly, as relentlessly and as long as possible. The theater's devoted audience, shoe-horned into minuscule troughs masquerading as benches, knows what it's in for and loves every minute.

There's a good reason for that. Led by artistic director Valery Belyakovich, the once-underground theater-studio still retains the excitement and energy that has made it a Moscow legend for fifteen years. And Belyakovich's new dramatization of *The Master and Margarita*, Mikhail Bulgakov's classic novel of devilish Moscow mythology, will not disappoint the faithful.

The key strengths, as usual, center around the grandiose, operatic mass scenes and the small core of accomplished actors who move as freely in their director's theatrical visions as, well, Mario Andretti around a hairpin curve. Specifically, they are the pop-eyed, sunken-cheeked Viktor Avilov, as Woland, the prince of darkness who turns Moscow on end to prove the existence of Jesus and the Devil both, and Vyacheslav Grishechkin, Sergei Belyakovich and Vladimir Koppalov as the exquisitely street-wise members of his retinue.

Things run thinner where it concerns the title roles. Irina Podkopayeva and Pavel Kulikov are very earnest and nearly as bland as Margarita and her beloved Master, whose novel, about Pontius Pilate and the execution of one Yeshua Ha-Notsri, landed him in an insane asylum. The actors weren't helped by the script. Except for Margarita's presiding over the wild, ritualistic and tastefully risqué Satan's Ball, they are mostly reduced to standing in corners and narrating their own parts. And since they dominate the second and third acts, the weakest is held for last.

Uneven as it is, this performance has plenty of stirring moments. Many are created simply, through the mastery of the oldest tricks in the book: Face-making, exaggerated gesturing, top-of-the-dial sound levels and all of it done at a breakneck speed. Particularly impressive is the way Belyakovich conquers the limitations of his cramped stage through the use of lighting.

Bulgakov's four intersecting plot lines get a full-blooded treatment. All the characters (39 plus extras) and all the famous scenes are there: From the initial meeting of Woland with the soon-to-be beheaded Berlioz and the hack poet Ivan Bezdomny (kudos to Alexander Naumov), to the black magic seance at the variety theater, and the complete intrigue of the luckless Pontius Pilate, whose fate it is to order the death of a soft-spoken prophet. Valery Afanasyev's taut, severe rendering of Pilate provides the crucial counterweight to the proceedings' reckless abandon.

The bottom line is that if you are claustrophobic or have weak nerves, *The Master and Margarita* is not for you. But if your idea of fun is pushing it to the limit, have at it. Only don't blame the guy behind you for jabbing his knees in your back—he can't help it. And take a cushion. That fifth hour of the performance can be a hard ride.

(September 1993)

Ivanov and Others, Young Spectator Theater

The delays plaguing Genrietta Yanovskaya's rehearsals of *Ivanov and Others* throughout most of last year finally seemed to be over. As September dawned, word was that Moscow was in for a treat well worth the wait. Then all began unraveling.

Just days before the first performance, one of the lead actors was found shot to death in his car. In a state of shock and grief, Yanovskaya, the artistic director at the Young Spectator Theater, immediately took on the grim task of preparing a replacement. She pushed back the opener a week and set to work. Then, with two days left to the rescheduled premiere, hearts skipped a beat again. Sergei Shakurov, the production's Ivanov, was rushed to the hospital.

This time the outcome was benign. Shakurov left the hospital on the morning of the opener and played his heart out that night.

For as long as this spell-binding production of Anton Chekhov's *Ivanov* is remembered—and that should be a long time—the tragedy and difficulties surrounding it will be a part of the legend. The rest will be more "mundane": Plain and simple, this is a riveting piece of theater.

Forget all the languid, "Chekhovian" adjectives in use ever since Chekhov himself railed at the tedium most theaters cultivated when staging him. Yanovskaya flew in the face of convention at every turn, sending full-blooded, willful, yet tragically flawed characters down the paths usually traveled by phlegmatic whiners. The result? Without violating the playwright's exquisitely subtle patterns of paradoxes and contradictions, she tapped into the nerve center of his genius for pinpointing the humor and horror lurking in almost every human endeavor.

She recalibrated the tone of Chekhov's early play by replacing several minor characters with others from his more famous dramas. Such lonely, abandoned and comic odd-balls as Charlotte, from *The Cherry Orchard* and Waffles, from *Uncle Vanya*, echo and illuminate in miniature the sense of alienation and powerlessness gripping Ivanov and the other principles.

Viktoria Verberg plays Ivanov's rejected wife Anna—the Jewess who abandoned her faith and family for love—with the vengeance, not of a woman scorned, but of one who believes utterly, even desperately, in the power of the love that consumes her. Naturally, it is to no avail. Shakurov's honest, wisely realistic and even compassionate Ivanov simply does not love her anymore. He is appalled at himself, but no sense of guilt can make him do the impossible: He cannot revive the past.

The future beckons to Ivanov briefly in the form of Sasha, a forthright, intelligent young woman whose longtime admiration for her troubled neighbor has ripened into love. Oksana Kiryushchenko's Sasha attracts Ivanov with her beauty, her bold sense of purpose and her refusal to be duped by the wagging tongues of gossips. But, ultimately, she too is doomed to failure.

The explanation this production offers is as obvious as it is endlessly complex. Love is not all you need. One needs also know how to be loved. But, suggests Yanovskaya, even if those conditions are fulfilled, the greatest enigma remains: Does anyone really need another's love?

As posed here, that is no tattered cliché. It is a harsh, corrosive truth that is reflected in Sergei Barkhin's rusty set of metal walls and shaky columns. Yanovskaya offers moments of respite in the reassuring sounds of nature or short, comic interludes, but more characteristic are the jarring bursts of fireworks that, like passions, fizzle out as quickly as they flare up.

Superbly acted from top to bottom, this carefully orchestrated production is a revelation: about Chekhov, theater and human nature. Mark it the first hit of the young season.

(September 1993)

The Blessed Island, Chekhov Art Theater

Ingredients: (1) The revival of *The Blessed Island,* an obscure play by the important Ukrainian playwright, Mykola Kulish. (2) A blend of big-name veterans and talented young blood from the Chekhov Art Theater. (3) A tender, loving touch from director Nikolai Sheiko.

A recipe for success? Well, more like the makings of a passingly pleasant, ultimately forgettable soufflé.

Kulish's play is an ethereal comedy, dashed with healthy doses of mad farce, that looks at the effects of the Bolshevik Revolution on a traditional Ukrainian family. Its dramatic impulse derives from the suddenly very timely, relentless fear of a godless and lawless future that grips the reasonably pious Savvaty Guska, his flabbergasted wife, Sekleteya, and their motley brood of seven strong-headed daughters.

Originally titled *Thus Perished Guska,* the play contributed to Kulish's arrest in 1934. The subsequent fates of both play and playwright are hazy. Kulish died in the camps sometime between 1937 and 1942. As for the play, some say it was lost and only recently rediscovered, while others claim it was published in 1960. Whatever the case, it has remained something of a mystery. That isn't especially surprising. It is no musty masterpiece.

The story is simple to the point of transparency. The Guska family, joined by their newly-returned governess, Ivdya, watches in terror as the Bolsheviks confiscate their neighbors' houses. A visit from a young family friend, Pierre, an ex-student from Kiev, gives them momentary respite, but their angst is cranked up again when a mysterious Bolshevik agent is given a room in their very home. Finally, at Pierre's urging, they "escape" to an idyllic, uninhabited island, untouched by politics.

Presumably lacking a better way to liven things up, Kulish leaned heavily on "revolving-door" scenes involving the daughters. In one, like mechanical dolls, they awaken from sleep and recite their dreams. In others, they pop up on stage one-by-one to flirt with the handsome Pierre and bicker amongst themselves (the first time, begging Pierre to save their daddy; the second time, thanking him—prematurely—for doing it).

By the grace of his impressive girth and massive talent, Vyacheslav Nevinny finds in the hard-pressed Guska a man of warmth, sympathy and endearing limitations. Given the thin material (aside from drilling a peep hole in the agent's wall, Guska hardly ever does anything), Nevinny relies almost entirely on his own endearing personality and infallible comic instincts to keep things afloat.

Also effective are the perky Darya Yurskaya, who charms as Akhtisenka, the angelic and scheming, youngest daughter, and Irina Apeksimova, as the momentously silent Khristenka, the daughter who vowed to remain silent until the Bolsheviks are gone.

But there just isn't enough of a play to latch onto. Sheiko stirs things up in the first half with plenty of frothy stammering and stamping, but it's too much show and too little substance. In the second half, he effectively plunges us into a strangely soothing natural preserve, but the outcome is formulaic and predictable.

Mart Kitayev's sets parallel the predominant atmospheres. An empty platform, stuffed above and below with random, homey objects, supports the busy first act. A simple and beautiful atmosphere, created primarily by subtle lighting and an enormous hanging plant, adorns the second.

The Blessed Island may provide some insight into Kulish's personal drama as one who rejected the Revolution as energetically as he had once accepted it, but it does nothing to enhance his reputation as a writer.

(October 1993)

Bérénice, National Youth Theater

Amidst the competition, chaos and crossfire that characterizes the diversity of the local theater scene—it certainly isn't immune to all the broader trends—there is a fledgling movement gathering steam. It might be described as "the smaller the better."

Small stages, adapted apartments, buffet rooms and even corridors have hosted some of the most interesting productions in recent years. Now we can add stairwells to the list.

What better metaphor for the decline of love and the ascent of power than a stately, dimly-lit stairway, lined with flickering candles in blood-red cups? Especially when the tiny audience of 40 views part one from the floor up, part two from a side stairwell on the central landing, and part three from the top of the stairs peering down into an abyss. The play inspiring that move is Jean Racine's *Bérénice*. At its best, Alexei Borodin's brief production of it at the National Youth Theater is like the tense, hot breath of two lovers doomed to part.

Racine's tragedy—about the star-crossed bond between the newly-crowned Roman emperor, Titus, and his beloved Bérénice, the Queen of Palestine—has been praised for its exacting simplicity ever since it appeared in 1670. It is a full-blooded, neoclassical tragedy on an intimate scale. This production's setting, devised by Borodin with designer Stanislav Benediktov, combines with the buffered intensity of the committed young cast to do a fine job of embracing that seeming contradiction.

The play begins with its only digression, as Titus's friend, Antioch (Alexei Vesyolkin), secretly admits he loves Bérénice. Antioch then confesses to her in person, but she rebuffs him, remaining unshakably true to her betrothed. From there the action develops with the swift, unwavering momentum of an arrow aimed at the heart.

Titus's first appearance reveals in sum all that is about to happen. His subjects will not abide a foreign empress, and, to maintain the stability of the state, he must reject her. Not yet suspecting Antioch's divided loyalties, Titus arranges to send Bérénice away with him.

Nina Dvorzhetskaya and Yevgeny Dvorzhetsky in Racine's *Bérénice* at the National Youth Theater, directed by Alexei Borodin, 1993. Photo: Alexander Ivanishin

As the emperor trapped by duty, Yevgeny Dvorzhetsky puts to excellent use his lean, lanky body, his rolling voice and heavy-lidded eyes. In him, Titus-the-man and Titus-the-head-of-state are engaged in a perfectly-matched duel to the death. Only through the sheer force of will can he break with the only woman he has ever loved, knowing he will love her forever. His voice echoing in the tunnel of the staircase, and his motionless, expressionless face barely illuminated by the candle he unceasingly holds before him, Dvorzhetsky is the picture of bitter, hopeless resignation.

Nina Dvorzhetskaya's Bérénice is every bit the crippled emperor's match. She is neither a suffering wallflower, nor a woman simply ruled by her devotion to a man. In her firm rejection of Antioch's advances, we easily detect the pride and pleasure her sexual power affords her. She does not merely love Titus; he is a fitting object for her passion. All the greater is her agony when she comes to realize the tragic fate in store for her.

Except for the setting, Borodin was tastefully conservative in other aspects of his direction. His actors wear conventional Roman togas and speak the verse text with the proper regal intonations. Most of the time they do it well. They move in a mildly stylized manner that evokes comparison with the well-known gestures of Roman statues.

This *Bérénice* is marked by a cold, pristine beauty that is constantly shaken by white-hot, subterranean emotions. It is a fine example of making a "rigid" classic come to life in a modern context.

(*October 1993*)

The Inspector General, Theater na Pokrovke

A reputable New York critic once admitted doubting that the classic Russian comedy, *The Inspector General*, is even stageworthy. First, he quoted the famous opening line, uttered by a provincial mayor: "I have invited you here, gentlemen, in order to communicate a most unpleasant piece of news: A government inspector is coming to visit us."

Added the critic sourly, before deftly nullifying the theatrical value of Nikolai Gogol's play about a traveling innocent who is mistaken for a lofty representative of the tsar: "A play can't begin so baldly."[1]

Well, granting that East is East and West is West, it probably follows that bluntness for one is intricacy for another. In any case, at a recent performance of the spectacularly imaginative and highly visual new production of Gogol's play at the Theater na Pokrovke, one impressed spectator was heard to mutter, "Man, that guy could write!"

Indeed. To say nothing about his ability to penetrate the catacombs of human pride, foolhardiness, obsequiousness and chicanery. And his unerring flair for giving the grotesquely comic a short, wrenching twist that makes you suddenly wonder, "Is this funny, or is it something else?"

In his new staging, Sergei Artsibashev focused on the "something else." From the mayor's stuttering, angst-laden first line, to his genuinely moving admission in the finale that he, like everyone around him, has been exposed like an emperor with no clothes, this production is tinted with alarm and foreboding. Couched in that tonality, the play's humor, of which there is a non-stop stream, strikes with doubled force.

Not planning it, or even really realizing it, a young boob named Khlestakov humiliates a town-full of self-important bureaucrats and shatters the romantic dreams of the mayor's wife and daughter. Out of cash, and with nowhere to go, he is stuck, starving, in the local hotel. When word comes that an inspector general is on the way, the mafia-like officials decide he must be the one. They lavish him with attention and bribes, only to learn too late that they got the wrong man.

The performance of Khlestakov by Sergei Udovik is stunningly unexpected. Even while clinging perfectly to Gogol's quirky plans, Udovik creates what is certainly one of the most unorthodox, eccentric interpretations of this character ever. Moreover, he does it with thrilling virtuosity. Rubber-faced, lizard-like and strangely ambivalent, he passes instantly from fear to rage, from innocence to foppery. Completely at the mercy of his

---

[1] Stanley Kaufmann in *Theatre Criticisms* (1983), 73.

ape-like servant Osip (Oleg Pashchenko), he utterly bamboozles everyone else.

As the Mayor, Yury Lakhin is winningly shrewd, sinewy and forceful, deviating from this character's usual blustery, bumbling manner. That makes his groveling before Khlestakov all the stranger and ultimately amplifies his tragic aura. He neither sees nor cares that his wife (Valentina Svetlova) and daughter (Yelena Starodub) are locked in a steamy, subterranean duel behind his back. Their goal is less to win the ravenous Khlestakov than to capture the family sexual bragging rights.

The whole production rides on alternating and competing atmospheric waves: the officials' dim-wittedness, Khlestakov's opportunism, the Mayor's intrigues, his ladies' quickened sexuality. To them Artsibashev added another: the sense of dignity that is so inaccessible to the characters. It is borne by four beautiful, spectral women who silently wait on both the bureaucrats and the small audience of 30.

The Inspector General is not only stageworthy. When staged well, it is a tour de force. The production at the Theater na Pokrovke is proof of that.

(*October 1993*)

The Bumbarash Passion, Tabakov Theater

War may be one of the least humorous things humans have contrived, but that doesn't mean it is ill-suited to comedy. Idiocy in any form is a comic artist's dream.

Take the new production of Yuly Kim's *The Bumbarash Passion* at the Tabakov Theater. It is not only a powerful and sensitive story about the mindlessness of war, it is also very funny. To a point, of course. At any rate, it is the almost non-stop mirth that makes the underlying drama—and the tragic ending—hit like a leaded boxing glove.

Vladimir Mashkov staged the play as a maelstrom of wacky events that unfold in a whirl of movement (kudos to choreographer Alla Sigalova), spirited folk music (arranged by Roman Berchenko), deafening gunfire and billowing smoke. Several scenes are played out as circus interludes, replete with pratfalls and sleight-of-hand tricks. The mad

action on the minuscule stage constantly threatens to spill into the front rows of spectators.

Bumbarash (Yevgeny Mironov) is a blithe country boy who does his duty and joins the Russian Army to fight the Germans during World War I. But he soon realizes that doing the right thing isn't always the right thing to do. After he "gets volunteered" to scout the enemy lines in a balloon and is nearly killed when shot down, he sneaks home to resume his peaceful life.

But the course of events has outstripped him. His brother Gavrila (Sergei Belyayev), thinking Bumbarash was killed, married his "widow," the fair Varya (played with touching innocence and inner strength by Anastasia Zavorotnyuk). Worse yet, Bumbarash learns that a revolution has taken place and now everyone is at war.

Gavrila joined an unaligned band of thieves. Another brother, Yasha (Alexander Mokhov), is fighting for the Bolsheviks. Bumbarash's former superior in the tsarist army (Alexei Neklyudov) is leading a regiment in the White Guard. Naturally, Bumbarash is trapped in the three-way crossfire.

Mironov centers the performance with a well-balanced mixture of irrepressible energy and poignant vulnerability. His fine voice and deft coordination easily allow him to make the numerous songs and dances seem a natural extension of his character's personality.

As Bumbarash's terrified Bolshevik brother, with permanently screwed-up eyes and a tight-lipped scowl, Mokhov gives us something rarely seen these days: a deeply sympathetic portrayal of a revolutionary. Outfitted with bottle-bottom glasses, flappy red pajamas and an ever-present bomb he doesn't know what to do with, he is the picture of benign helplessness.

The set by Alexander Borovsky—charred wood walls and a long table with benches attached to it—highlights the performance's darker side with pristine simplicity. The half-burnt table symbolizes what happens to the home hearth in times of war. The roving bands of brigands, revolutionaries and soldiers each preempt it for their own use, while it also functions as a hide-out and a prison for the beleaguered Bumbarash.

Yevgeny Mironov and Alexander Mokhov in Yuly Kim's *The Bumbarash Passion*, based on a story by Arkady Gaidar, Tabakov Theater, 1993. Directed by Vladimir Mashkov. Photo: Mikhail Guterman

Kim's play is a clever adaptation of some stories by Arkady Gaidar (that's right, grandfather of Economics Minister Yegor). He might have been a bit more ruthless when deciding what to cut. The scenes involving the leader of the bandits, Sofya (played with jarring voracity by Olga Blok-Mirimskaya), are rather repetitious. But, on the whole, the brisk scene changes and snappy dialogue are on the mark.

The Bumbarash Passion does for modern Russian audiences something like what *M*A*S*H* once did for Americans. It punctures the "heroic" myths of an old war to remind that the grand myths about new ones are just as silly.

(October 1993)

Slingshot, **Roman Viktyuk Theater**

Roman Viktyuk, that phenomenal theatrical equivalent of the populist pulp romance writer, is at it again. And present-day Viktyuk is good at nothing if not "doing it again."

You've seen his actors scaling the sets like apes in *Lolita*. You've seen them madly, and ponderously, puncturing holes in paper walls in *A Mystery Play*. In *Two for the Seesaw* you heard the theme song trotted out so many times you thought you'd never get that wispy little Chaplin tune out of your head.

Welcome to *Slingshot*, the director's most recent repetition, er, production. When the actors are not climbing the membrane-thin walls (designed by Vladimir Boyer) or slashing holes in them, they are sailing out over the front row seats on an oversized swing, propelled by the distraught strains of "The Show Must Go On," that Queen song that just won't go away. Maybe the sound engineer was given a broken record, because the song is repeated eight, that's right, eight times in the course of the performance.

Slingshot was written by Nikolai Kolyada, who is fast becoming the most-produced young playwright in Moscow. It depicts the relationship between Ilya, a thirty-three year-old man confined to a wheelchair, and Anton, a flighty nineteen year-old who befriends him and looks after him. The first barriers fall as they admit their experiences with women have been less than satisfactory. Later, they are brought closer by the blustery appearances of Larisa, Ilya's girlfriend-on-the-way-out. But, recognizing real love— even when you land in its lap—is not easy. Anton only realizes that when it is too late.

Viktyuk himself admits in the program notes that this is not Aeschylus or Shakespeare. But, as a strictly formulaic male bonding or gay play, it is at least built solidly. You wouldn't know that to judge by Viktyuk's staging. This is unquestionably the weakest in a series of increasingly vapid outings from the first Russian artist to seriously violate the gay taboo in 70 years.

Many of Viktyuk's first openly gay or, at least sexually-ambiguous, productions in the late 1980s were mesmerizing visual poems. *The Petty Demon, Phaedra* and *The Maids* bewitched with their rich suggestiveness. They were criticized as much as praised for the obvious reason: Viktyuk's homosexuality was (and still is) too unsettling to too many. But they were accomplished works of theatrical art.

Slingshot is a junk box of heavy-handed signifiers. Sergei Makovetsky's wooden Ilya talks with a false, gruff voice, letting us know he's trying too hard to be "male." Dmitry Bozin, as Anton, is adept at striking poses, tossing his long hair flirtatiously and stripping off his shirt every time we are supposed to understand the pair is sexually attracted. During the half-dozen dream scenes, the men ride the huge swing, energetically thrusting their crotches at the audience. (Get it? Get it?) When Anton "plugs" an electrical appliance into Ilya's excited heart, it goes on. Seriously. Yekaterina Karpushina's Larisa is dumb and insensitive: "You're worse than broads!" she jealously yells at the two.

The slingshot of the title refers to the little weapon Ilya keeps for fun. He likes to sit at his window and pop holes in his neighbors' windows. It is probably his way of protesting against the facades people erect around their private lives. This production of *Slingshot*, utterly lacking in taste and artistic vision, fails to tell us anything of value about that timeless and enigmatic feature of the human experience.

(November 1993)

N. V. Gogol's Marriage, **Hermitage Theater**

Mikhail Levitin's new production of *N.V. Gogol's Marriage* at the Hermitage Theater is a classic case of a classic gone wildly wrong. His fantasy on the themes of Nikolai Gogol's play, *The Marriage*, and story, "The Diary of a Madman," opens new horizons in the concept of overkill.

Levitin's well-deserved reputation rests on his off-beat creations that—like strange sculptures assembled from bits of trash—are filled with false starts, loose ends and weird turns that somehow progress with coherence and beauty. The victory of such productions as *Don Juan*, *An Evening in a Madhouse* and, especially, *The Beggar, or the Death of Zand*, comes, in part, because Levitin teeters precariously on the brink of chaos. We applaud him when, time and again, he recaptures his balance with a snap of his fingers and a winning smile.

The flip side is what happens when all the bits of trash only add up to a junk pile, and the tightrope walker keeps hitting the net face first. With some exceptions, that's what we get in *N.V. Gogol's Marriage*.

Why splice these two different works? Because both tell of meek, sensitive men whose wounded relationship to the world is partially expressed through their horrified fascination with the opposite sex? It's a little like merging *Richard II* and *King Lear* because both are about distrustful kings who squander their kingdoms. There's some sense to it, but who needs it?

It begs saying immediately: Boris Romanov's solo performance of the madman Poprishchin might be brilliant anywhere else. His gaunt face, darting eyes and furtive movements create a painfully tender portrait of a man gradually being consumed by madness. He eavesdrops on dogs, steals their correspondence and eventually fancies himself the King of Spain. He flutters among the spectators when in action and slinks into a grandiose cloth and rope tree hovering above the audience when the characters from *The Marriage* resume their action on stage.

But here, Poprishchin's constant appearances are only a major irritant for repeatedly slamming on the brakes in this very long performance. Meanwhile, the scenes from *The Marriage* bog down in an overabundance of mimic interludes, shrieking voices and physical jokes.

The idea is to renew Gogol's text about Podkolesin, a man whose passing, romantic wish to get married turns into a nightmare when his crude friend, Kochkaryov, takes control of his courtship with the retiring Agafya. Instead, the play's humor gets such a drubbing, all the air is punched out of it.

Much of potential value is drowned without a trace. Viktor Gvozditsky's dreamy, reticent Podkolesin is nearly evicted from the play. The overworked shenanigans in the scenes involving his three rivals for Agafya's affections, and the lengthy additions from "The Diary," dilute his role considerably. Then, Levitin stood him back-to-audience to deliver his entire final monologue.

Larisa Panchenko, as Agafya, and Alexander Pozharov, as the rival suitor Zhevakin, create some touching moments of frightened, sensitive people violated by the vulgarity around them. Pozharov is especially tragi-comic as he sadly bemoans his 17th rejection.

But those are rare exceptions in a performance whose tone is set by frantic, mock rape scenes, urinating jokes, and lots of hands choking throats. More in keeping with Levitin's overall design is Vladimir Gusev's Neanderthal-inspired interpretation of Kochkaryov.

Harry Hummel's spectacular set—which places the action somewhere between the interior of a tasteful Russian estate and a Robinson Crusoe paradise—and Svetlana Kalinina's beautiful, detailed costumes create a gorgeous backdrop against which this blustery, fractured production hits bottom with a thud.

(November 1993)

The Title, **Sovremennik Theater**

In the Sovremennik Theater's newest offering, *The Title*, a money-grubbing Russian girl travels to Italy to join forces with a gentle, unemployed Italian communist in order to get rich by selling her title of nobility to a Japanese buyer.

A knockabout farce? A sardonic satire? Well, not quite. The laughs and barbs bog down in so much significant sentimentality that we don't get much farther than a halfway comedy.

Playwright Alexander Galin and director Galina Volchek are equally answerable for that. Galin frequently reigns in his wacky characters by stopping them in mid-action and plunging them into interminable, heartfelt discussions about love, dreams or what it means to be Russian. Volchek, uncertain whether Galin had written a parody or a realistic drama, played both ends off the center: She created a performance that alternates streams of delirious caricature with oh-so-serious dramatics.

As in any good satire, the play isolates characters who are recognizable types rather than representations of real people. Galin's situations and characters are so blatantly, even ecstatically improbable that they can only be intended as caricatures.

The fast-talking, gold-digging Natasha (Yelena Yakovleva) eschews no deception to get what she is after. She is at constant odds with her bumbling, good-natured lover Pietro (Igor Kvasha), whose idea it originally was to sell off her title at a tidy profit. Natasha's mother, Nina Meshcherskaya (Lilia Tolmachyova), is the epitome of the ever-suffering, ever-deceived and ever-forgiving Russian soul, while her blowzy artist boyfriend Sergei (Sergei Garmash) is the very picture of Russian stridency and excess.

But there is just too much going on here with too little substance to support it. Galin wanted to serve up a thick brew of Russian treachery, backwardness and largess whose pungent aromas would sharpen when mixed with the stereotypes of western behavior; stinginess, pettiness, naiveté and openness. What he concocted was a watery alphabet soup.

Pietro is the prototypical western misfit who only found himself in Moscow. He went to school there, had friends there, had a job there, and had a purpose there. At home, with his child and sick wife, he can't find a job or a reason for living. That is why he borrows the money to bring Natasha and her mother (who holds the documents proving the family's nobility) to Italy. He'll sell off the papers for more than they're worth.

But Natasha's mother—who naturally thinks Pietro is a millionaire—brought along her boyfriend, a grumpy, insecure genius. He makes Pietro's life a nightmare by drinking up his last lira and subjecting him to moral tirades.

Yakovleva puts a hard, farcical twist on the role of the prostitute somewhat similar to the one she created in *Intergirl*, one of the best-known films of the perestroika era. She may or may not be a prostitute here, but she employs the same method of using an unsuspecting foreigner to escape her Russian home. The only member of the cast who sticks unwaveringly to a parodical style of acting, she ultimately suffers for it. In a production that works too hard at being meaningful, she impresses as one-dimensional.

Igor Kvasha copes well with the thankless task of performing in broken Italo-Russian, and does a nice job of informing his dunderhead character with warmth. The problem is that it often seems he and Yakovleva are performing different plays. Similarly, Tolmachyova is simply wonderful as the meek, though strong-willed Nina, but there is no way of believing she could even understand, let alone love Garmash's sullen, unimaginative artist.

Designer Alexander Borovsky's set sums things up. It is a monotonous, rain-drenched Italian street scene consisting of a high, imposing wall, a few plastic chairs and the closed awning of a café.

(November 1993)

The Wood Demon, Malaya Bronnaya Theater

Sergei Zhenovach, whose production of Anton Chekhov's *The Wood Demon* just opened at the Malaya Bronnaya Theater, needs no introduction for Moscow theater buffs. He is one of just a few new directors to establish a solid reputation and an admirable following in the post-perestroika era.

Some critics called Zhenovach's intimate 1992 productions of *King Lear* and *The*

Abyss signs of a major talent maturing. With last spring's spectacular staging of *The Miller Who Was a Wizard, a Cheat and a Matchmaker*, he showed a fabulous flair for the rhythms of folk wisdom and humor. In the eyes of many, it made him the heir apparent to the crown of Moscow's Best.

While joining in the praise for *The Miller*, this critic frankly found *Lear* to be the ideal cure for insomnia and *The Abyss* to be a grueling test of one's tolerance for tedium. *The Wood Demon* is more of the same.

The play, an early version of *Uncle Vanya*, flopped so badly after its premiere in 1889 that Chekhov went into hiding out of shame.

The two works share similar dialogue, but a few crucial plot changes make them vastly different. In *Uncle Vanya*, Ivan Voinitsky turns his frustration and anger on Serebryakov, his thankless "benefactor," and tries to kill him in a mad moment of farcical ineptitude. In *Demon*, Yegor Voinitsky simply goes off stage and quietly shoots himself.

In *Vanya*, Voinitsky's niece Sonya must dig deep within herself to find a reason to go on when she realizes she can never have the man she loves. Her forced transference of her affections from Doctor Astrov to her beloved, defeated and wronged uncle is the crux of one of the most powerful plays ever written.

The finale of *Demon* shows Sonya, who has forgotten her now-dead uncle, joining in bliss with her beloved Khrushchyov, a rashly righteous medical student. Meanwhile, as another pair of reluctant lovers also agrees to marry, professor Serebryakov's bored young wife Yelena suddenly returns home all-smiles after having run away two weeks ago.

Chekhov was testing the limits of dramatic clichés, but he wasn't yet master enough to create either a good parody or a convincing new form. The same might be said of Zhenovach.

How else does one explain the first 30 minutes of this performance? Trapped in and often hidden by Yury Galperin's obtrusive, cage-like set, the players take a leisurely afternoon breakfast. They sit calmly, chat quietly, clink their glasses and chew their food well before swallowing. It is all terribly lifelike.

Some will call it a delightfully subtle play at and with the notorious "Chekhovian languor." Perhaps, but when a half-hour scene is this realistically inert, it seems more honest to call it boring.

The cast consists primarily of Zhenovach's regular group of gifted young actors. But they are so busy splitting directorial hairs of subtlety, they usually fade into obscurity. Sergei Taramayev sinks the harrumphing Serebryakov in a forced, guttural voice and a few repetitive gestures of the arms. Irina Rozanova plays the professor's wife Yelena as a lifeless, marble statue. There is no hint as to why she so attracts Sergei Kachanov's faceless Voinitsky.

The brightest moments are provided by Sergei Batalov, as Waffles, the eccentric neighbor. He gives a wonderful performance of a man so pathetically sentimental, he can't help but be endearing. Nadezhda Markina nicely plays Sonya as a young woman in the process of discovering her dignity.

But ultimately, if the strong suit of *The Wood Demon* is its subtlety, it is a victim of its own success. There's too much "smart" artistic theory here and too little theater.

(December 1993)

Murderer, Theater u Nikitskikh vorot

The newest offering from the Theater u Nikitskikh vorot, *Murderer*, a dramatization of Fyodor Dostoevsky's *Crime and Punishment*, highlights the main strengths and weaknesses of this diligent, even zealous little playhouse.

Artistic director, playwright, composer, designer, and all-around renaissance man of the theater, Mark Rozovsky packs enough raw talent, vision and energy to fuel at least another hundred besides. Which brings us right to the weaknesses. Rozovsky's presence is so overwhelming and his plans are so ambitious, that his actors often look like they are two and a half steps behind their sprinting leader. In fact, the *maître* himself sometimes seems to get ahead of his own shadow.

So it is with *Murderer*. Rozovsky's adaptation and staging of Dostoevsky's kinetic novel is bold, imaginative and slick. The play embraces with almost miraculous efficiency the sprawling story about the former student, Raskolnikov. His fixation on an idea about the moral gulf separating "ordinary" and "extraordinary" people leads him to test his theory by murdering an old pawnbroker.

But the play is so seamless and dramatically hermetic that it loses the ragged, gasping intensity of the original. Furthermore, the youthfully earnest cast may be admirably enthusiastic, but it is dreadfully lacking in the depth or understanding needed to bring this complex work to life.

The biggest question is not why Rozovsky changed the superficial appearance of the novel so much, but, why didn't he change it more?

His refusal to be a slave to the chronology and the bare plot of the original was a decision well taken. He shuffled scenes like decks of cards, often using late occurrences early—in order to orient the audience—and often unifying several different, but thematically connected scenes. At times there may be four or even five scenes in progress simultaneously, with the characters easily moving from one to the other.

That was an effective way of recreating the polyphonic, or multi-voiced nature of Dostoevsky's novel. It also lent itself well to creating the impression that much of what is transpiring is the product of Raskolnikov's overactive imagination, the aspect Rozovsky wanted to bring out most. Raskolnikov (Alexander Miloserdov) makes that clear at the outset by announcing, "This is a confession." In fact, we never even see the actual murder or the victims; that would have been too naturalistic.

The orientation on Raskolnikov's internal world was handled nicely with the presentation of the mysterious Svidrigailov (Ernest Marchukov), a self-admitted debauchee and the former employer of Raskolnikov's sister. He appears in a devilish guise from behind a mirror, dramatically emphasizing his own claim that he and Raskolnikov are darkly linked.

But almost everywhere else the inexperience of the actors and the smooth all-inclusiveness of the script undermine rather than facilitate our attempts to believe in what is happening.

Except for Sonya (Svetlana Sergienko), the spiritual innocent who was driven to prostitution by need and who becomes Raskolnikov's only link to possible regeneration, most of the other characters are reduced to just one or two substantial appearances.

With such a large cast, that makes for too many hurried, merely illustrative scenes. Neither Raskolnikov's sister Dunya (Viktoria Zaslavskaya), his friend Razumikhin (Alexander Stolyarov) nor his enemy, the infuriatingly patient police investigator, Porfiry Petrovich (Alexander Ivanov), have enough stage time to expand the scope of the performance. These characters needed either to be cut entirely or given more flesh.

One can't help but admire *Murderer* for the conviction its creators feel for their work. The problem is, their heartfelt belief never succeeds in passing from the stage to the audience.

(December 1993)

Tsar Boris, Maly Theater

A popular playwright was recently overheard bitterly criticizing the Maly Theater.

"They claim it's their tradition to play the classics," he scoffed. "But they made their name in the 19th century by discovering or supporting contemporary writers. Now all they do is play hundred-year-old discoveries and support the memory of the dead."

On the surface, the Maly's recent premiere of *Tsar Boris* does little to refute that outburst. Written 125 years ago, the play's first and only previous production at the Maly was mounted 95 years ago.

But, with all due respect to the disgruntled modern playwright (his point is actually well taken), one would be hard-pressed to find a more timely work than this splendid verse tragedy. It tells of a Russian leader named Boris, whose good intentions bring him to ruin, and his country to war. More importantly, the Maly's powerful

Vasily Bochkaryov as Boris Godunov in Vladimir Beilis's production of A.K. Tolstoy's *Tsar Boris*, Maly Theater, 1993. Photo: Alexander Ivanishin

production of the play makes its date of origin and even its specific content seem secondary.

Tsar Boris is the final part of a trilogy written by the 19th-century poet, Alexei Tolstoy. (He is usually referred to by his initials, A.K., to avoid confusion with another Alexei Tolstoy who wrote in the 20th century, and he is of no relation to Leo.) His first two plays examine the reigns of Ivan the Terrible and his meek son, Fyodor. The third chronicles the fall of Boris Godunov during the Time of Troubles at the dawn of the 17th century.

In places, the parallels with the present are striking.

Godunov was not only the first tsar to be elected (by a council of the nobility), he was also a reformer who opened Russia to the West, and sought to minimize the political influence of a tightly-knit few. But when his enemies, led by Prince Shuisky, joined forces with an insolent upstart who claimed to be the rightful heir to the throne, Godunov was overthrown.

That was made possible because of the popular belief that many years before, Godunov had ordered the murder of Dmitry, Fyodor's younger brother and the only heir to the throne. Capitalizing on the unrest caused by Godunov's changes, a renegade cleric declared himself Tsar—the False Dmitry—and marched on Moscow supported by Polish and Russian forces.

Modern historians tell us that Godunov probably had nothing to do with the death of Dmitry. But through the arts, the legend became one of the most famous "facts" of Russian history. As recreated by Tolstoy, and as performed under the direction of Vladimir Beilis at the Maly Theater, it is certainly one of the most gripping.

With a sprawling cast of 38, the performance has its share of rough spots. It occasionally bogs down in secondary plot lines, especially early on, and at times the displaying of the beautiful costumes seems to be the most important task at hand.

But all snaps into focus when Vasily Bochkaryov takes the stage and begins to work his magic in the role of Boris. (He will perform in turns with Viktor Korshunov.)

Seldom does one see a single actor take such complete control over such a stageful of people.

Simply put, Bochkaryov is what lifts things from the level of interesting social commentary to the level of high human drama. His Godunov is an unsolvable knot of contradictions in which we see every nuance of each of his internal twists and turns. He is intelligent, but makes elementary mistakes. He is sensitive, but too easily resorts to force to prop up his slipping authority. He has no illusions about what it takes to wield power, but, in the end, is paralyzed by guilt.

Bochkaryov is the uncontested heart and soul of this complex production about eternal Russian problems. But a handful of exquisite performances in secondary roles help make this more than a one-man show. Eduard Martsevich turns in a delightfully obsequious Prince Shuisky. Balanced perfectly between spinelessness and raw ambition, he invariably finds ways to do Godunov's every bidding in the tsar's presence, while doing everything possible to undermine him when he is absent. Yelena Doronina, as Godunov's sister, and Nikolai Annenkov, as Lup-Klyoshnin—the man who actually murdered Dmitry—give brilliant cameos that deepen the impact of Godunov's spiritual crisis.

The doomed tsar's personal tragedy is reflected well in the doubt that arises even in those he loves; his fiercely loyal son (Alexander Bely) and daughter (Tatyana Skiba).

Iosif Sumbatashvili's grandiose set is both a stylization of the interior of a throne room, cathedral, dungeon or monastery, as well as a constant, eerie reminder that something is frightfully amiss. Its semi-spherical wall and ceiling is dotted with overlapping heads from icons that are expressed as gaping holes which seem to have been scorched into the material with fire.

Lighting designer Anatoly Remizov did a superb job of illuminating the stage in various shades of white, gold and silver. And the music, drawn from works by Georgy Sviridov, paints haunting, aural pictures of each scene's dominant theme.

Maybe the Maly is hopelessly stuck on the classics. But when it does them this well, who cares?

(*January 1994*)

Banana, Moscow Salon

The opening of a new arts center, the Moscow Salon, not only brought to town the most recent play by one of the world's best playwrights, Slawomir Mrozek, it marked the return of one of the city's prodigal sons.

After several disastrous projects in Moscow and some time spent cooling his heels in the West, director Roman Kozak is back with a playful interpretation of Mrozek's *Widows*, which Kozak rechristened *Banana* for the Moscow run.

The play, about two widows whose recently-deceased husbands had too much in common, was an excellent choice for the young Kozak who, essentially, finds himself in the position of having to mount a hometown comeback.

Mrozek's sublime dramatic simplicity, his crystalline sense of humor, and his intellectual clarity have always made for plays that grab quickly and affect deeply. *Widows*, or *Banana*, is blessed with most of the expatriate Polish writer's usual strengths. Furthermore, it has an added gentle warmth that is undoubtedly the result of Mrozek having recently survived a death experience.

Supported by a strong team, Kozak captured the play's whimsy and wisdom nicely. He gave free rein to the non-stop (and right-on-target) skewering of people's vanities and the small-talk they hide them behind. But the point was at least as much to savor human foibles as to ridicule them. Consequently, the eventual intrusion of death is not so terrible as it is alluring.

Roza and Lotus (played with marvelously muted comic timing by Yelena Shanina and Larisa Kuznetsova) are the two widows who start by commiserating in a café about their husband's funerals, but soon learn they were each other's husband's lover. Thanks to their haughty waiter's belated delivery of notes from each of the men, the women learn their husbands died not of food poisoning or a

cold, as they had thought. They died, it seems, in a duel.

The action then switches back to the incident which put the two men, Romeo (Maxim Sukhanov) and Tristan (Alexander Baluyev), on a deadly collision course. There, in the same café, in the presence of the same snippety waiter, they encounter a gorgeous, silent woman. But the more each of them pursues her, the more it becomes clear that she is the one pursuing them.

Alla Sigalova, who also choreographed the imaginative dance scenes, is wonderfully vampish as the mysterious figure of death. And Valery Garkalin is superb as the wacky, maybe even god-like waiter who takes almost sinister joy in getting everything wrong, and whose careless discarding of a banana peel has dire consequences.

Designer Pavel Kaplevich created the airy, beige set consisting of three round tables under huge pineapple-like lamps. Its clean lines and lightly humorous appearance are the ideal environment.

The success of *Banana* is especially satisfying because Kozak's ten-year career has been checkered, to put it mildly.

He first gained attention in the mid-1980s as an actor and director at the little Chelovek Theater-Studio. But subsequent attempts to go big-time brought him only trouble.

He founded the heralded Fifth Studio at the Chekhov Art Theater in 1990 only to see it flop within a year. Then, in another highly-publicized move, he took over as the artistic director at the Stanislavsky Drama Theater in autumn 1991. Ten months later, smitten by bad notices and insistent whispers that he was in over his head, he resigned and headed West.

Now, *Banana* suggests that the confidence some showed in Kozak a few years ago was justified. It and the Moscow Salon are an encouraging new beginning.

(*January 1994*)

Russian Eclipse, Pushkin Drama Theater

Paris in the 'twenties, the Russian provinces in the 'teens, a flighty actress, a heedless soldier, a servant of dubious intentions, and

Maxim Sukhanov, Alla Sigalova and Alexander Baluyev in *Banana*, Roman Kozak's 1994 production of Slawomir Mrozek's *Widows* for Moscow Salon. Photo: Mikhail Guterman

an investigator who is obsessed with a messy old incident that won't go away.

Those are the key ingredients of *Russian Eclipse*, the newest entry at the Pushkin Drama Theater. When distilled into a laconic list, they sound like the makings for a sprite mystery. But that's in principle. In deed, the performance is decidedly less than engrossing.

What happened was that Yelena Gremina's admirably intriguing play (originally entitled *The Case of Cornet O*) got flattened by a production that confuses mystery with melodrama.

Gremina—a young playwright who is destined for big attention next month when her play *Behind the Mirror* opens at the Chekhov Art Theater starring Galina Vishnevskaya—packed all of her characters into a sort of love quadrangle that begs to be treated with a wink and a healthy dose of irony.

Take, for instance, inspector Anton Castelli. Gremina certainly saw him as somewhat comical, too serious and self-indulgent.

His opening monologue is a wonderful parody of the embittered and nostalgic Russian émigré. Although he behaves like a boor, he never can figure out why his wife Anna, a provincial actress, abandoned him for Alexander, a slightly distrait cornet in the Russian army. And Castelli doesn't quite understand that his second wife Lukerya, who once was Anna's servant, has wrapped him around her little finger.

Even the images of Paris we get in the course of this play, which travels freely back and forth between the present and the past, suggest the author's tongue is planted slyly in her cheek. For Castelli (Andrei Tashkov), who lives there in exile in the 1920s, Paris is a dirty, debauched, pigeon-infested hole. For Anna (Olesya Doroshina) and Alexander (Konstantin Pokhmelov), whose stormy love affair unfolds in Russia in 1914, Paris is the Dream; the only earthly place where they can escape to perfect harmony.

The escape, naturally, proves impossible when Alexander—accidentally or not—kills Anna with a pistol she loaded and gave him herself. It is Castelli's job to solve the murder, and ultimately it becomes his life-long obsession to understand it.

Beyond the complex, but neatly-constructed plot, there are quiet but insistent echoes of the instability in pre-war Russia, of the coming revolution and of Russia's inevitable future descent into a period of murky turmoil. Among them are three "epistolary" digressions, during which Alexander's cousin Mika (Yevgeny Pisarev) writes enthusiastically about a coming eclipse that will be total only in Russia. Europe, he says, is calling it the Russian eclipse.

By replacing the original title with *Russian Eclipse*, and by his efforts to justify that shift in focus, director Vyacheslav Dolgachyov violated the fabric of the play.

Not surprisingly, it balked. Its intrigue turned to sentimentality and its gentle parodies turned maudlin. Meanwhile, its echoes of history and politics, effective in the original for the very reason that they are sketched only lightly, become too emphatic.

Excepting Yelena Novikova, who gives a well-defined and nicely paradoxical performance of Lukerya, Dolgachyov elicited nothing but clichés from his actors. The same can be said of the two silent tango dancers (Yekaterina Sibiryakova and Andrei Sukhov, choreographed by Larisa Dmitrieva). Dolgachyov added them for mood, but their barely competent performance only squelches it.

Margarita Demyanova's stark black set, sliced from left to right by a slanting stretch of white cloth, resolutely but falsely suggests that the production is something from the avant-garde.

(*January 1994*)

Oresteia, directed by Peter Stein

The applause that first greeted the end of the marathon performance was earnest but subdued. Then a curious thing happened. The expressionless Peter Stein energetically bounded on stage to join his cast for the curtain call.

The appearance of the acclaimed German director was just what the audience of nearly 1,000 was waiting for. The hall suddenly came alive. Applause turned to cheers, and cheers turned to a prolonged and enthusiastic standing ovation.

After eight on-again, off-again years of scheduling, financial and ideological barriers, Peter Stein's eagerly anticipated production of Aeschylus's trilogy, *Oresteia*, had at last become a reality in Russia.

The project was originally banned in 1986 by Soviet Defense Minister Dmitry Yazov, who objected to a German director bringing a Greek drama to a stage belonging to the Soviet Army. In an ironic twist of fate, Yazov is now awaiting trial for his role in the 1991 attempted coup and Stein, 57, one of Germany's best-known directors, is receiving an overdue hero's welcome in Moscow.

The often workman-like, occasionally spectacular performance at the premiere was reduced almost to the status of a sideshow, however. While the actors gamely fought off a professionally concealed case of the opening night jitters, the high-powered, high-profile audience was in its element.

Roving television and radio crews stirred the biggest excitement before the show and during intermissions. They hungrily stalked the theater's corridors, swooping down on every familiar face in search of the perfect sound bite and creating mini-traffic jams as rubbernecks gathered to gawk at the celebrities.

Some of them, like television personality and theater director Mark Zakharov, hung around only long enough to say they had been there.

During an interview at the first of two intermissions, Zakharov called Stein an "outstanding director" and predicted that his "debatable staging" will require "much study in the future." As soon as the camera lights were off, Zakharov donned his coat and left.

He was not alone. As the second part got under way, the crowd had thinned by about ten percent. Still, most of the audience, including the politicians Gennady Burbulis and Vladimir Shumeiko, stuck it out to the end.

What they saw was an uneven performance jointly produced by the International Confederation of Theater Associations (Moscow), Hahn Productions (Munich) and the Russian Army Theater that frequently

failed to sustain momentum, but which, at moments, almost unexpectedly burst into brilliance.

The first part, *Agamemnon*, tells of King Agamemnon's triumphant return from Troy, and of his murder by his wife, Clytemnestra. After a delightfully playful prologue in which a scout peered suspiciously from on high at the spectators filing into the hall, this three-hour segment progressed heavily and slowly, taking its cue from Moidele Bickel's gray and black set and costumes.

Yekaterina Vasilyeva, who would electrify the hall with her performance of Clytemnestra in the second segment, struggled early on to match her incendiary temperament with the mannered style of the Greek tragedy.

The initial breakthrough came as the first intermission was already nearing. Natalya Kochetova gave a searing performance as the seer, Cassandra, who predicts that Clytemnestra will kill her and Agamemnon both. Kochetova left the stage to the applause of the suddenly awakened audience.

The evening's unquestioned highlight was the second segment, *The Libation-Bearers*, in which Orestes, the son of Agamemnon and Clytemnestra, returns home to avenge his father by killing his mother and her new husband.

His saber poised at his mother's breast, ready to fell her at any moment, Yevgeny Mironov's Orestes seemed to exceed the limits of mental endurance as he withstood the cajoling, the pleading and the verbal manipulations of Vasilyeva's white-hot, stunningly intense Clytemnestra. But withstand her, he did—*The Libation-Bearers*, like *Agamemnon*, ended with the display of two more bloodied corpses.

The third segment, the *Eumenides*, is famous for its model of a modern judicial system that replaces the cycles of revenge. Written 2,500 years ago, that is the element which so many have said makes the present production of *Oresteia* in Russia so timely.

In this cathartic conclusion, Stein showed a splendid sense of humor. After the newly-created court absolves Orestes of responsibility for murdering his mother, the jurymen erupt into a comical, knock-down, drag-out brawl. Looking more like a scene from the nightly news than from a Greek tragedy, it drew a burst of healthy laughter from the spectators.

Pre-opener expectations about this *Oresteia* ran extraordinarily high. The Russian press's frequent, worshipful references to Stein as "the Master" put the director in a difficult position. He had to produce a work of genius or disappoint.

The slow-building response at performance's end clearly indicated that many were underwhelmed. But the enthusiastic reaction awarded Stein personally was a clear sign that, at least for the moment, few were holding that against him.

And when the emotional actors inundated the beaming Stein in a sea of bouquets, the atmosphere even took on the smell of hard-earned success.

(*February 1994*)

Bashmachkin, Bogis Agency and *The Seagull*, Commonwealth of Taganka Actors

February looks to be the busiest month of the theater season. Not counting Peter Stein's landmark production of *Oresteia*, which opened at the Russian Army Theater in the waning days of January, there are no less than seven new shows now opening at major venues throughout the city.

The onslaught began with two productions that are as totally different in spirit as they are in quality.

One, the Bogis Agency's *Bashmachkin*, is an intimate, one-man show that is conceived and performed with rare talent and delicacy. The other, a crude, Gargantuan swipe at Anton Chekhov's *The Seagull*, is shockingly inept. It is the first entry from the Commonwealth of Taganka Actors, the group that broke away from Yury Lyubimov at the Taganka Theater last year.

Bashmachkin, an adaptation by Alexei Burykin of Nikolai Gogol's classic story, "The Overcoat," is only the second offering from the creators of last year's soaring *Nijinsky*. As in the previous production, they once again bypassed the services of a director.

Every element of this staging—from Alexander Feklistov's evocative acting and Sergei Yakunin's scrupulously intricate set, to Yegor Vysotsky's spare, unsettling music—interconnects with the precision of clockwork. It may not have the ability to electrify as *Nijinsky* did, but its purpose is different: This is a fascinating attempt to study human tenderness as if through a high-powered magnifying glass.

Bashmachkin is a penniless scribe whose only "friends" are the words he works with, and the tattered, insignificant objects with which he lives. With their "moral" support, he has insulated himself from the outside world. Even his frightening encounters with his superiors—represented ingeniously by a series of furiously animated desk drawers—cannot shake him from his eccentric, but uncorrupted existence.

His downfall comes when he must replace his threadbare overcoat. After reconciling himself to walking more lightly in order to economize on shoe soles, he finally arranges to buy a new coat. But as he proudly promenades about St. Petersburg, it is stolen from under his nose. That is a blow from which he cannot recover.

One might argue that the interpretation tends too much towards the sentimental. By skipping Gogol's famous ending, wherein something resembling Bashmachkin's ghost comes back to haunt his tormentors with a vengeance, it loses most of the irony of the original.

Ultimately, however, that cannot tarnish the eloquence and conviction that characterize this production as a whole. Feklistov's nuanced, finely-textured portrayal of Bashmachkin is a tour de force of acting that leaves virtually no room for objections.

The same cannot be said about *The Seagull*. As performed by the former Taganka actors, it is a startling hodgepodge of misjudgments, bad taste masquerading as beauty, and plain ignorance of theatrical laws.

It is directed by Sergei Solovyov, the well-known filmmaker who recently stated he has lost the desire to work in cinema. Apparently he is under the delusion that the theater offers him a safe haven until his cinematic inspiration returns.

Alexander Feklistov in *Bashmachkin*, Alexei Burykin's dramatization of Nikolai Gogol's "The Overcoat", Bogis Agency, 1994. Photo: Mikhail Guterman

Solovyov made his professional theater debut last season with a vapid *Uncle
Vanya* at the Maly Theater. Now that he
has mauled *The Seagull*, he is talking
about staging the rest of Chekhov's major
plays.

That is a threat capable of curdling one's
blood.

Nothing in this production even approximates the discrimination and subtlety of
Chekhov's play about the aging actress,
Arkadina, and the constellation of talented
or would-be talented people who surround
her.

Granted, one thing will go down in the
history books. There may never have been
such a breathtaking stage environment as the
one designed by Alexander Borisov and
Vladimir Arefyev. The problem is that it is a
film location, not a theatrical set.

Across its vast expanses the actors
are incapable of making contact even among
themselves, let alone with the audience. The
actual wading pond which stretches the
entire width of the stage, the croaking frogs,
rising moon, misty rain, shimmering
woods and three-story, terraced country estate, merely crush everything under their
weight.

The acting is uniformly bad. Nina
Shatskaya, as Arkadina, unremittingly confuses histrionics with inspiration. As her
lover, Trigorin, Nikolai Gubenko (the last
Soviet Minister of Culture) squeezes out
emotion as if it were toothpaste in a tube.
Igor Gotsmanov is utterly lifeless as
Arkadina's son, Treplev. As Nina Zarechnaya, the delicate and tragic "seagull" who is
used and discarded by Trigorin, Yelena
Korikova is almost invisible.

There is no getting around it: This *Seagull*
is an extraordinarily expensive piece of
amateur work. It is a bad beginning for the
actors who claimed they were unfairly ignored by Yury Lyubimov.

As for Sergei Solovyov, he would be well-
advised to pause for a moment of reflection. The professional stage is no place for
dilettantes, no matter how grandiose their
ideas.

(*February 1994*)

The Importance of Being Earnest, Fomenko Studio

Style, elegance, wit, youth and beauty. Combine them more or less coherently and the
result can't help but please. That is the chief
principle behind the Fomenko Studio's new
production of Oscar Wilde's *The Importance
of Being Earnest*, which could easily have
been retitled *The Importance of Being
Fashionable, Come Hell or High Water.*

Still, this "theatrical demonstration" held
at the Zaitsev House of Fashion works on
the whole.

You might even say it works in spite of
itself. How else can you explain its undeniable attraction as it runs roughshod over
Wilde's spectacular verbal fireworks?

Wilde's send-up of the conventions of
farce and melodrama lampoons the refined
manners of polite society and celebrates its
intrigues. Its plot of romances—fueled and
frustrated by concealed identities—achieves
a happy resolution when the society lioness,
Lady Bracknell, unexpectedly identifies
the orphan, John Worthing. He had been
masquerading as an Ernest in order to win
the hand of Lady Bracknell's daughter,
Gwendolen.

These and other complications are but a
divine excuse to show off the famous cascades of Wilde witticisms.

But director Yevgeny Kamenkovich shook
a good deal of the bubbles out of Wilde's
champagne before serving it.

His young actors' rapid-fire speech could
not be further from the spirit of the original.
It creates the impression that the players
don't always understand what they are up
to, and it leaves none of the open air that is
the life force of humor. Some of the actors
are plain tongue-tied, and there is nothing
less witty than a fumbled punch line.

And then there is the setting of the runway in the surprisingly bland demonstration
hall at Zaitsev's fashion salon. The actors
either pose statically or parade back and
forth before the audience, not because the
action requires it, but because that is how
they show off Dmitry Cholak's gorgeous and
wildly outrageous costumes.

Madlen Dzhabrailova and Kseniya Kutepova in Oscar Wilde's *The Importance of Being Earnest*, directed by Yevgeny Kamenkovich for the Fomenko Studio, 1994. Photo: Alexander Ivanishin

At the premiere, Zaitsev himself gazed on happily. And indeed, despite the flaws and ragged seams, there is still enough elegance, beauty and youthful energy here to make a very pleasant evening of theater.

Most responsible for that are the utterly charming Ksenia Kutepova, as Gwendolen, and the comically urbane Yury Stepanov, as Worthing's gaudily rakish friend, Algernon. Both have a splendid, instinctive feel for the nuances and pastel shadings of comedy which usually remains sensible even amidst the shallow surroundings.

More monotone, but still effective are Madlen Dzhabrailova, who gives a pert performance of Algernon's sweetheart, Cecily, and Galina Tyunina, whose vampish Miss Prism is both Cecily's governess and the reason why Worthing became an orphan 28 years ago. Dzhabrailova is especially good when she and Kutepova both suddenly think they are courting the same man.

Kutepova's twin sister, Polina, plays a heavily mannered, mannequin-like Lady Bracknell, while Rustem Yuskayev, winning smile aside, creates a relentlessly incoherent Worthing.

This is the Fomenko Studio's first professional outing. It was formed last fall around a group of graduating students, and it continues to perform its uneven repertoire of student productions.

One wonders why its famed artistic director, Pyotr Fomenko—who has staked his name to the studio—delegated the honor of first production to another? Whatever his reasons, the results are mixed.

This *Earnest* occasionally impresses as an amateur show dressed in expensive clothes. On the other hand, it also proves that a few sparks of talent can cast a lot of light. To the studio's credit, that is the most lasting impression.

(February 1994)

A Hotel Room in the Town of N, Meyerhold Center

One hundred and forty-two years after his death, Nikolai Gogol is on a roll.

Several of his plays and prose works have already provided highlights this theater season. Now, hot on the heels of the Bogis Agency's excellent *Bashmachkin*, based on a story by Gogol, the Meyerhold Center brings us a wonderfully imaginative dramatization of his classic comic novel, *Dead Souls*.

Gogol's novel follows the peppery, picaresque adventures of the roguish Chichikov, who travels Russia's bumpy back roads buying up the worthless identification papers of dead serfs at "bargain" prices. He wants to amass what will look like a fortune on paper. After all, no one will ever find out that all of his property is phony, will they?

Dead Souls probably did more than any other literary work to define the incongruities of the Russian character and the Russian experience. And with its spectacular caricatures of oafs, cheats, brutes and fools, it has often been adapted for the stage.

That is just where Valery Fokin took an enlightened detour when he scripted and directed his new version. Calling it *A Hotel Room in the Town of N*, he skipped all the famous characters except Chichikov, and bypassed the adventures. Instead, we get a revealing glimpse into Chichikov's peculiar, inner world.

Fokin and designer Alexander Velikanov created an ingenious setting for Chichikov's world. It is a "total environment" that turns the spectator into something of a fly on the wall.

Velikanov built a box and placed it in the back corner of Moscow's largest exhibition hall, the former Manege. The interior realistically depicts a cramped, dim hotel room in which the audience is spread around the perimeter. In order to enter the room before the performance, each spectator steps over the splayed legs of Chichikov's thick-headed, sweetly snoring lackey (played with perfectly heavy flair by Igor Lyakh).

But no one knew better than Gogol that a realistic portrayal of life in Russia is worthless without a surrealistic undercoat. And Fokin brilliantly uses all the means available to theater to transform, violate and reassess the deceptively simple setting.

Outside the box, musicians from the Mark Pekarsky Percussion Theater move about freely as they perform the eerie, silence-laden score by Alexander Bakshi. The result is that at times Chichikov's room seems to be floating in space.

Occasionally, in comically disturbing, dream-like scenes, the musicians and other supporting cast members burst into the room through holes in the walls or furniture. The action and lighting further expand the "stage" to include the spaces below the floor and atop the ceiling.

Fokin's script, which shows Chichikov only as he reacts to recent outside encounters or as he primps for the next one, makes a minimum use of words. That gives Avangard Leontyev endless, minute opportunities for improvisation in his interpretation of Chichikov. He savors every detailed moment.

Leontyev is capable of turning the eating of a pea, the plucking of a nose hair, or even a yawn, into a symphony of expressions, gestures and moods. His Chichikov is attractively self-satisfied, arrogant, vain, and woefully alone. He is both blessed and tormented by the same thing: He lives exclusively in a world of his own invention.

This production is a wise, funny, often sad, and always respectful look at the Russian character through the prism of an author who knew Russia better than most. But even more important, it is talented and engaging theater.

(February 1994)

The Chairs, Contemporary Play School

Like most of the plays by Eugene Ionesco, *The Chairs* is both a witty prank and a powerful, metaphysical parable. The story about the sweet, nonagenarian husband and wife who frantically entertain a household of non-existent guests, is as packed with raucous, physical humor as it is with incisive insight into the harsh mysteries of the human experience.

Sergei Yursky, one of Russia's most respected actors for 25 years, has long wanted to take a shot at the play. After three decades of working up to it, he finally joined with the Contemporary Play School and his wife, the fine actress Natalya Tenyakova, to realize his dream.

He probably waited too long. For all the production's warmth and for all the affection Yursky and Tenyakova openly show for their characters, the result is only modestly successful.

Ionesco himself wrote that the aged characters must be played by young actors with the stamina to race about madly, interacting with the imagined guests who are represented by empty chairs on the stage. Unable to do that, Yursky and Tenyakova focused on their characters' touching, inner simplicity. Gaining a good deal in sentiment, they lost as much in the humor and angst of the original.

Yursky's naive old man, with his frumpy manner and weathered face as though chiseled in stone, is a child lost in the awkward body of an adult. He is certain that he had the secret and the power to save mankind, but nobody ever paid him any mind.

As his loving and supportive wife, Tenyakova reassures him that he is so talented, he could be anything he wants to be. The irony is that when he can't even properly strike a match to light a kerosene lamp, she merely stretches her hands out before her and lights it as if by magic.

Finally, the old man resolves to invite a houseful of prominent people to hear a lecture based on the wisdom he has acquired in life. But, before the lecture can be delivered, death appears as the evening's star guest, taking the old pair together. That, and the illiteracy of the orator they leave behind, guarantees that whatever secrets the old man possessed will remain forever unknown.

There is always a problem in transferring Western metaphysics to Russian soil. The European who is alienated from his surroundings is almost always a total exile. He is not only rejected by men and society, but by God and nature, too. The Russian, no matter what the tribulations, invariably retains links at least with nature. It is one of the primary sources for the legendary Russian soul.

That is just what limits this version of *The Chairs*. Lacking the sufficient theatrical energy, it is too soulful to capture fully Ionesco's bite.

(March 1994)

The Beggar's Opera, Vakhtangov Theater

The newest from the Vakhtangov Theater is called *The Beggar's Opera*, although it is not John Gay's famous 18th century ballad opera. It is actually *The Threepenny Opera*. But, wait a minute; it's not really Kurt Weill's and Bertolt Brecht's popular political musical, either.

Sure, the composer's and playwright's names are on the program. And, in a faint echo of Brecht's trademark use of political placards on stage, they even hang above the stage amidst a sea of misspelled London street signs.

But one would be hard-pressed to find more than a few shreds of Brecht's biting social commentary buried in this decidedly unengaged performance. And one wonders: How did the cast and production company manage to make Weill's spectacular, jazzy score so flaccid and tuneless? Imagine hearing the great "Mack the Knife" reduced to the level of an anemic pop song.

Director Gary Chernyakhovsky probably tried too hard to please his audience. Maybe he thought that since Russian life is so politicized these days, a socially oriented work would do the trick. But, with everyone so tired of politics, he proceeded to strip away all but the "human interest" angle.

After all, as the shyster Mr. Peachum sings, man does not live by bread alone: there's also selfishness, spite, fear and slander.

What's left are the broadly-sketched trials and tribulations of the thief, Mack the Knife (Igor Lagutin). He marries Polly (Natalya Moleva), a shyster's daughter; fakes marriage to Lucy (Vera Novikova), the constable's daughter; but is in love with Jenny (Yulia Rutberg), a perky prostitute. When Polly's mom (Maria Aronova) enlists Jenny to get Mack arrested and hanged, the only thing that can save him is the newly-crowned Queen. She does.

It's worth saying now: The premiere came just days after Moscow's October 1993, putsch-2 rebels were pardoned and released from Lefortovo prison. Were the production truly Brechtian, this coincidence of theater and life couldn't have missed getting a rise from the spectators. Instead, the diehards who still remained when the finale rolled around were as impassive as they had been all evening.

Even when Constable Brown (Viktor Zozulin) muttered that he fought in Azerbaijan side-by-side with Polly's father (Vladimir Simonov), it barely produced a ripple in the audience.

Okay, so it's Brecht without politics. That's possible, too. At least there's the great music and endless opportunities for cabaret-style dance to liven things up.

Think again. For all the singing (supervised by Tatyana Agayeva), there is precious little music. While effectively striking pretty-boy poses, Lagutin sings in a voice that wavers between the expressionless and the flat. Simonov occasionally shows energy, but not much musicality. Moleva and Novikova can be downright screechy.

Chernyakhovsky deserves praise for avoiding the horrid practice of lipsynching. But next time, he ought to choose a cast that can sing. Yulia Rutberg is the only one of the lot to display at least some musical instinct and talent.

The cliché-ridden dance numbers staged by Larisa Chumachenko fare no better. Lacking in rhythm, discipline and snap, they mostly resemble chaotic, random movement. Only Rutberg and the sprightly Grigory Siatvinda, as one of Mack's cohorts, do more than literally go through the motions.

The cramped action is confined to a red, hand-pulled, double-decker bus that serves alternately as Peachum's shady establishment, Mack's abode in the stables or the constable's prison. (The program lists no designer.) While the actors struggle to conquer the bus's moving parts, the inviting expanses of the Vakhtangov's stage go to waste.

Call this production what you will, it still comes out a two-bit operetta.

(March 1994)

The Beggar, or the Death of Zand and *Yelizaveta Bam*, Learned Monkey

The Learned Monkey theater was founded in the fall of 1992. Its troupe was drawn from graduates of the Shchukin Institute, and its main reason for being was a hauntingly beautiful one-act play called *The City of Mice.*

Lacking a sense of direction, to say nothing of money or a place to call home, the theater exhausted its first season mounting an amateurish, all-male version of *Romeo and Juliet.* Most of the current season has gone into producing, on one bill, two curious, early Soviet plays, *The Beggar, or the Death of Zand* by Yury Olesha, and *Yelizaveta Bam* by Daniil Kharms.

The result, though rough at times, is a reminder why these young actors were encouraged to stay together in the first place.

It is no coincidence that the new production is directed and co-scored by fellow-graduate Eduard Radziukevich. He was also the mastermind behind *The City of Mice.* But Radziukevich is not alone; several talents emerge in the course of this performance.

Konstantin Plotnikov not only assembled *The Beggar* from Olesha's unfinished play and other works—including the famous novella, *Envy*—he also gives an intense performance of the nameless beggar, an uncompromising figure whose bitter conflict with Zand essentially occurs on the level of the supernatural.

Zand is a writer whose willingness to anticipate the public's needs made him popular, but left him dissatisfied. When he is confronted by the beggar—who may be real or a dream—the facade of his comfortable world begins crumbling immediately.

The beggar's call to promote "useless" romanticism in an age of social upheaval sounds seditious to Zand. And, indeed, Plotnikov, with his sunken eyes and curled lip, defends his position with the vengeance of a saboteur. Viktor Bakin's interpretation of Zand bears less personality than his contribution as co-author of the production's pulsing, introspective music.

The carelessly constructed but cleverly designed set by Grigory Belov and Nikolai Titov depicts an oversized, angled bed that allows for some fine shadow scenes behind the "sheets."

The evening's second act is a freewheeling version of the wacky, disconcerting *Yelizaveta Bam.* Maybe no one will ever figure out what this play is about, but that is half the point. Its fascinating incoherence, echoing the beggar's "useless romanticism" in the first act, is its own self-justification.

Two men (Bakin and Dmitry Voronin) come to arrest Yelizaveta, but no one knows why or even cares. In a structure that smacks of the keystone cops meeting the theater of the absurd, the play's six characters rattle off jokes, bog down in digressions and occasionally make sense.

Tatyana Ulyankina creates a wonderfully vulnerable and divinely aloof Yelizaveta, who is as intrigued by the mad turn of events as anyone else. Alexander Zhigalkin, as her absent-minded father, holds comic court when he is not trying to escape the two thugish orderlies from a psycho ward (Alexei Khardikov and Sergei Didyayev).

There is no denying that this young team lacks experience. But some good ideas and plenty of unbrushed talent still make these performances winners.

(March 1994)

Behind the Mirror, Chekhov Art Theater

Following a handful of performances at the end of February, opera star Galina Vishnevskaya is again ready to resume her much talked-about experiment as a dramatic actress. The place is the Chekhov Art Theater, the play is Yelena Gremina's *Behind the Mirror*, and the day is April 1.

No doubt, some will see the resumption date as a sign. The Art Theater administration did its best to keep the press away from the first performances, and there's no point in hiding why: The advance scuttlebutt was that Vishnevskaya wasn't cutting it.

Indeed, at the special press showing four days after the premiere, the critical cognoscenti shared a good many crooked smiles, knowing nods, and whispered "I-told-you-so's."

But the view from here says the joke is on the doubters. Bluntly put, Vishnevskaya knows what to do on a stage, whether she is a polished dramatic actress or not. Her natural, majestic carriage and her imposing operatic mannerisms lend an impressive authenticity to her performance of Catherine the Great.

Moreover, director Vyacheslav Dolgachyov did a fine job putting Vishnevskaya in surroundings that minimize the dangers and maximize the opportunities to show off her considerable powers. His biggest misstep was to insist she play the German-born empress with a thick German accent. It sounds especially silly when Vishnevskaya forgets and slips momentarily into her natural speech.

But this is an old-fashioned show—a star vehicle—and, as such, it is thoroughly enjoyable.

Gremina's wise play focuses on Catherine's personal side—her world "behind the mirror"—as she makes her way through her fifties. Although she has lost none of her spark, her famous lust for power and men has softened somewhat, her subtle sense of humor has long since ripened, and her desire for a sense of belonging in the world is giving her no peace.

Designer Margarita Demyanova set the tone well. The stage is sprinkled with mood-creating children's implements, and the back, mirrored walls occasionally rise to reveal another world beyond them.

As is the custom at court, the empress's lady-in-waiting plucks a ripe young man, Sashenka, from the officers corps and readies him to serve as the sovereign's entertainment. To everyone's amazement, Sashenka (Sergei Shnyryov) takes his mission so seriously, he actually falls in love with Catherine, whom he affectionately calls "mama." For her part, Catherine's heart is also unexpectedly snared by the youth's beauty and innocence.

As Countess Bruce, the lady-in-waiting, Tatyana Lavrova adds to the mix an enigmatic, seductive and faintly comic air that keeps the action working on several levels at once. Her character is an ageless, but slightly aging beauty who also appears to be smitten by the pliable young officer. She gladly accepts when Catherine asks her to test the youth for loyalty, and is visibly disappointed when he passes the exam with flying colors.

Perhaps that disappointment is what eventually leads the Countess Bruce to drive a wedge between the two unorthodox lovers, and then to play a key role in their tragic and final separation.

Much of the credit for this production's success goes to the play itself. Aside from its well-crafted script, its strong female point of view provides a fascinating twist on the usually male-dominated genre of the historical play. Not only are the traditional sexual roles reversed throughout, but Gremina captured Catherine's nuances as no man probably could.

If Vishnevskaya paints her portrait of Catherine with broader strokes, so what? She does it with an attractive, regal flair.

(*March 1994*)

The Supper, Tabakov Theater and Chekhov Art Theater

The idea of a film director escaping the current crisis in Russian cinema by turning to the theater is becoming a commonplace. It is cheaper, it is quicker, and there is a safe bet the product will get seen—something almost no filmmaker today can count on.

The most recent to jump the fence is Andrei Smirnov, whose theatrical debut comes with *The Supper*, a joint production of the Tabakov Theater and the Chekhov Art Theater.

Smirnov's reputation rests primarily on his 1971 film classic, *The Belorussia Station*, a bittersweet look at old friends who lazily confront the passing of their youth. *The Supper* will not reserve the director a place in the pantheon of stage greats, but it is perfectly competent, if uneventful.

The biggest obstacle to popular success will be the memory of the audience.

The show stars two well-known actors, Oleg Tabakov and Armen Dzhigarkhanyan, as famous historical figures who meet to discuss the past and future over a late supper. One of last season's most exciting entries, *The Possible Meeting* at the Chekhov Art Theater, used an almost identical structure. However, *The Supper*, which is certainly an attempt to capitalize on the popularity of

The Possible Meeting, is only a pale reflection of that spectacular production.

This time the principals are Joseph Fouché, the resilient French Minister of Police under several regimes, and Talleyrand, the unscrupulous politician who served revolutionary and counter-revolutionary forces with equal faith.

Their meeting occurs in 1814 as Napoleon's grip on Paris has slipped. The streets are filled with marauders and the two resourceful men, between whom no love is lost, are hammering out an agreement about how to split whatever power will not be seized by Ludwig XVIII.

The performance is more literary than theatrical, something one suspects is owing at least as much to author Jean-Claude Brisville as to director Smirnov. The lame Talleyrand (Tabakov) spends most of his time immobile in his chair, while Fouché (Dzhigarkhanyan) has little choice but to sit uneasily or to circle the elegant dining room—designed by David Borovsky—like a wild beast on a tether.

The result is similar to a radio play, with the "action" consisting almost entirely of the two rivals' sometimes witty, sometimes wickedly aggressive, intellectual game of nerves. In that light, Dzhigarkhanyan is best suited to the production's style. His rumbling bass voice, his weathered, hard-cut facial lines, and his cutting stare all help create a badly-needed physical sense of drama.

Another weakness is the almost line-by-line parallels between the political realities of France in 1814 and Russia in 1994. Fouché's maneuvers to keep his secret police afloat and Talleyrand's promises to dissolve parliament sound almost like headlines from *Izvestia*. So much so, it can be downright distracting.

If Andrei Smirnov ever makes a film of *The Supper*, he would do well to give lots of close-ups of Dzhigarkhanyan's face. That is where most of the drama in this encounter takes place.

(April 1994)

The Brothers Karamazov: Tomorrow the Trial, Sarkisov Theater Group

There is something attractive in the recent tendency to make theater in apartment-museums. Sure, the reasons are mostly logistical: It gives a director without money or a home a place to work. But the aged, homey atmosphere of a great artist's former living quarters can't help but give a performance an added touch of class.

That is certainly the case with the Valery Sarkisov Theater Group's production of *The Brothers Karamazov: Tomorrow the Trial*. It is played in the tiny Onegin Hall of the Stanislavsky Memorial Museum, dedicated to one of the great directors of the 20th century.

The spare, intimate surroundings are ideal for this always sincere, occasionally compelling adaptation of Fyodor Dostoevsky's great novel about three brothers, each of whom inherited his father's insatiable passions in his own way.

Sarkisov (who directed and wrote the dramatization) ably distilled the swirling original into a series of philosophical monologues and dialogues. They take place after the lecherous father Karamazov has been killed, and his oldest son Mitya is in prison, ready to stand trial for the crime. Dostoevsky's almost voracious, dramatic prose usually fills in well for the lack of action.

The production focuses on the pious Alyosha (a sympathetic but wobbly, young Gleb Podgorodinsky) and the painfully agnostic Ivan. With his slick, bold smile, the towering Denis Karasyov is good at capturing Ivan's energetic pride, but comes up short when digging inside to find his spiritual angst.

Such characters as Mitya, the mysterious Smerdyakov and others appear in episodic roles that set or frame the production's themes of faith and grace. The actors in the episodes provide the best moments.

In his single scene as Mitya—innocent of murdering his father, but guilty of threatening to do it—Vladimir Steklov shows an enormous capacity for emotional intensity and salt-of-the-earth wisdom. As the epileptic Smerdyakov—the real murderer who thought he was carrying out Ivan's orders—Valery Yaryomenko finds just the right mix of arrogance and sycophancy.

Irina Lukovskaya sparks early comic fireworks as Mrs. Khokhlakova, the eccentric mother of Liza, the lame girl whose "beautiful, childlike soul" has been eclipsed by her bitterness, and who plays risky, coquettish games with the Karamazov brothers. Alyona Kolchugina's too-cute Liza is really more effervescent than obsessed with dark ideas.

The uncontested highlight is Valery Garkalin's "vulgar little devil," who appears as an apparition after Ivan learns the truth about Smerdyakov. Witty, persnickety, impatient and ingratiating all at once, Garkalin uses the intimacy of the setting to extend his velvety embrace from Ivan to the audience as well.

Aside from some chairs, the only real prop in Vladimir Kovalchuk's set is a small wooden railing on wheels. The actors roll it around, jettison it, or stand at it, as at a courtroom balustrade, to make their confessions.

Although uneven, this adaptation of Dostoevsky's urban, Russian tale is effective. And Stanislavsky's tasteful old apartments give it the ring of authenticity.

(April 1994)

The School for Wives, Mossoviet Theater

The good, old-fashioned human desire to laugh has led a lot of theaters to take on the plays· of Molière in the last few seasons. In most cases, the laughs have been pretty scarce.

Now, a winking, blinking, over-the-top production of Molière's *The School for Wives* at the Mossoviet Theater has solved that problem. From the opening, heart-on-sleeve French chanson to the final mass chaos scene, this show is so saturated in parody and camp, it squeezes laughs out of air.

Airy—if not downright thin—is just what most of Molière's comedies are. Of course, the playwright also had a genius for depicting situations that reveal the ABCs of human behavior. *The School for Wives* is no exception on either count.

It focuses on the lecherous, silly Arnolphe, who wants to marry his pretty, young ward, Agnès. She wants to marry Horace, who is so stupid that he incessantly plays into his rival's

hands. Arnolphe's friend, Chrysalde, and his servants, Alain and Georgette, provide comic complications, while some puffed-up relatives arrive at the end to untangle everything.

Obviously, the fun isn't the story, it's watching it unfold. And, despite some sudden dead spots when burlesque becomes overkill, this production doesn't just unfold, it blossoms. Director Boris Milgram staged a joyous, unapologetic attack on all the clichés that have become attached to Molièrian comedy over the last 300 years.

With more than a hint of Molière-meets-*La Cage aux Folles*, the male characters delight in their sexual ambiguities. Bewigged, berouged, and beset by frequent gasp attacks, they milk the text and all of its suggestions for every comic drop. It's all set in a head-spinning variety of styles that weds the vaudeville, song and dance, silent films, floor shows at old Intourist hotels and those inept, unintentionally hilarious Soviet musical movies of the 1970s.

As the shifty, cross-eyed, scrawny Arnolphe, Yevgeny Glyadinsky is the ideal overripe heavy. He is suspicious, possessive, petty and pompous. The lanky Andrei Mizhulis—in tight tights and a near-bursting codpiece—is superb as Horace, Arnolphe's sworn enemy. Gullible and endearingly weird, this Horace, with his awkward, spasmodic movements, is faintly reminiscent of a bell-rung cherub with clipped wings.

The picture-perfect Darya Feklenko creates a sweet, giggling Agnès, while the team of Margarita Shubina and Yury Cherkasov plays Georgette and Alain with well-timed give and take.

But the tone is set by Valery Yaryomenko's sparkling Chrysalde-as-transvestite. Whether he is belting out a tune in French or English, whether he is accompanying himself on the piano or the accordion, or whether he is hobbling on crutches or flying across the stage, the lightning-quick Yaryomenko is in total control of himself and the audience. His character is essentially a helping verb in Molière's play, but in Milgram's production of it, he is the tongue-in-cheek heart and soul.

Alla Kamenkova created appropriate visual surroundings. Her playful set is

Valery Yaryomenko in Molière's *The School for Wives* at the Mossoviet Theater, directed by Boris Milgram, 1994. Photo: Alexander Ivanishin

essentially an empty, yellow-draped, wooden stage built upon the stage. At moments, another stage behind it mirrors the goings-on. Her costumes undergo clever "progressions." They are realistic period costumes early on, but take on increasingly contemporary lines as the action develops. Eventually, in the energetic finale, the actors appear in outlandish parodies of 17th-century dress.

You may never have seen Molière played like this, but that's the point. This is no museum piece; it is daring and irreverent. It is also very funny. Which would have suited Molière just fine.

(*April 1994*)

The Car in Flesh, "Safo" Russian-French Theater Center

The Car in Flesh, featuring the former Soviet film star, Yelena Koreneva, and performed in a real car sales showroom, had all the makings for being fun and unusual. In fact, it never gets out of first gear.

But before distributing the blame for that, let's put things in perspective.

From 1974 to 1982, few actresses in the Soviet Union matched Koreneva's charisma. She was a genuine lyrical heroine in a very unlyrical era. She was funny, perky, pretty, a bit daft and, most of all, she was penetratingly sincere. That quickly made her a star, but it ended just as quickly when she did the unthinkable: She married an American and fled Moscow.

Now, after a decade of anonymity, Koreneva is making a comeback, and *The Car in Flesh* is the vehicle she chose to ride.

It was a bad decision.

Pyotr Gladilin's wafer-thin play, saturated with humorless double-entendres about men and cars, smacks of inspired amateurism. It consists of a half-dozen scenes linked by a male chorus (Vladimir Golyshev) whose sung texts partly introduce and partly obscure what is to follow.

The story emerges in chat. Over a 20-year period, Veronika (Koreneva) and Masha (the delightfully tough and eccentric Yevdokia Germanova) gossip about the hunks and bums they're either chasing or escaping. But this girl-talk sounds so much like shop-talk, we can't tell whether they mean men (with "broken starters"), airplanes (that "can't get it up") or automobiles (that "smoke a lot").

While Masha pursues pilots who can't get off the ground, and computers that memorize her nude photos, Veronika struggles through bruises and a pregnancy from a rough fiancé. Masha finally fixes her up with an older man whose distinguishing feature is his shiny, new Lincoln Mark VIII.

That provides the requisite love scene, with Koreneva awkwardly sliding and crawling all over the Lincoln. (Real car buffs cringe as the hood and top visibly and audibly buckle beneath her). When the old man dies, Veronika inherits the car, although by that time it's been standing, smashed, in the garage for 10 years. Still in mourning, she considers blowing her new fortune on a lotful of new cars, but suddenly changes her mind: She senses that her beloved Mark VIII is jealous.

Director Yevgeny Kamenkovich did nothing to incorporate the performance into the environment. Why do we spend 90 minutes staring into the car dealership's sales offices? They needed either to be used for more than occasional, pointless run-throughs, or curtained off, like the rest of the showroom. The actresses' stage placement was given no thought. Half the time, they are not even visible.

Koreneva, whose biggest success was in film, is clearly ill at ease in her return to the stage. She works valiantly and at times the familiar spark shines through. She was well served by the expressive Germanova, but, for her next project, she needs better material and a new director.

(*April 1994*)

The Oginski Polonaise, Roman Viktyuk Theater

Some people get famous by catching waves; some do it by making them. There isn't much doubt about which category Roman Viktyuk belongs to.

Yelena Koreneva in Pyotr Gladilin's *The Car in Flesh*, directed by Yevgeny Kamenkovich in an actual auto salon, 1994. Photo: Mikhail Guterman

Viktyuk became a celebrity midway through the perestroika era by creating a powerful trend in Russian theater. His splashy, titillating productions threw back the curtain on decades of sexual repression. They weren't just erotic, they were boldly and proudly homoerotic.

The best had an intense, suggestive, almost narcotic draw. But recently, they were becoming increasingly garish, cheap and slapdash.

Then came last week's premiere of *The Oginski Polonaise* by Nikolai Kolyada. It is tinged with doubt, introspection, sadness and maybe even exhaustion. The performance is rough and occasionally drags, but it comes from the heart. That is a welcome change after the self-satisfied brassiness that had crept into such productions as *Lolita* and *Slingshot*.

Viktyuk's non-realistic approach, echoed in Vladimir Boyer's set centered around a bridge-like staircase-to-nowhere, suits Kolyada's play well. It tells of a troubled woman who returns to Russia after a decade in the United States, and finds that old acquaintances have become strangers. But it is not a mere treatment of people's biographies. It is an opportunity to sketch the current outline of Russian life and the Russian character. (A recent production of the play at the Malaya Bronnaya Theater took the realistic tack and flopped.)

Lyudmila Maksakova is superb as Tanya, the ambassador's daughter who fled to New York after her parents were murdered in Central Asia. She gives a powerful, unsettling performance of a woman plagued by vulnerability and hyper-sensitivity. Her attempt to reenter Russian life is essentially an attempt to reenter childhood, and, ultimately, it is just as futile.

In Tanya's absence, her parents' apartment was seized by a neighbor, Lyudmila (Lyudmila Pogorelova), her uncouth husband (Valery Simonov), and their cohort, squirmy, but sympathetic Vanya (Oleg Isayev). They are happy to take Tanya's gifts and borrow her money, but don't want to lose what they now consider their own. Lyudmila suggests putting Tanya away in an asylum.

They are most irritated by David (Yaroslav Zdorov), the American transvestite Tanya brought to Moscow. His otherness—"What is he? A man or a woman?"—is too much for them to handle.

Drifting in and out of the picture is Tanya's mysterious old flame, Dima. He calls himself a one-eyed monster and, as played by Sergei Makovetsky, there is something to that.

After waiting for Tanya for nine years, he "buried" her a year ago, erecting a stone bearing her name next to her parents' graves. Now, he cannot overcome his deep-seated hostility towards her. His embraces are rough and his attitude sarcastic, his only attempt at tenderness—when she is confused and thinks she is with David—smacking of rape.

The strength of this production is that nothing is as it seems and it gives no answers to the questions it poses.

Tanya is probably not crazy, but in the madness of Moscow she may be. Dima, cold and even brutal, is kind and gentle when handling a beautiful white swan. The "intolerant" apartment squatters appear with dignity and grace as Tanya prepares to leave Moscow again. All of these ambiguities are reflected in the enigmatic character of David.

The Oginski Polonaise does not reach the heights of Viktyuk's best. But it has an attractive, thoughtful subtlety that turns around his recent downward slide.

(May 1994)

The Magnificent Cuckold, Satirikon Theater

This is what theater lovers wait for, sometimes for a whole season or more. If you are one of them, this is what makes you smile and shake your head in approving disbelief. It is what catches the breath and stirs the heart.

This is Pyotr Fomenko's production of *The Magnificent Cuckold* at the Satirikon Theater, his first outing since he sent critics scurrying for superlatives and spectators clamoring for tickets with last season's brilliant *Guilty Without Guilt* at the Vakhtangov.

Maybe *Cuckold* is not as perfect. Maybe it's a little more frayed at the edges, like the

Konstantin Raikin and Natalia Vdovina in Pyotr Fomenko's production of Fernand Crommelynck's *The Magnificent Cuckold*, Satirikon Theater, 1994. Photo: Mikhail Guterman

thick, twisted hemp ropes that hang from the balconies encircling the stage. Maybe, at moments, it's a bit more raw and nervous, taking its cue from the leading man and lady, who bring to life Fernand Crommelynck's relentless and heart-wrenching story of lovers doomed by the intensity of their love.

But even if all that is true, none of it is criticism. Growing inexorably from a joyous idyll into a disturbing view of passion gone wrong, this is a production of breathtaking inspiration.

Since it was written in 1920, many have called *The Magnificent Cuckold* an inconsequential play that has enjoyed a few sterling productions. The most famous was Vsevolod Meyerhold's farcical staging in 1922, under the title of *The Magnanimous Cuckold.* Employing Meyerhold's acrobatic style of acting, called biomechanics, it went down in history as one of that great Russian director's finest works.

Now, Fomenko brings his unique brand of flowing lyricism to the play, creating another bona fide masterpiece for a new generation to savor. So convincing is his vision, one can't help but wonder why the Belgian dramatist's play is usually dismissed so easily.

In part, Crommelynck wrote a masterful variation on the theme of the Fall. Only, here, the husband tempts his wife, while, even in disgrace, she remains essentially untouched by sin. Of course, the point is not the loss of divine grace, but the terrible consequences of breaking human trust.

As Bruno, the compulsive husband who combats his mad jealousy by driving his wife, Stella, into the arms of every man in town to test her fidelity, Konstantin Raikin runs the gamut of emotions from playful tenderness to lurid madness.

He starts out with a hypnotic, charismatic energy, his public boasts about his wife's most intimate charms coming across as only a hairline violation of decency. But from that moment when he, even to his own horror, suddenly strips off Stella's blouse in front of her cousin Petrus (Alexander Korzhenkov), he tips the scales into the realm of the possessed.

It is characteristic of this explosively temperamental actor that even his early, most loving moments are subtly streaked with the dark shadow of what is to come. But his biggest triumph is his final scene. Aged, broken, and driven insane by his obsession, Raikin's Bruno achieves a strange state of vulnerable purity even while cranking his merciless persecution of Stella up another notch.

Neither the silent protests of Bruno's guitar-strumming friend Estrugo (Fyodor Dobronravov) nor the disdain of Stella's jealously protective nurse (Marina Ivanova) have the slightest effect on him.

Fomenko gambled when picking the actress to play the part of Stella. And he hit the jackpot.

Making her professional debut, Natalia Vdovina is as fresh and delicate as a fragrant spring breeze, the picture of a child of nature. Her faithfulness and trust in Bruno are wholly believable, in part because her light, sexual coquettishness with others early on is so innocently instinctive.

When Bruno locks her in a hideous mask, and then outright forces her into promiscuity, she fulfills his desires, not because she is so submissive, but because she is so genuinely in love. Never a "fallen woman"— although she is castigated by society—she is cruelly trapped like the caged bird in whom she confides so gently in the opening scene.

Vdovina's gradual transformation from an unspoiled innocent into a troubled, experienced and haunted woman is powerful indeed. With her natural wholesomeness, her irrepressible energy, and her unshakable sense of right, she sets the tone for the entire production.

And this is a production which is as cleanly designed, as perfectly executed and as thoroughly thought-through as they come. Fomenko has made a name for himself as a director of impeccable taste, who pays extraordinary attention to even the finest, most insignificant detail. *The Magnificent Cuckold* is no exception.

In it, everything and everyone is wrapped in a shimmering veil of evocative, sensory effects that, like fine spices, highlight every aspect of the compelling drama. Tiny bells tinkle quietly when brushed against. Fine, scented powder billows down in bursts from a narrow chute above the stage. The actors cavort in a bath, the water splashing up over the edges, and they playfully spray misty clouds of water, which, thanks to the superb lighting, hang like gossamer in the air.

Staged in the round, the action also takes place on balconies above and behind the spectators, as well as in the corridors outside the small, 100-seat hall. Designer Stanislav Morozov's warm, rustic environment, decorated only by a strange, windmill-like contraption hanging over a washtub, consists mostly of unvarnished wood.

The suggestive lighting (Andrei Rebrov), the exquisite, lacy music (Galina Pokrovskaya), and the imaginative costumes (Maria Danilova) round out a production whose compositional aspects are nothing short of spectacular.

There can be little doubt about it now. Some 30 years into his career, Pyotr Fomenko has seized the spot of Moscow's number one director. *The Magnificent Cuckold* is glorious proof of that.

(*May 1994*)

Hamlet, Anton Chekhov Theater

Leonid Trushkin, of the Anton Chekhov Theater, will take a lot of flak for squeezing *Hamlet* into a one-act play. He will also get skewered for turning Shakespeare's contemplative hero into a sneering, angry rebel.

That always happens when a director takes liberties with a classic, even when calling it a "version" as a caveat.

But that's nonsense, really. Hamlet has been played as Hammy T, the prince of rap, a gay and a woman. He has even been paired with a dog, as in a recent New York show that cast a Golden Retriever as the faithful Horatio.

Trushkin's mistake wasn't in shaking up Shakespeare, it was in doing it badly and bathetically. He created neither a parody nor a pared-down, modern *Hamlet*. A frantic show that would have been better titled *Postcards from Elsinore*, it performs like a whistle-stop on a five-day, package tour of six Shakespearean towns.

You can almost hear the tour guide's pitch: "We'll skip the ghost, bypass the traveling actors, and do a drive-by of Ophelia. But don't worry—we'll take in *To be or not to be* and a few other favorites too."

A pioneering and highly successful practitioner of commercial theater in Moscow, Trushkin did succeed in one of his primary tasks. He avoided even the vaguest hint of a hesitating Hamlet.

He cut most everything that gives Hamlet a past, stripping him of psychological subtlety. He broke the play into transitionless episodes, buffering them with blackouts. Then he fortified it all with Vladimir Davydenko's frenetic music that plays like a record of *Bolero* stuck on the final grooves.

The result was Hamlet with an agenda. Hamlet the lone conspirator. At moments even, Hamlet on a rampage.

But, for all his bluster, Sergei Shakurov's Hamlet is an exercise in cold, professional acting. He is glib, agile and smooth. Yet he neither moves nor convinces, because he plays the Danish prince from the neck up only. Dropped into what amounts to an odd collection of Hamlet highlights, he probably had no other choice.

This Hamlet never doubts who killed his father: The performance begins as he knowingly sways above the heads of the murderous Claudius and Gertrude on a pendulum-like chandelier (designed by Boris Valuyev). He knows he is surrounded by spies: The truncated parts of his old friends Rosencrantz and Guildenstern make them into petty snitches. He knows what he must do: Revenge and "justice" are the tracks this locomotive runs on.

Ophelia, reduced to two scenes, drowns herself more as a sign of solidarity with her wronged suitor than out of insanity caused by rejection in love.

Still, not counting the retina-threatening blast that rocks the house in the finale and showers the front rows with ash (don't wear your white suit!), there is one genuine, heart-stopping moment.

It comes thanks to Viktor Proskurin, whose rock-hard Claudius has a searing moment of revelation when suddenly admitting the evil of his deed. Proskurin's midpoint monologue is a flash of brilliance in a murky sea.

The rest of the cast ranges from the competent to the amateur. Suffice it to say that, in this context, even an actor as fine as Lev Durov merely illustrates Polonius, the eternal, buffoon-like, court sycophant.

(*May 1994*)

Dear Liar, **Vakhtangov Theater**

Dear Liar at the Vakhtangov Theater renews one of those nice little traditions that distinguishes any self-respecting theater town.

In this case, it is a play that twice in the past has let pairs of popular actors bask in the glow of appreciative audiences. The leisurely, bantering Vakhtangov production, starring that venue's longtime favorites, Yulia Borisova and Vasily Lanovoi, is Moscow's third. It will not rival the legends of the famous earlier productions, but it is a warm, satisfying show.

Written by Jerome Kilty, the accomplished American actor, director and playwright, *Dear Liar* is a play in letters; a chronicle of the unique relationship that bound George Bernard Shaw to his semi-secret love, the actress Mrs. Patrick Campbell.

It was a union made to be dramatized, for in the headstrong, scandalously independent Campbell, the crusty, opinionated writer met his match.

Kilty structured his version of the story around the couple's copious, 40-year correspondence, filling in key gaps with an occasional face-to-face meeting. After starting with an epilogue, where we learn how the letters were saved after Campbell's death, it drifts back to the first time Shaw saw her perform. Then there is his writing of *Pygmalion* for her; her marriage to another; the death of his mother, and her son; his rise to fame and her descent into poverty.

Director Adolph Shapiro unobtrusively smudged the teasingly vague boundaries between the characters' real and epistolary worlds. The two jealously keep their distance when together, while their freest, most intimate moments occur only as they express themselves in letters.

The limits of the production are bound up in its strengths.

One suspects that the real Shaw and Campbell sparred harder and sparked hotter than what Borisova and Lanovoi show us. Certainly Lanovoi's Shaw is a bit too cold, and Borisova a tad too precious. If you are searching for accurate historical echoes, you might consider the pair miscast.

But the actors are far from lacking personalities of their own and, regardless of whom they are portraying, they create their own effective dynamic.

Borisova, who is also the leading lady in the Vakhtangov's hit production of *Guilty Without Guilt*, is an endlessly charming actress. Her sing-song, schoolgirl's voice and her wholesomely coquettish manner would melt the hardest heart. It is astonishing to think she made her stage debut in 1949, for she is the eternal picture of youth—fresh, quick and agile.

Here, she plays a pixy Mrs. Campbell who is characterized primarily by her light, cascading laughter and her sparkling eyes. Still, beneath the breezy surface is the soul of a fiercely independent woman. Despite her love and admiration for the great playwright, nothing will stop her doing what she wants to do.

It is a wonderful moment when Borisova defiantly turns a somersault to show how offended she is at Shaw's calling her a "veteran of the stage."

Lanovoi, the harsh, angular lines of his face still making him as ruggedly handsome as when he first appeared in 1957, plays Shaw as an enigmatic introvert. His biggest flaw is that he seems bereft of humor, although he has some fine dramatic moments.

Especially moving is the scene in which he sardonically claims to be in a humorous mood while describing his mother's cremation. Lanovoi plays it with an edge, bringing out fully the hard emotions of the experience.

Designer Tatyana Selvinskaya created a languorous, even voluptuous environment, draping the walls in copies of Matisse, and scattering the stage with stray objects of elegance.

Were *Dear Liar* a rainbow, it would not arch high in the sky, although its pastel colors would still catch the eye.

(*May 1994*)

I'm Better off Speaking, **Taganka Theater and Shchukin Institute**

I'm Better Off Speaking, a two-actor show affiliated with the Taganka Theater, is a genuine sleeper.

It boasts no celebrities and has had no publicity. Essentially, it is a student work created at the Taganka Theater Studio of the Shchukin Institute.

But a lot of big-hype, big-name shows can't match the power and sincerity of this inspired composition about the Jewish experience in Russia.

Much of the text is culled from the poetry of Joseph Brodsky, especially his early poem, "Isaak and Avraam," with smaller portions drawn from the Old Testament, Vasily Grossman's novel, *Life and Fate*, and *The Dybbuk*, the classic play of the Yiddish theater. There are even some timely-told "Jewish jokes," and most of the haunting songs are sung in Hebrew or Yiddish.

This potpourri makes for fleeting, even tattered scenes that are occasionally obscure in isolation. But taken as a whole, they acquire a profound, cumulative significance.

The main reason it works so well is simple: The acting team of Yelena Laskavaya and Igor Pekhovich (who also directed and created the script with Laskavaya and designer Maria Orlova) is blessed with a rare combination of talent, vision and harmony. From the first instant when Laskavaya's strong, soaring voice arises in the darkness, and the dignified, but ever-so-slightly apologetic Pekhovich appears in a lone spotlight, the pair is in complete control.

For the next hour plus, they lead us on a moving journey through the historical events and personal experiences which have forged the uniquely Eastern European Jewish character. The abundance of music—both actors have wonderful voices—binds the performance and supports its resilient atmosphere.

Of several standout moments, two are unforgettable.

One captures the stoic Laskavaya reciting what the Nazis have forbidden Jews to do. Her eyes heavy with sorrow and her smiling lips expressing an indomitable will, she says they cannot walk the sidewalk or eat anything but potatoes. The scene's full impact comes when we realize these are a mother's last words to her absent son as she awaits death.

Equally powerful is Pekhovich's reading of what amounts to a mathematical list describing the decimation of Jews in Europe during World War II. He delivers it with a rhythmic solemnity usually reserved for high prayers or poetry. Upon finishing, the lights go black and he sets the list afire. As it burns out, he lightly bats the sparking ashes into the air.

Not all are ready for this honest and deeply ethnic performance. I counted 10 disgruntled spectators who stomped out of the hall noisily. One even shouted a few choice words in parting.

Pekhovich isn't surprised. He explains that the least receptive audience they ever faced was at a dress rehearsal for a hall of elderly Jews. Few people of any nationality are really ready to face the truth, he says.

Odd. For the truth is wonderfully cathartic when told as beautifully as in *I'm Better Off Speaking*.

(June 1994)

What a Lovely Sight!, **Malaya Bronnaya Theater**

Avid supporters and grimacing critics of *What A Lovely Sight!* at the Malaya Bronnaya Theater will surely agree on one thing: This exercise in florid nostalgia is hands down the weirdest show of the season. And the view from here says weird is good.

Moscow has probably never seen such an inflated look at the excesses—and the undercurrents—of the official image and droning monotony of the Brezhnev years. Once it gets over an irritatingly feeble start, *What A Lovely Sight!* goes bursting past parody and careening beyond burlesque. Ultimately, it is a wicked travesty of clichés about youthful hope, familial duty and social commitment.

But don't go searching it for arrogance or cynicism. What makes it click is its affection for the life it ridicules so relentlessly. Director Artyom Khryakov fearlessly ripped back

Vladimir Yavorsky and Tatyana Oshurkova in Artyom Khryakov's production of Alexei Arbuzov's *What a Lovely Sight!* at the Malaya Bronnaya Theater, 1994. Photo: Mikhail Guterman

the facade of Alexei Arbuzov's play, written early in the so-called era of stagnation.

The story centers around the bright-eyed, bushy-tailed Vasya, a "wonderful, young man" with a weakness for women named Milochka. He lives in a happy community of loving friends and family, all of whom wish everyone the best.

Arbuzov, from the 1930s to his death in 1986, was one of the finest official Soviet writers. And he knew well the value of fairy tales, as a bare recounting of his play's plot reveals.

When Vasya's second wife, Milochka-2, dumps him for his best friend Seva, his father refuses to take him back in. Vasya then rudely brushes off the teenaged, crush-stricken Milochka-3, and accepts a transfer suggested by his cloying boss. He finally abandons Moscow for the far-flung town of Ustegorsk.

It is a strikingly desolate picture, really. But Arbuzov camouflaged it masterfully with an odd menagerie of dauntless, militantly positive heroes.

Khryakov added a lethal dose of poison to the author's pen, turning irony to mockery. He did it by changing expected intonations in speech, shifting pauses, inserting pantomimes, rearranging actors' entrances and exits, and cutting two minor characters. Couples engage in hilarious, acrobatic sex as they spout hifalutin speeches about social duty.

Deadly serious, the entire cast oozes a sticky, inspired optimism that both sends up and celebrates the youth-oriented Soviet culture of the 1950s and 1960s.

Khryakov coaxed fine performances from everyone. Olga Sirina is gracefully silly as the superficial Milochka-2. Tatyana Oshurkova is perky and sympathetic as Milochka-3, whom Vasya not only rejects, but even abuses when he takes illicit advantage of her willingness to please. Ivan Shabaltas plays Seva with winningly pompous macho, while the orange-haired Antonina Dmitrieva is delightful as the nosy elevator operator who is mother to all.

Vladimir Yavorsky labors to hold Vasya's plaster-cast smile in place in the first act, but eases into things thereafter. His smoothly

enthusiastic acceptance of "exile" is effectively double-edged.

Konstantin Kravinsky is superb as the television announcer who is literally trapped in a t.v. set, and who unflappably ticks off agricultural achievements, delivers poetry lectures and gives gardening lessons.

The black-box set and "tasteless" period costumes by Irina Akimova create the perfect visuals. Everyone's clothing is carelessly splashed in bronze, suggesting that these are people on their way to becoming monuments, or, on the contrary, that they are monuments in the process of decay.

Might this be the start of a nostalgia kick? Certainly the realities of Soviet life are taking on an attractive glow for many as they fade in memory. And this production is handled so as to delight the pros as much as the cons.

However, chances are that *What A Lovely Sight!* is a one-of-a-kind show. It would be tough to duplicate anything as outlandish as this.

(June 1994)

When Irish Eyes Are Smiling, Theater u Nikitskikh vorot

Mildred Jenkins is pretty sure she is still alive.

She would feel more certain if Don, her twenty year-old boarder with a latent sadistic streak in him, didn't keep reminding her that people get forgotten before they die. And if her arrogant former boyfriend from upstairs hadn't dumped her after using her to get his fake flower business going. And if her memories of childhood weren't so frustratingly elusive.

But in Athol Fugard's *People Are Living There* nobody gets any slack. It may not be fair, but that's not the point.

At the Theater u Nikitskikh vorot the celebrated South African writer's play is given the misleading title of *When Irish Eyes Are Smiling*, echoing the song Milly uses to try pumping up everyone's spirits at her rather grim birthday party. But that change neither softens the play's hard message nor dulls its biting story.

It is an impressive debut in the dramatic genre for director Mikhail Kislyarov, whose previous experience was as a choreographer at the Pokrovsky Chamber Musical Theater. He put his mastery of dance to good use in a few dreamy scenes that momentarily allow characters to escape the limits of their daily lives, but his feel for drama is equally strong.

Also on the mark is Marina Kaidalova, who turns in a first-rate Milly, the crusty, middle-aged landlady whose loser renters, Don and Shorty, are about her last link to the outside world.

Holding her momentum almost through to the end, Kaidalova gives Milly a tough, tenacious streak and a raw, cutting edge which don't exclude some revelatory moments of weakness and doubt. With a little better pacing of her performance, she might avoid a drop in intensity as the action reaches its climax, but that's nitpicking, really. By any measure, Kaidalova is excellent as the woman with almost nothing left to lose.

Don and Shorty, outcasts both, are on a collision course. And their point of impact is roughly that same gray area of despair which Milly inhabits.

Don (Pyotr Tataritsky) is a cynical and painfully disillusioned introvert who takes revenge on the world's lack of joy by telling everyone the honest, caustic "truth." Fueled by his readings of Freud, Don thinks he knows why Shorty's six-month marriage to Cissy (Yelena Sokolova) is already on the rocks: She hasn't let Shorty touch her yet, he suggests.

Shorty (Dmitry Osherov) is a mild-mannered mailman who repeatedly gets his pay docked for losing letters, and who tries bolstering his shaky self-confidence by taking up boxing. A wide-eyed innocent and the constant butt of jokes, he maddens everyone all the more for being so forgiving.

Despite their differences, Milly, Don and Shorty are closely bound by their almost continual state of mutual animosity. That is most clear during Milly's tragi-farcical birthday party. She arranges it to prove she still exists, but it quickly bogs down in bitter personal attacks among the participants.

Using several stop-action scenes, Kislyarov doesn't let us forget Milly's origins. The stage lighting (by Yelena Michurina) goes sharply to yellow and a silent young girl (Dasha Velikanova) in a white dress takes the stage to dance a bit or simply watch the other characters unseen. These scenes from Milly's "secret" past are low-key and effective.

Inna Kudina's apartment interior, with the kitchen spilling onto the floor in front of the audience, is purposefully nondescript. The costumes by Natalia Kostygova are literally topped off by Milly's crazy, electric-powered birthday hat.

When Irish Eyes Are Smiling, focused around Marina Kaidalova's willful Milly, captures well Fugard's tale of the down but not-quite-out.

(*June 1994*)

Confession of a Son of the Age, Ostrovsky Oblastnoi Theater

A local critic not long ago proudly praised Vladimir Klimenko, who goes by the professional name of Klim, as "Moscow's most boring director."

It was a point well taken on all scores.

Indeed, probably no one else today can match Klim's aesthetic submersions into silence, motionlessness and meaningless detail. And yes, for all the thought and theory that surely entails, it has a way of getting seriously boring.

Klim's latest opus is *Confession of a Son of the Age*, a three-day marathon of plays by the French poet Alfred de Musset.

More to the point, it *was* his latest, since the last two segments of the trilogy closed after just three showings each. The unsuspecting administration at the Ostrovsky Oblastnoi Theater, which commissioned the work, didn't quite know what to make of so much "experimental" theater.

Remaining in the venue's repertoire is *Candelabra*, while *Love Is Not to be Trifled With* and *Venetian Night* will be performed only rarely for select audiences.

Actually, *Candelabra* differs only slightly from the others, sharing their ethereal, actionless form. Also like them, it is a talky play about the mind games that bind or separate the sexes. But with a more recognizable plot than the others, and staged with a bit more theatricality, it is somewhat more accessible.

True, much of the credit for that goes to Larisa Lomakina, whose spectacular, suggestive sets play with a model of a three-story house and its garden. They are first seen through shimmering, transparent curtains, and later are echoed in sparse, geometrical objects.

The two canceled shows were the measure of Lomakina's achievement. The continuing evolution of the decorative elements in *Love Is Not to be Trifled With* was the key reason that production's aggressive tedium remained palatable. However, when Klim abandoned all decoration but a few pieces of wicker furniture in *Venetian Night*, he left his actors as emperors and empresses with no clothes. The cavernous, bare stage required heroic efforts from director and cast alike, but they were not up to the task.

Very briefly, *Candelabra* concerns Jacqueline (Maria Katayeva), whose lover, Clavroche (Yury Morozov), wants to outwit her suspicious husband, André. Similarly, André (Mikhail Rogov) hopes to drive a wedge between the lovers.

Enter the inexperienced Fortunio (Andrei Astrakhantsev), whom Clavroche foists on Jacqueline as a decoy, and whom André sets on his wife to occupy her time. Naturally, the two fall in love, creating not a love quadrangle, but a love candelabra.

The performance begins with extended, "incidental" action. A flashlight shines out of the miniature house into the darkness. A man in a tux sweeps the garden grounds while another strolls by. A third knocks on the door and is let into the house, where we see silhouettes of a love tryst in progress.

The airy piano music and the mysterious movements in the shadows create an intriguing atmosphere. But it is short-lived. Neither Lomakina's set nor the tasteful use of music are enough to give meaning to the protracted scenes of expressionless, lethargic characters rambling on in toneless voices.

The actors seldom do more than sit, stand or walk. Their rare attempts to create visual images with statue-like poses seem irrelevant and even unintentionally comic. An occasional temper tantrum from Jacqueline, and a few dead-pan, humorous songs from Fortunio provide some relief from the aimless drifting in and out. But most of what we see is secondary. Klim is really only interested in the dense text.

Candelabra is clearly intended to appeal to the intellect, or even the subconscious. For all its pretentiousness, it is an interesting idea. As a performance it is very long.

(July 1994)

The Caucasian Chalk Circle, Irene's Happiness, The Good Person of Setzuan and *A Christmas Carol*, Rustaveli Theater

In 1915, when Sandro Akhmeteli was still pondering the steps he would take to revolutionize the Georgian theater in the 1920s, he described the visual image which, to him, was most Georgian of all: "The Georgian," he wrote, "walks exquisitely, his gait is light... And he carries his whole body freely and erect, barely swaying." Akhmeteli criticized his contemporaries for "failing to grasp the Georgian's gestures, [failing] to sense the rhythm of those gestures, and [failing] to create on stage the kind of movement that would capture the Georgian atmosphere."[2] Although his experiments would last barely ten years before he was murdered in 1937 by his enemy Lavrenty Beria, Akhmeteli's brief stint as the artistic director of the Rustaveli Theater (1926–1935) had an enormous impact on Georgian theater in specific, and Soviet theater in general. That could not be made any more evident than by the exhilarating month of performances which the current incarnation of the Rustaveli put on in Moscow in June 1994. Under the guidance of Robert Sturua, the Rustaveli has become a world-class theater by honing to perfection the very principles Akhmeteli set forth eighty years ago.

It is impossible not to stop a minute and say a few words about the extraordinary

---

[2] Quoted in Natela Urushadze, *Sandro Akhmeteli* (Moscow: Iskusstvo, 1990): 34.

courage and vigor of the Rustaveli's entire staff and troupe, which for two years has continued to make theater in the midst of a bloody civil war. Even now, as the shooting has moved out of Tbilisi, the actors often spend the night at the theater after rehearsals, since it is too dangerous to go out on the streets after dark. For that same reason, the theater performs only Saturday and Sunday matinees. And yet, the Rustaveli has not just survived, it has thrived.

Of the four productions brought to Moscow (shown in twenty performances), three were new. Charles Dickens's *A Christmas Carol* (directed by Otar Egadze and Levan Tsuladze), Bertolt Brecht's *The Good Person of Setzuan* (directed by Sturua) and David Kldiashvili's *Irene's Happiness* (directed by Andro Yenukidze) all opened in 1993 or 1994. Brecht's *The Caucasian Chalk Circle* (directed by Sturua) has been in repertoire since the mid-1970s, but it played as if it had just come off previews. All the shows brilliantly reflected the forces now at work in Georgia. *Irene's Happiness* was a scorching look at the explosive Georgian temperament, while the other three bore the stamp of almost belligerent, if occasionally despairing gaiety. The subtext in them all was that life—and theater—can hold their own against death and destruction.

The tour fittingly opened with *Chalk Circle*, Brecht's parable of love, selfishness and selflessness set during a civil war in ancient Georgia. Sturua's tremendous ability to blend and alternate sweeping, mass scenes with intimate moments was signaled immediately. A man and a woman entered through an oversized gate upstage and methodically made their way across the dimly lit stage to the forestage. She sat down to a piano at stage left, while the burly, dignified Storyteller (Zhanri Lolashvili) ceremoniously announced what was to be performed. He then sauntered back to the gate. Just as he was about to open it, a frenzied crowd burst through it onto the stage. While they noisily danced and caroused, the Storyteller led them in a song as he, or others, would subsequently do with regularity. Lolashvili, who served as something of an emcee and "unseen" mover of the entire performance,

epitomized Akhmeteli's description of the Georgian gait as "exquisite, free, erect and light." Holding his head high and his torso stiff, Lolashvili invariably walked with slow, high strides that suggested the gait of a thoroughbred horse, while his arms were always free and fluid. The movements of the other actors were less rigidly stylized, although there was an element of stylization everywhere, giving all the actors' performances the feel of being parts of a unified whole.

The highly disciplined actors carefully kept within the limits of their typecast characters without becoming stereotypes or losing their humanity. As Grusha, the peasant woman who saves and raises the murdered governor's abandoned baby boy, Tatuli Dolidze was sincerity and commitment incarnate. Yet that didn't stop her from occasionally wishing quietly that she were on her own again. As Grusha's fiancé Simon Chachava, the towering, square-jawed Kakhi Kavsadze was the picture of reserved pride and dignity, his attempt to save Grusha in the finale by claiming to be the boy's father coming across as a humble, yet chivalrous gesture of love. Scenes involving Grusha's roly-poly brother (Dzhemal Gaganidze) and her scrawny, deceitful husband Yussup (Ivane Gogitidze) were presented and performed as sterling comic skits.

Meanwhile, the third act was a rolling, comic tour de force thanks to the prodigious talents of the great Ramaz Chkhikvadze, who played Azdak, the town-drunk-turned-judge, with the same volcanic power that he gives his legendary King Lear. With his spectacular operatic voice, his uncanny timing, and his bottomless well of energy, Chkhikvadze was a clown on the loose, a madman looking for a wall to hit. What he hit was the pinnacle of comic acting.

The set by Georgy Alexi-Meskhishvili implied a forlorn outpost. Battered fortress walls lined the walls of the large, empty stage, the center of which often revolved, delivering or carrying away actors in statue-like poses. A few artist's implements stood bunched at forestage right (the Storyteller's "studio"), a messenger occasionally appeared atop a kind of Trojan horse, and spare props such as a bed, a wash tub or a scaffold

Ramaz Chkhikvadze in Robert Sturua's production of Bertolt Brecht's *The Caucasian Chalk Circle* for the Rustaveli Theater. Moscow tour, June 1994. Photo: Mikhail Guterman

(in Act III) were brought in from time to time. But the stage was primarily an open platter that served up the actors and the action.

Irene's Happiness, written by David Kldiashvili in 1897, and set in a Georgian village in the early 19th century, tells the story of the headstrong Abesalo, whose obsession with the beautiful Irene leads to tragedy. Originally written as an exploration of social differences (Abesalo is a nobleman, Irene the daughter of a commoner), director Yenukidze deftly refocused the work into a stinging, probing expos of the Georgian national character.

The story's impact derives from its simplicity. While visiting the relatives of a friend, Abesalo is smitten by the young Irene whom he takes that very night. No one lifts a finger to defend the half-horrified, half-fascinated girl (played with beautiful dignity by Nino Kasradze), and when she becomes Abesalo's wife, she tries her best to be obedient. That, however, only infuriates her husband, whose wrath is soon turned on everyone.

Zaza Papuashvili was simply stunning as Abesalo, creating a character whose sexual passion was merely a weakly veiled inclination towards wanton violence and destruction. (He first admits to having fallen under love's spell while drunk and brandishing a pistol in his hand.) But Papuashvili's triumph was to find in Abesalo's black, intoxicated fury such a profound, complex spirituality, that he precluded anything so simplistic as outright condemnation of his actions. His guilt was further shared by Irene's father, who aided the abduction; by his friend and Irene's relative, who turned a blind eye while admitting it was wrong; and even by Irene's fiancé, who protested only within the bounds of propriety.

The small audience for *Irene* was split into two separate blocks and seated at the back of the stage, looking across Shmagi Sheklashvili's set of a 19th-century hut into the empty hall of the Vakhtangov Theater, where all the tour's performances were held.

All began serenely as a woman read and an old man lay in bed. Irene sat down to play the piano. Suddenly, she hit a sour chord and the lights went bright. With a terrible rumbling and screeching, the theater's massive fire wall came down, trapping the actors and the audience on the stage.

As the performance moved on, the sense of claustrophobia that caused was quickly forgotten. Until the finale, at least. Then, all the characters scattered frantically while the frenzied Abesalo sought someone to vent his rage on. Too old to run, Abesalo's servant fell murdered, stabbed in the back. As the dead body lay at center stage, the fire wall was lifted with the same deafening roar, revealing the entire cast spread throughout the parterre and balcony. They stood and applauded the audience who sat in stunned silence on the stage.

Irene's Happiness literally turned the audience around, making it a part of the theatrical act and showing its complicity in the violence depicted in the performance. Then, by pulling the actors off the stage and putting them in the traditional position of spectators, it celebrated theater's ability to transform and transcend.

Sturua's production of *Good Person* was a natural extension, and brilliant development of the devices which went into *The Caucasian Chalk Circle*. Alexi-Meskhishvili, with Mirian Shvelidze and Shota Glurdzhidze, echoed the set from that earlier work, once again lining the stage perimeter with battered walls, and using a revolving platform in the middle of the essentially empty stage. A modest bamboo hut stood on the extreme edge of the platform and a rickety elevator shaft ran up the back left wall, allowing for the entrance and exit of the bumbling gods.

Like *Chalk Circle*, it also began with an "announcement," this time from Wang, the water seller, and was followed by a horde of people pouring onto the stage through the gate at the back. The entire cast raced to the edge of the forestage in tiny, choppy steps, bid the audience hello and goodbye and then disappeared as quickly as they had come. That wave of energy, motion and good-natured irony was the preface to what lay ahead.

Good Person took the theatrical elements of *Chalk Circle* to an entirely new level. It was an astonishing display of brilliantly modulated music, movement, lighting, decoration, costumes, make-up and rhythmic speech patterns. The lighting alternated between soft, smoky blue and harsh, bright spots, while the spectacular music ranged from a thrilling version of Beethoven's *Ode to Joy*, to jazzy tunes from the 1930s. The music, whose high volumes seemed to give it a spatial quality, was used in choppy fragments that excited, teased, and then frustrated when it was abruptly cut away to dead silence. The make-up and costumes only hinted occasionally at the Chinese setting, with some characters wearing heavily stylized clothes and make-up, and others appearing in modern, casual dress.

Once again, the "swaying, rhythmic gestures" which Akhmeteli said characterized the Georgian national image were at the center of everything. It seemed that hardly a twitch or a blink had not been carefully choreographed—showing off influences from Charlie Chaplin to, perhaps, Pina Bausch and the organized chaos of *West Side Story*—and yet Sturua's splendid ensemble of actors made the whole thing look improvised. There was Levan Berikashvili's slinking hunchback Wang; Baia Dvalishvili's strange, puppet-like Mrs. Yang, with her darting eyes, squeaky voice and hopping gait; and Nana Shonia's elegant Shin, who invariably moved in long, loping strides and angular, twisting torso movements.

Sturua displayed a masterful ability to shift control of the performance from one character to another, creating the perfect approach to Brecht's highly-populated play. Just as important, every one of his actors, whether playing a lead or a cameo, was ready and able at every moment to shoulder the responsibility of carrying a scene.

But for all the intricate teamwork and all the outstanding individual performances that went into *Good Person*, the show belonged to the young Nino Kasradze, who was breathtaking as Shen Teh/Shui Ta. Agile and graceful, at once smolderingly sexual and chastely wholesome, Kasradze was filled to overflowing with a deep sense of humanity, compassion and tenacity. She seemed to have the taut reflexes of a hummingbird, while displaying nerves and a will of steel. She moved

in complete freedom among Sturua's bouncing, skipping and swaying motions—which ebbed and flowed like the snippets of music—creating a riveting visual picture with a profound emotional impact.

As Kasradze's chief partner, the grounded flier Yang Sun, Zaza Papuashvili retained the same explosiveness he showed in *Irene's Happiness*, but this time he colored it with dumb arrogance and irresistible romantic charm.

The latter was never more evident than in the final seconds of Act I and the first moments of Act II, when Shen Teh and Yang Sun fall in love. The actors' inspired tenderness and burning inner joy were a sight to behold in Sturua's simple, but gorgeous handling of the scenes.

As Act I drew to a close, the pair stood almost hanging over the edge of the stage, gazing into each other eyes and holding each other in a light embrace. But before one could register the image, they broke the spell, sprightly stepped apart from each other and stared into the audience with the slightly tired, but grateful look of two actors ready to go rest for a twenty minute intermission. The ease with which they stepped out of character created a genuine theatrical shock; after all, it was played so beautifully that you were left there still believing it was all true.

Act II began with a reprise of the opening scene, only this time it was just Shen Teh and Yang Sun, not a crowd, that raced the distance from the back wall to the forestage. There, they briefly rubbed noses and teased each other for having fallen in love. Kasradze flashed an impish look at the audience and then they both went racing back to the gate in the back wall, awkwardly throwing off their coats as they ran in leaping bounds. Standing framed in the huge opening, and backlit in smoky blue, they struck a long pose in a gracefully arched, back-bending embrace. It was a spectacular, two-part scene that epitomized the theatricality, the warmth and the inspiration of this masterful production.

A Christmas Carol, in Shota Glurdzhidze's lovely design telescoping a view of Scrooge's detail-filled office in the open trap of the forestage with scenes from snow-bound

London in the back, was a luscious, cream-filled pie that topped off the tour splendidly. Originally staged as the Georgian civil war was escalating, directors Egadze and Tsuladze may have chosen this guileless parable of wrong and right as a talisman of hope. If so, it was a splendid choice, for it was exceptionally beautiful and cathartic. And, as always, the Rustaveli troupe was at its whirling, swirling best from top to bottom.

Karlo Sakandelidze's Scrooge went the road from cruel, grumpy miser to a wonderfully kind, little old man without missing a single transition or without hitting a single false note. Temur Chichinadze played a blustery, Napoleonic Ghost of Christmas Past, while Lela Alibegashvili was an utterly delightful Ghost of Christmas Present. A self-deprecating, would-be ballerina who constantly tripped over her own feet, she emanated such kind generosity and believed so sincerely in Scrooge's innate goodness, that even he fell head over heels in love with her.

Perhaps most characteristic of the entire Rustaveli ensemble was Murman Dzhinoria as Marley's ghost. On stage for only a single, brief scene, Dzhinoria poured so much concentrated energy into his grandiose, lock-joint bucket of bones that his exit provoked a sustained ovation from the audience.

Robert Sturua, leaning in equal measure on his own spectacular, innovative ideas and on the strength that tradition provides, has assembled an extraordinary team of actors which is capable of effortlessly running back and forth between a whisper and a scream. Put simply, he has created what is surely one of the great theaters of the world.

(*Fall 1994, Slavic and East European Performance*)

1994/1995 SEASON

The Red Devil Battery Sign, Gogol Drama Theater

The Gogol Drama Theater's new production of Tennessee Williams's *The Red Devil Battery Sign* continues Moscow's recent infatuation with the great American playwright. It is the writer's sixth play done within the last year, and there are more to come.

True, this mini Williams boom has been a quiet one, mainly because most of the productions have been remarkably feeble. *Battery Sign*, for all its distinguishing features, is no exception.

In this case, the problems start with the play itself. Written in 1975, it bombed in Boston despite a cast headed by Claire Bloom and Anthony Quinn. Closing after a rocky ten-day run, it really has never been heard from since.

The program notes at the Gogol Theater try blaming this embarrassing moment for Williams on American political intolerance. The contention is that the drama's veiled and overt references to secret surveillance, the Kennedy assassination and the use of drugs by the government against its internal enemies made it too controversial.

Maybe so. But *Battery Sign* has bigger problems than that: It is obscure, clichéd and, even by Williams's standards, overwrought. Rather than seek a coherent thread in the murky sea of the play, director Sergei Yashin indulged in its excesses almost gleefully.

The story revolves around Woman Downtown—a tormented, nameless woman who may be a mental patient under observation, or a political renegade who knows too much—and King, a Mexican band leader who is down on his luck. They meet, sparks sort of fly, they fall into a kind of pseudo-sexual, huggy, outlaw love, and, colored by the haze of alcohol and drugs, it all leads to tragedy.

A detailed sub-plot about King's suffering wife, their daughter and her lover, goes too far afield. We simply can't muster interest in them, especially with the supporting cast constantly driving for drama through bold poses, cocked eyebrows and meaningful stares.

As Woman Downtown, the tall, attractive Larisa Borushko was strapped by her director in an unnatural, slurring manner of speech, and, for much of the evening, stripped of all but the flimsiest lingerie. But for a few fleeting moments, when she valiantly struggles to achieve sincerity, the biggest impression one is left with is that the actress has been pawed by an insensitive director.

Oleg Gushchin, who showed a flair for subtlety two years ago in the Gogol's workmanlike production of Vladimir Maximov's *Far Away... In Other Lands*, gives a forced, one-dimensional performance as King. Whenever he begins panting heavily, you can be sure his character is agitated again.

Yelena Kachelayeva's lounge-lizard costumes are even more vulgar than anything the United States had to offer in the 1970s, and choreographer Alexander Pepelyayev's Latin American boogie numbers are as stiff as they are mercifully obscured by smoke.

The neon Red Devil battery sign, looming over the stage as a grotesque devil's face, is presumably intended to symbolize the evil and crassness lurking on the underbelly of American life. Crass might also be a fair choice for describing this play and this production.

(September 1994)

God May Be All Around, Hermitage Theater

Mikhail Levitin's production of Alexander Vvedensky's *God May Be All Around* at the Hermitage Theater is the continuation of a young, but healthy tradition.

For much of the last decade, Levitin has used the stage at the Hermitage to explore the legacy of a small though important group of unorthodox Russian writers who were active in the late 1920s and early 1930s.

Calling their little collective the Oberiu, they wrote poems and plays which subsequently became known as the clearest expression of the absurd in Russian literature. But since the key members either died early or were killed in the camps, and since almost none of their writings were published, the Oberiu was known only among a select few for nearly 50 years.

Levitin began turning that around in 1982, when he staged a popular show called *Kharms! Charms! Shardam! or the School for Clowns*, based on the works of Daniil Kharms and other Oberiuty, as the members themselves were called. Since then, Levitin has not only recovered many "lost" works, he has expanded the influence of the Oberiuty by applying their strange and playful tactics to the works of unrelated writers, sometimes with good results.

After the director's recent forays into Molière, Lewis Carroll and Nikolai Gogol, *God May Be All Around* is a venture back into the heart of the Oberiu.

Vvedensky's verse play is full of delightful nonsense, clever word play, wondrous, childlike observations, and—spirited away beneath the jocular surface—some crystal clear observations on nothing less than the nature of life and death.

To the extent that the piece can be said to have one, the plot concerns a young man, known as Ef (Sergei Shchepachyov), who gets the idea he wants to "fearlessly" witness a public execution. The catch is that the execution becomes Ef's own, as the crowd holds him down and lops off his head.

Only then does Ef acquire a name, Fomin, and something of a biography, as he wanders in confusion among a horde of beggars, nymphets, tsars, clocks, cows and bulls in search of comfort and an explanation of what has happened to him. One of the liveliest individuals he encounters is the eternally tap-dancing Dead Man.

Fomin's meeting with Venus is only marginally satisfying for both: She is old and flabby now, while his lack of a head, to say nothing of one of his key organs being dysfunctional, makes him less than attractive to her.

Designer Harry Hummel outfitted the dimly-lit small stage eclectically and theatrically, often using bits and pieces of props from other Hermitage shows. The audience

is right in the thick of things, being seated in narrow rows around the perimeter of the action.

But despite its strong points—the text, design and direction all work well together—this production is better in theory than in fact.

The musical segments (led nicely by Andrei Semyonov at the piano) are often sung sourly, and the dances (choreographed by Tatyana Borisova and Sergei Tsvetkov) are often more chaotic than energetic or expressive.

The problems lie chiefly with the young cast, almost all of whom are members of Levitin's most recent graduating class at the Russian Academy of Theater Arts. Hardworking and energetic, they don't command the irony, insight and chutzpah needed to give Vvedensky's words the proper edge.

Levitin himself seems well aware of this shortcoming: He interrupts the curtain call to implore the audience's indulgence for his inexperienced charges.

Be that as it may, *God May Be All Around* has its moments. And the primitive simplicity of Fomin's concluding speech about why things exist, even catches a wave of genuine inspiration.

(September 1994)

The Death-Defying Act, Tabakov Theater

A clown tentatively enters the ring, ties a rope around his neck, climbs a ladder and, when he reaches the top, tries to play a jazzy riff on the sax.

The problem is that the act is such a killer, indeed it kills him as he tumbles down in a shrieking heap on the arena floor. Then, as if by magic, the body is suddenly surrounded by four other frightened clowns. But as they start bickering in animated whispers about what to do with the body, and what they're going to do without their late, great comrade, we begin to notice that their memories, their movements and their aspirations are strikingly similar.

The Death-Defying Act, a magnificent new play by Oleg Antonov at the Tabakov Theater, is an allegorical story about a man who appears to have succumbed to his own inner battles. With its razor-sharp acting and

Vladimir Mashkov's production of Oleg Antonov's *The Death-Defying Act*, Tabakov Theater, 1994, with Andrei Smolyakov, Sergei Belyayev, Vitaly Yegorov and Andrei Panin. Photo: Mikhail Guterman

Vladimir Mashkov's imaginative direction, it surely will be one of the top shows of this season. This production, making the most of spectacular music, lighting and magic tricks, not only acts on the mind and the emotions, it overwhelms the senses.

Antonov created a sparkling quartet of characters, each with his own severe limitations, but all with clear-cut, fully-developed personalities. Whether it is the shifty Red (Andrei Panin), the sensitive Whitey (Vitaly Yegorov), the devilish Blackey (Andrei Smolyakov) or the endearing Fatty (Sergei Belyayev), all are as united by their secret desire to break free of one another as they are bound by their past misfortunes or their nagging dreams for the future.

Mashkov took Antonov's clever, incisive play and applied to it the principles of the distinctly Russian tradition of clowning. More pensive, resigned and philosophical than its western counterpart, Russian clownery has no fewer pratfalls and thumps on the head, but it plays them in a minor key, invariably just barely concealing the disturbing tone of fateful revelations soon to be made. That is the very essence of *The Death-Defying Act*, which might be described roughly as a play about achieving freedom and discovering limits.

Paralleling—or at least parodying—the problems some Russians have faced in breaking with the past, Antonov's lovable clowns repeatedly mouth admirable sentiments while pulling nasty tricks on one another. When pressed by his penniless friends to give them money, Whitey is unmoved: "Everyone pays for himself," he snaps aloofly. "That's what freedom's for!"

In the end, freedom is an unattainable dream, at least if the only way it can be achieved is by every man selfishly fending for himself. Like burning filaments released from the confines of a light bulb, the four clashing personalities are capable of burning brightly only for an instant, before quickly running the risk of burning out altogether. It is when they realize that they cannot exist without one another that they "resurrect" the dead clown who comes back to pull off his "death-defying act" to the mad ovation of the crowd.

But it would be a gross error to reduce this spectacular production strictly to the level of a simple allegory. The world of the four clowns, as temporary and dependent as it may be, is so complex, so convincing and so much fun, that the spectacle of it all is an end in itself.

And as sheer spectacle, *The Death-Defying Act* has no peer among current Moscow shows. The magic tricks, performed brilliantly by the entire cast, are worthy of the finest circus acts. Flying balls of light, fiery explosions in mid-air, handkerchiefs that take on a life of their own, and a chopped off-arm that comes back to life, are only a few of the dazzling deceptions.

The most astonishing element of this show may be Yefim Udler's swirling, sculptural light. Using heavy smoke and dense spots of hot and cool colors, Udler gave the light an actual physical presence, its floating, marble curls assuming the form of columns, impenetrable walls or layered curtains which interact beautifully with Alexander Borovsky's set of red, wooden walls and trap doors.

Add to that the haunting, pulsing music selected from Michael Nyman's compositions for Peter Greenaway's films, and you have a genuine feast for the senses, a rare and delightful theatrical treat.

(*September 1994*)

The Seagull, Lenkom Theater

Chances are, no one has ever determined scientifically which great playwright most often gets played badly. But if someone ever tries, Anton Chekhov will surely contend for the crown.

Witness Mark Zakharov's sputtering new production of *The Seagull* at the Lenkom Theater.

The director, famous for his booming, boisterous productions, has publicly stated that his purpose was to avoid the proverbial, "boring Chekhov." And while he sets off no cannons (as he did in *The Marriage of Figaro*) nor caves in the ceiling (as he did in *The Wiseman*), in *The Seagull* he does give Chekhov's fascination with unrequited love a new twist.

Here, lovesick people don't pine for intangible objects of desire, they paw at them comically, nervously fiddling to undo buttons, or clumsily throwing a leg around a reluctant partner. The sighs, which indeed mar so many Chekhov productions, are usually replaced with bitter anger or arrogance.

But it's not the ideas that went wrong—Zakharov's interpretation may be even more justifiable than most—it's their realization that fails to convince.

The director wasted a brilliant half of a cast by subordinating it to barely competent performances in the leads.

Casualty number one is the scintillating Inna Churikova—certainly Russia's finest actress—in the role of Arkadina, the aging queen of the stage whose wanton vanity and irrepressible energy have alienated her from her son Treplev, a sensitive, would-be writer.

As Trigorin, Arkadina's straying lover and a famous author, the next casualty is the sublime Oleg Yankovsky, whose brilliant performance in Andrei Tarkovsky's film classic, *Nostalgia*, is only one in a career of stage and screen highlights.

Also nearly lost in the shuffle is the splendid Leonid Bronevoi as Dorn, the not-quite-yet-cynical doctor who might infect someone with common sense if only someone were listening. Bronevoi's rumpled, charmingly self-indulgent style has made him one of Moscow's top actors for nearly 30 years.

But for all the importance this trio has in *The Seagull*, it is a play about youth; its hopes, its dreams, its mortal dangers. The self-destructive young Treplev and his beloved Nina Zarechnaya—who aspires to be a great actress like Arkadina, but ends as Trigorin's discarded mistress—are the play's reasons for being.

And that is why this production falls flat.

Dmitry Pevtsov is grossly miscast as Treplev. The admirable talent he has shown over

Inna Churikova momentarily gets the better of Oleg Yankovsky in Anton Chekhov's *The Seagull*, directed by Mark Zakharov, Lenkom Theater, 1994. Photo: Mikhail Guterman

the years in the physical, acrobatic elements of his profession has often been enough to conceal his weakness at giving a role depth. But here, the actor's attempt to interpret his darkly contemplative and hypersensitive character comes off as boyish and meek.

No less overmatched is the director's daughter, Alexandra Zakharova, in the role of Zarechnaya.

While she did bring something to the shrill, rosy-cheeked and earthbound Countess Almaviva in *Figaro* two years ago, Zakharova is a washout as Chekhov's fragile, searching heroine.

Perhaps realizing his younger actors could not hold their own against their more accomplished partners, Zakharov minimized the competition, and crippled the show. Churikova is often positioned with her back to the audience, and sits hidden behind a curtain when delivering Arkadina's famous line about her fans showering her with adulation in Kharkov.

Sure, for a few fleeting moments at the end of the first act, Churikova and Yankovsky are brilliant as she jealously tries arresting his character's inevitable drift toward Zarechnaya. They even make the clumsy sexual gymnastics foisted on them seem natural. But it's not enough.

The beautiful sets by Oleg Sheintsis consist of a spectacular, silvery lake scene, created ingeniously by strings drawn tautly across the stage, and a rich interior that perfectly conjures the atmosphere of a fin-de-siècle Russian drawing room. They provide welcome distraction in the many moments that need it.

(*October 1994*)

Love Is Not To Be Trifled With, Mossoviet Theater

Something is going on upstairs at the Mossoviet Theater. And a long way up it is, too.

Alexander Lenkov in Mark Weil's production of Alfred de Musset's *Love Is Not To Be Trifled With* at the Mossoviet Theater, 1994. Photo: Mikhail Guterman

To get there, you climb four flights of stairs, passing even the nosebleed seats of the huge mainstage, and ducking under a low-hanging, well-padded obstacle on your way to the distant fifth floor. But once you've caught your breath, you're likely to be glad you're there.[1]

Here, on the small "Stage Beneath the Roof," situated literally under the angled roof of the building erected in 1959 and hidden away from the city hum in the Aquarium Garden off of Triumphal Square, the Mossoviet Theater mounts its most unusual shows.

Nothing is always perfect, of course, but the intimate, upstairs space increasingly seems to be hosting interesting work. Now, following last season's delightfully campy *School For Wives*, a strangely appealing production of Alfred de Musset's *Love Is Not To Be Trifled With* provides another good reason to make the vertical trek.

Mark Weil's talented and elusive production probably could use a disclaimer. It isn't the show for the once-a-year spectator.

Musset's atmospheric 19th-century verse play, about a pair of young lovers testing the strength of their love and coming to regret it, is rich in allusions and unspoken subtexts. But that is just where Weil has done such a nice job.

Together with choreographer Georgy Gusev, Weil gave a tangible sense of rhythm to the flow of action, pacing things with whirling dance interludes performed to snippets of jazz and Mahler. The whirling sensations are echoed even in the entrances and exits of the actors, who often disappear on one side of the stage and reappear seconds later from the opposite side.

The play's ironic treatment of certain types in "good society"—the sensitive Baron, his son's tipsy tutor, his niece's eccentric tutor, the caring priest—is turned to excellent comic use through exaggeration. That leaves the more psychologically realistic principals—Perdicante (Andrei Sokolov) and his sweetheart, Camille (Yevgenia Kryukova)—to occupy a kind of island of intensified emotions.

To test his faithfulness, she enters a nunnery, while, to verify her resolve, he falls into an affair with the common-born Rosette (Marina Kondratyeva). At their best, the short scenes of sexual sparring, seduction and intrigue create a mesmerizing sensation of intellectual erotica. They are always at least sincere and believable.

As the Baron who longs to see his son and niece joined in marriage, Yury Kuzmenkov is endearingly sentimental and at a complete loss to understand what has stricken his beloved charges. Especially effective is Alexander Lenkov, who turns in an uproarious, cross-sex interpretation of Camille's tutor, the wacky Dame Plouche.

Perhaps suggesting that everything may be occurring in the imagination of an artist who plays the role of the Chorus (Alexei Osipov), Danila Korogodsky suggestively outfitted the stage with stray implements from an artist's workshop and some odd-sized furniture.

Even if *Love*'s whys and whats are not always clear, that isn't what is most important. It is a suggestive, funny and provocative production that often bypasses the mind and affects the heart.

(October 1994)

Mozart and Salieri. Don Juan. The Plague, Lithuanian International "Life" Theater Festival

Eimuntas Nekrosius must wonder what Moscow really thinks about him. When the Lithuanian director brought to the Russian capital his new interpretation of some of Alexander Pushkin's Little Tragedies, *Mozart and Salieri. Don Juan. The Plague*, the reactions among many in Moscow's theatrical *beau monde* were predictably old.

When the final curtain was drawn at the end of the first of two showings at the Mossoviet Theater (November 2 and 3, 1994), hordes of familiar faces belonging to critics, actors and directors were seen making a mad rush for the exits. The vast majority of those retreating never bothered to

---

[1] This space was redecorated in 1995 and furnished with elevator access.

applaud. By the time of the curtain calls a few seconds later, there were already major traffic jams at the theater's two side exits. Meanwhile, about half of the audience staged a scattered, but demonstrative ovation. The response clearly echoed that which greeted Nekrosius's Moscow showings of *The Nose* in 1991, although I was told by the critic Olga Galakhova that the reception on night two was significantly more friendly.[2]

The staging of Pushkin, a production of the cumbersomely-named Lithuanian International "Life" Theater Festival, and organized in Moscow by the Theater of Nations, is vintage Nekrosius. As always, it is dense with visual and aural stimulants; beautifully lit (by Romas Preinis); designed sparsely and suggestively with a myriad of odd, unexpected objects (by Adomas Jacovskis); filled with a tensile, intellectual humor; and consists of two very distinct and occasionally competing languages. One is the performed text, the other is what might be called "parallel action": the extraordinarily expressive action which often is as self-contained as pantomime, but never as limited.

I found the first act, *Mozart and Salieri*, to be especially effective. Featuring Nekrosius's longtime star Vladas Bagdonas as Salieri and the ethereal, almost Christ-like Algirdas Latepas as Mozart, it was a theatrically beautiful segment that made the utmost of the actors' thoughtfully ironic mannerisms couched in long stretches of silence and intense physical activity.

---

[2] Adding to the picture of Moscow's complex relationship with Nekrosius was a February 1993 performance of his *Pirosmani, Pirosmani* by the Lithuanian State Youth Theater. One of several entries in a small festival honoring the director Andrei Goncharov (of whom Nekrosius was a student), it played to an audience of maybe sixty or seventy enthusiasts at the Mayakovsky Theater which has a capacity of 1230. Many had seen the production on previous tours, but that hardly explains the abysmal attendance. It should not be forgotten that just a few months earlier, in October 1992, Nekrosius backed out of the first Anton Chekhov International Theater Festival at the twelfth hour, stating that his production of Prosper Mérimée's *Carmen* was not yet ready.

The opening images, crisply metaphorical without being overdone, were especially memorable. Salieri kneeled in front of a piano clicking and clacking away furiously at an abacus, and tapping harshly on the piano's keyboard cover. Once this prolonged, musical overture had created a clear sense of rhythm, Mozart entered dressed in a swaying cape. His nonchalant, even gallant, manner immediately clashed with Salieri's busy, self-centered, narrow-minded activity. Mozart splashed his hand in a vessel of water, did a little dance step and then, with a broad, free wave of his hand, sent a spray of water in a glistening arch across the perfectly-lit stage. After Mozart ridiculed Salieri goodheartedly, plucking at his sparse hairs, it became apparent that the piano was missing a leg and was standing upright only because Salieri was kneeling with one cocked leg supporting the weight of the left front corner. Mozart pulled Salieri out from under the piano, putting the broken leg back in its proper place. Salieri, in muddled confusion, tapped at Mozart's forehead, as though it were an abacus, the sound resonating throughout the entire theater. Suddenly, Mozart seized Salieri's abacus and hurled it on the floor, breaking it into pieces.

A detailed, blow-by-blow description of this kind could be continued almost indefinitely. (Especially striking was the much later scene when a despairing Salieri retrieved the scattered beads of the broken abacus as though he were trying to salvage lost musical notes.) But what is so effective is not so much the narrative of the action, as the role that the action played in the performance as a whole. Aside from what I have called the "overture," everything described here ran concurrently with the actors' dialogues and monologues. It was a parallel, simultaneous and independent detour from the text, which, thanks to the vision of the director and the talent of the actors, nevertheless remained an integral element of the whole. Two sets of images—one linguistic, one visual—ran side by side, occasionally competing with one another, more often deepening and filling each other out.

Other moments worthy of mention included the sights and sounds of Mozart almost demonically ridiculing Salieri while he detuned the piano and hacked joyously at the keys, emitting distraught notes. Finally, he cranked one wire so tightly it snapped. But even here, the genius was still able to create music, for Mozart picked up the broken wire and began twirling it over his head like a lasso. He delighted to the pulsing, musical sounds it made, laughing and dancing as Salieri stood by bowing in a prayerful pose.

In the finale, after Salieri had killed Mozart, he made a death mask, glopping a bunch of freshly-made clay over his rival's face. When the mask had set, Salieri, holding a candle, removed it and measured it to his own face. Suddenly, Mozart arose in a darting motion, kissed Salieri and quickly blew out the candle.

Through these rich layers of parallel action, Nekrosius informed Pushkin's text with a mass of unexpected nuances, giving Pushkin's brilliant, intricate verse play a bold theatricality which it has probably seldom had in performance.

The second act, consisting of most of *The Stone Guest (Don Juan)* and some short excerpts from *A Feast in the Time of Plague (The Plague)*, was much longer and, to my sensibilities, suffered some from repetitiveness. More than just reviving echoes of sounds and images from the first act (as it often did effectively), it occasionally seemed to get hung up in playing with those elements for their own sake. But be that as it may, Nekrosius's unmistakable signature remained visible every step of the way. And the finale— a slow, seemingly endless, rhythmic, twirling fade that had most of the cast deliberately, but joyously dancing out a kind of pagan ritual over the soaring sounds of Orthodox hymns—was a stunner, plain and simple.

Partly through the essentially humorous character of the hyperactive Girl (Dalia Micheleviciute), probably an "escapee" from *A Feast in the Time of Plague* who occasionally stuffed her mouth with food and frequently ran about the stage rolling a metal disk in front of her with a stick, Nekrosius softened the high solemnity of Don Juan's meeting with Donna Anna and her dead husband, the Commodore. But he sacrificed little of the play's force, less treating

the legend's cold drama of revenge and death, than exploring Don Juan's spiritual relationship to the events in which he, as performed by Algirdas Latepas, is a player.

If the story's focus sometimes seemed to blur in an overabundance of images and signs (was Tauras Cizas's Don Carlos really supposed to look like Peter the Great, and if so, was that really necessary?), the visual impact of its performance seldom did. All of the movement, from the swaying and dancing of Laura (Viktoria Kuodite) to the acrobatics of Leporello (Andrius Belobzeskis) was handled with the utmost grace and precision.

In a clever nod to one of Pushkin's better-known fetishes that was just as sexual as it was humorous, Nekrosius placed Donna Anna (Rimante Valiukaite) kneeling on a stool with her back to the audience, to whom she slowly and sensuously bared the soles of her feet.

That image was repeated in the finale, though with a shift from a significance of sexuality to one of mortality, when the stunned Don Juan, dead or dying, sat flat-legged on the floor with his sockless feet facing the audience. It was faintly revived again moments later as Leporello began turning the pages of an enormous book. Inside, on every page of the book, were clear, black foot marks, indicating someone's uninterrupted forward motion from the beginning to the end. At least as I read it, the implication was that, although ended, this man's life had clearly left its mark. Meanwhile, to the accompaniment of the rhythmic, whirling dancing and the increasing volume of the Orthodox hymns, Don Juan's face ever so gradually lost its look of horror, acquiring in its place an expression of peace and acceptance.

Whatever its flaws, Nekrosius's production of Pushkin's Little Tragedies is unquestionably an important addition to the oeuvre of a major European director.

(Spring 1995, Slavic and East European Performance)

100 Years of Cabaret, Bat Cabaret

Elegant Moscow. Sentimental Moscow. Witty and charming Moscow. Where do you go to find it?

Natalya Trikhleb, center, leads the actors of the Bat Cabaret in a spirited tap dance in Grigory Gurvich's 1994 production, *100 Years of Cabaret*. Photo: Mikhail Guterman

Right there in the heart of the city, on the corner of Pushkin Square at the Bat Cabaret. Where Grigory Gurvich, the big man with a big mission and an even bigger heart, works the kind of magic that has the power to shape a city's personality.

Since reopening the legendary pre-revolutionary theater in 1989, Gurvich has made it a mecca for the elite; a haven for the fashionable. His first two shows, *The Reading of a New Play* and *I Tap About Moscow*—both written and directed by the man himself—show off his extraordinary flair for mixing music, humor, history, politics and autobiography into a honey-laden brew that intoxicates without ever leaving a hangover.

Gurvich may be a sucker for the sentimental, but there isn't a sappy bone in his body. Style, grace and wit are the words his personal dictionary begins with; a black tux and bowtie the bedrock of his wardrobe.

Now, to celebrate the fifth anniversary of his theater's revival, Gurvich has mounted *100 Years of Cabaret*, his tribute to the styles of entertainment he loves best: French torch songs, American dance and Italian comedy. All of them are introduced by Gurvich himself, who easily moves back and forth between his roles of emcee and occasional actor.

Let's say it up front: This one doesn't have the flow of the earlier productions. As a kind of overview-of-the-genre show it was planned that way, of course. When Gurvich introduces an aria sung by the utterly divine Natalya Trikhleb, he says flatly: "Why shouldn't I have opera in my variety show if that's what I want?"

He's right, of course. And boy, can Trikhleb sing! But with a structure like this, the show has to jump-start its momentum again after almost every number.

Another problem is a minor slip in Gurvich's usually exquisite sense of timing. Several skits—such as a one-armed Frenchman joining with a one-armed German to play the accordion—straggle on long after the punch line has been hit; some are packed with more filler than fun.

But Gurvich has the ultimate trump card up his sleeve: his own personality.

Call him the sultan of suave, the wizard of wit, or the king of charisma, but when he takes the stage to the slinky accompaniment of Roman Berchenko at the piano, he soothes everything over. He isn't just the show's author, he is its heart and soul.

Meanwhile, amidst the uneven collection of sketches, some are as good as ever. The best include a wildly energetic medley of American pop from Elvis Presley to Chubby Checker; some thunderous, top-flight tap-dancing; and a beautifully-done interactive film skit that has actors climbing onto and off of the screen a la Federico Fellini or Woody Allen.

But the star is Gurvich. Were there such a thing, he would be Mr. Moscow, the man who brings warmth and respect to the town he loves. And, a few slips notwithstanding, it is always a pleasure to watch him do it.

(November 1994)

The Wedding. The Anniversary, Yermolova International Theater Center

Before Anton Chekhov wrote the great plays that made him one of the most popular and enigmatic playwrights of the 20th century, he wrote a bushel of one-act plays bursting in equal measure with knockabout humor and pathos.

Thanks to director Alexei Levinsky, we now have a relatively rare opportunity to see two of them, *The Wedding* and *The Anniversary*, at the Yermolova International Theater Center. With the much-publicized and heavy-handed *Seagull* running across town at the Lenkom Theater, Levinsky has provided a chance to skip the hype and get down to Chekhov.

Performances are held on the "Free Stage," a narrow nook where spectators and players are separated only by a yard of floorspace rigged with a solid row of bright footlights. The actors occasionally pose at stage's edge, peering hazily and quizzically through the light into the hall, and creating something of a one-way window effect. It lets us study in detail the peculiar expressions and idiosyncratic behavior of the endlessly sympathetic losers who inhabit these little plays.

Both are short and sweet, displaying the Chekhov signature of efficiency and clarity. *The Wedding* captures the flavor of a wedding reception where what is most important isn't who got married, but who is attending. *The Anniversary* depicts a disastrous day at a bank office celebrating its fifteenth anniversary: A despairing, if also belligerent, widow drives everyone mad demanding money the bank has nothing to do with.

Levinsky went after a loose, amateur-like feel in the performances and came up with a rough, clunky warmth that produces a nice mix of the lyrical and the grotesque. In both plays he gives us menageries of people who are funny, pathetic and quite painfully alone, yet modestly sure that something makes them special.

That is best exemplified in *The Wedding* by Fyodor Valikov's softly eccentric performance of Captain Revunov-Karaulov, the reception's key guest. A total stranger, and totally unaware of what is going on, he was dragged in off the street to imitate the general that the groom demanded be present as part of the marriage agreement.

Valikov plays the retired captain as a clear-headed simpleton with a big heart. But when he realizes how he has been used, his aching sense of indignation recasts everything in a new light.

Also effective is Gennady Galkin's Kharlampy Dymba, a lonely, russified Greek whose litany of comically clichéd truths about life in Russia and abroad almost pass for wisdom in this company.

Echoes of these two outcasts are easily discernible in the character of Khirin in *The Anniversary*. He is the lowly, defeated and soured clerk who can't abide even hints of frivolity but who, in the excellent interpretation of Andrei Kalashnikov, clings tenaciously to his dignity.

Even so, he is no match either for his fastidious, air-headed boss (Vladimir Mashchenko) or for the rampaging widow Merchutkina (Alexandra Nazarova) who quietly but relentlessly drives the poor clerk over the edge.

Designer Viktor Arkhipov gave the illusion of expanding the stage by placing upstage angled panels of tin-foil mirrors that

A scene from Alexei Levinsky's production of Chekhov's *The Wedding*, Yermolova International Theater Center, 1994. Photo: Alexander Ivanishin

reflect muddy images of the actors. He painted most of the props in a flat gold, forcing the spectators to turn to the actors for color and variety, and underscoring the performance's human impact.

(*November 1994*)

Misha's Party, **Chekhov Art Theater**

Misha's Party, one of a trio of new shows at the Chekhov Art Theater, is unusual for a host of reasons.

Most uncommon is that it is the joint project of two playwrights who write in different languages—the Russian Alexander Gelman and the American Richard Nelson. Gelman's participation is unexpected for another reason too: a prolific author of plays on industrial and production themes in the 1970s, he became a symbol of the perestroika

cultural crisis when he completely abandoned the theater after 1984.

That crisis saw the number of contemporary plays produced in Russian theaters plummet, making this production of *Misha's Party* a notable rarity. Which brings us to the final surprise: When contemporary plays are this fun and this funny, you can't help but wonder why everybody isn't doing them. This observer hasn't seen such frequent bursts of laughter in a Moscow theater in ages.

Misha's Party, conceived by Gelman and Nelson together before each wrote his own play, is a brisk, well-made theatrical sitcom. The situations are far-fetched without being annoying, and the characters, though bordering on caricatures, are well-defined, sympathetic individuals.

Misha has turned 60. To celebrate, he invited to the Ukraine Hotel his young fiancée Lida, plus his two former wives Katya and Natasha with their husbands Fyodor and Valery. Also there is Mary, an American actress whose granddaughter Susie has disappeared across the river at the Russian White House.

That normally might not have concerned the crusty Mary, but this is no normal situation: The date is August 20, 1991, Gorbachev is locked up in Foros, Yeltsin is holed up in the White House and everybody—most of all the democrat-slandering Fyodor—is waiting for a KGB attack at any minute.

But there really isn't much politics here, except as comic fodder, and that was the authors' well-considered intent. This story reminds us that every person's life—History and other people notwithstanding—is that person's own greatest gift. Misha (the splendid, sad-eyed Stanislav Lyubshin) sums it up perfectly: "My life is short. These coups will take place over and over again, but I will only be 60 years old once."

And yet, Misha has a whopper of a surprise up his sleeve. After unveiling the plans of a new house he built on the Volga River, he drops the bomb: He wants all his wives—past and future—to live there with him.

Oleg Yefremov directed this sometimes sentimental and always comic stew from a proper distance, letting the excellent cast show off their abundant talents at will, painting the wacky goings on in broad swaths and bright, primary colors. Tatyana Lavrova's Katya is the pouty, still hurt first wife; Anastasia Voznesenskaya's Natasha is the adventurous home wrecker-turned-second wife; Yevgenia Dobrovolskaya's Lida is the sensitive, empathizing young woman who fell for the charming elderly ladies' man.

Alexei Zharkov creates a sympathetic toughie as Katya's thick-headed husband, while Andrei Myagkov is a spectacular bundle of nerves as Natasha's would-be screenwriter husband. Now an émigré living in the U.S., when he learns that Mary's son is a big Hollywood producer, he nearly comes apart at the seams between chasing after Mary and trying to retrieve his wife from Misha.

The corn of this comedy is tempered by Nelli Seleznyova's Masha, the ignored daughter whom Misha must learn to love, and Olga Barnet's guileless Mary, who tries saving Misha's party from ruin when things get out of hand, instead inadvertently ruining everything.

Boris Messerer's set turns a slice of the Ukraine Hotel into a three-ring circus, dividing the stage equally into Misha's and Mary's suites, and the corridor between them.

Misha's Party is neither especially deep nor challenging. Its considerable strength is that in drawing a picture of contemporary Russian life, it tells simple truths clearly, simply and with a wonderful sense of humor.

(*November 1994*)

Lou, The Russian State Theater Agency

After a two-hour performance of the world premiere of *Lou*, his new one-actress play, a noisy hour of congratulations, and a few glasses of champagne, the Australian playwright hushed the crowd to make a toast.

"When I wrote this play," David George said in well-prepared Russian, "I knew I had to find an actress with the heart, mind and soul to play it. I knew I needed a Russian actress."

With the help of David Smelyansky's Russian State Theater Agency, the actress that George found was Yelena Koreneva, the former Soviet film star who spent ten years in the United States and is now working to revive her acting career at home. Viewers last saw her this spring in *The Car in Flesh*. *Lou* is an incomparably better play, and once this still raw production picks up some steam, it may well provide the showcase Koreneva has been seeking.

George's play is almost certain to bring him international recognition. It is feminist without being doctrinaire; it is intellectual without being pretentious; and it teases sexually without the vaguest hint of vulgarity. The playwright chose a fascinating heroine and wrote an intriguing monologue that lets her speak out at various points in her life, from her youth to her last minutes before death.

At times, such as in Lou's visit to Leo Tolstoy, it descends into name-dropping and fact-listing, but more often it is concerned with revealing a unique personality.

Lou Andreas-Salomé was an intelligent, fiercely independent woman who had a knack for shocking society and capturing the hearts of great men. Born in Russia in 1861, she moved to Europe 20 years later, beginning her long line of amorous conquests, the most celebrated of which were Friedrich Nietzsche and Rainer Maria Rilke. Her long friendship with Sigmund Freud at the end of her life—Lou herself was a practicing psychiatrist and a much-published author—produced a copious and fascinating correspondence, as well as influencing his theories of sexuality.

Koreneva, whose sublimely lyrical film persona was so endearing for always slightly slipping into silliness in just the right proportions, usually handles her complex heroine well. The actress has matured, become wiser and more cautious in a way that suits her. That helped her create her finest moments at last Friday's premiere—the scenes devoted to Lou's old age.

As directed by Yevgeny Kamenkovich, the production is attractive, if static. It is well served by Pyotr Gladilin's set, primarily consisting of books stacked on the floor and a white European "skyline" on the back wall, and Sergei Skornetsky's excellent lighting which casts shadows that separate or merge with the actress at key moments.

The biggest problem on the opening night was a lack of momentum. The choppy scenes—the playwright's way of creating dramatic movement—never came together in a unified whole. At times visibly struggling with the volume of text, Koreneva seldom got inside her character, settling instead for creating an effective facade. Nevertheless, Koreneva is a charismatic, talented actress, and her performance in *Lou* is ultimately satisfying.

(*November 1994*)

Boris Godunov, **Chekhov Art Theater**

Read the program notes to the Chekhov Art Theater's new production of Alexander Pushkin's play in verse, *Boris Godunov*, and you will quickly sense that something is wrong.

Oleg Yefremov, the show's director, its star actor and the longtime artistic director of the theater, writes passionately about the great risk of staging this, Russian literature's most enigmatic play about the enigma of power in Russia, and about the theater's duty to do it. Yefremov outlines the parallels between the present and those historical eras identified with the names of Godunov, Ivan the Terrible and Joseph Stalin, and concludes that Pushkin's poetry, created on the basis of "real life," provides a way for "theater to survive in troubled times."

It all sounds very impressive, and let there be no doubt about Yefremov's sincerity. But his compulsive need to justify himself so weightily even before the performance begins, hints loudly that the show itself doesn't say what he wanted it to. And that surely is the case.

This *Godunov*, featuring Yefremov as the tsar whose reign from 1598 to his death in 1605 gave way to a crippling, eight-year power struggle, is remarkably flat and disorganized. Unable to corral the cast of more than seventy into a unified ensemble, Yefremov left all those scenes which don't concern his character to develop helter-skelter. Meanwhile, he plays the tragic Godunov with such monolithic, leaden grief that he drags the show to a halt, rather than giving it meaning.

Almost unbelievably, things occasionally get so bad that one wonders whether this isn't an amateur exhibition and not the product of one of the world's most famous theaters. Actors imitate emotion and agitation with meaningful facial expressions and guttural voices. Secondary actors stand by looking as though they're wondering whether they'll ever get their money out of the crashed MMM pyramid scheme. (For comparison, watch Sergei Shnyryov's carefully nuanced silent scenes as Godunov's son, Fyodor.) Mass battle scenes are "fought" lethargically and clumsily by a mix of student extras and pros.

Godunov's chief rival is Grisha Otrepyev, an opportunistic young monk. When he hears the legend that Godunov murdered the infant heir to the throne, Dmitry, in order to seize power, Otrepyev flees to Poland where he gathers an army to support his bold and false claim to power.

As played by Mikhail Yefremov, the director's son, this Otrepyev is utterly unconvincing. The actor repeatedly strikes poses rather than penetrating his character's surface, and blusters rather than mustering genuine audacity.

The evening's only sustained bright moment comes thanks to the delightful comic team of Vyacheslav Nevinny and Andrei Myagkov playing the tipsy priests who unknowingly escort the fugitive Otrepyev to the Lithuanian border. But even this success is as much a sign of the failures around it as it is anything else. So masterfully natural are the massive Nevinny and the wispy, straggly-haired Myagkov, their scene looks like a drum-tight vaudeville number played in a morgue.

The unusual set by Boris Messerer needed a better production to show it off. The walls are draped with black material striped in gold, giving the illusion that the stage is enveloped in an enormous, crude fur coat. Hanging from the flies are two huge screens that move and twirl on a circular track, and on which are projected old sketches of Moscow, fragments of icons, folk art and illuminated manuscripts.

Life at the Chekhov Art Theater has been rough in recent years. Occasional successes like *The Possible Meeting*, *Behind the Mirror* and the recent *Misha's Party*, have alternated with mediocrities such as *The New American*, based on the works of Sergei Dovlatov, and resounding flops such as *Woe from Wit* and now *Boris Godunov*. In any case, anyone interested in the Godunov legend is better off going across town to the Maly Theater, where Vasily Bochkaryov works theatrical wonders in the title role of A.K. Tolstoy's *Tsar Boris*.

(December 1994)

Without Mirrors, Contemporary Play School

Nikolai Klimontovich has waited a long time to see a Moscow theater produce his play,

Without Mirrors, written during the springtime of perestroika in 1986. Over the ensuing 8 years, several theaters rehearsed it, but Iosif Raikhelgauz at the Contemporary Play School—who himself spent several years working on the play—is the only director who could get it as far as a premiere.

But if Raikhelgauz deserves an "A" for effort and stick-to-it-iveness, what he created can only get an "F" for flop. It strips Klimontovich's strange, allegorical fantasy of everything but its bare, purposefully silly plot, leaving behind a plodding, excessively literal and utterly unconvincing performance.

The action occurs in a run-down dacha where the young Pavel (the pointlessly fidgety Mikhail Yefremov) has retreated for a winter's eve with his even younger girlfriend (Olga Gusiletova). But, before things get beyond some banter about Pavel's forebears and the kind of lives they once led, a woman named Anna (Olga Yakovleva) makes an unexpected appearance. Confusing Pavel for his father (the electricity has conked out) Anna reminds him of the night they spent together here 20 years ago. The young man plays along with the blunder, pretending to be his dad and drawing out the details of the old tryst by feigning faulty memory.

Klimontovich transcended the impossibility of the situation with a bit of magic. When Anna is shocked to see that Pavel looks no different than he did 20 years ago, the resourceful young man claims to have invented an ointment that returns youth to aged bodies. He convinces Anna to try it too, and, with no mirrors around to prove otherwise, she buys the ruse.

It's great theatrical magic, one chimerical stroke brushing aside reality, and making way for flights of fancy that are no less persuasive than dreams. But, as handled at the Contemporary Play School, there is no magic; there is only the bald dictate of the text and a cast that doesn't believe in its own powers of transformation.

As the show progresses, it is buried under a pile of questions to which it resolutely refuses to give answers.

Does Anna really believe in the ointment? If not—as it would seem here—then what is she doing? Why does the young Pavel go to such lengths to deceive her? (Can it really be just because he is a smart aleck?) What compels the bland young girl to go along when she walks in to find the odd scheme in full motion? With no hints of answers to any of these questions, one can only wonder what an idiot Anna's lover must be to sit out in the car waiting for her for two hours with only an occasional meek beep of the horn to remind her of his existence.

Yakovleva is one of Moscow's best-known actresses. Her performances for the great director Anatoly Efros in the 1970s and 1980s are considered classics and her role as Josephine in last year's revival of Efros's *Napoleon* I at the Mayakovsky Theater brought her to the public eye again after several years spent in France. But no amount of past accolades can hide her flat failure to make Anna even marginally believable. Yefremov and Gusiletova are equally uninspired, while Vladimir Kachan's Sonya, an old woman, is beyond explanation or redemption.

Only Albert Filozov's single scene at the end as Pavel's father hints that this play might conceal beneath its surface an interesting exploration of youth, aging, love and death. But by the time he appears, even magic couldn't save this show.

Boris Lysikov's set plays with mirror images by splitting the audience in two and seating the spectators face to face across a narrow stage depicting an interior with transparent walls.

(*December 1994*)

Anton, All the World International Theater Center

With so few contemporary Russian plays making it to the stage these days, it is cause for a minor celebration when one does. Especially if it is done as sincerely as Yury Volkov's production of his own play, *Anton*, playing irregularly at the House of Actors and other venues around town.

Anton was the name of Volkov's grandfather, a man that the playwright suggests in a narrated prologue might have been a writer were it not for an exhausting, unhappy

marriage, and for his arrest which led to his death in the camps in 1936. So, while the play actually takes its name from the great Russian writer Anton Chekhov, it is the specter of Volkov's grandfather that transforms it from a mere stage bio into a work shaded with the intimacy of personal attachment.

It isn't surprising that Volkov was intrigued by Chekhov, certainly one of the most fascinating figures in the rich pantheon of Russian cultural giants. The grandson of a serf who bought his own freedom, and the son of an oppressive, impoverished shopkeeper, he was a striking example of one who, to use an only partially adequate American phrase, pulled himself and his family up by the bootstraps. He was a man of extraordinary will, focus and talent, all of which he used to a degree that only a select few can.

That, as strictly applied to Chekhov's flourishing as a writer, is the crux of Volkov's play. He explores the personality of a man willing to make hard decisions and painful sacrifices in order to sustain his literary gift. A favorite and an admirer of women, he avoided binding ties until a late and very long-distance marriage. A devoted friend and a lover of good company, he essentially remained a loner until his death.

Volkov traces these traits with persuasive efficiency, portraying Chekhov (Andrei Smolyakov) in various states of entanglement, either with such women as the Blonde (Olga Chernook), the Dazzling Woman (Nadezhda Butyrtseva), and the Meek Woman (Vera Kharybina), or with his two friends, the moody painter Isaac Levitan (Kirill Kozakov) and the colorful writer Vladimir Gilyarovsky (Igor Zolotovitsky).

The scenes with Levitan and Gilyarovsky are especially insightful, revealing both Chekhov's distaste for the kind of florid philosophizing of which the great landscape painter was capable, and his lack of interest in the frivolous escapades of which Gilyarovsky was such a champion. Not overlooked is the close, highly complex relationship between Chekhov and his sister, Masha (Marina Shvydkaya), on whom the writer was so jealously dependent that he went so far as to sabotage her own potential marriage.

Volkov's decision to direct his own play—a common move in the West, but rare in Russia—produced admirable if unspectacular results. As would be expected, the play is treated with care and insight, while a more experienced director might have got more from the actors.

Smolyakov's sympathetic Chekhov—thoughtfully obsessed with his privacy and genuinely regretful that literature leaves no room for other "lovers"—provides a solid center supported by performances ranging from the effective (Kozakov and Zolotovitsky) to the earnest. Characteristic of this raw production is Vera Kharybina's nice scene as the neighbor woman Dunyasha following her barely competent interpretation of the Meek Woman shortly before.

Nikolai Epov's set on a platform raised over the front rows of seats keeps things clear and simple. Beside Chekhov's stand-up desk are stacks of papers, his doctor's bag and a curtain hung in a tight ring that allows actors to hide and make "unexpected" entrances.

Anton is an elegy for a grandfather; an exploration of one of Russia's most innovative writers; and, perhaps, an act of self-encouragement on the author's part. If the performance doesn't always share the play's reach, it is still noteworthy for its conviction.

(December 1994)

White Columns, Commonwealth of Taganka Actors

White Columns, Nikolai Gubenko's free adaptation of the bitterly satiric prose of Mikhail Saltykov-Shchedrin for the Commonwealth of Taganka Actors, is destined for controversy.

Many will hail it as a merciless exposé of Russia's ills. Others will attack it as a sensationalist, political broadside. They all will be right. But there is no denying that Gubenko, an actor, film director and the last Soviet Culture Minister, has unfailingly captured in his first-ever theatrical staging the bile, the chancres and the malevolence lurking beneath the surface of contemporary Russian life.

That is not an evaluation. In fact, this relentless, even savage production is so self-contained and so self-justifying, it almost defies evaluation.

Yes, Gubenko skillfully plays with rhythms of motion and creates striking visual images; and yes, the acting on the whole is strong. The powerful music selected from Shostakovich, Schnittke, Rachmaninoff and others is used well, while Anatoly Remizov's harsh lighting amidst a sea of darkness gives a menacing feel to Alexander Orlov's "unstable" set of enormous architectural columns which fall and rise around a long banquet table that niftily transforms into a stylized orator's soapbox or a parliamentary dais.

But that is not what you take away from this performance. Instead, you are haunted by the disturbing memory of its unending stream of stupid, vile, unredeemed and unredeemable people.

There is the sadistic Doctor (Tatyana Zhukova-Kirtbaya) who rules her insane asylum with a whipping stick ever at hand; there is Sila Terentich (Vyacheslav Pilnikov), the sinister old leader of the asylum inmates who is replaced by Pyrkov (Lev Butenin), a Yeltsin clone whose revolution "destroys his homeland to get praise in foreign newspapers" before plunging everything into chaos; there are the corrupt members of a "secret society" whose underground congress turns into a black farce before Pyrkov strong-arms them into submission.

Wandering in horrified amazement through this Danteesque assemblage of thugs with names like Mr. Shyster and Mr. Bootlicker, is the young Provincial, who drank himself to death out of despair. But his demise in a drunken stupor gives him the power to return for a look at the living. Often accompanied by his cloying friend Prokop (Mikhail Lebedev), that is what he does, giving the production its episodic nature. Andrei Kaikov plays the dead man as a sensitive innocent, providing some rare moments of harmony.

The text, compiled by Gubenko with help from Leonid Filatov, is about as subtle as a flying mallet. Heavily salted with telltale words such as "parliament," "referendum," "reforms" and "constitution," there is no mistaking that Saltykov's 19th-century prose has been updated. So bleak and bilious is the picture it paints, it leaves nothing and no one unscathed. And its anguished, cynical view of Russian power-plays certainly assumes that the director included himself among the targets.

Two years ago, under the banner of defending the rights of neglected actors, Gubenko helmed a noisy rebellion against Yury Lyubimov at the Taganka Theater. In a series of celebrated court battles, he won control of the Taganka's new stage, which he occupied with his newly-formed Commonwealth of Taganka Actors.

It was a typical example of destruction and division in the name of progress. While the Lyubimov half of the Taganka has continued to founder, the Commonwealth's first production of *The Seagull* last winter was an unmitigated disaster that has played only rarely since. *White Columns*, the venue's second show, is significantly better, although its overwhelming pessimism implies that Gubenko may only have won a Pyrrhic victory over Lyubimov in the Taganka wars.

Be that as it may, *White Columns*, cannot be ignored. It may often be unpleasant, but it is always ruthlessly honest.

(*December 1994*)

Pygmalion, Sovremennik Theater

If George Bernard Shaw had lived another six years, he most certainly would have turned his poisonous wit on Alan Jay Lerner and Frederick Loewe. All they did in 1956 was nearly eclipse forever Shaw's celebrated play, *Pygmalion*, by turning the story about the professor who makes a lady of a lowlife into *My Fair Lady*, one of the most memorable musicals of all time.

Then George Cukor put the final nails in the coffin by making the deservedly awardladen movie of the musical with Rex Harrison and Audrey Hepburn. Ever since, Shaw's story without the songs, and without Harrison and Hepburn, somehow seems lacking.

At any rate, those are the kinds of thoughts Galina Volchek will be stirring with her new production of *Pygmalion* at the Sovremennik Theater.

Volchek went the star route, casting the enormously popular Valentin Gaft as Professor Henry Higgins, and Yelena Yakovleva as the flower girl Eliza Doolittle.

But this pairing, like Volchek's direction, is surprisingly bereft of inspiration and chemistry. *Pygmalion*, of course, is less sentimental than *My Fair Lady*, and Shaw didn't mess with happy endings, but the Higgins/Doolittle twosome is one of the great theatrical duets. However, Gaft and Yakovleva often play their characters like singers reading different pages of a score.

Yakovleva provides the show's best and worst moments, hitting dead bottom in her galling early scenes as the guttersnipe with the impenetrable Cockney accent. Lacking the opportunity in Russian translation to play with English, she compensates with a bundle of awkward affectations. It's not a bad idea in principle, perhaps, but as Yakovleva snorts, sniffles and grunts with her head scrunched into her shoulders, she looks less like Eliza than Quasimodo from *The Hunchback of Notre Dame*. It is so irritating that one can only ask what Volchek was up to when the actress was rehearsing her part.

Once free of the need to imitate ignorance, Yakovleva finally can blossom. Especially effective is her first outing in society after perfecting Higgins's beginning lessons in elocution. The actress not only transforms into a beauty, but attains fine comic control. Her glances, pauses and gestures reveal the irony of one who is playing a game well and knows it. Thereafter, she wavers from time to time between excess and monotony, but usually radiates a believable and vulnerable elegance.

Gaft's Higgins is a melange of all the famous Gaft mannerisms. He is arrogant, powerful and brusque, spitting out his lines with machine-gun speed. The problem is that he emanates as much conviction as a gunslinger popping cans off a fence: He never misses, but he's never in any danger, either.

Ultimately, the lack of danger is what deflates this romantic comedy. Imagine a near-kiss scene done so matter-of-factly that the only logical outcome is for the kiss not to be consummated. Well, it happens here twice with the passion meter never registering a blip. When this Eliza finally walks out on this Higgins, the only mystery is, what took her so long?

The supporting cast, led by Valery Shalnykh's soft-natured Pickering, Galina Sokolova's loud Mrs. Higgins, and Valery Khlevinsky's blustery Alfred Higgins, helps fill out the plot.

Even the excellent designer Pavel Kaplevich underachieved. His imaginative costumes in shades of violet are beautiful, but his set is smarter than good. Depicting opposing halves of two moving buildings that never quite come together, it seems little more than an obvious metaphor.

Whether it be Loewe's marvelous melodies or Shaw's syncopated romantic conflicts, this *Pygmalion* leaves you wondering where the music went.

(*January 1995*)

Goodbye, Deadmen! Hermitage Theater

Goodbye, Deadmen! at the Hermitage Theater is the latest of Mikhail Levitin's projects in reviving the Soviet drama of the 1920s and 1930s. This time the object is Isaac Babel's neglected play, *Maria*, written in 1934. And, as usual, Levitin gives us even more.

Stuffed around the cracks are four interludes using either Babel's short stories or a tragi-farcical folk song to loosen the tight structure of the episodic play in eight scenes. That, plus a handful of tactful liberties taken with the play itself, creates a sometimes disorderly, always evocative show that embraces, rather than merely depicting, Babel's look at people doomed to extinction.

The world of *Maria* is inhabited by the noble tsarist general Mukovnin and his daughters Katerina and Lyudmila, and a crew of shady characters led by Isaac Dymshits, a Jewish blackmarketeer making hay in the chaos of civil-war ravaged Russia. The clash of these two social strata, both with their roots in tsarist Russia, is nothing compared to the threat they face from the Bolsheviks. In fact, they are so endangered, they almost find themselves coming together involuntarily out of self-defense.

The urbane, high-strung Isaac (Viktor Gvozditsky) is courting the frivolous, young Lyudmila (Yelena Kotikhina) largely as a means of rubbing shoulders with nobility. Katerina (Darya Belousova), looking every bit a cadaver before her time, is horrified by her sister's loose behavior, but powerless to stop it. Their ailing father (Boris Romanov) is tragically caught in a typically Russian vice: Oblivious to the fact that his kind is soon to be swept away, he seeks to understand the social chaos buffeting him rather than oppose it.

Hanging above them is the specter of the eldest daughter Maria, whom Babel never brings into view. The apple of her father's eye and her sisters' favorite, she is also a volunteer in the Red Army. The author used her aura to signal his own impartiality and understanding of social change, blurring the line dividing negative and positive forces.

Levitin, enjoying the luxury of hindsight, is not so unbiased. From time to time he brings on a ghost-like figure to the edge of the stage, her sorrowful air undercutting her family's reverential talk of her.

In his interpretations of the others, Levitin followed Babel to the letter. Whether it is Isaac and his scraggly band or the fragile, slowly deconstructing Mukovnin family, everyone in this universe is complex, vulnerable and endowed with dignity.

Boris Romanov's exquisite General Mukovnin gives a poignant, inner light to this constellation of mismatched partners on a journey to ruin. The actor's performance is so subtle, it seems one can even hear the thoughts behind his careful motions and transparent voice.

Viktor Gvozditsky, whose Isaac is as elegant, sinister or powerless as the situation demands, steps out of character to perform a superb reading of Babel's story, "Di Grasso," about a boy entranced by a traveling Italian actor. It has nothing to do with *Maria* per se, but everything to do with invoking Babel's razor-sharp brand of anti-sentimental sensitivity.

The final scene of a young couple taking over the abandoned Mukovnin apartment is vintage Levitin. Babel wrote of workers moving furniture; Levitin has riff-raff madly and vainly struggling with a piano. It is a comically penetrating symbol of harmony squandered by those who cannot fathom it.

Meanwhile, the joyous epilogue is an apologia for all those who cannot survive. Everyone climbs into a carriage that rumbles slowly out of the hall, the riders smiling, throwing confetti, and waving goodbye to the applauding spectators.

Harry Hummel, as always, designed a set that is equally graceful and fragmentary, while Svetlana Kalinina created luxuriously detailed costumes.

Levitin is a champion of excess. He loves piling on layers, tacking on addendums, and throwing spotlights on trivia. When it works, as it usually does in *Goodbye, Deadmen!* it creates a syncopated feast for the mind and the heart.

(January 1995)

The Persecution and Assassination of Jean-Paul Marat as Performed by the Inmates of the Asylum of Charenton under the Direction of the Marquis de Sade, Theater u Nikitskikh vorot

Since staging an exceptionally strong version of Anton Chekhov's *Uncle Vanya* two years ago, director Mark Rozovsky has been treading water. With the exception of *Murderer*, his own superficial dramatization of Dostoevsky's *Crime and Punishment*, he has repeatedly turned over the stage at his Theater u Nikitskikh vorot to other directors, with only mixed success.

Now Rozovsky is back with a new production of Peter Weiss's *The Persecution and Assassination of Jean-Paul Marat*—the full title of which continues, *as Performed by the Inmates of the Asylum of Charenton under the Direction of the Marquis de Sade.* (The play is often billed, as it was in Peter Brook's famous 1964 version, as *Marat/Sade.*)

But this effort only suggests that Rozovsky is still looking for the secret to get him moving again.

Weiss's play is a scorching, philosophical treatise centered by an ongoing dialogue between the egalitarian revolutionary Marat and the supreme individualist Sade. Flitting around them is a group of fourteen crazies who, depending upon the whim influencing them at the moment, are either in accord with or in opposition to the two principals.

Rozovsky, who began his career in the 1960s running the amateur student theater at Moscow University, staged the play as if it were a topical revue. He invariably gave punch-line stress to lines about parliamentary strife, revolutionary chaos, and corrupt defense and finance ministers. His use of the attendant crazies as a chorus of clowns further softens the play's impact. The move might have worked had the purpose of the jesters been to deepen a sense of alienation, but instead, in all their circus-like clamoring for freedom, they merely create goofy foils for Marat and Sade.

Marat, propagating the virtues of a moderate republican form of government, is played by Sergei Desnitsky, who seems to be the only actor Rozovsky will cast in a leading role these days. Solid and capable, though lacking variety, Desnitsky brings the same workman's reliability to each of his now numerous roles. Here he plays Marat—sitting in his bath and waiting to be stabbed by Charlotte Corday—with characteristic aloofness, perhaps confusing weary disillusionment for thoughtfulness.

More effective is the young Igor Senko as the deliciously disgusting Marquis de Sade, who declares that equality among humans is impossible: Humans, he says, are the cruelest, most dangerous and most insane of all beasts. Usually reclining in a chair in front of the stage, his nervous twitches, curling lip, graceful gestures and sated gaze create a persuasive image of a man absorbed in a philosophical vision. For all his outer calm, Senko's Sade burns with an inner fire.

But, as news of the revolutionary strife taking place in Paris (or is it Moscow?) leaks into the asylum, Marat and Sade can never achieve a real duel. Each merely presents his views in alternating monologues that are undercut and broken up by the other inmates' amateurish antics.

Tatyana Shvets created an appropriately pristine interior of a hydropathic asylum, with Marat's bathtub at center. Light designer Yefim Udler once again proved he is the best in the business with his jarring, unusual colors that take on spatial qualities.

But, with minor exception, this *Marat* is confused and lackadaisical. It just is not the kind of material which Rozovsky's unquestionably sincere but undeniably limited team is capable of handling.

(*January 1995*)

Great Expectations, National Youth Theater; and *Pip*, Novy Drama Theater

Two recent adaptations of *Great Expectations*, Charles Dickens's classic novel about Pip, the country orphan who learns some hard lessons about life in the jungle of London, show the opposing conclusions and similar problems that can arise in various interpretations of a single source.

Using a stiff, narrative-heavy dramatization by Wilma Hollingberry, the National Youth Theater created one of those shows that primarily gives a speed-read of a big book. At the Novy Drama Theater director/adapter Vladimir Sedov did radical surgery, excising the sentimental scenes of Pip's childhood, and discarding Dickens's hint at a happy ending. The result was an atmospheric, if not always convincing, production that bears resemblance to the alienated worlds of, say, Luigi Pirandello or Jean Genet.

At the Youth Theater, director Alexei Borodin and designer Stanislav Benediktov recreated all the unchanging drabness of Pip's world. The spacious stage simultaneously depicts the interiors of Joe Gargery's home, where Pip grows up, and Miss Havisham's neighboring residence, where Pip falls hopelessly in love with the cold-hearted Estella. Right there in the center is the grave of Pip's mother. Simple prop changes turn the same set into the office of the lawyer Jaggers; the London apartment Pip shares with Herbert Pockets; a street before the city prison; or the river bank where the police finally capture Pip's mysterious benefactor, the ex-con Magwitch.

Damir Ismagilov's dim lighting barely keeps a spot on the action, leaving the impression that a cavernous, murky darkness is ever ready to swallow everyone and everything.

The monotony of the visuals is duplicated in the acting. Lifeless internally and static externally, the actors may be more or less engaging at any given moment but none among the cast of over 30 ever acquires an independent life that exists outside of reference to Dickens's book. The novel's sentimentality, rather than its human drama, is what is referenced most often.

Sedov's version is more interesting, although it ultimately lacks the flesh and blood needed to bring it to life. Its simplified title of *Pip* signals a refocused story and, indeed, it has none of Dickens's social commentary. This is a concentrated, revisionist exploration that quietly but insistently raises questions about Pip's real nature: Is the source of his inability to find his way among people the fact that he is gay but does not recognize his inclination?

Hints abound that it is so. Pip repeatedly misses the subtle signs of homoerotic attraction tendered by his roommate Herbert. The same aura colors his dealings with the gently affectionate Magwitch, who here is less a renegade criminal than an enigmatic man of refinement.

In that light, Pip's attraction to the unresponsive Estella looks increasingly like a consequence of his own inner confusion. In Dickens, Estella's frostiness is the product of Miss Havisham's severe tutelage; Sedov's revision seems to suggest she is what a gay man sees when forced to look upon a woman as a sexual subject.

But that all works on such a deeply subliminal level, it never musters an impact. The actors' stylized movements and speech—intended to mesmerize—are more effective in theory than execution. Most often they just plunge things into dense tedium. Only Irina Manuilova, as the majestically dignified Estella, and Vladimir Levashyov, as the soft-spoken, avuncular Magwitch, capture the ambiance Sedov appeared to be after.

Sedov's bracingly effective minimalist set consists of little more than a high, angled, steel wall at center stage. Svetlana Arsenyeva's severe, usually monotone costumes, and Dmitry Smirnov's sparse, evocative music round out the production's strong suit: its idea and its trappings.

(*January 1995*)

The Victors' Feast, Maly Theater

It was a long wait, but Alexander Solzhenitsyn has finally seen the world premiere of *The Victors' Feast*, a play he wrote 43 years ago, staged against all his expectations in Moscow.

The rest of the audience at the Maly Theater on Wednesday had a shorter wait. It took just over three hours before the final curtain fell and they got what they had really come to see.

The cast of 20, joined by director Boris Morozov, were lined up single file across the stage taking their first bows, when the shouts of "Author! Author!" began reverberating through the hall. Morozov hurriedly placed a sturdy little white ladder in front of the left corner of the stage and Solzhenitsyn bounded up onto the stage from his seat near the aisle in the seventh row.

Beaming almost like a little boy, the 1970 Nobel Prize-winning author seemed somewhat abashed at first, almost feverishly passing on to the actresses the endless stream of bouquets heading his way, and embracing the director and the actors in bear hugs. But if there were a few awkward moments among those now sharing the stage, the spectators never hesitated. They immediately stood and greeted Solzhenitsyn with a thundering ovation which, after several curtain calls, gave no indications of letting up.

However, the applause quickly died down as the writer, whose voluminous works have come to symbolize the Russian struggle against communism, stepped forward and raised his left hand. Standing almost directly beneath the large, gilded symbol of the hammer and sickle still hanging dead center in the Maly's proscenium arch, and flanked on either side by two smaller emblems above the side stalls, Solzhenitsyn explained how his play—about some officers in a Soviet reconnaissance unit in Eastern Prussia at the end of World War II—had come about, and what its first ever performance in 1995 meant to him.

He began by noting the "amazing coincidence" of the premiere falling on January 25, the 50th anniversary of the day Soviet troops encircled the German army in Prussia, and the very day on which the action of *The Victors' Feast* takes place. He wrote the play, he continued, 43 years ago without the benefit of a pencil or paper. He was in a labor camp in Ekibastuz and he composed the

work in his head, rhyming the dialogues so as not to forget them.

"I never thought I would live to see it performed," Solzhenitsyn said, adding that he certainly never expected to see it staged in a Russian theater. Referring to his own experience as a captain in a reconnaissance battery in the Soviet Army before his arrest in February 1945, he stated that he was especially happy that a new generation of Russians could now see that Soviet officers during World War II were not lacking in ideals or convictions and that they too, had been "thinking people."

Solzhenitsyn concluded by saying he hopes to see Russia "happy and healthy, as it, alas, is not today." At that, he stepped back into the line of actors and the thunderous applause picked up where it had been interrupted and continued on again through several more curtain calls.

It clearly was the highlight of an evening in which the performance played second fiddle to Solzhenitsyn himself. Accompanied by his wife and a small band of photographers and television cameramen, he turned heads and gathered a crowd as he arrived at the theater 30 minutes before curtain time. When he entered the hall to take his seat 15 minutes later, he was greeted first by an ovation, and then swamped in a sea of photographers and autograph hounds, all of whom he obliged good-naturedly.

The Victors' Feast, obviously in large part autobiographical, takes place in a German castle occupied by the officers of an artillery intelligence group. As the action develops, it becomes clear that none of the officers bears any loyalty to Stalin or communism and that they all expect major changes to take place when they return home.

Like so much of Solzhenitsyn's writings, the play is marked more by a schematic presentation of ideas than by artistic finesse. The verse dialogue is simplistic and often clumsy, so that despite highly professional performances from the entire cast, neither the characters nor their actions ever really come to life.

But none of that mattered to the crowd of about 900. They were there to celebrate the triumphant appearance of a former enemy of the people on the stage of Russia's oldest and most storied dramatic theater.

(January 1995)

Talents and Admirers, **Theater na Pokrovke**

Sergei Artsibashev has traveled the world with his languorous, deceptively lazy productions of Russian classics, his little Theater na Pokrovke garnering praise on tours and capturing prizes at theatrical festivals. But nowhere has he lived as modestly and quietly as in Moscow.

For years, while waiting out the construction of a new stage just off the Garden Ring, Artsibashev and his troupe have occupied a few rooms on the top floor of an obscure building tucked in the back corner of a muddy courtyard two blocks north of the Yelokhovskaya church. There they have performed their acclaimed interpretations of Anton Chekhov's *Three Sisters*, Nikolai Gogol's *The Inspector General* and Ivan Turgenev's *A Month in the Country* in the biggest room they had, a "hall" that, with a shoehorn, seated 30.

That will all change this month when the Theater na Pokrovke finally takes up residence in its new home.[3]

And when it does, one of the first performances will be the theater's most recent effort, Alexander Ostrovsky's *Talents and Admirers*. It is a vintage Artsibashev production which may not add anything new to the director's vocabulary, but which offers a refined summary of his strong points.

Artsibashev is adept at peeling back the cutting edge of risk buried in understatement and nuance. At times he carries things to such extremes that he teeters on the brink of plunging headlong into amateurish tedium. His actors chat confidentially in barely audible voices, mutter under their breath during seemingly empty pauses and chuckle at inside jokes. They make no effort whatsoever to project or broadcast anything to an audience by the usual theatrical means.

It is a dangerous game in which Artsibashev stays on top by infusing his productions with a strong sense of purpose. In his hands, literary characters and dramatic figures come to life, acquiring the warmth and subtle contradictions that make villains lovable and heroes believable.

Ostrovsky's spirited backstage melodrama—about a young, 19th-century provincial actress's struggles with her chief rival, and their demanding and fickle admirers—is ideal material for Artsibashev to work his magic on. The great playwright packed his play chock full of the usual, heady swirl of treacheries, intrigues, unbridled squabbles and secret heartbreaks; Artsibashev renewed Ostrovsky's fascinating people by skipping past appearances and going at them from the inside out.

As Negina, the young actress who sees her popularity disappear almost instantly when she turns down the rude advances of a pushy fan—in our age it is called sexual harassment—Natalya Grebyonkina is filled with trembling innocence and a well of indignant pride. Close to her bluntly practical mother (Nina Kiryakova), and finding temporary refuge in the sincere, but uninspiring affections of a lovestruck tutor (Valery Nenashev), Negina is nevertheless all alone in a cutthroat world.

Negina's rival, the slightly older and significantly more experienced Smelskaya, is ever ready to take advantage of Negina's slips in popularity with the rich men whose primary business is the pleasure of courting actresses. As played by Yelena Borisova, Smelskaya is imposing, frivolous and quietly sly, but never lacking a last-minute soft spot even for her competition.

In fact, while the two actresses publicly remain the rivals Ostrovsky intended them to be, a few brief moments—such as their lighting up cigarette butts together, or singing a quiet duet—reveal their silent mutual respect and deep, sisterly solidarity. It is one of the subtle shifts which Artsibashev typically introduces to foil stereotypes and suggest the unexpected.

With its downplaying of the obvious, its emotional scenes that quietly implode rather than explode, and its insight into human

---

[3] The move actually took place in May. See the June 1995 review of *Scenes from a Marriage*.

nature, *Talents and Admirers* does not conquer, it persuades. And, like other productions by Artsibashev, it does that well.

(*February 1995*)

Madame Bovary, Mossoviet Theater

Chalk up another winner for the Mossoviet Theater, which has recently emerged as Moscow's liveliest large playhouse. Whether in majestic costume dramas on its mainstage, or in more experimental shows on its intimate "Stage Under the Roof," the Mossoviet has repeatedly pushed the right buttons to keep its audiences happy.

The newest outing, a sweeping dramatization of Gustave Flaubert's *Madame Bovary*, is almost certain to be the venue's most popular yet. A tear-jerker that never shies away from the emotional release of comedy, it may be formulaic, but its formulas are honed to perfection.

Director Yury Yeryomin (he also wrote the dramatization) made brilliant use of Maria Rybasova's grandiose, two-tiered set with a revolving lower half that allows a multitude of visual angles on the interior of the provincial home of doctor Charles Bovary (Yevgeny Lazarev). Not only does the decoration provide the same kind of rapid setting changes that are usually the property of cinema, but it also echoes Emma Bovary's true mental state: At key moments, the rooms spin away, leaving the despairing Emma (Olga Ostroumova) to face a gaping, black void.

For all the complexity of the setting and the elegance of Viktoria Sevryukova's costumes, Yeryomin packed his production with simple details whose effects are powerful and far-reaching.

Early on, Emma's lover Rodolphe (Alexander Goloborodko) tip-toes across gravel spread in front of the kitchen window, the faint crunching sounds he makes implying the superficial tact that he and Emma observe as they slip into an affair. But by the time Emma has descended irreversibly into despair and deceit, her young lover Leon (Dmitry Shcherbina) races carelessly across the gravel, making a harsh racket that might be the sound of a life gone wrong.

Ostroumova's Emma first appears as a dreamy romantic whose discontent with her uninspiring husband and her narrow life seems quite harmless. Girlish and light-headed, she flinches in fright when she realizes that her boredom is about to drive her to adultery. But once the step is taken, there is no turning back. She overwhelms even her more cautious lovers, growing to hate her husband with a cold, cutting ferocity.

If the actress does not always lay bare the inner motivations of a trapped, lonely and limited woman, she does an impeccable job of showing us the crumbling facade.

As Emma's fawning husband in baggy pants, Lazarev is less the disgusting figure his wife sees in him, than a sympathetic softy who doesn't realize it was his tragedy to marry the wrong woman. Walking in a permanent crouch and always ready to throw himself at Emma's feet, Lazarev's Charles is a man with an immeasurable heart and a finite imagination.

Brilliant throughout, the actor is stunning when, for a brief moment, he thinks he has pulled off a complex operation that will make him famous and wealthy. He bursts into an uncharacteristic, heart-rending dance of joy that is as short-lived as his happiness will prove to be.

In keeping with this production's well-crafted emphasis on the paradoxes of human nature, Vladimir Sulimov is believably charming as the salesman who drives Emma into crippling debt, while Anatoly Adoskin is kindly and sympathetic as Homer, the busy-body druggist who symbolizes the pettiness of provincial life and inadvertently supplies the poison that will resolve Emma's problems.

(*February 1995*)

An Old Man Wanted to Leave His Old Woman, Contemporary Play School

It may be jumping the gun to say it now, but the view from here says this season's most endearing, heartfelt production will be *An Old Man Wanted to Leave His Old Woman* at the Contemporary Play School.

Semyon Zlotnikov's simple, funny, and, ultimately, poignant play is a sterling foundation for old-fashioned theater at its most moving and most convincing. And as co-directed by Iosif Raikhelgauz and Albert Filozov, there isn't a false move or a superfluous stroke in this look at what happens when an old man gets it into his head at age 78 that he can't live with his wife of 52 years for even one more day.

But let's be honest. Neither the fine play nor the sensitive direction could possibly have worked so seamlessly without the incomparable duet of Maria Mironova and Mikhail Gluzsky playing the embattled oldsters. That goes equally for their superb performances and for the sentiment factor they bring to the show.

Mironova began her illustrious career in 1927, and for decades was one of the Soviet Union's most beloved satirical actresses. In recent years she has had precious few opportunities to take the stage. Gluzsky, who began a bounteous film career in 1939, has also been a stranger to the stage of late. He was a longtime member of the Film Actors Theater, which, due to internal squabbles, essentially fell apart a few years ago.

All the clichés fit. Like a bottle of fine wine or your favorite slippers, this pair has only gotten better and become more lovable with age. There is a lot to be said for their talent—they know what they're doing up there on stage, and like pros, they don't let you know they know it—but the real cornerstone of their performances is heart.

Mitya is an old crank who, in his youth, wrote a dissertation about *Don Quixote* but now is immersed in the severe philosophy of Leo Tolstoy. His wife Vera is a former nurse with a big heart and buckets of good sense that won't let her take Tolstoy or Mitya too seriously. And that is what brought things to a head.

Struck by the misfortune of asking too many questions too late, Mitya has decided that, like Tolstoy, he is unhappy and must go off to live out his last days alone. The rich, comic banter courses like electricity while Vera packs her husband's bag and he justifies himself with thunderous grandiloquence. But the air quickly thickens when Vera horrifies Mitya with her admission that during the war she kissed a lieutenant who even "dragged her under the stairwell."

For Mitya, it is the final proof that he has lived a life of lies, and he cuts loose a string of "truths" that shatters even his indulgent wife: He never did love her, he sputters.

With equal doses of affection and penetrating insight, Zlotnikov observes his couple through breakups and reconciliations, his flawlessly natural dialogue concealing the situation's tragedy behind laughable particulars. As happens in life, there is no knowing how these people really lived and what compromises they made. But there is no doubting they deserve the peace they seek.

Boris Lysikov set the action in a neatly cramped apartment whose walls gradually disappear, ultimately leaving the pair one-on-one. The powerful finale features beautiful lighting from Igor Kurakin, as a series of harsh spots follow Gluzsky's slow movement around the motionless Mironova who is washed in a serene, silvery blue.

After last week's premiere, the two actors were greeted by a sustained standing ovation that had the surprised Mironova fighting back tears and the ecstatic Gluzsky doing a happy jig. Both were fitting responses to that rarity, a truly wonderful show.

(February 1995)

Jacques Offenbach, Love and Troo-La-La, Young Spectator Theater

When Jacques Offenbach created the modern operetta, the world changed forever. With its aggressive frivolity and its unapologetic foolishness, it is the genre every sophisticate loves to scorn. And yet rare is the spectator crabby enough to sit through an operetta and walk away with anything but a grin stretching from ear to ear.

All of that came to mind during the weekend premiere of *Jacques Offenbach, Love and Troo-La-La,* an adaptation of Offenbach's *Bluebeard* at the Young Spectator Theater. While the show never quite mustered the punch and rhythm it was aiming for, it still made for a gay and colorful spectacle.

As usual, director Genrietta Yanovskaya went out on a limb. If she drew raves and razzes last season for populating Chekhov's *Ivanov* with characters from all that writer's plays, this time she took a troupe of dramatic actors, dressed the men in tuxes, the women in revealing frills, attached radio mikes to their waists, and sent them out to sing and dance.

Then, to crank things a notch tighter, she wrote the character of Offenbach himself into this two-pronged bouffe about a flower-girl who is really a lost princess, and a baron with a blue beard who marries virgins and does them in on their wedding night.

The addition was a stroke of near-genius on two accounts: It tinted the feather-light proceedings with an unexpected lyrical depth, and gave reason to bring Yevgeny Sarmont on stage. He makes his first appearance as Jakov Eberst, the mild son of a synagogue cantor. But as snippets of the can-can push through the solemn strains of Jewish hymns, he is drawn to another world, where he takes the pseudonym of Jacques Offenbach.

There, Offenbach is as much at home amidst the bright costumes and extravagant people, as the actor is a natural in playing him. Hair flying, arms flailing and eyes blazing, Sarmont looked every bit like a half-pint Beethoven on helium, racing about the stage, barking at his actors, flirting with his actresses, and conducting a phantom orchestra in a mad, grotesque solo that brought down the house.

The *Bluebeard* that Offenbach wrote, and the one we see played out here under his wacky direction, is a fluff-ball of melodramatic clichés. There is the lost princess (Arina Nesterova) who loves a shepherd who really turns out to be a prince (Alexander Zhukov); there is the king's physician (Olga Demidova), who poisons propaganda ministers and searches for the lost princess; and there is the alchemist (Igor Gordin) who serves Bluebeard by poisoning his baron's brides and searching for his next victims.

All of them, and many more including those long thought dead, finally unite in a bash that culminates with—count 'em—eleven symbolic weddings and a can-can. The main pair consists of Anatoly Salimonenko's arrogantly handsome Bluebeard, decked out in white, and his sixth, not-so-virginal bride (Viktoria Verberg), dressed to kill in red.

Yanovskaya's intrepid troupe gave it their all. But, aside from Sarmont, only the winning Nesterova fits her role to perfection. She has just the array of a soaring voice, an impish heart and a springy step that are so essential to musical comedy.

Scenes lacking those two players often relied for effect on Svetlana Logafet's pretty costumes, Sergei Barkhin's bright, if somewhat chaotic, music-hall decorations, and the professional skills of a cast doing what it was not really cut out to do. The dances, attributed to Sergei Vinogradov, consisted of little more than kicking legs and waving arms.

Still, even if this show occasionally struggles, it has more than enough bubbly joy and light-hearted fun to send sophisticates and skeptics home with a happy smile.

(*February 1995*)

Teibele and Her Demon, Chekhov Art Theater

In its new production of *Teibele and Her Demon*, the Chekhov Art Theater has dipped gloriously into a thick concoction of mysticism, sexuality and righteous justice as only could have sprung from the mind of Isaac Bashevis Singer. Based on the story by Singer, and adapted for the stage by Eve Friedman, the play is a riveting ghost story for adults, rife with the rich rhythms of foreboding fantasy and liberating humor that are so characteristic of Singer's village Jews.

Under the direction of Vyacheslav Dolgachyov, the performance sweeps on like a relentless wind, especially in the impeccable first act, before unexpectedly losing some thrust as things move to a culmination. Still, it remains a moving, gripping production by any standard.

That is true in large part thanks to Margarita Demyanova's exquisite double-decker set in which a sparse country scene, with its deep, swirling skies, sits atop the cozy, inviting interior of a woman's bedroom.

Teibele (Yelena Maiorova) is a beautiful young woman who, having been abandoned by her husband, is the object of much attention among the men in a small Polish village in 1880. But as the legal wife of a man who has never been proven dead she remains untouchable.

That, plus Teibele's fertile imagination, her fascination with biblical demons, and her frank talks with her gullible friend Genendel (Natalia Yegorova), all combine to set her fantasies afire. None of it is lost on the lovesick Alchonon (Sergei Shkalikov), a woebegone teacher's assistant whom Teibele despises, but who eternally hangs around the well by her house just to watch her. He finally resolves to visit her one night in the guise of the "demon" Gurmizach, a daring move that has brilliant success and shattering consequences.

Dolgachyov handled the strong erotic nature of the story with immaculate good taste. Shkalikov's Alchonon-as-Gurmizach repeatedly appears stark naked, although it all remains quite chaste thanks to the actor's deft movements, the well-timed draping of a sheet as he spins or writhes, and the murky, shadowy lighting by Igor Yefimov.

In fact, Dolgachyov joyfully parodies the audience's expectations of titillation by having the dreamy Maiorova prepare for bed with a luxuriously slow, mesmerizing striptease. But for every layer she peels off, there seem to be two more to go, and she finally crawls into bed still clothed from neck to ankle.

Maiorova is superb at creating an internally uninhibited, even irrational heroine for whom maintaining the proper appearances, at least at first, is entirely natural. She has no qualms about misleading the forbidding rabbi (Vyacheslav Nevinny), who comes to perform an exorcism. Indeed, she is thoroughly content to exist in a world of her own where the sanctity—and sexual satisfaction—of dreams is inviolable.

Alchonon, who transforms beyond his own expectations when becoming the invading Gurmizach, is not so flexible. Loving Teibele deeply, he needs more than their nocturnal trysts can offer. Shkalikov is especially good as the glib demon whose thunderous daring never entirely excludes a bewildered sense of humor.

These are the strongest scenes, with the electrified Teibele savoring her double life,

the pining Alchonon suffering from it, and both of them charging ahead like runaway horses. The later complications—Alchonon's friend Menashe (Boris Shcherbakov) finding a way to force Teibele to marry the hated teacher, and Alchonon's vain efforts to get his new wife to recognize in him her beloved Gurmizach—occasionally bog down in less-than-convincing realistic detail and eclipse some of the magic.

But, having said that, you can forget the reservations. *Teibele and Her Demon* remains to the end a compelling, compassionate fable of desire, dreams and the doomed efforts of people to transcend the limits of reality.

(*February 1995*)

Amphitryon and *Uncle's Dream*, School of Dramatic Art

Showings of two vastly different works at Anatoly Vasilyev's School of Dramatic Art renewed suspicions that, at least in Moscow, the renowned director has found a way to make everything look the same. Whether it was in Molière's *Amphitryon*[4] or in excerpts from Dostoevsky's *Uncle's Dream*,[5] Vasilyev's static actors declaimed, shouted and giggled in monotone recitals that were almost identical in style, conception and performance to those used in excerpts from *Joseph and His Brothers* in 1993, and the staged Platonic dialogues in 1991.

The problem would seem to be that Vasilyev has misjudged his talent and confused his mission, something that was confirmed especially in the excerpts from *Uncle's Dream*. There, for the first time in the 1990s, an actress of major talent walked onto Vasilyev's Moscow stage, and for the first time in as long the director's minimalist ideas took legitimate form, at least at times.

The actress was Mari Töröscik, the Hungarian star of stage and screen who played Maria Alexandrovna in Vasilyev's 1994 adaptation of *Dream* at the Budapest Art Theater. That production received mixed notices

---

[4] Held December 24, 1994.
[5] Held February 23, 24, 25, 1995. I attended the last of them.

in the Hungarian press,[6] but the actress was so taken with her director that she accepted his invitation to come to Moscow to work with his students for six weeks at the beginning of 1995.

As in Budapest, the Moscow version consisted of excerpts from various chapters, most of which were dialogues and all of which were performed by actors "trapped" in chairs. Throughout the 3-hour performance, they stood only to enter or exit, with the sole exception being when Töröscik once walked a short loop behind her chair before sitting down again.

Aside from Alexander Anorov (who also impressed as Amphitryon's servant in *Amphitryon*), not a one of Vasilyev's actors could raise the performance above the level of a beginner's learning exercise as they traded among themselves the limited number of roles. This was made all the more apparent by Töröscik's fluid and subtle mastery of nuance, expression and energy. Her Hungarian-language performance of Moskaleva, the mother who wants to marry her daughter to the most advantageous match, was gripping and profound.

What all this indicates is that Vasilyev has a rare and undeniable talent for working with talent. He has shown that repeatedly over the years in his productions starring gifted actors. The best known among them include *Solo for a Clock with Chimes* at the Moscow Art Theater (1973), *The First Variant of "Vassa Zheleznova"* and *A Young Man's Grown-Up Daughter* at the Stanislavsky Theater in 1978 and 1979, respectively; *Cerceau* at the Taganka Theater in 1985; and *Six Characters in Search of an Author*, originally staged in 1986 with Vasilyev's students as a "diploma production" at the State Institute of Theater Arts (GITIS), and later made the first production of the School of Dramatic Art when it was

founded in 1987. But by this time Vasilyev's temperamental nature and his continuing drift away from the idea of a theater for the public, had caused his core of talented, established actors to move on to other theaters and other projects, and had, essentially, left him alone. He further alienated old friends and loyal colleagues by attacking Russian actors as selfish, and criticizing the Russian system of theatrical education for ruining, rather than raising actors.

That is what prompted him to found the School of Dramatic Art, a hermetic world where, in theory, he planned to create a new strain of actor. However, the reality has been that he experiments on his students with ideas which he only takes before the public in rare productions abroad. Moscow spectators, if they can get on the invitation list to the infrequent showings, see nothing but parts of works-in-progress which, until now, at least, have never been brought to conclusion.

Meanwhile, Vasilyev has spawned a strange hybrid of actor who, with rare exception, bears a striking resemblance to a robot, and who seldom gets a chance to perform in public. It is certainly only prudent and fair to allow that these students may yet blossom. But as the years pass and the young actors show no signs of acquiring even the most elementary aspects of individuality—on the contrary, they consistently move farther from it—it is equally prudent and fair to suggest that Vasilyev may not be the teacher he hoped to be.

Whether he does not trust his actors with the freedom of natural mannerisms, or whether his goal is nothing less than to reinvent the ABCs of acting, Vasilyev limits his charges to a bare minimum of expressive devices. With the actors seemingly nailed to their chairs from beginning to end, *Uncle's Dream* is an exception, of course. But in *Amphitryon*, as it was in *Joseph* and the Platonic dialogues, the actors seldom do more than sit or stand stiffly as they speak, and they seldom interact physically.

Most striking—or, perhaps, most irritating, depending upon one's point of view—is the highly stylized speech that all of the actors have learned as if by rote. It is a choppy

[6] Tamas Koltai wrote of the show which premiered April 9, 1994, that "professionals and the lazy half of the public could not swallow it; it stuck in their throat." Quoted in Alexander Sokolyansky, "Anatoly Vasilyev postavil "Dyadyushkin son" v Budapeshte," *Moskovsky nablyudatel*, Nos. 9–10 (1994): 12–14.

manner of chant in which at least minor stress falls on every word, no matter what its semantic value, and every word is separated from those around it by a mini-pause or hesitation. By and large, those words which receive major stress are pronouns and the conjunction "that." The following hypothetical text is an attempt to express in writing the rhythmic effect of such speech:

YOU. SAID. *THAT. I.* WAS. THE. ONE. *THAT.* GAVE. *HER.* THE. RIGHT. etc.,

Within these structural boundaries, the actors may dip into a whisper, carry on at a more or less regular volume, or, as is most apt to occur with the actresses, rise into a hysterical, guttural yell. But in all cases, the basic rhythm remains the same. While superficially creating the feel of a philosophical dialogue, over a period of time, this inflated, oratorical style actually begins bleaching the text of meaning.

The delivery of the text, if it is not done in anger, is usually accompanied by grins and laughter as if the actors were responding to inside jokes. Frequently, when two actors are carrying on a dialogue, other actors sit by silently, laughing and grinning among themselves or, more rarely, turning to the spectators to draw them into the process. It is not uncommon for the young actors to slip out of character (or at least to pretend to) and laugh heartily at some moment in the text or the action which they apparently find amusing. All of this mirth, having precious little to do with what is being said or done, is most apt to arouse in one the desire to rephrase Tolstoy's damnation of Leonid Andreev as, "These actors continuously try to amuse me, but I am not amused." Meanwhile, actors left out of the action for extended periods are even capable of slipping into their own world and staring blankly into space.

Against this backdrop, which at its worst in *Uncle's Dream* was downright amateurish, Mari Töröscik was living proof that Vasilyev is capable of inspiring talent. Even confined to her chair at stage right, she commanded an extraordinary freedom of spirit and depth of understanding, both of her own character and of those whom she opposed. Her facial expressions, her gesturing hands, her hunching of her shoulders, her shifting in her chair as she occasionally snapped up her dress to cross or recross her legs, all blended into a compelling physical portrait of an indomitable, willful and wily woman. And, of course, behind the flawless physical image which the actress created, there was the fire of the director's vision shining in her eyes. Never did Töröscik resort either to the grinning masks or the oratorical style of her partners. She was a brilliant palette of shades and tones, effortlessly turning Vasilyev's form into content.

The scenes from *Uncle's Dream* were performed to mark both the 8th anniversary of the founding of the School of Dramatic Art, and the reopening of Studio One on Povarskaya Street (formerly Vorovsky Street). And as Vasilyev had already shown in his delightfully whimsical and theatrical design of the new stage at the former Uranus movie theater, the renovated Studio One is a minor masterpiece of modern theatrical architecture.[7] The ceiling in what used to be a basement room was removed, uniting the cells of two stories and creating an extraordinarily tall, narrow hall. On the upper half of the walls (stage right), the apertures which used to be doors are now small loges fenced off with low wooden railings. Natural light pours in through the windows above and below at stage left, while theatrical light is aimed through the former door openings. The thickness of the walls has been increased, so that the artificial light entering from side stage appears to the audience reflected off the backside panels of the apertures. At the end of the room farthest from the stage, a diagonal slice of the former ceiling/floor was left in place, creating a small balcony that hangs over the wooden, tiered rows of seats below. The new, high ceiling is divided into four panels that are painted in an eclectic range of colors and styles including the medieval Russian icon

---

[7] For a description of the stage at the former Uranus, see the 1993 discussion of *Joseph and His Brothers*.

and European Renaissance. Upstage, just a few feet from the back wall, stands a low white, wooden partition with modest, decorative Ionic columns at either side and framing a doorway at upstage right. Signaling Vasilyev's nearly religious attitudes toward theater, many of the doorways leading in different directions from the spacious, carpeted coatroom are thick, narrow, low and arched in imitation of those that might be found in a monastery. The new Studio One and the existing stage at the Uranus comprise the two finest modern theatrical spaces in Moscow and, in my opinion, are Vasilyev's greatest contributions to Russian theater in the 1990s.[8]

Amphitryon was performed at the Uranus stage shortly before Töröscik came to town. It exhibited the same basic limitations of *Uncle's Dream*, but also revealed in rare moments the sparks one expects from a Vasilyev production. In any case, it had a greater sense of play than I have seen in other recent works. As if it were a mix of *Joseph and His Brothers* and *Uncle's Dream*, the performance began on chairs placed on the floorspace in front of the stage. However, in time, the actors—once again working essentially in pairs reciting dialogues—began to stand and move about not only on the floor, but on the stage as well. When on stage, the actors shared space with a row of spectators who had been personally seated and arranged by Vasilyev before the performance began.

Molière's text was cut and performed so that it became a kind of philosophical tract about the nature of identity, with Amphitryon's servant at the center. The other main thrust—which has been a key in all of Vasilyev's recent works—was the war between the sexes, trimmed to its most basic and most confrontational. The costumes, similar to those in *Dream*, mixed styles from 18th-century France, New York or Chicago in the 1930s, and Oriental motifs. In one brief, gorgeous moment, Amphitryon's servant signaled the fall of night using two 15-foot poles with long, blue streamers attached to the ends. Standing at the edge of

the elevated stage, he waved the poles in circles that carried the streamers nearly to the ceiling, right up to the faces of the spectators sitting in the narrow, upper balconies, and dropping them all the way to the floor.

Still, the performance was seldom able to break free of the stiff oratory and the borderline smart-aleck masks. There were a few attempts to incorporate the moves and gestures of the martial arts, but the actors performed them clumsily and sloppily. One scene featured simultaneous dialogues in which three different pairs, as though singing in the round, began delivering the same texts at staggered intervals, so that at the middle of the scene there was nothing but a screeching roar emanating from the stage. I have seen this device used well by Viktor Sibilyov, a graduate of Vasilyev's directing course, whose Sibilyov Studio enjoyed a short flight of creativity in the early 1990s before falling apart in the spring of 1994.[9] In Sibilyov's hands it was handled in a mesmerizing hush from which the key words seemed to emerge as if by chance so that the meaning of the dialogue came through with unusual force. As done in *Amphitryon*, the result was little more than senseless cacophony.

The case of Sibilyov is germane to the problem of Vasilyev because it once again raises questions about the director's value as a teacher. The fact is that the vast majority of directors which Vasilyev has turned out have either followed in his footsteps so closely that they can't acquire their own identity, or they have not been able to function in the real world. For a short time, Sibilyov was a "transitional" figure who broadly imitated his teacher while also bringing his own clear vision to the process. But he was eventually tripped up by another quality that Vasilyev instills in all of his students: a disdain for the practical elements of theater life. With no money whatsoever, Sibilyov was too proud to ask for it and too proud to accept any conditions attached to the financing or housing

---

[8] The Uranus has since been remodeled again.

[9] See my "Recreating a Tradition: Moscows's Sibilyov Studio," *Slavic and East European Performance* 12 (Spring 1992): 20–29.

that were occasionally offered him. In the end, he fell victim to an idealistic dream that art can exist outside of life.

Several graduates from Vasilyev's directing courses have never moved on to practice their profession, choosing instead to remain in the safe confines of the School of Dramatic Art in the capacity of assistants. Of those in Moscow who are most often linked with their teacher, only Boris Milgram has forged his own style with a couple of intriguing productions at the Mossoviet Theater: *First Love*, based on the writings of Samuel Beckett, and Molière's *The School for Wives*.

The others, Vladimir Klimenko (known as Klim) and Boris Yukhananov, have gathered small, but loyal followings primarily because they have remained so faithful to the Vasilyev style. Yukhananov's two-day, seven-hour fantasy based on *The Cherry Orchard* utilizes the same endless Vasilyev grins and giggles with the difference that Yukhananov builds them into a relentless, sarcastic irony. Klim, whether in an adaptation of Gogol's *The Inspector General*, or in a three-day trilogy of plays by Alfred de Musset running a total of 12 hours, imitates Vasilyev's static, motionless style, expanding it even farther through interminable pauses and the barely audible muttering of the actors. Invariably, even the most hostile spectator at one of these shows will admit that the Vasilyev pupils are not bereft of interesting ideas, but even the most die-hard fan will surely be caught yawning before the evening is over.

It is too early to count out the value of Vasilyev's work at the School of Dramatic Art if for no other reason than talent should never be counted out. On the other hand, the trends marking the last eight years are undeniable. Since opening his school with a ready student production that toured the world (*Six Characters*), Vasilyev has not created a single finished production in Moscow. The vast majority of directors he has turned out have been ineffectual due to their inability to break his grip on their imagination. His sporadic showings of scenes, excerpts, public rehearsals and the like, clearly indicate that he misses contact with seasoned actors and is not able to raise inexperienced actors to a

level that would correspond to his own. Unlike a true teacher, who helps students find their own keys to self-expression, Vasilyev appears able only to impose his will on others.

More than anything, Mari Töröcsik's marvelous performance in *Uncle's Dream* left one wondering what Vasilyev might be capable of if he once again had access to Albert Filozov, Alexei Petrenko, Vasily Bochkaryov, Yelizaveta Nikishchikhina, Natalya Andreichenko and the other splendid actors who were once his partners in creating some of Moscow's best productions of the 1970s and 1980s.

(*Summer 1995, Slavic and East European Performance*)

The Simpleton, Laboratory Theater

Sergei Kokovkin wrote his first play, *The Simpleton*, when the Kremlin was sending an onslaught of tanks and troops to subdue some pesky renegades. That action, which caused a lot of hand-wringing, but no coherent response from the world at large, was greeted locally with nothing more than a ripple of dissent followed by silent concurrence.

No, it was not December 1994 as the Chechnya campaign was beginning; it was 1968 when Soviet tanks were rolling into Prague.

And that is why this fine play has only now come to light. Twenty-seven years ago Kokovkin showed it to one of the Soviet Union's leading playwrights, who said something like, "This is a great play. Put it in your desk drawer and leave it there."

That's what Kokovkin did, continuing on with his acting career before once again succumbing to the impulse to write. Since the 1970s, he has penned several plays that have been staged by well-known directors ranging in style from Kama Ginkas to Roman Viktyuk.

But as contemporary life has increasingly revealed an underbelly streaked with the same kind of corruption, lies, fear and silence that has frequently pervaded the Russian experience, Kokovkin felt the time to stage *The Simpleton* had come. Again.

So it is that the play has finally made its bow at the small Laboratory Theater under the author's own direction.

It is an allegory about those who—believing fully in their independence—enthusiastically do what they are told; seldom question orders; and, if they do have doubts, either reject them or find they are utterly incapable of exerting their own will.

Such a state of affairs is entirely natural for the world these people inhabit, for they are actors in a theater. In fact, in this world, the more obedient you are, the more perfectly you carry out commands, and the more effectively you transform into another being, the better respected you are.

This is no mere variation on Shakespeare's claim that "all the world's a stage." Deceptively merry in the circus-like atmosphere and puppet-show ambiance of Irina Balashevich's set and costumes, it is a constricted, finite and, ultimately, sinister universe.

The Director (Vladimir Shevyakov) hands out roles as if he could do otherwise if he wanted. The Leading Lady (Natalya Kislitsyna), the Heroine (Olesya Potashinskaya), the Raisonneur (Alexander Mazurenko) and the Stand-In (Valery Zadonsky) all play their parts as if they had the power to play others. Impersonating a daring rebel, the Simpleton (Sergei Nazimov) finds he cannot rebel against his role.

They are the victims who, in their impotence, perpetrate the evil of their world. And they are carefully manipulated by the diabolical Fop (Boris Tokarev), who coerces the Simpleton into setting the theater afire, and the brutal Fireman (Andrei Starodumov), who sets in motion a trial that sentences the Heroine to death.

The absurdity and the malevolence of the trial scenes clearly capture the play's essence. The Fireman, perhaps the figure most removed from the business of theater in any playhouse, seizes control of everyone with the crack of a whip and a slogan declaring that "art demands sacrifices." But even more shocking is what happens when he apparently dies in a fall from a ladder: The actors refuse to stop the trial, although they know there is no reason to continue.

Eventually, the Simpleton makes one last effort to break free. But, trapped in a mask he cannot remove, and unsure that his words are even his own, he has no recourse but to lament bitterly that he is "a dead man among the dead."

The Simpleton is a solid, convincing performance of a remarkable play whose grim and highly theatrical vision has acquired the distinctive glow of timelessness in the quarter century since it was written.

(*March 1995*)

No One Writes to the Colonel, Stanislavsky Drama Theater

It happens. The team whose last show was a runaway hit gets together for a new one and expectations run high. There are problems and delays set in. Anticipation builds. Then the show opens and you wonder whether it isn't a new version of *The Emperor's New Clothes.*

No, this time, at least, the show at the Stanislavsky Drama Theater is *No One Writes to the Colonel,* based on the novella by Gabriel Garíca Márquez. It stars Pyotr Mamonov, the ex-rock star who was spectacular in *Bald/Brunet* a few years ago. It features Denis Burgazliev and Lyudmila Lushina, Mamonov's partners in *Brunet,* a show that still plays to packed houses at the Stanislavsky. And while he has been demoted to Mamonov's "co-author" of the production, it also boasts the participation of director Oleg Babitsky, whose guidance was crucial to the success of *Brunet.*

It would be easy to say that *Colonel* flopped because of the expectations. It would also be untrue. The real culprit is a tangible sense of misplaced hubris on Mamonov's part and an astonishing lack of focus both in Viktor Slavkin's dramatization and in the non-existent direction.

Mamonov, whose spastic act as the leader of the legendary pop band Zvuki Mu endeared him to rebellious Soviet youths, has perhaps become too used to being loved for being weird. He used the same persona to excellent effect in *Brunet,* and he uses the same persona—again—to dismal effect in

Colonel. How many times can you wash dishes in the same greasy water?

Drooling and jerking about the stage, Mamonov hogs the spotlight while the rest of the cast are left as props to keep attention on the star. It worked beautifully in *Bald/ Brunet* because Daniil Gink's excellent play was about a strange man trapped into living a staccato life on the off beat. But what does it have to do with Marquez's retired colonel, a mild-mannered man who has been waiting in vain for 15 years to begin receiving his pension?

There is none of Marquez's loping, intoxicating magic realism in this performance that, instead, seems intent on creating a bleached imitation of the tragiclownery of the theater of the absurd. In place of the thoughtfully stubborn, quietly righteous colonel we usually get a nerd or a buffoon.

In García Márquez's story, the colonel's tragedy is amplified by the fact that his son was killed 9 months ago at a cock fight, while the petty town mafia has coerced the grieving father into continuing to raise his dead son's rooster until it is ready for the next fight. Penniless, the colonel and his increasingly intolerant wife are forced to starve in order to feed the rooster.

At the Stanislavsky, García's nuanced constellation of people surrounding the colonel is strictly one-dimensional. Diana Rakhimova, confined to sitting stiffly in one of two positions for the entire show, is a dignified, but impenetrable wife. Burgazliev's Doctor, rather than being the bearer of politically seditious conscience, is a goofy stick man in an aviator's suit. Marquez's shady local thugs emerge here as hoodlums with a Chechen tinge.

The whimsical, eclectic set and costumes are par for the course for designer Pavel Kaplevich. Act I is performed around a monstrous stuffed figure resembling a dinosaur or a snail, while Act II gives us two stark, elevated platforms against a swimming-pool blue background. However, like so much in this show, there is no telling what their purpose is.

In the rare moments that Mamonov drops his geeky facade, he shows flashes of

power. But they invariably fizzle immediately as he rips back into self-indulgent self-celebrations. The result is a self-parody that borders on the embarrassing. Next time, make this man of raw talent work with a director!

(*March 1995*)

The Hussy, Malaya Bronnaya Theater

In what is shaping up as the year of Dostoevsky—at least in quantity of productions if not in quality—the most grandiose enterprise belongs to Sergei Zhenovach.

The director's newest, *The Hussy* at the Malaya Bronnaya Theater, runs nearly four hours but comprises just one-third of a projected trilogy fashioned after Dostoevsky's four-part novel, *The Idiot*. Coming soon are the second and third installments, *The Impoverished Knight* and *Russian Light*.

The Hussy is typical of Zhenovach. It is lengthy, talky and understated. It is an attempt both to conjure the bliss of curling up on the sofa for a long, uninterrupted read, and to recreate life's flow of trivial events which, adding a few unexpected explosions, make an absorbing pattern of interconnected biographies.

That is the theory, at least. The reality is more banal, occasionally resembling an illustrative, television mini-series. But if Zhenovach didn't entirely avoid his frequent nemesis—tedium—he does intrigue us at times. *The Hussy* slightly shifts the focus on some of Dostoevsky's passionate characters, showing them in a more lighthearted vein.

That is especially true of Sergei Taramayev's wonderfully strange and sensitive performance of Prince Myshkin—the "idiot" who has returned to Russia after spending four years abroad for treatment of epilepsy and/or mental problems. One of Dostoevsky's most fascinating portraits, Myshkin is a "near-perfect human" who never dissembles, never suspects evil of others, and sees the essence of people's souls.

Straying from the traditional portrayal of an intense, Christ-like Myshkin, Taramayev plays something of a grinning idiot. More than a little goofy with his tousled hair,

Sergei Taramayev as Myshkin in Sergei Zhenovach's production of *The Hussy*, part one of his trilogy based on Fyodor Dostoevsky's novel, *The Idiot*, at the Malaya Bronnaya Theater, 1995. Photo: Alexander Ivanishin

sparkling eyes and a never-ending smile draped across his face, this Myshkin forms an ideal, if unprecedented, image of Dostoevsky's wide-eyed, childlike hero.

Homeless and penniless, Myshkin reenters Petersburg society by promptly getting mixed up in the scandalous affair involving the haughty beauty, Nastasya Filippovna (Irina Rozanova). This "hussy" is being pushed by her stable of admirers to marry the lowly Ganya (Sergei Perelygin), while also being pursued relentlessly by the wild Rogozhin (Sergei Kachanov).

Myshkin first hears of Nastasya from Rogozhin on the train ride home, learning more about her at the Yepanchin home, where he comes to recommend himself to the lady of the house, a distant relative. He finally meets the "hussy" herself at the home of Ganya's parents, where she makes a flamboyant appearance, and later he almost becomes her fiancé for a brief, heady moment during her shocking birthday party.

Only the lazy have not accused Dostoevsky of crafting overwrought melodramas, so it is not surprising that Zhenovach succeeds best when exploring personalities instead of plot.

Perelygin's calculating Ganya quietly reveals an unexpected depth, while Lev Durov's performance of Ivolgin, Ganya's half-broken, half-senile father, is a tragicomic triumph. Equally impressive is Sergei Batalov as Ferdyshchenko, everyone's laughingstock whose deep-seated sense of honesty is satisfied by his ready admissions of dishonesty.

But too often this production drifts aimlessly. Muted by the director's insistence on including what appears to be every word of Dostoevsky's dialogue, it is also unable to define clearly the character of Nastasya Filippovna.

Rozanova is seldom the willful, misunderstood figure from the novel, rather seeming a mean, petty tease. Large, imposing and with an impenetrable, marble beauty, she far more resembles Hélène from Tolstoy's *War and Peace* than one of Dostoevsky's "infernal" women. Her biggest scene—when she coarsely rejects Ganya, is humbled by Myshkin's marriage proposal and then runs off with Rogozhin—is so lacking in drama, it does little more than guide the narrative to its conclusion.

Yury Galperin's multi-layered set, featuring a moveable train coupe on the forestage and several views of Petersburg interiors that are revealed or transformed through the use of flowing, velvet curtains, is efficient and beautiful.

Ultimately, Sergei Taramayev's fine performance puts an interesting twist on *The Idiot*, although *The Hussy* remains too listless to capture the real Dostoevsky.

(*March 1995*)

Summer Folk, **Stanislavsky Drama Theater;** *The Barbarians*, **Vakhtangov Theater; and** *The Final Ones*, **Tabakov Theater**

Maxim Gorky was the dean of Soviet literature. Labeled in 1901 by Lenin's newspaper, *The Spark*, as a "writer of the protesting mass," he was earmarked by Bolshevik ideologues to become the prototype of the communist writer, a figure supposedly combining Leo Tolstoy's sweep and Anton Chekhov's insight.

A friend of Chekhov, Gorky was also his epigone, churning out upwards of 20 plays that brashly copied the great writer's structures, but utterly lacked their extraordinary sensitivity. Many were called masterpieces, while most deservedly disappeared from repertories by the end of the 1980s. But this season, coinciding with Russia's most difficult year for reform since the advent of perestroika, has seen an abrupt surge of interest in Gorky's drama.

It began in early winter with the Stanislavsky Theater's *Summer Folk*, and has now continued with *The Barbarians* at the Vakhtangov Theater and *The Final Ones*

at the Tabakov Theater. Ready to join the pack in April is *The Enemies* by the Commonwealth of Taganka Actors.

What seems to have happened is that—like many others ranging the country's social spectrum—some of the directors whose sensibilities were formed within the Soviet aesthetic, have decided to go back to the formulas they know best. Even in the grayest years of stagnation, Gorky's turbulent characters provided a safe outlet through which to vent dissatisfaction. And now that discontent with everything from the president to the price of baloney has reached new heights, Gorky has come in handy again.

That is clearest at the Vakhtangov and Tabakov Theaters. Arkady Kats's production of *The Barbarians*, an exploration of jaded morals among members of the pre-revolutionary intelligentsia, repeatedly trots out those trusty lines that are guaranteed to get a murmur from the audience. Whether it is a clammy brute's claim that "people are getting more petty, and crooks are getting more powerful," or an old drunk's threat that, "You can't destroy me! I am indestructible!" it all sounds like something from a dusty quote book.

Adolph Shapiro's version of *The Final Ones* is no different. Once again Gorky-the-teacher admonishes us with impassioned speeches and maxims about human nature that are stuck in characters' mouths like cigars between the lips of a dime-store Indian. The grim story tells of an aristocratic family in tsarist times divided by cruelty, lack of love, lies and political obscurantism. Acted with exhausting overkill, the characters are never real people, but merely examples or signs to be deciphered.

Only Vitaly Lanskoi's treatment of *Summer Folk* attempts to reassess Gorky rather than simply play him by the book. Portraying another doomed cluster of family and friends from the prerevolutionary intelligentsia, this is the best Chekhov copy of the three plays now running. Its people fall in love, argue and philosophize, never quite realizing that a social cataclysm is set to sweep them away.

If Lanskoi couldn't make a mediocre play good, he at least washed it with an affection that is not typical of Gorky. Aside from some occasional bathetic pity for oppressed young girls, the writer seldom got closer to his people than a jarring, brotherly slap on the back.

The generation gap in Moscow theater, reflected in the Gorky revival, is best exemplified by developments at the Tabakov Theater. It began the season with the spectacular, innovative *Death-Defying Act*, the product of a young author, Oleg Antonov, a young director, Vladimir Mashkov, and a young cast. In *The Final Ones*, Shapiro's heavy direction and the plodding performances of his well-known actors, Oleg Tabakov, Olga Yakovleva and Yevgeny Kindinov, all point back to a well-trodden road.

(*March 1995*)

Krechinsky's Wedding, Sarkisov Theater Group; and *Foma Opiskin*, Mossoviet Theater

Moscow's theatrical excursion through the past to glimpse the dark side of the present continues apace. And as time goes on, some of the views are getting increasingly grotesque and oppressive.

This time the spotlight falls on two works from the 1850s—Alexander Sukhovo-Kobylin's play, *Krechinsky's Wedding*, and Fyodor Dostoevsky's novella, *The Village of Stepanchikovo*. Both were written under the influence of the comic genius of Nikolai Gogol, and both are scathing satires of Russian-style cheats, frauds and boors.

The intent of the Sarkisov Theater Group is to present *Krechinsky* as an exorbitant burlesque of familiar types. Meanwhile, the Mossoviet Theater plays *Stepanchikovo*, re-titled *Foma Opiskin* after the lead character, as a grinding portrayal of insidious evil.

Valery Sarkisov's production of *Krechinsky* is acted in a room of the Stanislavsky Memorial Museum, essentially using the existing surroundings as decoration. The extravagant, flowing costumes in flowers, paisleys and stripes, by Yelena Stankeeva and Alexei Kamyshov, extract the action from the 19th century without fixing it specifically in the 20th.

Krechinsky (Valery Yaryomenko) is a card sharp who needs money to pay old debts and fund new ones. Muromsky (Alexander Ilyin) is a country squire with a big estate and a marriageable daughter, Lidochka (Oksana Samokhvalova). When they come together under the not-so-quiet guidance of Lidochka's fashion-mongering Aunt Atuyeva (Irina Lukovskaya), it is a recipe for disaster.

Yaryomenko's Krechinsky is vain and coldly diabolical, while his sidekick Rasplyuyev (Vladimir Steklov) is the typical picture of the banality of evil—lazy, greedy and morally void. Ilyin's Muromsky, a short-tempered bluster with a bark much worse than his bite, is no match for their scheming.

But this show is uneven to the point of being rocky. Despite well-defined performances from Ilyin and Steklov, most everyone else seems preoccupied with admiring their own extravagant poses and expressions. Sarkisov created a few nice moments by standing his actors at a lectern to deliver monologues as introspective confessionals, but, ultimately, *Krechinsky's Wedding* founders in a fusillade of eccentricity.

In *Foma Opiskin* at the Mossoviet, director Pavel Khomsky did not only churn out another in that venue's growing line of elaborate costume dramas. He also plunged us headlong into a simmering cauldron of perfidy and feebleness. What he couldn't do was keep the laughter in Dostoevsky's darkly comic novella from slipping into a derisive and off-putting smirk.

Foma Opiskin (Sergei Yursky) is a rootless man who seizes control of an entire household through high-minded speeches and clever psychological manipulation. Surrounded by fools, cowards and people who just don't care, he faces few obstacles in crushing his friend, Rostanev (Yevgeny Steblov), in whose house he lives as a guest, and whose life he has turned into hell.

Yursky, the renowned actor and director who has just celebrated his 60th birthday, pours everything he's got into his role. But for all the energy, and all the agility he shows in navigating the humongous, 20-foot sofa that is the centerpiece of Enar Stenberg's set, Yursky may have overdone it. His heavily distorted speech, overstated, angular movements, and pop-eyed stares are used so relentlessly that at times they become a source of irritation.

Steblov's cringing and anemic Rostanev, like most of the professionally executed performances in the show, drives so deeply into caricature and exaggeration, that there is little room left for humor.

Opiskin takes such delight in every rogue's wicked pass and every fool's stupid move, that there is something almost pathological in it. Sure, the point was to vividly portray depravity. But this show wallows in it so gleefully, at times it even seems to savor it perversely.

(March 1995)

The Metamorphosis, **Satirikon Theater and the Meyerhold Center**

Just over a year ago Valery Fokin created one of last season's outstanding productions, *A Hotel Room in the Town of N*. A free adaptation of Nikolai Gogol's novel, *Dead Souls*, it was performed inside a specially-constructed box at the Manezh Exhibition Hall.

Now, at the Satirikon Theater and with a different cast, Fokin has applied the same total environment ideas to Franz Kafka's story, "The Metamorphosis."

Once again, as though trekking the winding stairs to a ride at Disneyland, spectators pass into a fascinating, artificial world. Again, strange, suggestive music by Alexander Bakshi wafts in from different angles as though it were hanging in the air and drifting on the wind. And, as in *Hotel Room*, the spoken word has been reduced to a role subordinate to expressions, sounds and movement. Displaying rich imagination and liberating insight, these are the flourishes on the director's personal artistic signature.

The Metamorphosis tells the harrowing tale of Gregor Samsa, a conscientious employee, obedient son and loving brother. We first see him bidding good-night to his family and meticulously packing his bag for an early departure on a business trip the next day. But the mundane flow of his life is horrifically interrupted in the morning: When he awakes, he finds he has turned into an insect.

Few sights this season will be as chilling and as theatrically exhilarating as that of Konstantin Raikin's Gregor slowly coming to at daybreak on his back in his hard, narrow little bed.

Preceded by a long, sleepful pause that is so deathly silent you can hear the air hum, the scene slowly begins unfolding as Gregor vaguely notices that both his arms and legs are cocked stiffly in the air. Raikin, at close range before every one of the 65 spectators, brilliantly runs the gamut of possible emotions several times—from confusion and alarm, to comic relief that it is all a dream, to the unspeakable horror that the nightmare is a reality. It all finally comes home to him when he hears in terror that his voice has been replaced by a guttural ticking sound.

The subsequent story, in as much as there is one, follows the reactions of Gregor's family, and the states of mind into which Gregor himself is thrown. Once over the initial shock of his transformation, he even begins delighting in simple pleasures and coping with the peculiarities of his new life.

But such aspects of normalcy cannot last for long. Gregor's domineering father (Fyodor Dobronravov) chases him away by throwing apples at him, while his crushed mother (Marina Ivanova) makes one weak effort to accept her son's new form before giving in to disgust and terror. The family maid (Anna Yakunina) teases him sexually only in order to humiliate him more.

Gregor's beloved, violin-playing sister, as performed by the graceful Natalia Vdovina, tries somewhat harder to reconcile herself to what has happened. But when Gregor ruins her music recital by crawling into the living room and frightening off the invited guests, she cruelly rejects him too, denying him his final source of familial love, and shattering his last link to life.

The multi-planed environment designed by Vyacheslav Koleichuk functions superbly as a realistic setting that instantly takes on the attributes of an imagined space by lowering the floor to turn Gregor's room into a dungeon-like pit, or shifting the lighting on the family's living room which we only see through a sheer screen.

A scene from Valery Fokin's dramatization of Franz Kafka's "The Metamorphosis" for the Meyerhold Center and the Satirikon Theater, 1995. Photo: Alexander Ivanishin

At times there is a sense that *The Metamorphosis* is so focused on minute, suggestive detail that its spectacular facade lacks an inner ballast. But such suspicions are fleeting. Fokin, together with his production team and the splendid Konstantin Raikin, have come in with another triumph.

(*April 1995*)

Love in the Crimea, Chekhov Art Theater

There may not be a more significant new play produced in Moscow this season than *Love in the Crimea* at the Chekhov Art Theater.

Written by the great contemporary Polish playwright, Slawomir Mrozek, *Crimea* caused a scandal after its world premiere in Poland a year ago. Its French premiere last November was greeted with tremendous interest, and now it is Moscow's turn.

The local show will undoubtedly evoke responses similar to those in both Poland and France. At times brilliant, at times bleakly obscure, and at times irritatingly silly, it will get plenty of attention one way or the other.

The play examines three eras of Russian life in three acts. The first observes a constellation of friends and lovers at a Crimean resort in 1910. The second picks them up in the late 1920s as they, at least superficially, are busy building socialism. The final act catches them in the early 1990s, when thugs and American mass culture have all but disfigured the old resort town. Over the years, some characters age, others do not.

Mrozek's most controversial move was to handcuff directors by appending to his work ten interdictions forbidding changes in the text, design, music and structure of the play.

In Roman Kozak's production, it is easy to distribute the praise where things work well. Specifically, the first act is a stunning, atmospheric deconstruction of the mores of the Russian intelligentsia and of Chekhovian drama.

Set in designer Valery Levental's gorgeous, art nouveau sanitarium overlooking the Black Sea, and given a spectacular inner sheen by lighting designer Damir Ismagilov, the performance is buoyed by brilliant ensemble acting and Kozak's filigreed direction. Intellectually comical, leisurely rambling and deeply heartfelt, it is equally reverential to and skeptical of the Russian penchant for talk and philosophy.

Mrozek delights in teasing us with "Chekhov jokes," and Kozak proves a master at giving them form. Characters repeatedly become trapped in philosophical ruminations that they can't escape; a shuffling babushka interminably lugs around a samovar; a gun hanging on the wall can't help but be fired; and offstage, the three Prozorov sisters try to leave for Moscow but can't quite do it. Later, a telegram comes from Lopakhin informing that a cherry orchard is up for sale.

Center stage is Alexander Feklistov's sweeping, aching performance of the mysterious Ivan Zakhedrinsky. Ironical, occasionally cutting and always adrift in the world, he loves the young Tatyana (Diana Korzun) who is grateful for his affection, but nothing more. His rival is the perennially disillusioned intellectual, Pyotr, who, in Pavel Belozerov's probing interpretation, takes on the harsh angles of a loving caricature.

Impossible to summarize accurately, the complex, suggestive first act signals that a masterpiece is in the making. But it is a false sign.

The second act is a shallow parody of Soviet clichés. Zakhedrinsky is now a bumbling deputy minister of culture, and his beloved, elusive Tatyana is his typist. Other characters have become either an excursion guide, a janitor, or a big-time bureaucrat. There are murky attempts to explore Zakhedrinsky's desires and jealousy in dream scenes that quote from Shakespeare's Midsummer Night's Dream and Othello, while Lenin, who barged into the first act

prematurely, is now a paper-maché statue propped against a phonograph.

The crass final act gets triter yet. Zakhedrinsky, now a former political prisoner, returns to find the once-idyllic resort run by an old camp-mate who exports prostitutes to the West. An enormous, floating figure of Catherine the Great bares her breasts, and an American flag hangs from a Russian Orthodox church.

Rather than giving us a new perspective on the dilemmas of these complex times, both acts merely pick on the familiar for easy laughs.

It is hard to say whether the author or the director bears the prime responsibility for the show's abrupt degeneration. But whatever the case, along with the excellent cast, they both can share the plaudits for the scintillating first act.

(April 1995)

Immersion, Bogis Agency

When the Bogis Agency independent production company first appeared on Moscow marquees two years ago it immediately served notice that its credo would be quality. Its production of *Nijinsky* was one of that season's best shows, and the following year it came in with another big winner called *Bashmachkin*. Both shows raked in prizes, rave reviews and full houses.

Bogis's newest show will not match its predecessors in any of those categories. *Immersion*, written by first-time playwright Natalya Boiko, is too modest theatrically and too personal to inspire large numbers. Furthermore, Irina Borodulina's direction (she also plays the female part in this two-actor show) is self-effacing to a fault.

But for all of that, *Immersion* is an admirable piece of work, mainly because of its makers' tangible sense of sincerity and commitment. They have the energy and undisciplined talent of youth, and that alone makes them interesting.

The show's three scenes run just over an hour, touching briefly and obscurely on a few moments in the uneasy relationship of a young woman and man. Unable to stay together, they are equally incapable of making a break. Often—especially in the first scene with its voices coming out of the ether, its fragmented memories and its image of the young man as a bear—the setting appears to be the interior of one of the young woman's dreams.

Most important, as already tipped off in the title, *Immersion* is a journey into its heroine's unguarded thoughts.

Borodulina nicely captures the feel of a young woman wandering in the blank spaces between hope and resignation. Wearing a charming smile and speaking in her uplifting, half-laughing voice, the actress in her best moments also saves room for a nagging sense of doubt. We see in her the consequences of being simultaneously tugged in different directions: She is attracted by happiness, wanting to believe in it, but she does not really believe it is possible, nor does she even know what it is.

We never quite learn who this woman is. We know that she cherishes a toy train she has kept from childhood; we know she corresponded with a man she did not see once for ten years; we know she is writing a tragic novel about skindivers; and we know she is 30 years old, although she says she's just 27. But none of that really brings us any closer to understanding her.

Also at a loss to make sense of her is her lanky boyfriend. As played by Dmitry Pavlenko, he is sensitive and gentle at heart, if also an impostor. He claims in the first scene to be a harmless bear, while we learn in the second that he is an ex-con. After his wife left him, he started sneaking peaks at the letters one of his neighbors kept receiving from a far-off admirer, and that is how he fell in love with the mysterious woman.

Naturally, nothing is that straightforward in this story that largely consists of unspoken thoughts and unfinished conversations. And since the performance lacks a sense of dynamic movement or rhythm which might have made things more coherent, it has a tendency to drift aimlessly, relying solely on charm to keep the audience's attention.

Designer Viktor Arkhipov provided an effective black box set with a network of elastic strings stretching across the floor. They represent both the webs in which the pair becomes entangled, and, with the help of Sergei Skornetsky's bright cross-lighting, the river in which they eventually immerse themselves to end their troubles.

Immersion is primarily attractive for its honesty and freshness. That refers not only to Boiko's sketchy but intriguing play, and the unassuming performances by Borodulina and Pavlenko. It also includes the Bogis Agency itself, which has shown again that a key component of quality is having the courage to take risks.

(April 1995)

The Inspector General, Pushkin Drama Theater

From start to finish, the Pushkin Theater's production of *The Inspector General* is filled with unexpected twists. Characters are boldly reinterpreted, scenes are reshuffled and the action has been moved from a room in the house of the town mayor to the yard outside his estate.

Even the fabled dumb scene in the finale, with all the characters caught in a frozen pose of fear, is taken out of the show itself and moved to the curtain calls.

But despite having two powerful actors in the leading parts of the Mayor and Khlestakov—the Petersburg fop who is mistaken for an inspector general—the cast at large is not up to the task of reinventing Nikolai Gogol's classic comedy of corruption, opportunism and stupidity. This show ultimately leaves you suspecting that the director's innovations sounded best when they were still on the drawing board.

Director Yury Yeryomin shied from leaping directly into the play's famous opening salvo when the Mayor announces to the assembled civic leaders the "unpleasant news" that an inspector general is headed their way. Instead, he begins the action with the third-act scene of the Mayor's wife and daughter bickering over beauty secrets, and only later casually returns to the traditional opener as the Mayor saunters in wearing a self-satisfied grin.

It is a radical change that slows the play's rhythm considerably, and signals immediately that there are plenty more surprises to come.

Alexander Porokhovshchikov in Nikolai Gogol's *The Inspector General* at the Pushkin Drama Theater, directed by Yury Yeryomin, 1995. Photo: Mikhail Guterman

Despite the colorless mother–daughter spat, the alterations seem well taken at first. That is so thanks entirely to Alexander Porokhovshchikov's expansive, knowing and razor-sharp rendition of the Mayor.

Every bit the thug-with-a-heart, the barrel-chested actor easily and even benevolently reigns over the rascals who run the town's key institutions and make a good living at it. He is a supremely self-confident man who knows exactly how one keeps a grip on money and power, has no qualms about doing it, and hasn't the vaguest fear that anyone else could possibly outwit him.

But outwitted he will be, and if that weren't galling enough, the agent of his downfall will be the penniless, petty clerk Khlestakov. He simply lets the Mayor and his men self-destruct, before proposing marriage to the Mayor's impassive daughter and skipping out of town.

In the appearance of Khlestakov, Yeryomin once again took major liberties. Rather than wait for Gogol's introduction of him in the second act, the director inserted flashes from that act into the Mayor's opening scene, so that the key moments of the first and second acts unfold simultaneously, and create a kind of mystical bond between the two principals.

An even bolder shift is Viktor Gvozditsky's devilish, aggressively irrational interpretation of Khlestakov. But that is where the limitations of this unorthodox production begin to surface.

An actor of great power and range, Gvozditsky is most effective when bottling up his explosive nature. His interpretation of Khlestakov, however, is punctuated by a string of emotional outbursts bordering on the hysterical. Like a shrill note held too long, it becomes monotonous and even off-putting.

The actor was not helped by Yeryomin, whose reading of Khlestakov as a satanic figure trivialized the complexity both of the character as well as of the predicament he puts everyone into.

Gvozditsky's strained pungency is set off even more by the utter blandness of the rest of the townsfolk. Only Sergei Agapitov shows personality in his lively performance of the bumbling landowner Dobchinsky.

Tatyana Glebova provided attractive costumes mixing classical reserve and an underlying sense of humor, while Mart Kitayev designed the unremarkable set depicting the Mayor's courtyard.

For all of its interesting ideas, this *Inspector General* is quite rough and disjointed. Were it not for Porokhovshchikov's commanding presence at the center, it likely would fall apart altogether.

(April 1995)

The School for Wives, Taganka Theater; and *The Imaginary Invalid*, Yermolova International Theater Center

Over the last few seasons a tiny number of writers has accounted for an inordinately large number of the productions done on local stages. Dostoevsky, Gogol, Ostrovsky and Chekhov have consistently led the Russian parade. Among foreign writers, the names of Luigi Pirandello, Harold Pinter and especially Tennessee Williams have cropped up time and again.

But maybe the most popular of all has been Molière. Now, two more versions of the Frenchman's comedies indicate there is no danger of his dropping out of vogue soon.

The Taganka Theater's *The School for Wives*—Moscow's third rendition in two years—is a wild romp that aims for fun and hits it. Meanwhile, the Yermolova International Theater Center produced an intriguingly stark, modern approach to *The Imaginary Invalid*.

At the Taganka, director Alexei Kiryushchenko pulled off the theatrical equivalent of slipping a ship in a bottle. The actors, performing a shortened text in rapid-fire style, play on a stage barely big enough

to hold them and the only notable piece of decoration—a lacy, pink structure that looks as much like a woman's armoire as the facade of a country house.

It is a breathless leap into hyper-theatricality, with the players ecstatically laughing too hard, weeping too loud, and opportunely bursting into song. Physical humor, from the cornball to the bawdy, and moments of inspired silliness, such as everything coming to an abrupt halt for a character to leisurely chase a butterfly across the stage, make for non-stop crazy action.

Kiryushchenko boldly attacked the story of a virile youth acing out a middle-aged man for a girl's attentions, retaining its satire of human follies, but making a delirious celebration of "provincial" theatrical shenanigans his main focus.

As Arnolphe, the pot-bellied *gentilhomme* out to marry his ward Agnès, Alexander Karpov is a bundle of jealous nerves, while the grinning Andrei Butin, who is constantly straightening the disobedient wig on his head, plays his rival Horace with as much endearing, thick-headed simplicity as arrogance.

Matching the uniformly energetic cast are Oleg Stepchenko's dazzling costumes, as busy as bee-hives with bows, buttons, frills and folds everywhere. The masterpiece is Agnès's dress, looking every bit a lampshade cut from a bed spread.

In *The Imaginary Invalid*, director Alexei Levinsky achieved a very different kind of humor, relying on his familiar style that might be called existential clownery. Levinsky loves a good joke as well as anyone, but he invariably couches it in unconventional surroundings.

Here he was aided by designer Viktor Arkhipov, whose essentially empty set creates its bracing atmosphere by the backdrop which a diagonal streak splits into black and white halves.

The performance begins with the actors doing tap-dance exercises—playing on Molière's designation of his play as a "comedy-ballet"—and bits of jazz and hip-hop subsequently crop up frequently. There are silent movie-like chase scenes, graceful pantomimes, slow-motion games of catch, and all the while the dialogue is spoken in markedly contemporary intonations.

Everything takes its cue from Sergei Dreiden, a splendid St. Petersburg actor brought in to play Argan, the hypochondriac who would marry his favorite daughter to a medical apprentice in order to have his own doctor in the family. Phlegmatic and stubborn, Dreiden's anti-hero is actually a man more in sync with his own world than appears. In fact, it is the world around him that is bad for his health.

Providing crystal-clear counterpoint is Tatyana Rudina as Toinette, Argan's eccentric servant. Brash, wily and decisive, she sees to it that the fragile Angelique (Natalya Seliverstova) escapes the rigged marriage and is given to her goofy, but beloved Cléante (Dmitry Pavlenko).

Even if the second act of *Invalid* flags as it gets too wrapped up in curiosities, this outing remains one of note.

(*May 1995*)

Your Sister and Captive, Russian Army Theater

In the wake of the Russian Army Theater's new production of *Your Sister and Captive*, a play by the St. Petersburg playwright Lyudmila Razumovskaya examining the personalities of Mary Stuart and Queen Elizabeth I, conversations about the moribund state of contemporary drama are bound to heat up again. Most of them will miss the point.

In truth, this show, staged by Alexander Burdonsky and starring two of the Army Theater's most popular actresses, borders on the intolerable. It is maddeningly superficial, unforgivably pompous and painfully long.

Little of that has anything to do with Razumovskaya's play. She wrote an intense chamber piece that sheds a penetrating, modern light on two of the most intriguing figures in the history books. For her, Mary and Elizabeth are not so much queens as types of women.

Mary, Queen of Scots is impulsive, emotional and irrational. Her love is passionate, her jealousy furious, and her forgiveness generous. She is a risk-taker, ruled and doomed by the whims of her desires. Elizabeth is infinitely more cautious, always keeping herself in check so as not to lose her grip on England.

Diametrically opposed in character, the two women who address each other in letters as "your sister and captive," are presented by Razumovskaya in an appropriately schematic manner.

Act I encompasses the young Mary's disastrous affair with the earl of Bothwell leading to the murder of her second husband, Henry Darnley, while Act II observes Elizabeth after Mary has been locked away, but her threat to the English throne has not subsided. The short third act unites the two on that day when Elizabeth reluctantly orders Mary to be beheaded.

Razumovskaya created a cruel world in which some men relish the brutal roles of rapists, murderers and usurpers, while others are weak and ineffectual, if occasionally sincere. That, however, is less the author's conviction, than it is her pointed observation. In any case, as is common in her plays, the question of survival for women is always a matter of making harsh, abhorrent decisions, and often one of plain self-denial.

Burdonsky, whose previous outing was an anemic, pseudo-musical copy of *Evita* called *The Diamond Orchid*, failed to illuminate the play's complex characters. He staged a showy historical chronicle replete with pantomimic dances buffering each of the scenes. We almost never see the "whys" of the dueling sisters' behavior, being blinded, rather, by a trite facade of "whats" and "hows."

Alla Kozhenkova's stereotypical imperial costumes, and her set consisting of a forest of shiny, cold black columns that suggest the halls of a castle, also orient the performance to appearances rather than substance.

Alina Pokrovskaya, as Mary Stuart, was handed the most difficult and thankless task of all. For the two hours of the first act, she must play a woman perhaps half her age, often enough engaging in sexual acrobatics that simply do not suit her. It is the kind of gross miscasting that can only evoke empathy for the actress and raise serious questions about the director's competence.

Pokrovskaya works diligently, but more often than not she replaces impetuosity and tragedy with hysteria, and confuses changeability with inconstancy.

Lyudmila Kasatkina's Elizabeth is mannered and slow to warm up in a way that suggests a kinship with the calculating queen. Whether teasing, surreptitiously interrogating or preparing to execute her young lovers, she recognizably illustrates what we expect from her. But the actress also displays a certain coldness and penchant for striking poses that keep her from fully revealing what makes her heroine tick.

Your Sister and Captive is another example of good modern material going to waste in the hands of a director who really doesn't know what to do with it.

(*May 1995*)

The Freeloader, Yermolova Theater

The Freeloader at the Yermolova Theater begins with the crystalline tinkling of a high-pitched bell. The small, curtainless stage depicts the exquisitely detailed and richly furnished drawing room of a provincial, 19th-century Russian estate. Tiny, carefully wrought figurines stand on small, elegant tables, and the walls are decorated with miniature landscapes.

Were it not for the forbidding influence of the so-called fourth wall—that invisible veil separating actors from spectators—you might well be tempted to leave your seat in the hall and cross the homey, inviting stage to find out whom the bell is summoning.

That, of course, is just what Vladimir Andreev was after when he staged this early and largely forgotten play by the great novelist Ivan Turgenev. Aided by designer Vladimir Serebrovsky and an excellent cast, he revived the long-gone life of another era, and plunged us right into the heart of it.

It is an old-fashioned story, and one of the charms of Andreev's version is that it is played as straight as an arrow. Irony and caricature, like fine spices, are used only in slight pinches, so that what we get are highly individualized people and moving situations that may be out-of-date, but are all the more striking for their historical veracity.

Vasily Kuzovkin, the "freeloader," is an impoverished landowner who for years has lived in the home of a now deceased neighbor, waiting in vain for a court battle over his land to be settled. His status had always been something of a domestic jester, but now that Yelena, the young lady of the house, has brought home a new husband, his situation has taken a turn for the worse. In the past he at least had certain ties to the old master, but now he is essentially an unwanted stranger in a stranger's home.

As the old Kuzovkin, Vladimir Zamansky shows an uncanny ability to get under his character's skin, reflecting his humiliation, his sadness, his humor and his dignity. Small in stature, with large, gentle hands and probing eyes, Zamansky is impeccable as the man who has subordinated all of his pride and desires to the necessity of subsisting in the shadow of his life's brightest moment and biggest shame: He is, in fact, the father of Yelena (Vasilisa Pyavko), although almost no one believes him when the secret finally slips out.

That secret, and the complications which arise when it is revealed, are mere levers in the traditional plot. What gives them the power of insight is the way they reveal the inner workings of different personalities.

Viktor Sarakvasha is infuriatingly ruthless as Tropachyov, the superficial and mean-spirited neighbor who delights in humiliating old Kuzovkin for sport. As Pavel Yeletsky, Yelena's self-satisfied groom, Alexei Sheinin works finely in the gray areas floating between muted cruelty and half-hearted kindness, propriety and priggishness. He can't quite condone Tropachyov's pitiless tricks, but he enjoys them too much ever to stop them in time.

Meanwhile, a whole other universe exists in what may have been the production's biggest success of all: the cares and behind-the-scenes world of the servants. Their stifled whispers, doused smiles, rustling dresses and hurried glances add up to a symphony of sights and sounds that make the life in this house endlessly fascinating and touchably real. Especially eye-catching are Yury Kazakov, as the butler who is obsequious to his masters and a boor to his underlings, and

Maria Zhukova, as the sensuous, eternally grinning maid.

Anything but a mere museum piece, *The Freeloader* is a well-turned miniature, a Faberge-egg of a look back at a very different Russia which we may think we know, but which we seldom see in such clear and close detail.

(May 1995)

My Poor Marat, Mossoviet Theater

What is it with plays by the late Alexei Arbuzov these days? The once-fantastically popular Soviet playwright had completely disappeared into oblivion until his *What a Lovely Sight!* was revived with unexpected and resounding success a year ago at the Malaya Bronnaya Theater.

This year it is his 1965 play, *My Poor Marat*, in a strikingly fresh interpretation at the Mossoviet Theater, which has suddenly got people talking enthusiastically.

Marat, Lika and Leonidik are teenagers during the siege of Leningrad. Utterly alone, and thrown together by circumstance, they become fast friends whose relationship deepens and becomes inextricably tangled over the course of the next 20 years. Arbuzov undeniably created a disarmingly ingenuous story, but there is no denying either that his situations and characters still bear that mushy, generic Soviet stamp.

Enter Andrei Zhitinkin, who happily and with a healthy dose of self-irony tabs himself "Moscow's most scandalous director." That surely is overstating it, but Zhitinkin has indeed garnered his share of detractors, in part for brashly fiddling in semi-taboo subjects, but more for churning out some garish spectacles that have had as much substance as cotton candy.

Maybe Zhitinkin has slowly been inching towards that moment when he would finally put it all together, or maybe *My Poor Marat* is an inadvertent detour in an uneven career. Whatever the case, it is a scintillating show that entertains as completely as it reveals the inner workings of three fascinating and highly modern characters.

That's right, modern. The play's action runs from the early 1940s to the early 1960s,

but one of Zhitinkin's several triumphs was to forge a thoroughly contemporary atmosphere without violating the historical fabric of the original. Marat, Lika and Leonidik are recognizably kids of the war generation and adults of the 'sixties generation, but they are presented through a filter with a 1990s sensibility.

Arbuzov wrote about a love triangle in which two men fall in love with a woman who loves one, but marries the other. Zhitinkin complicated things considerably. You'll never find the proof, but hints abound right and left that Marat (Alexander Domogarov) and Leonidik (Andrei Ilyin) are as much in love with each other as with Lika (Larisa Kuznetsova).

Confused glances, lingering embraces, little secrets kept from the inquiring Lika, and Marat's refusal or inability to return Lika's love—all of these moments and more clearly open up the possibility of a homosexual twist to the play. But it is the ambiguity of things which gives the production its emotional and cathartic thrust: The real point is that all of them love each other, and that there is no way of putting labels on their love.

Domogarov and Ilyin turn in wonderfully sensitive performances that capture all the ragged edges of uncertainty, and all the clumsy grace natural to young men trapped by true love.

And then there is Larisa Kuznetsova's incomparable Lika. A Roman candle of energy, excitability and impulsiveness, Kuznetsova also has the range that allows her to flawlessly plumb the depths of a resilient woman who overcomes life's hard knocks by the force of will. Her thrilling, liberating and comic performance tops off the all-around first-rate production.

The costumes and set by Andrei Sharov, at first entirely in varying shades of white, attractively suggest the purity and innocence of the characters and their insular world. Bits of color only begin creeping in later when life's realities also intrude.

My Poor Marat is an ideal example of how to go about finding the new in the old. Arbuzov's play supplied a touching, well-crafted basis, and Zhitinkin yanked it into

the present with a boldly modern interpretation that never abuses its sensitivity.

(*May 1995*)

Scenes from a Marriage, **Theater na Pokrovke**

It took a long time but it finally happened. After several false starts, snags and
cancellations, the Theater na Pokrovke has
opened its new location.

Situated where Pokrovka Street crosses
the Garden Ring, it occupies the first two
stories of an oldish apartment building, the
first floor making a clean, well-lighted foyer,
and the second floor housing dressing rooms
and a performance space that seats about 60.

Ending years of planning and reconstruction, it is a triumph for Sergei Artsibashev,
the venue's artistic director, mastermind and
one of Moscow's most respected directors
of that lost generation hanging precariously
between the twin peaks of "young" and
"well-known."

And even if the new location has its drawbacks, they at least fit the theater's newest
show, Ingmar Bergman's *Scenes From a
Marriage*. While Bergman's characters
struggle with their imploding marriage on
stage, spectators can occasionally catch the
sounds of real married life drifting down
through the thin insulation from the apartment above.

Scenes From a Marriage, written as a
television drama, was a natural choice for
Artsibashev. His deliberately uneventful
stagings have always played with laconic
cinematic technique, his actors being more
apt to flash an icy glare than shout in anger,
or to turn slowly than spin and race across
the stage.

The approach works well when applied to
theater texts because it flies in the face of
theatrical histrionics. You expect one thing
and get another, and in the space between
the two there is a universe of opportunities
for revelation.

The successes in *Marriage* are more modest, although Artsibashev has remained true
to his style.

Juhan (Valery Nenashev) and Marianna
(Yelena Starodub) are the perfect couple; so

ideal, in fact, that a t.v. show did a spot
celebrating their happy life together. The performance begins as the t.v. interview over-
takes the broadcast of a Pavarotti concert on
a television set tucked high into the wall at
center stage, and we watch as the "live"
couple noticeably responds with more mundane candor than they had shown the camera.

Before long, it is the gritty, barroom singing of Tom Waits that sets the tone, undercutting Pavarotti's elegance and hinting
broadly at the untruths of Juhan's and
Marianna's public faces. More suggestions of
trouble ahead come when the couple's impetuous friends Katarina (Natalya Grebyonkina) and Peter (Oleg Pashchenko) break out
in a raw, marital spat as the foursome does
a loping, change-your-partner dance.

Bergman's script is merciless: Emotional
ruin, sexual discontent and moral decay float
carelessly just beneath the surface of civilized
facades. Artsibashev follows the author's
lead and reveals the sordid truth in an unwavering atmosphere of commonplaces and
banalities that are echoed even in Mikhail
Barkhin's purposefully nondescript apartment setting.

But that is where this production loses its
edge. As we careen with the characters from
crisis to crisis—abortion, infidelity, separation, a hostile attempt at reconciliation, divorce, and then finding love again only after
they each remarry and can cheat together on
their new spouses—we begin seeing the distinctive features of a soap opera.

The understated performances too often
bleach out the characters' motivations, leaving only the ragged facts of their relationship
to occupy us. And each time the warbling,
wheezing voice of Tom Waits cuts in again,
you sense that he is closer to the truth than
the actors.

Still, if this production does not show off
Artsibashev's signature at its best, there is no
mistaking its scrawl. He is a director with a
vision and a touch like no one else's in
Moscow, and that alone gives an intrinsic
interest to everything he does. The opening
of the new Theater na Pokrovke adds an
important new address to Moscow's theatrical topography.

(*June 1995*)

Ivanov's Family, **Pushkin Drama Theater**

The Pushkin Drama Theater's new adaptation of Andrei Platonov's story, *Ivanov's Family*, is so strong and moving, it can't help but bring to mind the problems that have plagued this venue for so long.

The Pushkin is often said to be jinxed. It occupies the building that once housed the great Kamerny Theater, founded by Alexander Tairov in 1914, but closed by a Communist Party decree in 1949. Tairov died a year later, a broken man. Some say Tairov's restless, angry spirit won't let his successors work in peace.

Then there's the version that the theater was built on top of a graveyard, a bad place indeed to locate a playhouse.

Whatever the reasons, few would deny that for a troupe and an artistic director with plenty of talent, successful shows are surprisingly rare visitors on the Pushkin's stage. Even when something of interest does turn up, there always seems to be that nagging "but," which brings you back to that jinx again.

That makes the success of *Ivanov's Family* all the more impressive: You wonder, what lengths did its creators go to in order to be this good?

For starters, director Yury Yeryomin turned everything around. Literally. The 60 spectators sit in a shallow semi-circle on the stage itself, looking at the ragged contours of the closed fire wall which blocks off any view of the empty hall behind it. And once the action gets going, the stage often spins slowly to the left or right, providing views of Valery Fomin's set; the modest interior of Ivanov's apartment and the birch woods outside it.

In a brief, incisive prologue, we first see the grizzled Ivanov (Alexander Yermakov) waiting for the train that will take him home after the end of World War II. He runs into Masha (Viktoria Lebedeva), a young family friend, whose freshness intoxicates his war-weary senses. But the encounter ends when he reaches his hometown, and finally,

Alexander Yermakov and Irina Byakova in Yury Yeryomin's production of *Ivanov's Family*, an adaptation of a story by Andrei Platonov. Photo: Mikhail Guterman

tentatively, he approaches the long-awaited reunion with the wife and 2 children he hasn't seen for 4 years.

That is when the dream begins unraveling.

Ivanov is greeted coldly by his young son (Fedya Novitsky) and when his wife Lyuba (Irina Byakova) comes home from work, they throw themselves into a clumsy embrace that says more about fear than passion.

Platonov's story, like an exquisite, fine-line drawing, traces the hopes, the desires, the doubts and the disillusionments that await this attractive, good and lonely couple. And Yeryomin masterfully brought those fragile moments to life. He trained a hungry, intrusive video camera on the characters, catching them in a rarely-interrupted flow of pained, thoughtful close-ups.

No matter which way the revolving stage turns the spectators, the large-screen monitor is always planted between them and the actors. It creates a tensile second reality, a tangible inner world that not only focuses the slow, pause-laden action, but gives it deeper meaning.

Ivanov and his wife struggle as much with their own demons as with each other. He is horrified to learn that, in a moment of despair, Lyuba broke down and had a one-night fling with another man, while Lyuba is appalled at her husband's misplaced intolerance. But the real pain for both is in the rift between the dreams they had of their meeting and the reality of it.

Platonov's "happy" ending of Ivanov aborting his anguished escape when he sees his children running after him, looks terribly trite in the context of this tough, honest production. But by that time, nothing can dampen the triumph wrought by Yeryomin and his first-rate cast.

Ivanov's Family may not be powerful enough to remove a 45-year curse, but it's the best thing; hands down, the Pushkin Theater has put out in five years.

(June 1995)

By the Light of Others' Candles, Stanislavsky Drama Theater

The premiere was still a week away and only a handful of people had gathered at the Stanislavsky Theater for a late morning dress·rehearsal of *By the Light of Others' Candles*, a new play for two actresses by Nadezhda Ptushkina.

Director Vitaly Lanskoi sat front row center in the tiny Zerkalny—or mirrored—hall of the Stanislavsky Theater, washed in weak waves of stuffy air by two small fans flanking him. As the guests filed in, Lanskoi reminded them that what they were about to see was not yet a finished product.

"We're still working here," he said shuffling some papers on a small desk in front of him, "so don't be surprised if I stop things or start shouting."

As it turned out, there was nothing to shout about, unless it was to raise a cheer for the actresses, the playwright and the director himself. The show, which opened on Tuesday this week, is a tough, wonderfully far-fetched, and killingly funny exploration of two diametrically opposed women trapped in an extreme situation. Their only way out is through tragedy.

Alla (Natalya Pavlenkova) is a frivolous, aimless girl of 21 with a heart as pure as it is changeable, and a slightly goofy, sublimely sincere personality that apparently attracts men like honey. Alexandrina (Tatyana Pushkina) is a jaded literary critic who, at age 56, admits she writes books that no one reads, has never loved anyone and knows nothing about sex.

This odd couple came together thanks to Alla's latest flame, a guy she swooningly calls her "guardian angel," but whom we easily recognize by her stories as a thug and a thief. Alla's mom is Alexandrina's housekeeper, so when the critic left for Germany on her latest junket, Alla sneaked into her apartment for a candlelight love tryst using the set of keys she stole from her mother.

But the resourceful boyfriend was after something more tangible than love: He cleaned all the valuables out of Alexandrina's apartment and disappeared.

We pick up the action as Alla is contemplating what to do next, and the critic unexpectedly returns home to find her crawling around the floor holding a pistol her boyfriend left behind. It is the beginning of a

Tatyana Pushkina and Natalya Pavlenkova in Nadezhda Ptushkina's *By the Light of Others' Candles*, directed by Vitaly Lanskoi for the Stanislavsky Drama Theater, 1995. Photo: Mikhail Guterman

most unusual story filled with crime—from robbery and torture to murder—friendship and the devastation of unexpected self-revelation.

Ptushkina masterfully and creatively manipulates the elements of the detective genre, using Alexandrina's daffy interrogations of Alla both as a means to narrating a delightfully convoluted story, and to revealing truths about the two women through spicy girl talk. Her uncanny ear for juicy, comic dialogue makes you wonder whether she doesn't spend most of her time eavesdropping on unguarded conversations in hair salons and bathhouses.

Alla, an unsullied soul, will say anything the critic wants to hear, if only she'll let her go. Alexandrina, seduced by the combination of her own loneliness and her hostage's loose tongue, constantly drives the talk deeper and deeper into dangerous territory. When she herself isn't spouting meaty, cutting phrases about men, women and the inadequacies of both, she is cruelly bent on destroying Alla's joyously unprincipled romanticism.

Tatyana Pushkina's eccentric performance of Alexandrina, with her gruff mannerisms, her rumble-to-a-scream voice and her venomously expressive face, is a sight to behold.

Yelena Kachelayeva provided the simple, but eye-arresting set depicting the chaotic remains of a plundered apartment, while the lighting by Arnold Kaye uses the hall's mirrored walls well.

By the Light of Others' Candles is fresh, bold and funny. That goes equally for Ptushkina's play—one of the best new plays of the season—and for Lanskoi's lively production of it.

(*June 1995*)

Waiting for Hamlet, Taganka Theater

What is going on at the Taganka Theater?

Yury Lyubimov, its renowned founder, only rarely deigns to visit Moscow from his home in Israel. Recently he staged his first new Taganka show in two years—Euripides's *Medea*—but it opened at a festival in Athens and then Lyubimov abruptly canceled four Moscow performances scheduled for June.

But make no mistake. The Taganka is stirring. Nestled among the repertoire of old standards, at least one of which has been running for 20 years, several unfamiliar titles have quietly appeared.

The most recent, an intriguing foray into Shakespeare called *Waiting for Hamlet*, has now joined productions of *The School for Wives* and *Without Columbine*, as well as last season's haunting *I'm Better Off Speaking*.

All were mounted by young members of the troupe or at least young people with ties to the Taganka through the Shchukin Institute, the school which originally spawned the Taganka in 1964. None has anything to do with Lyubimov, except that he has found no reason to exclude them from the Taganka marquee.

Waiting for Hamlet, directed by Alexander Moiseev, is a swift, imaginative gallop through the story about the Danish prince who learns that his father, the king, was killed in a court coup, but is unable to muster an adequate response.

Taking frequent liberties with the play, this production refreshens it rather than overshadowing or obscuring it. With the actors playing in a space teasingly reminiscent of a monastery, and dressed in an eclectic mix of medieval-style costumes and simple modern designs, everything takes on a sleek, abstract and contemporary look.

The men's jeans, jack boots and baggy black sweaters are an obvious nod to Lyubimov's famous 1971 production of *Hamlet* which starred Vladimir Vysotsky in the title role. Meanwhile, like so many of the best shows around town this season, *Waiting for Hamlet* plays to a small audience in an unorthodox setting: the foyer in the building's old wing where the Lyubimov/Vysotsky *Hamlet* was once performed.

Spectators, numbering over 100, sit in a semi-circle facing three sets of stairs, two short inclines leading to the coat racks and one long stairwell leading to the second floor. Every inch of possible acting space is used, including a corridor and fourth set of stairs to the audience's right.

When things commence, there is no need to wait long for Hamlet (the Shakespeare look-alike, Anton Lutsenko). He immediately takes a seat in a corner where he immerses himself in reading a book, oblivious to what is happening around him. The others whip crisply and lightly through the text, occasionally taking over his lines.

Standing on the long stairwell, candles in hand, the usurping King Claudius (Alexei Grabbe) and his new bride Gertrude (Yelena Laskavaya) lead the entire cast minus Hamlet in something like the Lord's Prayer. The text is Hamlet's famous "to-be-or-not-to-be" speech, which is repeated several times throughout the evening, elevating Shakespeare's immortal words to the level of a leitmotif.

The yes-man Polonius (Igor Pekhovich)—now serving Claudius with the same unprincipled goodwill that he presumably showed the last monarch—occasionally leads everyone in lilting songs and circular, spinning dances. It is as if to say, "everything is fine; we have no problems here."

When Lutsenko's Hamlet finally emerges from his reverie, he appears as a soft-spoken intellectual with a quick mind. He is not so much incapable of taking action—the traditional interpretation—as he seems doubtful that there is any point to it. And while this prince sees only too well the treacheries surrounding him, he never succumbs to despair or disillusionment.

Amidst the uniformly strong cast, Yelena Litvinova's memorable Ophelia is a standout. She is never the vague, romantic waif we so often see, but is alert, subtle and intelligent, a woman more than worthy to be Hamlet's match. Litvinova's final scenes border on the brilliant. Her descent into madness is never hysterical or pitiful, but is played with supreme understatement and concrete detail.

Is this *Hamlet*, together with the other new shows at the Taganka, the sign of a moribund theater coming back to life? It's too early to be sure, but there can be no doubt that the hallowed walls of one of the world's most famous theaters are attracting a new generation of talent.

(June 1995)

1995/1996 SEASON

Hoffmann, **Chekhov Art Theater**

Hoffmann, the new production which opened the season at the Chekhov Art Theater, is that rare instance of a modern play reaching the stage. Making it even rarer is that its author, Viktor Rozov, comes from a generation that has virtually disappeared in the 1990s.

Rozov, who turned 82 a month ago, was one of the top five Soviet playwrights in the 1950s and 1960s. In plays such as *Good Luck!*, *In Search of Happiness* and *Alive Forever*, he redefined the youthful Soviet hero and heroine of the immediate post-Stalin years with a more realistic, doubting and humane touch.

Alive Forever, in Rozov's own crystal-clear screen adaptation under the title of *The Cranes Are Flying*, won world-wide fame and a best picture award at Cannes in 1958.

But *Hoffmann*, at least as handled by director Nikolai Skorik, is not going to make anyone nostalgic for the past.

In fact, it is not even a new play in the full sense of the word, but rather a dramatization based on works by E.T.A. Hoffmann, the great German author of fantastic tales, and on a book about Hoffmann by Jan Miestler. It would appear that the primary source was Hoffmann's unfinished novel, *Tom-Cat Murr*, an "autobiography of a cat" that also includes the famous portrait of a composer trapped between the worlds of imagination and reality.

Whatever the case, in performance *Hoffmann* is a listless, disjointed and banal treatment of the torments which are visited on an artist.

Ernst Hoffmann (Andrei Panin) is haunted by his love for the beautiful young Yulia (Irina Apeksimova), to whom he is giving music lessons. Or so it seems. In fact, it is impossible to determine how real his love or their affair really is, since the line separating Hoffmann's life from his literary creations is hopelessly blurred.

Yulia enters his world most often as a figment of his imagination, a character created in his mind. It is Hoffmann's cat (Valery Nikolayev), dressed to the nines in frills and lace, who suggests that his master is in love with the girl while also discussing with him the merits of his latest novella.

Expressing satisfaction with the writer's literary progress, the cat briefly engages Yulia in a seductive dance before she slips away to Hoffmann's own embrace. That image is duplicated in a mirror-image by the cat and a mysterious, second female figure, echoing the play's central theme: the notion that for an artist, the created world is at least as real, if not more so, than "actual" life.

Hoffmann's experiences with his colorless wife (Tatyana Rozova) intertwine with the wild and fantastic goings-on of his imagination. Inflamed with jealousy, he "kills" Yulia and her fiancé, then rudely "intrudes" on their wedding night.

Ultimately, Yulia agrees to receive Hoffmann if he will "give her his reflection." He does, in the form of a doll, but sinks into a state of distraction which is dispelled only when a young neighbor girl "returns" his reflection by giving him a portrait she has painted.

Under Skorik's heavy-handed direction, the action breaks into incoherent episodes and creeps forward at a snail's pace. The actors, usually buried in darkness, speak in whispers which make a mystery of the text to all but those seated in the front rows.

The intent was to create an atmosphere of fantasy and enigma filled with the hushed excitement of desire and imagination. The result is a production that is far more boring than bewitching.

Best of all is the grandiose set designed by Skorik. The tall, angled red tile roofs of an old Germanic town thrust skyward like menacing spikes into the night. But the effective decoration only highlights the failure of this production. Rozov's play is too formulaic and Skorik's treatment of it is too unfocused.

(September 1995)

Medea, Taganka Theater

Yury Lyubimov hasn't exactly had it easy in the 1990s.

His few productions at the Taganka Theater, while bearing the unmistakable Lyubimov stamp, have not had the fire that once made him the Soviet Union's most famous theater director. Now a citizen of Israel, Lyubimov has long been working more in Europe than in Moscow, although his reputation is not what it was when he was deprived of his Soviet citizenship in 1984. In recent years he has staged several productions in Greece.

Then there was the messy divorce with Nikolai Gubenko who, with a rebellious party of actors now calling themselves the Commonwealth of Taganka Actors, won control of over half the real estate at the Taganka.

That battle, with its fallen heroes and behind-the-scenes back-stabbings, was at times worthy of comparison with a Greek tragedy.

Which brings us right to Lyubimov's newest show, Euripides's *Medea*, which opened in Moscow on Tuesday and Wednesday evenings. The local showings follow last May's world premiere in Athens, and the Russian premiere which took place this month during the Taganka's Siberian tour.

Medea tells of a woman who murders her own sons to avenge the husband who abandoned her. It is a tale of passion, plotting and treachery that can't help but cast shadows bearing a resemblance to the Taganka's own internecine strife. The idea of destroying one's own beloved creation out of spite and anger describes the situation at the beleaguered theater as well as Euripides's retelling of the Greek myth.

Lyubimov certainly intended to draw that parallel, just as he intended to echo recent developments in Russian politics.

David Borovsky's set might depict a war zone or at least the remains of one, with its sand-bag trenches and towering back wall of rotting metal. The men all wear camouflage khakis, while all the women except Medea look like travelers in the Holy Land in sand-colored robes.

But Lyubimov, one of the great practitioners of political theater in the 1960s and '70s, did something unusual in *Medea*. He drew his comparisons and then moved on, creating a breathtaking human portrait. You can catch or miss his metaphors about betrayal and revenge, but you cannot ignore his searing, devastating vision of the woman whose pride and fury knew no bounds.

And that is where another backstage tale comes into play, this time one of triumph.

Lyubov Selyutina has been a Taganka actress since 1977, never really having an opportunity to distinguish herself. Her small roles in Lyubimov's recent productions of *Electra* and *Zhivago* gave no reason to think she was capable of anything bigger.

Think again. Selyutina, as the statuesque, fiery Medea, is stunning and masterful. Cutting a striking, larger-than-life picture with her blood-red lips, burning eyes, streaming black hair and sweeping, almost geometrically-shaped gestures, she is equally impressive penetrating the motivations that lurk behind her heroine's wrathful behavior.

This is a once-in-a-lifetime performance, the breaking loose of talent which has been lying in wait for longer than patience usually can bear. Selyutina is a live wire of contained and nuanced fury from her first fleeting appearance—when she angrily snatches her black cloak from a woman who dares try it on—to the finale, when she ruefully, but victoriously stands over the dead bodies of her sons and the bent body of her broken husband, Jason (Yury Belyayev).

Frankly, Selyutina is in a class by herself. It is as if Lyubimov poured into her every last drop of his anger, frustration and talent, leaving him little to offer the others. He drew solid but unspectacular performances from Taganka old-timers Maria Politseimako (the nurse), Vitaly Shapovalov (the tutor) and Felix Antipov (King Aegeus of Athens), while his young actresses in the Chorus, even as they speak Joseph Brodsky's translation, are unmoving and uninspired.

None of that matters in the end. The prodigious performance by Selyutina is an experience not to be missed. She is so powerfully commanding that her presence alone makes *Medea* Yury Lyubimov's best Moscow production in the '90s.

(September 1995)

One Night, National Youth Theater

One Night at the National Youth Theater resurrects a well-known writer's small play which had remained in mothballs since it was written in 1942.

The writer was Yevgeny Shvarts who, between 1928 and his death 30 years later, penned some of the cleverest, most biting political fairy-tales in world literature. Usually, he used a Hans Christian Andersen story as his basis, that making him plenty popular with Soviet audiences and equally suspect in the eyes of the Soviet authorities.

One Night was an aberration for Shvarts. It was a realistic drama about contemporary life, in this case, the tribulations of people struggling to survive the Leningrad Blockade.

But as happened with Shvarts periodically, the play had problems with the censor. It seems the dramatist failed to recognize the heroism of those enduring the Blockade, instead creating what one cultural bureaucrat called "a little world of no interest to anyone."

That may have been a silly political reason to ban a play, but 50 years on, one is inclined to agree that *One Night* is not apt to keep spectators on the edge of their seats. The play bears the musty stamp of a drama painted by numbers. Its people are sympathetic, but precious; their predicament believable, but strictly formulaic.

Director Alexei Borodin went to great and imaginative lengths to work around the play's limitations. What he came up with was about half successful.

With designer Stanislav Benediktov, Borodin created an effective environment, placing the audience and the action in a basement beneath the stage. Surrounded by machinery, girders and gadgets, 35 spectators sit backed up against a crude brick wall and a chain link fence. A few "skylights" cut into the ceiling—that is, the stage floor

above—allow impeded views of the night sky. A small desk stands to the side, serving as the focal point of the action.

It all has the authentic ring of a war-time bunker, with Borodin adding a nice, human touch to facilitate transitions between the three acts: The first time around, actors serve the spectators glasses of warm, unsweetened tea, later handing out chunks of half-toasted black bread. In the finale, they bring out a glass of vodka for everyone so that all can join in on the small celebration which Lyagutin, the local handyman so longs to enjoy.

Shvarts tells the story of a mother who has cut across the front from a distant village in search of her daughter and son. Inquiries have led her to a building inhabited by some eccentric, good-hearted people and a small band of rambunctious teenagers. They are suspicious of the newcomer, wondering if she isn't a German spy, but over time they become involved in her personal drama.

The severe limitations of the play, which fairly falls over itself creating a neat crew of flawed-but-endearing people, threw up insurmountable obstacles for the cast.

At best, we get well-defined stock characters. That is true both with the comically blustery Arkhangelskaya (Lyudmila Gnilova), a pianist forced into the role of nurse by the war, and Olga Petrovna (Natalya Ryazanova), a persnickety busy-body whose job is to assist the house administrator, but more often muddles his affairs.

As Marfa, the woman looking for her children, Natalya Platonova is down-to-earth, while the young Mikhail Gorsky's performance of the spunky teenaged Shurik adds some welcome life.

The most thankless task belongs to Larisa Moravskaya, who must play Marfa's dying daughter—who doesn't die in the end, but gets up from her sick bed to rush back to her place at the factory.

One Night premiered on May 9, the 50th anniversary of V-E Day, playing only twice more before the end of last season. It is a conscientious, visually interesting production of a play that would have been forgotten were it not for the fame of its author.

(September 1995)

Russian Light, Malaya Bronnaya Theater; and *A School for Fools*, Fomenko Studio

Russian theater, perhaps more than any other in the world, loves to sidestep dramatic texts for its sources and inspiration. Novels, stories, poetry and every other possible literary form are fair game for the director who is looking for ideas to plumb.

We now can add two more dramatizations to the list: *A School for Fools*, a "theatrical composition" at the Fomenko Studio based on Sasha Sokolov's famous novella, and *Russian Light*, the final piece in Sergei Zhenovach's ambitious trilogy of Fyodor Dostoevsky's novel, *The Idiot*.

In its entirety *The Idiot* runs for more than eleven hours over three days, letting us draw some conclusions about its creator.

Slowly and without fanfare, Zhenovach has emerged in the '90s as one of Moscow's most popular directors. One might wonder how it happened, since with rare exception (notably his delightful folk-oriented production of *The Miller Who Was a Wizard, a Cheat and a Matchmaker*) Zhenovach totters precariously between subtlety and tedium, invariably setting his shows in agonizingly slow, real-life time.

But that has not deterred a loyal and constantly growing following from receiving Zhenovach as a kind of theatrical poet of the Russian soul. During the prolonged ovation after the premiere of *Russian Light*, an elderly woman was heard to say with firm and unmistakable pride, "Let everyone know what Russians are like!"

That heartfelt exclamation suggests an explanation for Zhenovach's popularity. His attraction is in what he says rather than how he says it. Excepting *Miller*, his productions are seldom visual, dynamic or challenging in the common sense of the words. What they are is honest and straightforward. They bring time to a halt, allowing their characters to open their hearts and commune with the spectator.

It is the equivalent of spending an afternoon with acquaintances over shashlik in the country, or an evening with strangers in a friend's kitchen. A Zhenovach show has the same instant sincerity and the same rambling aimlessness.

The trilogy based on *The Idiot* claims to incorporate every word of Dostoevsky's dialogue. What that means, of course, is that it lacks the great writer's spectacular narrative, his shrewd observations about character and his penetrating insights into motivation.

In the hands of a more theatrical director, those elements would be reflected in the acting. But here the light-handed Zhenovach is at a disadvantage. If an actor isn't blessed with the gift of getting inside a character, Zhenovach is unlikely to provide the key. In a large-cast show like *Russian Light*, with its 22 characters, that makes for a good deal of colorless, text-driven performances.

The biggest exception is the splendid Sergei Taramayev as the strangely childlike Prince Myshkin. Outwardly comic, his innate sense of integrity leads him to speak the truth even to those who neither value it nor wish to hear it.

He twice nears the brink of marriage in *Russian Light*—first to the headstrong young Aglaya Yepanchina (Anastasia Nemolyayeva) and then to the notoriously experienced Nastasya Filippovna (Irina Rozanova). But Nastasya pushes him aside in favor of the wild, possessive Rogozhin (Sergei Kachanov), as she had done once before in *The Hussy*, the trilogy's opener. It is a fateful move, for even in victory, Rogozhin kills her in a jealous fit.

One of Taramayev's finest moments comes during one of Myshkin's most suspect: At a social gathering he launches into an inspired, messianic and openly nationalistic definition of Russia's place in the world before collapsing in an epileptic fit.

Also impressive are Vladimir Toptsov, as the slippery and ungainly clerk Lebedev, and Lev Durov, as the passionately proud and humiliated General Ivolgin, whose highlight in life was meeting Napoleon as a child. Ivolgin's death—a flying leap into the arms of his teenage son—brings a breathtaking end to a small but virtuoso display of acting.

Those cases aside, *Russian Light*, like *The Hussy* and *The Impoverished Knight* before it, is essentially a meticulous piece of enacted literature. If that is what you seek, it offers plenty.

A School for Fools is one more inexplicable chapter in the ongoing saga of the Fomenko Studio. Founded in 1993 from a highly-touted graduating class at the Russian Academy of Theater Arts, it has yet to live up to its promise or to the talent of its renowned artistic director, Pyotr Fomenko.

Its first professional outing in early 1994 was an underwhelming stab at Oscar Wilde's *The Importance of Being Earnest*, while its next, a beautiful but strikingly vacuous production of Alexander Blok's *The Puppet Booth*, closed after just three showings last fall.

A School for Fools was directed by Yevgeny Kamenkovich who in recent years has repeatedly exhibited the desire to experiment with environment and has repeatedly shown he is incapable of doing it. This time the space is the "Blue Guest Room" at the House of Actors on the Arbat. The few stabs at transforming the room theatrically—actors crawling into a niche in the wall; bicycle riders circling the audience; and pupils sitting among the spectators—are awkward and ineffective.

Sokolov's brilliant novella about a schizophrenic boy who lives a fantastically rich life in his imagination is trivialized and reduced to a succession of obscure episodes in a near non-existent plot. The dramatization's unnamed adapter split the bifurcated hero into five characters, rubbing him clean of his startling flights of fancy, his nervous, burgeoning sexuality, and his soaring sense of wonder.

The cast consists of a new crop of mostly unremarkable students. Only Mikhail Krylov and Inga Oboldina, as manifestations of the hero, remind us of Sokolov's inner freedom.

The jury is still out on whether the Fomenko Studio intends to become a professional theater or remain a school for eternal students.

(*October 1995*)

Favorites of Fortune, Pushkin Drama Theater

Favorites of Fortune at the Pushkin Theater introduces an unfamiliar name to Moscow spectators, and gives them the opportunity to look at the shape of their own lives. The new play by Yelena Popova tackles the personal and domestic problems of some citizens of the former Soviet Union attempting to enter a new world.

For the most part, it is a look back at the sources of the present rather than an examination of what may come in the future. However, if there are any questions as to the author's point of view about what lies in store, they should be dispelled by her epigraph printed in the program.

"Any new life we may have," she writes, "is only a continuation of the old."

As the developments of the play reveal, that isn't so much a statement of pessimism as one of clear-sighted honesty. Times change only in so far as people do, and, as life tirelessly and repeatedly shows, people change very slowly if at all.

Under the direction of Yelena Dolgina, the story is delivered with warmth and understanding, if also a bit drably. Instead of revelations—that is, really getting into what makes these people tick—we usually see a slick picture of the events occurring in their lives. The situations are occasionally touching and usually comic.

The "favorites" of the ironic title are led by Irina (Nina Popova), the insightful, but somewhat aimless middle-aged daughter of a now senile ex-general, and Slavik (Alexander Yermakov), her estranged husband who still lives with her in the same large apartment. Formerly an up-and-comer in the Komsomol, the Young Communist League, Slavik now spends most of his time running around with a blank-headed girl (Natalya Korogodova) who is younger than his daughter by Irina.

This was once a family of privilege, although as one of the characters notes, the old general (Stepan Bubnov) was a man of limited talents who reached the top by being in the right places and saying the right things. It was presumably through his influence that Irina once had a good job—from which she has just been fired—and Slavik was such a star in the now irrelevant Komsomol.

All any of them have left now is the sprawling, three-bedroom apartment. And it becomes the focal point of a tug-o-war that can't help but remind one of the famous line from Mikhail Bulgakov's novel, *The Master and Margarita*, written in the 1930s: "Muscovites aren't a bad lot; it's just the matter of living quarters that ruined them."

Slavik is in no hurry to let go his interest in the apartment, so when Irina begins receiving her old flame Reutsky (Romuald Vildan), Slavik digs up dirt on him: Reutsky is married and an ex-con.

Seemingly hanging outside the fray is Nastya, Slavik and Irina's grown-up daughter. Played with a lively sense of humor and affection by Irina Byakova, she is a peacemaker early on until an unexpected turn of events proves her no better than the others: The old general's nurse, Wanda (Yelena Sitko), moves in with the old guy, setting up a new threat to control over the apartment.

As did Slavik with his "rival" Reutsky, Nastya moves quickly to drive Wanda out, rudely casting aside human feelings to keep the competition at a minimum.

Favorites of Fortune took First Prize at the 1994 European Play Competition out of a field of entries from 29 countries. One of over 20 plays written by Popova, a native of Minsk, Belarus, who has had seven plays produced in the former Soviet Union, it is her first to be staged in Moscow.

The production at the Pushkin does not reveal the excellence that the European judges apparently saw in the play, although it has its effective moments.

(*October 1995*)

Kings' Games, Lenkom Theater

Mark Zakharov made his fame by creating what some have called Moscow's answer to Broadway. His shows at the Lenkom Theater, which he has headed since 1973, are nothing if not brash, flashy and loud. He often works in the realm of the musical but even when he doesn't, showmanship and ostentation are the keynotes.

His first big splash came in 1974 with a romantic musical treatment of the legend about Till Eulenspiegel, the peasant prankster of German folklore. In the mid-1980's he struck again with the rock-opera *Yunona and Avos*, based on the poem by Andrei Voznesensky. These shows, like most at the Lenkom, also bore the light fragrance of unobtrusive political satire.

That now-standard fare of music, fun and politics was repeated in the 1993 production of *The Marriage of Figaro*, and is featured again in the new *Kings' Games*, which opened last week. However, where the lively *Figaro* was buoyed by some impressive acting and a clever play, *Kings' Games* bears the heavy stamp of a tired formula.

The story is based on Maxwell Anderson's *Anne of the Thousand Days*, a play about the ill-fated marriage between the feisty Anne Boleyn and the obstinate King Henry VIII. While running through numerous wives and lovers in hopes of siring a son and heir, Henry's heart is snared by the young woman who dares defy him. But for all its bluster, Zakharov's version of that clash of passions is remarkably tepid.

The blame can be spread evenly among all involved.

The adaptation by Grigory Gorin, known for his "Russianizations" of foreign works, is plodding and unimaginative, while the instantly forgettable music by Shandor Kallosh is neither melodious enough to be attractive nor adventurous enough to be interesting. It is, however, played very loudly.

The same can be said for the acting. With little action to speak of, the performance essentially consists of a series of confrontations in which the principals engage in booming conversations. The monotony is broken by a few energetic dance routines (staged by Alexei Molostov), although they rarely seem an organic part of the whole.

The biggest hole in this production is its utter lack of sexual fireworks. Whether strutting with a royal verve, buckling weakly like a child or singing in his expressionless voice, Alexander Lazarev, Jr., is cold, mechanical and inaccessible as Henry. His fashion-magazine good looks work against him, since they only highlight his lack of contact with Amalia Mordvinova's Anne Boleyn.

Mordvinova plays a kind of moderately contemporary queen consort who is more school-girl hip than tempestuous.

Zakharov desperately lunged for a semblance of sensuality by stripping Boleyn naked at the end of the first act and surrounding her with a bevy of topless ladies-in-waiting. As the follow-up scene to Boleyn's convincing Henry to reject the Vatican and setting himself up as the head of the English Church, it intends to synthesize the urges for sex and power. Instead it offers tasteless titillation.

The political satire comes in Leonid Bronevoi's dry-as-a-martini performance of Boleyn's uncle, the Duke of Norfolk. A schemer and a sneak, he is equally reprehensible, comic and endearing, providing the show's best moments. It is a minor miracle, since only one with Bronevoi's instincts could succeed with the clichés and queer jokes handed him in the text.

The set by Yury Kharikov (he also designed the imaginative, billowing costumes) is dominated by a monstrous spiked balloon that floats over the action like a tottering ship of state. Zakharov eventually sends it sailing over the spectators' heads as a forehead-thumping lesson: What happened in 16th-century England can happen to you, too, baby.

Kings' Games has plenty of bravado, noise, pomp and circumstance, but it's still a royal case of all show and no substance.

(October 1995)

Talents and Admirers, Maly Theater

Let's give praise where praise is due. The newly renovated Maly Theater affiliate on Bolshaya Ordynka may not be the Eighth Wonder, but it is at least a minor miracle.

Elegant and cozy, modern and traditional all in one, it is now easily Moscow's most graceful and inviting auditorium. From the powder blue neo-classical exterior to the soft yellows, grays and browns of the sleek, contemporary interior, this is a space that oozes class.

The marble floors sparkle underfoot, the plush carpets pad your step, the oversized tapestries and drawings entertain the eyes, while all of it is washed in a delicate light emanating from gorgeous cut-glass chandeliers that seem to drip rather than hang.

The hall is nothing less than exquisite. Actually quite large, with a capacity of 760, it has the feel of a warm, intimate enclosure wrapped tightly by two narrow, high balconies. The bordeaux velvet seats, like the lighter red velvet curtain, lend the hall opulence and comfort.

This is the kind of place that could anchor a tour guide's list of must-sees. Indeed, if the Maly uses it to put on shows like its anemic new rendition of *Talents and Admirers*, it won't be long before it becomes just another spectacular tourist trap.

Talents and Admirers is one of many "backstage" plays by Alexander Ostrovsky, the great 19th-century playwright and influential administrator at the Maly Theater who intimately knew actors, their problems and their obsession for the stage.

At the center of the tumult is Alexandra Negina, a poor, but popular young actress in a provincial troupe who has the daring and naiveté to spurn a pushy, graying and monied admirer. He, Prince Dulebov, wants to set her and her mother Domna Panteleyevna up in a fancy new apartment; she wants him to leave her and her young tutor boyfriend alone. That affront brings her misfortune, as the injured prince contrives to ruin her upcoming benefit performance, almost her only source of real income, and cancel her contract for next season.

As is typical of Ostrovsky, *Talents* is filled with villains, angelic innocents, mercenary creeps and romantic, but ineffectual purehearts, creating a melodramatic concoction teeming with life and laced with truth, insight and genuine human emotion.

And as is true of Ostrovsky perhaps more than any other Russian dramatist, the actors playing his full-blooded people are what make or break his plays. With a pair of exceptions, the cast at the Maly sinks this version of *Talents* in a sea of facelessness and clichés.

Director Vladimir Beilis started with his best idea, bringing out Vasily Bochkaryov, in the role of the director's assistant Narokov, to inaugurate things with the traditional three tinklings of a bell. Moments later,

Bochkaryov nearly steps out of character to deliver a monologue on his love for the theater.

When telling of having once rebuilt a theater, Bochkaryov pauses, smiling graciously at the spectators. It is a warm, effective moment linking play with reality. But things rush downhill from there.

Svetlana Amanova is listless and ponderous as Negina, the young actress who should be so fresh, innocent and fragile, neither encouraging one to believe in Negina's talent or her ability to attract so many admirers. As her mother, Irina Likso offers a bundle of tired, theatrical expressions and exclamations.

As Velikatov, the millionaire who convinces Negina to run away with him, Viktor Korshunov muddles the needed sense of mystery in colorless monotony.

Together with Bochkaryov, Afanasy Kochetkov provides the rare bright spots with his borderline grotesque interpretation of Gromilov, the quintessential tragedian. Masterfully overplaying the grimaces, the gestures and the bellows, Kochetkov draws a convincing—and hilarious—portrait of a man doomed to perceive the world tragically.

Those few scenes are the only ones in *Talents and Admirers* worthy of the magnificent surroundings in which they are played.

(*October 1995*)

Brothers and Sisters, The Cherry Orchard, Gaudeamus, Claustrophobia and The Devils, St. Petersburg Maly Drama Theater

One might justifiably say that the theater most know in the West as "the Maly" had never played in Moscow. The Maly Drama Theater of St. Petersburg—the Maly—last played the Russian capital in 1986. It was only a year later that artistic director Lev Dodin took his troupe on the first of what was to become a seemingly endless series of foreign tours that would bring the company world-wide fame. So, when the Maly began a three-week, October/November Moscow engagement, it had come in an entirely new capacity.

The tour began with the six-hour *Brothers and Sisters*, the last show to play Moscow, continuing with *The Cherry Orchard, Gaudeamus, Claustrophobia* and the ten-hour production of *The Devils*. Despite ample opportunities for local egos to be bruised (Russia's Culture Minister Yevgeny Sidorov drew guffaws at the opener by stating that Dodin is so famous in the West, nobody there even wants to hear about Moscow talent), the response from audiences and colleagues alike was unabashedly enthusiastic. Published rumors stated that the Maly papered the house for the first shows, leery that demand would be low. There was no need for that: Every show, including several added at the last minute, played to jam-packed, highly-appreciative crowds.

Brothers and Sisters, based on Fyodor Abramov's tetralogy of novels about the hard life in Russia's countryside during and after World War II, displayed the Maly's strong suit: its precision and disciplined energy. Although a decade old, the show still plays with new conviction and excitement.

Part One, detailing the struggles of the women to keep the village running while the men are at war, was especially effective. The whirlwind development of the episodic scenes, the near magic versatility of Eduard Kochergin's set which transforms instantly from a bathhouse to a loft, and the undeniable truth of the characters and their situations, all combined to ward off the nagging feeling that the show's quasi-realistic, sociopolitical approach, which Dodin admits he learned from Yury Lyubimov's productions of the 1960s and '70s, is now passé. At least in Part One, that mattered not. It was infused with a pulsing sexual power (signaled by the phallic wooden gates that repeatedly swung out over the first rows of the audience) which unfailingly kept the focus on the individual and the personal. Part Two, chronicling the village's descent into bureaucratic and political obscurantism, while executed splendidly, offered little that was not done better in the first segment.

Dodin could be called the bard of the Soviet underbelly. He delights—theatrically—in the excesses of that often spiritually and physically sick society. And it is in his

Igor Ivanov, Nikolai Lavrov and Tatyana Shestakova in Chekhov's *The Cherry Orchard*, directed by Lev Dodin at the Maly Drama Theater, St Petersburg. Performed in Moscow, autumn 1995. Photo: Ken Reynolds

production of *The Cherry Orchard* that we see in relief the limits and possibilities of that approach. This is a coarse, proletarian rendition of Chekhov in which the people look more like representatives of the genus of Homo Sovieticus than of the tsarist gentry. It is an approach that, like a muscular hand thrust in a lace glove, could have ripped to pieces the fabric of Chekhov's exquisite play. As it is, Dodin's version is a bit too heavy ever to truly fly, but the very quality that holds it back also gives it power.

Tatyana Shestakova's narrow, earth-bound Ranevskaya and Sergei Bekhterev's high-strung, small-minded Gayev are characters of little impact or consequence. But their absence, as it were, allows for an entirely different take: Thanks to Igor Ivanov's gritty, driven performance of Lopakhin—the merchant whose grandfather worked the cherry orchard as a serf, and who now buys the land to save it from falling to strangers—this *Cherry Orchard* is no nostalgic portrait of the dying aristocracy, but a rough, gruff exploration of a middle class emerging from a class of slaves. In alternating waves of hot and cold, Ivanov achieves the near impossible—playing the whole projected history of his character's family. In his hatred for his grandfather and his respect for Ranevskaya, we see his dual attitude to his past as a second-class citizen, while in his conviction that someone must save the doomed orchard, we see his flatly unsentimental responsibility before future generations.

The production's details—from the little pond which the characters constantly pollute unthinkingly, to Yepikhodov's absurdly squeaking shoes and the actors' frantic circling of the stage—bear the unmistakable imaginative Dodin stamp at every turn.

Gaudeamus is a melting-pot of Dodin's strengths. Exhilarating and moving, its 19 "improvisational" episodes convey the horrors and stupidities of army life with raucous humor and sobering frankness, expanding them into a metaphor for the brutalities of Soviet life. Alexei Porai-Koshits's snow-covered stage with holes that swallow up and regurgitate the unprepared recruits, their ignorant superiors and their victimized girlfriends, is a masterpiece of design

simplicity. The music ranging from Beethoven to the Beatles keeps the pace in constant flux, while the actors display their own musical talents when each takes up an instrument and they cut into a blistering, jazzy tune.

Satire, sarcasm and flights of lyrical humor predominate until the 15th, 16th and 17th scenes ("Corrida," "Bliss" and "Ecstasy") when the bottom drops out: The once innocent boys have descended into violence, drug abuse and rape. The emotional finale, "Academy," brings out the damaged, the dead and the offended, who launch into a stirring version of "Gaudeamus igitur..." ("Let us rejoice while we are young"). Through the cruel irony of this song being sung by those deprived of youthful purity, this scene achieves genuine cathartic power.

Claustrophobia is a sequel to *Gaudeamus*, and like most sequels, falls short of the original. Based on the works of a quartet of more-or-less contemporary Russian writers (Vladimir Sorokin, the late Venedikt Yerofeev, Lyudmila Ulitskaya and Mark Kharitonov), it is another technically brilliant, episodic tour of Russian/Soviet life, only this time an insane asylum replaces army barracks as the field of battle. Porai-Koshits again provided the spectacular setting, a white room that gradually deconstructs, allowing people to climb walls or penetrate them.

Criticism has arisen in Petersburg and Moscow that *Claustrophobia* was created as a potpourri of naturalistic clichés about Russian lowlife that would appeal to Western audiences and critics who only know Russia through horror stories in the press. I see no reason to accuse Dodin of such pandering, but he is vulnerable to criticism for gratuitously reveling in the odious. One scene depicting a couple in their kitchen—with its vomiting, spitting, violence and defecating—is so long and repetitive that it evokes disgust not for the ignorance that breeds such behavior, but for the showing of it. If there is a danger of becoming what one plays, Dodin came precariously close to crossing that line here.

Obscured in the murky, unredeemed darkness of this technically virtuosic show were a handful of bright moments. Particularly noteworthy were Oleg Dmitriev's penetrating performance of a skittish poet, and Maria Nikiforova's inspired interpretations of several lost souls.

Dodin's dramatization of *The Devils* is a tour de force of literary theater, manifesting all that genre's pluses and minuses. It truly brings Dostoevsky's menacing, funny and devastatingly insightful novel to life, although one tends to remain more impressed by the literature than by the theater, which always remains secondary in conception and execution. That said, it is hard to imagine a more chilling Verkhovensky—the two-faced, conniving ringleader of an underground revolutionary circle—than the one played by Sergei Bekhterev. His obsequious smiles and deceptively soft manner make his grim mission all the more sinister. Also impressive were Igor Ivanov's reeling, heart-on-sleeve interpretation of the comically pathetic Captain Lebyadkin, and Sergei Kuryshev's tragically innocent Kirillov, the youth who is "eaten" by his idea of becoming a god through suicide. As befits literary theater, most of the marathon production consists of monologues or dialogues which can be either riveting or tedious. They are more often the former thanks to Dodin's conservative, static *mises en scene* (in which a second or third party often adds a sense of tension by silently listening in), his excellent use of light to focus attention, and Eduard Kochergin's multifaceted set in which the four walls of various interiors also serve metaphorically as guillotine blades.

The Maly Drama Theater's Moscow tour was a major triumph, a spectacular display of a complex theatrical organism. Dodin's talented, powerful productions—despite their not-infrequent limitations—clearly place him among the best directors working in Russia today. But what puts him in a class by himself—and I suspect not only in Russia—are his extraordinary talents as an organizer and administrator. For 12 years he has not only held together a repertory theater of 50 actors and probably twice as many support personnel, he has pushed them to the limits of their talent and kept them there working productively at maximum strength.

There is a sense of overachievement to all of the Maly Drama Theater's productions (with the possible exception of the soaring *Gaudeamus*), and I mean that purely as a compliment. I have seen better acting and I have seen more intricate directing, but only when Robert Sturua brought his Rustaveli Theater to Moscow have I ever seen an entire theatrical team function on such a breathtakingly high level. Lev Dodin has earned his reputation as Russia's theatrical ambassador to the West.

(January 1996, Plays International)

A Trial Interview on the Theme of Freedom, Theater na Pokrovke

Maria Arbatova is one of the best known names from what might be called the phantom generation of playwrights—writers now around 40 who are widely published, highly respected, and have had many of their plays translated and staged abroad. What most of them have not been able to do, Arbatova included, is to get their plays produced in Russia and, especially, in Moscow.

Sergei Artsibashev's production of *A Trial Interview on the Theme of Freedom* at the Theater na Pokrovke, marks the first time in several years that an Arbatova play has been staged in the Russian capital.

For Artsibashev it is a natural step. While his best work generally occurs when he takes on the Russian classics, over the years he has also occasionally turned a sympathetic eye to contemporary writers. It is a mix that has won his Theater na Pokrovke an enviable, well-deserved reputation.

A *Trial Interview* would appear to occupy a special place in Arbatova's work. It transforms and recycles themes that the author has repeatedly touched on in well-publicized interviews given in her capacity not only as a writer, but as president of the Harmony Moscow Feminist Club.

Arbatova is an outspoken critic of the intelligentsia of the '60s generation and perhaps it is only fitting that the most interesting and believable character in her new play represents that group. Vadim Petrovich, played with a tangible undercurrent of wisdom, understanding and a touch of fatigue by Gennady Chulkov, is an elderly man with key connections and a rich past. We know little about him other than he was a communist big-shot and that he is the object of the title's "trial interview."

The interview is taken on the sly by the play's devil-may-care heroine, Margarita. She visits Vadim's apartment under romantic pretenses and, while getting him to look the other way as she supposedly changes a torn pair of stockings, she turns on a tape recorder in her purse. She prints the result in *Moskovsky Komsomolets*, the popular and feisty scandal-rag for which she is a star journalist.

But the treatment of the generation gap is only one of the play's facets. It also explores the foibles of modern relations between the sexes, the complex ties and jealousies among women friends, the frustrations of mother–daughter bonds, and briefly lights on the problems of the New Russian and the uncertainty of attitudes toward the West.

If that sounds like an overfilled grab-bag of topical subjects, that's probably because it is. Arbatova provided a recognizable romp through the A-list of contemporary issues but seldom went beyond surfaces. Artsibashev's low-key direction does little more than serve it up conscientiously.

Margarita (Yelena Starodub) is an energetic woman approaching her 35th birthday who has apparent success juggling a fistful of romantic relationships—a teenage lover, a separated husband, a New Russian suitor and a mysterious, unseen love who has emigrated to New York. Seemingly free as the wind (Vadim admiringly calls her a "holiday of disobedience") she is more likely a prisoner of her own nonchalance.

The other characters fight their own battles in search of freedom, the most engaging aside from Vadim being Margarita's friend Galya (Tatyana Shvydkova). Amazed at and inhibited by Margarita's success with men, Galya desperately wants a husband and a family, but gets cold chills when she's around a man.

The keenest insight comes from Vadim during his unwitting interview: He suggests that freedom consists in battling one's own complexes. It is a simple truth that reflects one way or another on everyone by the time things reach a climax.

Watching *A Trial Interview on the Theme of Freedom* is often akin to reading an issue of the newspaper Margarita works for: It titillates and amuses at moments, but doesn't really stick in the memory.

(November 1995)

The Masquerade, Chekhov Art Theater

A severe, passionate husband suspects his younger wife has been unfaithful, the sparks of his suspicions being carefully fanned into flames by an associate. The husband's jealousy peaks, his wife's protestations of innocence fall on deaf ears, and he puts her to death in a spasm of cold rage.

Shakespeare's *Othello*? No, it is *The Masquerade*, the best known of five plays by Russia's foremost Romantic poet, Mikhail Lermontov. But in place of Shakespeare's clearer, broader and undeniably more profound investigation of jealousy, treachery and purity, Lermontov peered into the disease of spiritual emptiness which had afflicted the aristocracy in the early 19th century.

Apparently the play also has a special resonance at the end of the 20th century. Nikolai Sheiko's new production of it for the Chekhov Art Theater is the third in Moscow in the '90s, following versions at the Art Theater's now-defunct Fifth Studio in 1990 and the Russian Army Theater in 1992, where it is still in repertory.

But the real shadow extending over Sheiko's interpretation (as at the Army Theater), comes from what is unquestionably the most storied production of the play ever: Vsevolod Meyerhold's legendary mounting of it at the Alexandrinsky Theater in St. Petersburg in 1917.

That opulent, atmospheric staging, whose elaborate set of curtains and backdrops by Alexander Golovin has entered the history books of stage design, premiered the night the February Revolution began: Meyerhold and his actors dodged bullets to get to the theater, and a spectator was killed at the door.

Sheiko opens with a human sculpture at the back of the stage that recreates Boris Grigoryev's famous portrait of two Meyerhold personalities, one in a staid tux and top-hat, the other in a flamboyant red costume. The figure in the tux steps down and staggers forward as two layers of curtains—one black and one white—hurriedly close behind him, bisecting the stage diagonally.

When the figure stops beneath an angled mirror on the ceiling, we recognize him as Viktor Gvozditsky, the actor who has played Meyerhold for a moment, but will play the jealous husband Arbenin for the next three hours.

However, by then the best of this visually intriguing, theatrically slack production is already behind it. The historical quotes in Mart Kitayev's multi-curtained set, Maria Danilova's spicy, playful costumes and the impressive use of space attributed in the program to Mikhail Kislyarov, are effective, although they can't transform what is essentially a routine outing.

The action alternates between intimate, generally effective scenes played on chairs in front of the stage, and intricate, choreographed scenes that unfold in the open spaces of the stage. These more frequent moments do little more than look nice.

Viktor Gvozditsky, easily one of Moscow's top five actors, is uneven as the former gambler and womanizer who is undone by his past. In his most thoughtful moments, using his mesmerizing voice to best advantage, Gvozditsky flashes the power for which he is known, but he is banal—and irritating—when unleashing his prodigious temper and shattering the fragile atmosphere.

More consistent, though not as spectacular, is Irina Apeksimova as the flirtatious Baroness who unwittingly sets the tragic events in motion. She finds a lost bracelet at a masquerade, giving it in a tender moment to the young buck, Prince Zvezdich (Vitaly Yegorov), who determines that it belongs to Arbenin's wife Nina, and so goes about pursuing the wrong woman. As Nina, Polina Medvedeva is as wholesome and colorless as milk, wearing a cloying, girlish smile that doesn't leave her face even as she dies of poisoned ice cream.

By the time of the appearance of the Stranger (Pavel Belozerov)—an old, offended friend of Arbenin, and possibly the mastermind behind the scenario which led to Arbenin killing his wife—this production has become too small to matter.

(*November 1995*)

The Main Thing, Riga Theater of Russian Drama; *I Can't Imagine Tomorrow*, Torikos Theater (Gelendzhik); and *National Governance in Shambala*, Omsk Drama Theater

The beginning of Moscow's 1995/96 season boasted more shows by touring companies than at any time in the 1990s. It was a luxury many thought had been lost for good. With government money short in recent years and the ties among the nations and former republics of the old Soviet bloc having broken down, tours from even nearby Russian cities had become a rarity. But the Russian Ministry of Culture (like the Moscow city administration) is again loosening the purse strings and international ties are being restored. The result in October and November 1995 was an influx of out-of-town shows so great that it was physically impossible to keep up with them all.

The key, though not the sole, organization responsible for the boom in visiting troupes was the Theater of Nations. Called the Friendship of Nationalities Theater in the Soviet era, it remains a state-funded structure with ties to the Ministry of Culture and the Russian Union of Theater Workers (STD). It is now located in the coveted old Korsh Theater building on Petrovsky Lane (formerly Moskvin Street). More a production company than a theater, it arranges and conducts festivals and individual productions throughout Russia, while supporting Russian projects abroad. In the two months between September 25 and November 27, 1995 alone, the Theater of Nations hosted in Moscow the Baltic States Theater Festival, showcasing eight theaters, the triumphant tour of St. Petersburg's Maly Drama Theater, featuring seventeen performances of five productions, and the Theatrical Omsk Festival, presenting six performances by four theaters.

During that same period, but independent of the Theater of Nations, Moscow's Maly Theater hosted the First International Festival of National Theaters, while there was a handful of other independent touring productions. With Moscow's own season getting off to a slow start, the best shows early on were provided by visitors.

As part of the Baltic festival, the Riga Theater of Russian Drama presented Nikolai Yevreinov's *The Main Thing*. It was directed by Roman Kozak, the 38-year-old Moscow director and actor who first gained attention at the Chelovek Theater-Studio in the early 1980s, and who recently became an assistant to Artistic Director Oleg Yefremov at the Chekhov Moscow Art Theater. Kozak, together with set and costume designer Andris Freibergs, did an excellent job of infusing an old-fashioned feel into a thoroughly modern production.

As though deliberately spurning Yevreinov's directions calling for a small, poorly-furnished room in Act I, Kozak employed the entire large stage at the Mossoviet Theater where the single performance was held. The back wall depicted a shallow balcony within an interior, entrance into which was accessed by a second-floor door and a steep, narrow stair protruding onto the stage. But for a smoking pot and a chair down front, there were essentially no other props. The color scheme of the decoration and costumes was almost solid black, while the atmosphere surrounding the Fortune Teller/Doctor Fregoli receiving actors looking for roles, was a mixture of mystery and farce. It took place in one of three small areas within the huge empty space—either at the back wall, at center stage, or all the way downstage. Walls of light, designed by Ivan Danichev, isolated the places which the actors occupied, creating highly pictorial scenes. The music was an eclectic selection ranging from Dave Brubeck and Louis Armstrong to Russian classical composers.

Act II more or less followed Yevreinov's lead, with the rehearsal-within-the-play being performed downstage. The actors, now dressed in white, were spread out almost in a flat line beneath the arch, with the huge open space behind occasionally being penetrated by the Barefoot Dancer or a perennially late pianist who repeatedly held up the rehearsal. Her dignified, unhurried treks back and forth across the stage created marvelous, comic pauses in the action which was usually played fast and loose as if it were a cabaret skit.

Acts III and IV ignored Yevreinov's plan for the stage layout, substituting a long, rather futuristic, see-through plexiglass structure divided into the rooms of the inhabitants of Maria Yakovlevna's boarding house. It occasionally spun in circles while silent but chaotic action took place inside and outside the cubicles. The actors often slipped into imitative movements, such as "playing" a non-existent piano when piano music was heard. Gestures and movements were frequently synchronized. Less farcical and more melodramatic than the first two acts, the concluding segments were perhaps less effective, although on the whole, the production remained a lively, interesting revival of a much-discussed, but seldom-produced play.

The Torikos Theater, from the Russian town of Gelendzhik on the Black Sea, brought to Moscow a penetrating production of Tennessee Williams's *I Can't Imagine Tomorrow*, a one-acter about a husband and wife confronting their disproportionate needs for one another. Co-produced by two Moscow-based organizations, the Russian State Theater Agency and the Bogis Agency, it starred two Moscow actors—Alexander Feklistov and Diana Korzun. Brilliantly directed and designed by Anatoly Slyusarenko, the artistic director at the Torikos, it may have been the best rendition of American drama I have seen on the Russian stage.

Two rotating floor fans stood at either corner downstage, their humming sound broken only by the light tinkling of bells hanging from one of the fans, while the only furniture left from Williams's directions were two straightbacked chairs. A row of seashells lay around the perimeter of a semi-circle of small, rectangular mirrors on the floor. Like the walls and ceiling, the floor was flat black.

The mirrors caught and refracted the light of bright, narrow spotlights which cut across the darkness like sabres. At times, a large, transparent bowl of water cast rippling rays of light on the walls and ceiling. In fact, the lighting by Sergei Tyutin was so material that it took on the qualities of another prop on stage.

Feklistov, as the man who is incapable of verbalizing his emotions, was dressed in Williams-like, off-white "clothes for a summer hotel." He was expressively static and frustrated. Korzun, as the slightly nervous, impatient, sharp-eyed wife, wore a short, billowing, white chiffon cape over light gray leggings. Sleek, graceful and modern, she was constantly in motion, tipping her head, spreading her arms out straight (with the light catching just the upper halves), cocking her legs or lithely twisting her body. She was everything her husband was not—fluid, fluent and free.

In late November, the Omsk Drama Theater put on a single performance of Alexei Shipenko's strange but wonderful *Natural Governance in Shambala*. A long, rambling work whose key characters of Brando and Liza appear in a myriad of times and places, it is probably best described as a dream play.

Liza, it seems, has died and been buried, but perhaps Brando has just put her to sleep in order to spirit her off to a hideaway in Tibet. There Hitler hosts a crazy banquet where we also encounter Napoleon, Mussolini, Karl Marx and Nostradamus. All of them are blown away by a crew of sub-machine-gunners headed by Stalin, or at least his look-alike. Drifting in and out of things are the Dalai Lama, Buddhist monks, Liza's parents, her father's mistress, and her cousin, a young officer in the Tsarist army who is in love with her and comes looking for her when he learns that she is not really dead.

Things begin and end with Liza's nude body lying on the autopsy table, suggesting that the whole thing has been a figment of Brando's imagination. But, at least in Vladimir Petrov's beautiful, well-acted production, the actress playing Liza (Anastasia Svetlova) comes out for the curtain calls dressed for the first time as the 11-year-old girl she is supposed to be. Suddenly, one wonders whether the play hasn't been her dream.

Designers Irina Akimova and Yury Ustinov gave the production a soaring, other-worldly feel. Layers of semi-transparent curtains with large, free-form patterns on them, cut across the stage allowing action to continue in one area while props or actors were removed or delivered in another. When in Tibet, the back wall was illuminated in a translucent sky-blue against which wind-swept white clouds hurried from one side to the other. The masterfully-lit stage was kept as if in a murky darkness, at least in contrast to the enormous, cinema-like sky behind it, the effect being that the action seemed to take place at the very top of the world.

(*Spring 1996, Slavic and East European Performance*)

The Execution of the Decembrists, Young Spectator Theater

Walking to your seat on a small grandstand on the black stage, you pass by handwritten signs directing you "to the execution." It is a wink of humor that will constantly reappear throughout an intense, coldly powerful show whose subject is anything but funny.

The Execution of the Decembrists, at the Young Spectator Theater, is based on historical documents concerning the gruesomely botched hangings of five revolutionaries who spearheaded the notorious, equally inept uprising against tsarist rule on December 14, 1825. When three men slipped through their nooses bloodied and broken but still alive, they were strung up and hung again.

The show was created and directed by Kama Ginkas, whose compelling production of *K.I. from "Crime"* last season won him the Crystal Turandot award for best director.

Ginkas plays with a rigid documentary style. The characters speak the language of interrogations, reports or letters from which the text has been cut and pasted, only occasionally emerging as flesh and blood in moments of anger or frustration. The story's considerable impact derives from the constant friction between the grisly tales we hear and the matter-of-fact, even mundane manner in which they are related.

The humor—call it dry or call it black—is vintage Ginkas, a master at making spectators laugh where they ought to cringe. Impeccably observant, he emphasizes the myriad of common incongruities which attend any human endeavor and can't help but elicit laughter, even as five men go to the gallows. Humor arises in the props, including corny museum-like exhibits of nooses and shackles, and in the aggressively inadequate representation of the condemned as white nightshirts on hangers with crude name-tags slung across the chests.

In the carefully wrought absence of pathos or sentiment, humor creates the initial human contact between the spectators and the players.

Those gathered to hash out why the execution went awry include Nikolai I, four surviving conspirators, and several witnesses or participants. Their reminiscences, monologues and outbursts are conducted by a figure called the Author. Olga Demidova plays the male character with a brusque, preemptive flair, frequently contradicting speakers or spinning around at her desk to stare skeptically into spectators' eyes.[1]

In a rare case of Ginkas pulling back the curtain on the documentary style, Demidova walks among the frozen figures, giving each, no matter what their role in the events, a sympathetic, forgiving caress of the head. It is a moving moment as a declaration of both historical atonement and artistic neutrality.

Whether it is the boyish, feeble Nikolai (Maxim Vitorgan) who cannot stop the execution, the prison warden (Igor Gordin) whose revulsion comes less from human feelings than from professional shame for the tragicomedy of errors, or the increasingly hysterical surviving Decembrists, all are players in a scenario much bigger than they are. Schnitzler, a German witness (Andrei

Bronnikov), quotes Kondraty Ryleyev, one of the condemned rebels, muttering that Russia "is a damned nation which can't create conspiracies, conduct trials or carry out executions."

Dmitry Suponin is brilliant as the young policeman whose conscience tells him he is a part of a despicable act while his official position makes him one of the executioners. His wide-eyed simplicity and common sense capture perfectly the banality and tragedy of one who sees evil but cannot oppose it.

As the comically droopy-eyed, so-called Participant by Duty, Vladimir Salnikov epitomizes the inert but responsive cog that makes any machine run. As Yakushkin, a conspirator given a 20-year sentence, Yevgeny Sarmont is his opposite, an unspeakably horrified, unbelieving knot of outrage.

This show lacks those few spectacular directorial touches which usually mark a Ginkas work, and at times it seems suspended in repetition. Still, every calibrated stroke bears the signature of a major artist. Tough and unrelenting, *The Execution of the Decembrists* cuts like cold, sharp steel. It is the season's first significant production.

(*December 1995*)

Romeo and Juliet, Satirikon

Konstantin Raikin is riding high at his Satirikon Theater. Two seasons ago he brought in Pyotr Fomenko to stage a breathtaking production of Fernand Crommelynck's *The Magnificent Cuckold*. Last year he invited Valery Fokin to create a stunning dramatization of Kafka's *The Metamorphosis*. Both shows starred the dynamic Raikin himself.

This time, showing he's no mere splendid actor doing a great job running his own theater, Raikin took the director's seat. Only judging by the unrelenting energy of his new *Romeo and Juliet*, one suspects he spent a lot more time roaming the stage inspiring his actors with his own vitality, than sitting back making notes.

This *Romeo and Juliet* is nigh onto perfect Shakespeare. The young, enthusiastic,

---

[1] When Demidova went on maternity leave, the role was taken over by Genrietta Yanovskaya, Ginkas's wife and the artistic director of the theater.

Marina Ivanova, Natalia Vdovina and Lidia Petrakova in Shakespeare's *Romeo and Juliet* directed by Konstantin Raikin at the Satirikon Theater, 1995. Photo: Alexander Ivanishin

talented cast rips into this, one of the greatest plays ever written about the glory and tragedy of youth, with conviction, excitement and intensity. Shakespeare's cascades of quotable quotes—translated by Boris Pasternak—spring to life as if they are being pronounced for the first time.

As if capturing a firefly in a jar, Raikin caught the fervor, the delightful silliness and the deadly seriousness of adolescents crossing the line into adulthood. Their burgeoning sexuality is reflected in the bawdy phallic images of unsheathed swords, stiff legs and the protruding shaft of a cart; their mindless, instinctive fury is portrayed in elaborate, spectacular fight scenes; their purity is echoed in the deep blue costumes and penetrating blue and orange light of the ethereal ball scene at the Capulet home where Romeo falls in love with Juliet.

Boris Valuyev's beautiful set echoes the characters' pristine states. An elementary, two-story structure of square, open cells stands at mid-stage. When the central cells move away and a pitch black curtain rises, we find ourselves on a strangely iridescent piazza in the center of Verona. Maria Danilova's colorful costumes mix in equal measure poofy folds and sleek, figure-hugging lines.

In these dazzling surroundings the jewel that shines brightest is Natalia Vdovina's spunky, whirling, volcanic Juliet. Vdovina became a star overnight with her exquisite debut in *The Magnificent Cuckold*, and she was brilliant again in *The Metamorphosis*. As Juliet, she establishes what we have suspected all along: The sky is her only limit.

In her first appearance, Vdovina emerges unexpectedly from a trunk like an infant from the womb, her innocent impetuousness making her less a young teenager than a spoiled baby-child. Filled with boundless, expendable energy, she flies madly to and fro, speaking too fast and confounding everyone.

Frivolous and self-centered, Juliet pays no heed to her first meeting with Romeo, gaily dancing with every boy at the ball. Romeo, played with touching, unblemished grace by Alexander Koruchekov, stands thunderstruck until the two are alone. He then plants a kiss on her lips which will seal their fate. In a hilarious moment, Juliet tears herself away, but before she can get far, Romeo's magnetic attraction brings her flying back for a grand, collisional kiss.

For all the show's well-placed, boastful sexual imagery, it is—as it should be—the kisses that are divine. The pair's nocturnal embrace, with Romeo dangling from Juliet's balcony seemingly held only by her kiss, leaves him speechless for most of the next scene and draws applause from the admiring audience.

As Juliet's nurse, Marina Ivanova is pert, sly and well aware of the emotions that are about to envelope her young charge. Alexei Yakubov delivers three masterful comic episodes as Peter, the nurse's blundering servant.

Vladimir Bolshov has the swaggering arrogance of a rock star as Mercutio, the hot-headed lad whose death Romeo avenges by killing the killer (Alexander Zhurman's Tybalt), thus deepening the Montague–Capulet feud when he had hoped his secret marriage to Juliet had ended it.

Romeo and Juliet is a triumph for everyone who took part in it. But it is Natalia Vdovina's sparkling Juliet, her magnificent transformation from a joyously silly child into a profound, sensuous, doomed woman, that lingers in the mind.

(*December 1995*)

Czech Photography, a joint production of the Russian State Theater Agency, David Smelyansky and the Lenkom Theater; and *Birthday with Crutches*, Mossoviet Theater

Can it be time to quit singing dirges for the contemporary Russian playwright? It has been one of the most popular themes in the '90s—there are no new plays and no new playwrights, or so the story goes.

Even if that is an exaggeration—several excellent productions of fine new plays have been mounted in the last few years—there is no denying that living writers have had a much tougher time getting their plays produced than dead ones.

Now, a glance at the city marquee shows that in the last three months, there have been seven premieres of new Russian plays. That is just one less than in all of the previous season's ten months. And judging by the announcements of upcoming shows, there are many more ahead.

The two most recent in the mini-wave are Alexander Galin's *Czech Photography*, a joint production of the Russian State Theater Agency, David Smelyansky and the Lenkom Theater, and Stepan Lobozyorov's *Birthday with Crutches*, at the Mossoviet Theater. Both are well-crafted, beguiling comedies with more than enough straightforward honesty to make them touching as well.

Czech Photography is a two-man show with extras starring Nikolai Karachentsov as Lev Zudin, a down-and-out, middle-aged photographer, and Alexander Kalyagin as Pavel Razdorsky, Lev's old partner. Both ran afoul of the Soviet authorities in 1968 when they published a female nude photo in a liberal Czechoslovakian magazine, *Czech Photography*, but only Zudin paid for it. He went to prison, while the more wily Razdorsky went on to snare the coveted post of Kremlin photographer.

We catch up with them in the present, as the wealthy, cynical Razdorsky has returned to his home town of Saratov to, as he puts it, make sure he is not forgotten. He rents out a restaurant on an old river boat to throw a huge party for the locals, but his meeting with the tipsy, quixotic Zudin puts a damper on things: He is forced to take stock of his life, something he seems unaccustomed to doing.

Under the direction of Galin himself, the actors skillfully milk the text for all its laughs and sentiment. Karachentsov may overplay the drunken mannerisms, but his nagging, puppy-dog tenderness and vulnerability are irresistible. Kalyagin repeats what has made him a popular screen and stage actor for 25 years—sincerity, bravado and split-second comic timing.

David Borovsky's set of a three-tiered paddle boat hanging over the edge of the stage, puts us right on board with the action.

Birthday with Crutches, directed by Yevgeny Lazarev—better known as one of the Mossoviet's best actors—and retitled from Lobozyorov's original *Family Portrait with a Stranger*, is a situation comedy that pokes fun at people's fears of the strange and unknown. A young man rents a room in a provincial Russian town from some friends of a friend, but both parties end up living in terror of the other.

The catalyst of their anxiety is the mutual friend, Mikhail (Vladimir Goryushin), who wants to keep the handsome visitor, Viktor (Dmitry Zhuravlyov), away from the family's pretty daughter Tanya (Marina Kondratyeva): Mikhail "informs" each side that the other is susceptible to psychotic attacks. From there on out, every hesitant effort to make friendly contact is mistaken for mad ravings.

Viktor asks for a phone number and turns everyone against him. Yury Kuzmenkov's Timofei, the man of the house laid up with a broken leg, invites Viktor to join his birthday party, but Viktor suspects he'll be poisoned. The crux of the problem is everyone's willingness to believe the worst of others, and the most gullible and meddlesome of all is Natalya Tkachyova's sweetly spiteful Grandma.

Czech Photography and *Birthday with Crutches* are lively, humorous and entertaining. If they aren't modern classics, they at least are further proof that good, solid plays are being written. It's encouraging to see some finally getting staged.

(*December 1995*)

Antigone in New York, Contemporary Play School

Any account of Leonid Heifetz's fine production of Janusz Glowacki's *Antigone in New York*, at the Contemporary Play School, must begin with a digression.

It was November last year when the theater world was shocked by the events that drove Heifetz from his position as the principal director at the Russian Army Theater.

The real story never came out, although the tip of the iceberg was sensational enough: A commercial group sought partial

Lyubov Polishchuk in Janusz Glowacki's *Antigone in New York* at the Contemporary Play School, directed by Leonid Heifetz, 1995. Photo: Mikhail Guterman

control of the Army Theater's enormous stage and hall, but Heifetz was opposed. A couple of thugs forced their way into his apartment, beating him up and threatening him with death should he set foot in the Army Theater again.

Heifetz's appeals for help to the Defense Ministry (of which the theater is an official branch) fell on deaf ears, so he took the threats seriously. He resigned December 9, 1994. After that, rumors had him leaving variously for Turkey, Germany and St. Petersburg. He did spend some time in Poland.

Now, *Antigone in New York* is an unmistakable sign that last year's horrors did not affect the director's artistic powers.

Glowacki's play is a tough but sensitive look at three bums of different nationalities in New York's Central Park. The expatriate Polish author has lived in the United States since 1981, and he captured well the harsh and humorous rhythms of the New York streets.

Sasha (Vladimir Steklov), who maybe once was a budding artist in his hometown of St. Petersburg, got dumped by his wife, and then ran into trouble doing pick-up work in Brighton Beach. Now he spends his time meticulously ripping out the pockets of his grimy blazer and contemplating going home to mother.

His park bench partners are Pchelka (Yevgeny Dvorzhetsky), a skittish, hyperactive, string bean of a Polish émigré whose breakdown seemed to come when he turned coward before a woman's love, and Anita (Lyubov Polishchuk), a cat-like Puerto

Rican who says she can't get back to her Brooklyn apartment because the authorities won't let her in the subway with her junk-filled shopping cart.

Vulnerable, confused and brutally lonely, they interact, but remain stray meteors in a cold, dark universe.

One thing giving them common ground is the recent death of John, a "Boston aristocrat" whom Anita apparently loved, and whose body she wants to save from an anonymous burial in Potter's Field. Echoing the mythical Greek heroine, Antigone, who insisted on burying her outlaw brother against the king's orders, Anita convinces the others to snatch John's corpse from the police and bury him "properly" in Central Park.

It doesn't matter that, when they drag in the body after a hilarious, adventure-filled night, it's the wrong one. Anita even pretends not to notice, since it's not John she wants, but an object for her unneeded affections.

Murphy (Valery Barinov), a New York cop, interrupts the action to give the official line on skid row losers: Don't believe the bleeding hearts, he warns, these people are criminals and trouble-makers.

The strong cast is led by Steklov's Sasha. This gritty, powerful actor can move mountains with the twitch of an eyebrow, and when he finds himself falling in love with Anita, you feel it too. Just as you feel his terror when his need for liquor ruins it all before it can get started.

Mikhail Barkhin's Central Park set, with its puny metallic and cement tree "growing" behind a long, diagonal bench, seems to echo the notion that even nature has turned against these people.

As one who recently found himself an outcast with nowhere to go, Heifetz handled the story with exceptional delicacy and taste, coaxing it along tenderly, and allowing the image of each character to emerge slowly like a photo in a dark room. His *Antigone in New York* is a moving treatment of the elusiveness of prosperity, and the unfathomable mystery that every human being is.

(*December 1995*)

A Theatrical Romance, Mayakovsky Theater

Over the last few years, the Mayakovsky Theater has settled into a groove that seems to suit its administration and spectators alike. Its newest outing, A *Theatrical Romance*, will not upset the status quo.

Like so many shows the playhouse has produced recently, *Romance* is a comfy, fluffy comedy delivered up by a mix of strutting stars of various magnitudes, backed by an eager-beaver supporting cast. It is slick, professional to a point, and has all the depth of a paint-by-numbers painting.

Now in his 28th year as the top man at the Mayakovsky, Andrei Goncharov almost astonishingly spent several years putting this show together. Astonishing, because it has the feel of something slapped together in a few weeks. Each of the actors churns out the same kind of shiny, packaged performance you can see them give in any number of other shows on the venue's list.

The hook in *A Theatrical Romance* is Natalya Gundareva, whose fame as a stage and screen idol is still going strong in this 24th year of her illustrious career. She plays Marya Ogneva, a wayward, early 20th-century provincial actress who returns to her husband after a long absence. But most of all, to the crowd's delight, she plays herself.

Strictly speaking, there is no Marya Ogneva here. We never really learn anything about her, where she is from, why she has been where she has been, or what makes her tick. Instead, we get a mini encyclopedia of Gundareva's famous mannerisms; her sparkling, easy stage personality, her catching, squealy laughter, her regal way of sitting or standing, and her penchant for staring ironically and searchingly into the audience rather than making contact with her partners on stage.

To show her off even more, Goncharov gave her a couple of romances to sing— which she does with ease and feeling—and had her maneuver her way through a few very elementary dance steps whose most characteristic features are a good deal of hand-waving (choreographed by Svetlana Voskresenskaya).

Before Gundareva makes her relatively late entrance, the stage is set by the people inhabiting the house to which Marya Ogneva is returning. Egged on by the scheming Yablokov (Roman Madyanov), Ogneva's impoverished husband Stepan (Igor Okhlupin) arranges with his young landlady Natalya (Tatyana Augshkap) to pretend that he is the wealthy owner of the house. They all think the actress is just passing through, but the fireworks, such as they are, begin when they realize she has come to stay.

Madyanov gives a solid performance as the fast-talking, comically sleazy Yablokov, while Okhlupin wavers between moments of flagrant overacting and some endearing, heartfelt scenes.

More complications arise between Natalya and Babin (Viktor Zaporozhsky) the young man who holds the promissory note to her house: They're in love but can't get past the bickering stage to admit it. This is the weakest link by far, with Augshkap's screechy Tatyana and Zaporozhsky's lifeless Babin lacking any discernible romantic rapport.

The lightweight play, usually called' *A Cuckoo's Tears* or *The Shot* (because of Stepan's clumsy attempt to shoot Babin in a jealous rage) is a 19th-century-style vaudeville written by Alexei Tolstoy. He was best known for his novels *Road to Calvary* (1921–40) and *Peter the First* (1929–45), and for his insistence on being considered a distant relative of the great Leo Tolstoy. It is one of some 40 plays that he wrote between 1908 and his death in 1945, none of which has found a permanent place in the repertory.

Goncharov, as in his frothy adaptation of Alexander Ostrovsky's *The Victim of the Century* last year, was most interested in appearances. He threw up a sturdy facade, but that can't dispel the feeling that this show's pseudo-folkloric style, with its music, dances and distinct caricatures of Russian types, has all the color, attraction and substance of a painting on a cheap tin souvenir samovar.

(December 1995)

The Black Man, Stanislavsky Theater; and Town Ho!, Chelovek Theater-Studio

The Stanislavsky Drama Theater has been using its relatively new small stage in its "Mirrored Hall" with relative success over the last few years. The Chelovek Theater-Studio has been playing on small stages for more than two decades, at times with resounding success.

Recent shows at these two venues bear witness to the kinds of experiments each is apt to try—and to the limitations that hold them both back.

In *The Black Man* at the Stanislavsky, principal director Vitaly Lanskoi put together a loose little tribute to honor the 100th anniversary of the birth of the poet Sergei Yesenin, while in *Town Ho!* at the Chelovek, Alexander Marchenko fashioned a musical and movement-oriented composition on philosophical themes related to the sea. Both are honest, sincere outings that probably have more meaning for the participants than for the spectators.

The Black Man takes its origin from Yesenin's poem of the same name, completed just six weeks before his untimely death—whether by suicide or more likely by murder at the hands of the secret police—at age 30 on December 28, 1925. The poem is a miniature summing-up, with Yesenin seemingly admitting that his excesses have led him to a deadend. Lanskoi padded this and other texts with excerpts from Chekhov, Pushkin, Gogol and Shakespeare, attempting to create a picture of a poet whose talent is losing the battle with life's mundane realities and harsh demands.

In a move that is never clearly justified, Lanskoi gives us two Yesenins, the unblemished kid (Kirill Grebenshchikov) who came bursting into St. Petersburg from the province of Ryazan, and the older, confused and doubting poet (Sergei Zemtsov) who has left in his wake a series of public scandals and broken romances.

The figure of the fresh young Yesenin, hovering primarily as a silent specter in the background to remind us of what has been lost, adds little but confusion to the proceedings. Meanwhile, the rather plodding

Zemtsov splits his time between laying out the facts of the poet's biography—in brief scenes with the women from his past collectively played by Anna Isaikina—and exploring the contours of his spiritual world. That is accomplished through his interactions with a mysterious visitor in white (Vladimir Sazhin), presumably the Black Man himself.

The whirlwind of facts we get—Yesenin's marriages to the actress-to-be Zinaida Raikh and to the American dancer Isadora Duncan, his drunken forays through night-time Moscow, and his bittersweet travels through Europe—merely put signposts on the map of Yesenin's life, providing no real insight into it. The confrontations with the mysterious visitor, sometimes played out in scenes from *Hamlet* or Pushkin's *Mozart and Salieri*, are performed too weakly to be revelations about a major poet's inner life.

Town Ho! takes its title from a phrase that sailors used to cry when sighting anything at sea but land, and is constructed around an excerpt from Herman Melville's *Moby Dick*, some French ballads and Joseph Brodsky's poem, "The New Jules Verne."

The sea here is a metaphor for the quest for meaning, a mysterious place that harbors every possibility but in which no traces can ever be left. As intriguing as that idea may be, it is almost impossible to translate into theatrical language, in this case, a kind of modern dance pantomime.

Tatyana Gorchakova and Lidia Safina spend most of their time capably making like fish to director Marchenko's plucky, swishy music, but to what end? The performance remains aggressively obscure and self-indulgent. Like anything done at this spry little theater founded in 1974 by Lyudmila Roshkovan and still run by her today, *Town Ho!* is partially redeemed by its tangible sense of conviction. But, like a meal of oysters and seaweed, it is definitely an acquired taste.

(*January 1996*)

Mrs. Lev, Contemporary Play School

What do fire and water, air and earth, and Leo and Sofya Tolstoy have in common? All are natural opposites that somehow found a way to coexist: the elements for millions of years, the Tolstoys for 48.

And it still isn't certain which of those competing pairs was rocked by more rifts and conflagrations. It is a fact that the Tolstoy union, which produced 16 children and some of the world's greatest literature, was one of the most complex, confrontational and painful famous-name marriages in history.

Mrs. Lev, a play by Sergei Kokovkin, produced by Boris Morozov at the Contemporary Play School, takes a stab at getting a fresh perspective on the troubled Tolstoy alliance. However, concentrating on the events of a single day shortly before Tolstoy's death at age 82, it emerges more as a homogenized illustration of marital discord than as the purging reevaluation of conflicting human forces that one suspects the makers had in mind.

The play's title, reproducing Leo Tolstoy's name in its Russian form, seems to hint ironically that history may have left Sofya in Leo's shadow, but now we are going to take another look. It happens only to a limited degree.

In the play's single day, Sofya is confronted with the latest in a long line of Leo's infidelities with local peasant women, and with the latest attempt by Tolstoy's advisor Vladimir Chertkov (Vladimir Kachan) to gain control of the rights to the great man's writings. Providing some comic relief is a British visitor (Sergei Yeremeev) who has come to record Tolstoy's voice for posterity on a newfangled recording machine. When he fails to turn the contraption off, he also inadvertently records a conversation that gives Sofya proof of Tolstoy's tryst with the young Tanya (Yelena Ksenofontova).

Kokovkin based his play on historical facts—Tolstoy's prodigious capacity for sexual escapades, Chertkov's shifty maneuvers to inherit Tolstoy's wealth for his own socially oriented schemes, Sofya's frightful position of seeing herself publicly pummeled and ridiculed in her husband's literature. He brings these facts together in a hypothetical setting and the result is a recognizable picture for anyone who is at least casually informed about Tolstoy's life; but it doesn't really offer any new insights.

Valentina Talyzina's Sofya, for all the sympathy she may attract, seems stubborn and narrow rather than feisty and trapped. She plays a woman wronged, practically determined to defend herself and the rights of her children, but never breaking out as a full-fledged personality on her own.

She comes closest when confronting her "rival" Tanya through understanding and sisterly friendship. Sofya falls into unguarded reminiscing, admitting she has "been mating" her whole life long. For a brief moment, we see her as a tragic figure, a person who has done all that society and her husband have asked of her, receiving only scorn in return.

Lev Durov, an explosive actor with an unruly white beard attached to his chin, is a dead ringer for Tolstoy. But his striking resemblance may even have worked against him. He so perfectly calls up our own preconceived notions of Tolstoy, that we see in him more of the myth than of the human being. And when in the end he seems to return as an apparition to narrate what will happen in the final hours of his life at the railway station of Astapovo, we realize that once again Tolstoy has overshadowed Sofya.

Tatyana Spasolomskaya's set depicts a rustic interior at Tolstoy's Yasnaya Polyana estate. Initially, we see it vaguely through a screen that also reveals a battle mural on the back wall, referring equally perhaps to Tolstoy's experiences in the Crimean War and his unsettled married life. The color scheme is of browns and blues, echoing the mix of the earth and the heavens that characterized his uneasy union with "Mrs. Lev."

(January 1996)

The Ball, Novy Drama Theater

Every once in awhile a show comes along that looks almost perfect. Great costumes, excellent performances, snappy directing, crisp writing, refreshing music, the works. One of those bright, entertaining shows that, as Russians say, you watch in a single breath.

The Novy Drama Theater's production of *The Ball*, Pyotr Gnedich's play about social

maneuvering complicated by love and embezzlement in the court of Peter the Great, is just such a show. Beautiful, buoyant and funny, it has the clarity and color of a masterful folk painting.

Director Andrei Sergeev is a designer by profession, his only directing experience coming as an occasional right-hand man to Boris Lvov-Anokhin, who in the middle of a storied career spanning four decades took over the Novy Drama Theater as artistic director in 1989. Sergeev made his professional bow as an artist at the Maly Theater in 1987, designing Lvov-Anokhin's popular production of Gnedich's *Lackeys*. Since then the two have been almost inseparable, and it is no coincidence that he has made his directing debut with another play by Gnedich.

The Ball was originally staged in 1912 but essentially disappeared after that; not the kind of track record that promises success for a first-time director. But with strong support from everyone involved, success was the result.

The unquestioned star of the ball is the delightful, charming and astonishing Vera Vasilyeva as Natalya Borisovna, an old-school widow who balks at Peter the Great's western innovations, refusing to attend a state ball with "drunken Germans," and relies on her youthful spunk to save her son's love affair from falling an innocent victim to politics.

Vasilyeva, 70, has the same disarming smile, fetching dimples and bottomless well of sincerity that immediately set her apart when she joined the Satire Theater in 1948. If anything, this universally beloved actress has since grown younger and stronger. She is grace and talent incarnate, a study in detail, concentration and truth, effortlessly illuminating every glance and gesture of her endearingly blustery heroine. This is that rare performer who defies description or criticism, and must be seen to be believed.

As rarely happens with a cast of 40, Vasilyeva's entrancing, nuanced performance is surrounded everywhere by top-notch work.

The first entrance of her youthful, love-struck son Pyotr Andreevich (Denis Bespaly), frizzed up in an orange costume and beehive wig to impress the pretty Frosya (Marina Yakovleva), is a spectacle in itself, and highlights Sergeev's shrewd delineation of caricatured types.

Frosya's family is headed by her embezzling father Matvei Sidorych (Anatoly Sutyagin) with a bell-shaped belly and the complexion of a cadaver. At 60 he is 30 years younger than his own straggly-haired, wheelchair-bound father Sidor Zotych (Igor Churikov), but not half as lively. His wife Zinovia (Natalya Bespalova) is a remarkable creature whose wildly exaggerated bust is barely enough to balance off the weight of her humongous rear end.

Budding bourgeois bums, they are heartily consternated when Natalya Borisovna gives them an ultimatum: If they attend the ball, she will not let her son marry their daughter. However, the seemingly hardhearted matriarch turns out to be a softy underneath, and when she learns that Matvei Sidorych has been caught stealing government monies, she quietly suggests her son pay the debt and saves the day.

The gala culmination is the wild ball itself, overseen by a wonderfully mock-serious Peter the Great (Vladimir Levashyov). It features a huge corps de ballet of fainting matrons, dandies in pink and flying cupids who cavort to the light strains of music by Jacques Offenbach.

Sergeev's own modern, minimalist set, aided by Viktor Vasilyev's strong side and top lighting showcase Natalia Zakurdayeva's colorful and comical period costumes, and the extraordinarily expressive makeup by Lyudmila Meyerhold.

This *Ball* is one not to be missed.

(January 1996)

Child of Another, Gogol Drama Theater

In *Child of Another*, the Gogol Theater has resurrected a playwright, Vasily Shkvarkin, who has not been heard from for decades. But if it makes for an interesting project in principle, in deed there is little to recommend it.

Shkvarkin was an anomaly if not something of a mystery in Soviet literature. An exquisitely polite and impeccably well-dressed man whose elegance was such that one memoirist wrote it seemed he was always wearing white gloves, Shkvarkin was an aesthete who virtually never took part in literary polemics or political life.

Having worked in a bank and the leather business before the revolution, he entered a playwriting contest in 1925, taking second prize. Over the next 20 years, he became the top Soviet writer of light comedies, beloved by audiences, ignored by the state and reviled by the critics. Something of a Neil Simon of his time and place.

By the time of his death at age 73 in 1967, Shkvarkin was pretty much forgotten, although *Child of Another*, his most popular play, was occasionally the object of revivals. First staged in 1933 at the Satire Theater, the play was performed at that venue a staggering 1,500 times throughout the '30s and '40s.

With a little good will and imagination it is even understandable today why the play was once so admired. The comic situations are honed to a sharp edge. The characters, though stereotypes, are lively. The dialogue, featuring ironic twists and the occasional double-entendre, is witty.

Precious little of that, however, comes through in Alexander Bordukov's bracingly superficial and shamelessly overacted production at the Gogol Theater. Things are not helped by Viktoria Nikonova's cartoonish set—a pale green, see-through dacha with crooked windows and walls, pale green lawn furniture, plyboard cut-out shrubbery and a green backdrop suggesting the surrounding forest.

Before long, one can't help but feel that the monotony of the visuals is drowning out what little life there may be lurking in the performance.

In the time-honored style of the 19th-century vaudeville, the play puts forth a budding actress who finds herself rejected by her lover and at odds with her parents. What was new in 1933 was a rather feminist twist: The headstrong girl purposefully worsens her situation to prove her independence. Bordukov shaved off most, though not all, of Shkvarkin's few direct references to "communist reality," but it was not enough to free the work entirely of the smell of moth balls.

Manya (Anna Bolshova) is the actress rehearsing the part of a girl who gets pregnant out of wedlock. When one of her suitors, Senechka (Dmitry Chopenko), overhears her repeating her lines, he takes it for the real thing and spills the beans to her horrified parents. It isn't long before Manya is also abandoned by her true love, Kostya (Andrei Bolsunov).

Manya, her sense of justice injured, decides to play the error for all it's worth, finding consolation in a real unwed expectant mother, Raya (Irina Rudnitskaya), whom she talks out of an abortion.

Before all ends happily, several layers of complications are added, with Manya briefly getting engaged to Raya's shifty former lover, Pribylev (Ivan Volkov). He is a road engineer who, when Manya learns the truth and rejects him, decides to flatten the dacha of Manya's parents to make room for a thoroughfare.

Bordukov staged it all in alternating waves of schmaltzy sentimentalism, monumental melodrama and screechy farce. If he was aiming for a kind of retro camp—a legitimate approach to a play like this—he missed the mark widely, landing smack dab in the middle of overkill and underachievement.

Child of Another, occasionally known in translation as *Father Unknown*, was once one of the most popular of all Soviet comedies. You wouldn't know that by the production at the Gogol Theater.

(*January 1996*)

The Sunshine Boys, Vakhtangov Theater

Willie is sick of Al and has been for half a century. He doesn't like the way Al pokes his finger in his chest, and he can't stand the way Al spits when making "s" sounds. In fact, he has a theory that Al specially thinks up words jam-packed with sibilants just to be able to spit at him as much as possible.

Willie and Al are Willie Clark and Al Lewis, former vaudeville stars who spent 43 years bickering off stage and bewitching on it as the famous "Lewis and Clark" comedy team. Now, after an eleven-year hiatus, the old geezers are getting together again to play their popular doctor sketch for a t.v. special on the history of comedy. The question is, can they stand working side-by-side one more time?

The play is Neil Simon's *The Sunshine Boys*, and it is pure Simon. On the upside that means a witty text and packed punchlines. On the downside, it means that dramatic development and character psychology are gaily washed away in the cascades of gags.

At the Vakhtangov Theater, director Andrei Zhitinkin took the best possible route in navigating the material: He cast a great actor in the central role of Willie, getting the most out of the jokes, while occasionally achieving a depth that isn't really indigenous to the frothy play.

Yury Yakovlev is now in the 44th year of an illustrious career that has brought him as much acclaim for his stage work as for his starring roles in film. With a year more of experience than Willie Clark, he knows all there is to know about life on stage and off.

Nevertheless, Yakovlev has not been a frequent guest of late on his home stage at the Vakhtangov. Until *The Sunshine Boys* came along, the only other show he could be seen in was the acclaimed *Guilty Without Guilt.* *The Sunshine Boys* has been staged as a vehicle for the actor, and, with his impressive talents pushing the pedals, it goes places fast.

Yakovlev's Willie is a spoiled man-child with charm. Pouty, selfish and vulnerable, he is the typical retiree from any number of old, formulaic Hollywood or Broadway comedies. Making life miserable for everyone around him—in this case, his loving nephew doubling as his suffering agent Ben (played with straight-on warmth by Oleg Forostenko), and his deceptively phlegmatic nurse (Maria Aronova)—we see through his cantankerousness if not to a heart of gold, then at least to a crusty old heart that still is beating.

Willie holds out on agreeing to the comeback engagement for the longest time. Fending off Ben's exhortations, he gives a

Yury Yakovlev in Neil Simon's *The Sunshine Boys*, directed by Andrei Zhitinkin at the Vakhtangov Theater, 1996.
Photo: Mikhail Guterman

rogue's gallery of imitations of Al at his worst behavior. Handled by a lesser actor, these moments of trite shtick could easily fall flat. Carried off by the slurring Yakovlev with his hip-hop limp, they are the triumph of an actor exercising his craft and having a blast at it.

When Al finally shows up at Willie's sparsely furnished Manhattan apartment (functionally designed by Ilonka Gansov-skaya), the pair eventually gets around to rehearsing the act—and getting caught up in old animosities. It's never quite certain whether Willie keeps flubbing his lines be-cause he's too old to remember, or because he's bound and determined to drive Al to distraction.

Mikhail Semakov's understated Al is the ideal sidekick. Quiet but stubborn, and de-manding but affectionate, he'd love to bury the hatchet after all these years. But he's leery that Willie has the same idea, and is aiming for his back.

Zhitinkin softened Simon's ambiguous ending, having the two old slumbering codgers jump out of their chairs to launch into a sword fight with canes. But by this time, the end isn't what's important. We've already had the pleasure of watching Yury Yakovlev put on an acting clinic.

(February 1996)

The Karamazovs and Hell, Sovremennik Theater

There is just about everything in the Sovremennik Theater's new adaptation of Dostoevsky, *The Karamazovs and Hell*, to guarantee success.

It was directed by Valery Fokin who in the last few years has reasserted himself as one of Moscow's top talents. As in his spec-tacular productions of *A Hotel Room in the Town of N* and *The Metamorphosis*, Fokin once again collaborated with Alexander Bakshi, a striking, unorthodox composer. Performing the lead of Ivan Karamazov is the young star Yevgeny Mironov, the recent winner of the best-actor Nika, Russia's highest cinematic award, for his performance in *The Moslem*.

For good measure, Mikhail Gluzsky, the popular film actor who impressed so in a rare stage appearance in last season's *An Old Man Wanted to Leave his Old Woman*, delivers two fine scenes as Zosima, Dostoevsky's archetypal vision of a wise priest. And Igor Kvasha, a leading actor and founding member at the Sovremennik, turns in an effective, grizzled, often humorous performance of Fyodor, the proudly debauched patriarch of the ill-fated Karamazov family.

So why is this show so flat and uninspiring? At least some of the answers are buried in what made the project so promising in the first place.

Yevgeny Mironov, a light, extraordinarily agile actor with a kind face and a winning, warm demeanor, is completely out of place as the hyper-intellectual Ivan. Fokin could well have titled this production *Ivan and Hell*, for its focus rests squarely on Ivan, his battles with the notion of a God who lets evil exist in the world, and his repeated encounters with a pair of badgering devils (Avangard Leontyev and Alexander Kakhun).

Mironov, remaining at heart a kind of congenial next-door neighbor, would have been much more on target as the pious, youngest son Alyosha (handled here routinely by Dmitry Petukhov). But with Mironov at the helm, the expected torque of Dostoevsky's descent into existential nausea never occurs.

Sergei Garmash delivers a sincere if unspectacular Dmitry, the sensual eldest brother, while Vasily Mishchenko is functional as Smerdyakov, the illegitimate brother who killed the father, thinking he was doing it with Ivan's blessing.

In the cast's partial defense, the play itself provides little to build on. Nikolai Klimontovich, who adapted the novel into 13 dramatic episodes whose chronology has been slightly reshuffled, seemed intent on picking on all the superficial signs which create the Dostoevsky stereotype, but do nothing to get inside the author's world.

The result is truncated literature merely transferred to the stage without any imbedded dramatic or theatrical devices capable of interpreting or remaking the original. Without that act of recreation, theater does not happen, and one might just as well read the book.

Fokin employed Bakshi's hissing, ticking and tocking music as he has before: having it emerge sometimes from behind the spectators' backs, sometimes from backstage. But where that was so effective in the controlled, small spaces of his last two productions, the effect is lost in the large hall at the Sovremennik. The music remains nothing but random sounds unable to muster a sense of atmosphere.

Furthermore, the dark, heavy set by Woldemar Zawodzinski is so metaphorical as to border on the trite. Its crumbling walls of a cavernous, "civilized" interior reveal layers of earth, rocks and roots breaking through, perhaps to hint that, like another of Dostoevsky's famous characters, these people live "underground." A see-through, terrarium-like coffin protrudes into the first rows of seats. From it the dead father emerges early on, leaving an empty space to which Smerdyakov will go when he commits suicide.

With all the Dostoevsky adaptations that have been appearing of late, *The Karamazovs and Hell* is just another in the crowd. As for Fokin, word is that he's already at work on his next project. Let's get on to that one.

(February 1996)

The Newspaper *"Russian Invalid,"* Dated July 18 . . . , Osobnyak Theater; and *Macbeth*, Bolshoi Drama Theater, both of St. Petersburg

Even before the March 30 opening of the Second Chekhov International Theater Festival, a marathon three-month affair featuring 35 productions from 18 countries, two touring shows from St. Petersburg once again pointed out that much of the best theater in Moscow in the 1995/96 season was coming from outside the city limits. One was Temur Chkheidze's grand, acclaimed production of Shakespeare's *Macbeth* for the Tovstonogov Bolshoi Drama Theater, while the other was Alexander Lebedev's almost minuscule staging of Mikhail Ugarov's play, *The Newspaper "Russian Invalid," Dated July 18...* for the Osobnyak Theater. They couldn't possibly have been more different in scope, theme and execution although both were equally interesting.

First into town was the Osobnyak Theater which on January 25, 1996 gave a single performance in a tiny hall at the House of Actors on the Arbat as part of the author's 40th birthday party. Mikhail Ugarov is one of the many writers of the "middle generation"—i.e., strictly speaking no longer "young," but still decades from being "old"—who have had a terrible time getting their plays produced. Ugarov's case has been complicated by the fact that his intellectual, highly literary plays are often perceived as lacking in theatricality. They all have been praised as masterful writing, although productions of them have been few and far between.[2]

After seeing the Osobnyak's version of *"Russian Invalid,"* one can't help but think that all the hesitation in regards to Ugarov is more than a little misguided. Lebedev's production drives right into the heart of the languorous play set in pre-revolutionary times, and comes out with a fistful of irony that makes the text and its characters sparkle with life.

Ivan Ivanovich (Dmitry Podnozov) is a bit of an eccentric who, in the two years that he has avoided leaving his apartments, has continued to live a life in his imagination that suits him just fine. Attempts by his edgy nephew (Lebedev) and his impetuous niece (Olga Teterina) to draw him back into the real world are fruitless; he is more than

satisfied by the vicarious pleasures he gets "going for walks" in front of his picture window and reading occasional letters from a woman who may or may not be attempting to get him to run away with her. He is waited on by a rather mysterious and, seemingly, quite independent nanny (Yelena Sevryukova) in a white costume and with her face covered by a veil.

The key components of Yevgenia Gurina's simple, curtain-draped set are a dinky divan-like train-car bench at center stage and the "picture" bay window on the back wall featuring the image of a horse. The set is "enhanced," so to speak, by an unidentified woman who comes out for a kind of prologue and recites Ugarov's extraordinarily detailed set descriptions, pointing to empty spaces or clearly inadequate props as if encouraging us to believe what we hear and not what we see. On either side of the stage are portrait galleries of great Russian writers and theatrical figures, Lebedev's own addition, perhaps intended to teasingly draw attention to Ugarov's reputation as a master of words and "unstageable" playwright.

The conflict between Ivan and his nephew Alyosha is to an extent generational, but more importantly it is one of aesthetics and world views. Ivan is neat, fastidious, reserved and cerebral, while the young, quick-talking Alyosha, who at least claims to be looking for a rich widow to settle his money problems, is crude, caustic and calculating. In many ways, this is a playing out of Ugarov's own position as a playwright in an age that has seen the aggressive vulgarity of mass culture become the norm. Ivan Ivanovich, perhaps like Ugarov himself, takes refuge in the seductive comfort of exotic words and rarefied thoughts, although he is anything but a psychological weakling afraid to face reality. His withdrawal is that of an aesthete, an active, conscious step. That becomes most evident as the production draws to a close and Ivan launches into a heated—and comical—tirade on his hatred for "stories with plots," and categorically rejects the idea of "endings."

Podnozov shines in this scene, emerging from his hiding place behind a plaid blanket

---

[2] Ugarov's published plays are: *Doves*, written 1988 (*Sovremennaya dramaturgiya* No. 3–4, 1993); *My Kitchenette*, 1989 (*Teatr*, No. 8, 1992); *Orthography According to Grot*, 1991 (*Sovremennaya dramaturgiya* No. 2, 1992); *The Newspaper "Russian Invalid," Dated July 18...,* 1992 (*Dramaturg* 1/1993); *The Ragamuffin*, 1993 (*Dramaturg* 3/1994); and *The Green Cheeks of April*, 1994 (*Dramaturg* 6/95). One play, an adaptation of Hans Christian Andersen, remains unpublished: *The Princess on the Pea*, written 1990.

with his face going red from frustration and the veins in his neck visibly popping out. He temporarily gets a grip on himself only when he drifts into a soothing description of a "bent lily."

By acknowledging the metaliterary basis of *The Newspaper "Russian Invalid," Dated July 18...*, and by having fun with it, director Lebedev drew out the substantial theatricality inherent in it. His modest but effective production leaves no doubt that Mikhail Ugarov is no mere author of *Lesedramen*.

In *Macbeth*, which played under the auspices of the Theater of Nations at the Mossoviet Theater February 22 and 23, Temur Chkheidze found a way to have the best of two worlds. He staged a relentless, sweeping social drama which, at the same time, never loses its human focus. Georgy Alexi-Meskhishvili's large but sparse, partly mechanical set (a moving platform on tracks on the stage level, and a narrow runway stretching from side to side high above the stage) highlights the former, while the actors, led by Gennady Bogachyov's compelling Macbeth, play the tragedy of believable people ground under by ambition, stupidity, intrigue and history.

Bogachyov, hairy, clunky and appearing enormous on stage, has a brute, almost animalistic simplicity about him. In that, there is almost even a glimmer of innocence or at least the kind of moral neutrality one would grant a wolf or lion. He is easily manipulated by Lady Macbeth, because he hasn't a shadow of her sophistication. When he finds himself on top of the heap, he accepts his position as entirely natural; when he must fight to retain it, he shuns no treachery. Then, as some vague memory of conscience seems to dawn on his Macbeth, the actor creates a fascinating and gripping picture of a man slowly self-destructing under the weight of his own bloody ways.

Early on, Alisa Freindlikh's Lady Macbeth is at a distinct disadvantage. Frankly, the fine and popular actress is too old for the part, and she often buries her character in flurries of overacting. But in her final two scenes she turns it all around and matches Bogachyov stride for stride right through the grisly end. Her descent into

sleepwalking insanity is played with a palpable, cutting tension, while one of the production's finest moments comes as her dead body is toted and tossed around by the grief-stricken, uncomprehending Macbeth. Freindlikh, nearly bald but for a few straggly wisps of hair, limp, pliable, and deathly expressionless, is a sight to behold.

In Chkheidze's version of the macabre finale, the dead Lady Macbeth sits propped against the wall at the front, left corner of the stage, holding her husband's bloody, severed head between her legs as if it were a newborn infant. Almost imperceptibly a smile begins to appear on her lips but in time it grows into a horrid, scowling grin. It is as though even she has realized that she is now free; the responsibility for the violence which she spawned has now passed on to Macbeth's murderer, Macduff.

(Slavic and East-European Journal, Summer 1996)

Tanya-Tanya, Fomenko Studio

Great theater is a matter of good combinations. The right play, the right director, the right actors in the right spots. When all of those things come together at the right time—as they rarely do—that's what makes success.

That is just what happened with *Tanya-Tanya*, the Fomenko Studio's marvelously airy and penetrating production of a brilliant new play by Olga Mukhina.

Since its formation on the basis of an acclaimed graduating class at the Russian Academy of Theater Arts in the fall of 1993, the Fomenko Studio has struggled artistically. Pyotr Fomenko, its renowned leader, has battled serious health problems and occasionally has been busy with other projects. Meanwhile, his former students have turned out some ambitious, but ultimately hollow productions, raising big questions about their true potential.

Tanya-Tanya, the studio's fourth professional outing, was prepared by the actor/director Andrei Prikhodko. But when the mid-January opener neared, things apparently weren't right. Fomenko stepped in, canceling the premiere, and took over for an intense few weeks of extended rehearsals.

Andrei Prikhodko and Galina Tyunina in Olga Mukhina's *Tanya-Tanya*, a production of the Fomenko Studio, 1996. Photo: Mikhail Guterman

So who gets to take credit for this probing, delicate and enthralling examination of the mystery of love now that it has opened? The answer is easy: Everyone involved.

The kudos must begin with Mukhina. At age 25, she is one of the youngest of the many talented playwrights to recently burst on the scene, belying the conventional wisdom that there are no good contemporary plays. *Tanya-Tanya*, Mukhina's second published play, is a work of breathtaking imagination and depth.

Cut into cinematic episodes that both stand alone and echo one another, the play draws back the curtain on the affections, desires and despairs of three men and three women gathered in one place, the hospitable home of Vasya Okhlobystin. Mukhina's colloquial language and her fateful situations buried in deceptively superficial chit-chat, create a dramatic world of razor-sharp clarity.

The actors are better matched to the people they play than in any of the studio's previous productions, inhabiting Mukhina's languorous, tactile world with persuasive honesty and sincerity.

Prikhodko is superb as Okhlobystin, a romantic who rudely discovers that advancing age is about to end the kind of life he is accustomed to. Charmingly gruff and always magnanimous, he toys with the lonely Zina (Galina Tyunina) but falls for the doll-like beauty Tanya (Ksenia Kutepova).

Tanya's husband Ivanov (Andrei Kazakov) is momentarily sidetracked by a pretty girl also named Tanya (Polina Kutepova, Ksenia's twin in real life), and when he turns his attentions back to his wife, it is nearly too late. Adding to the confusion of affections, Tanya and Ivanov's son (Kirill Pirogov) falls for the same girl as his dad.

Mukhina's constellation of lovers seem to soar weightlessly in a heady atmosphere of heightened passions, although that hardly means their skies are cloudless. On the contrary, hearts are broken inexorably and irreversibly as people dance and kiss, and champagne flows.

Especially impressive are Tyunina and Polina Kutepova as the two women aced out by Tanya's cool, marble beauty. Tyunina

captures perfectly Zina's spinsterly self-sufficiency and eccentricity, while Kutepova's transparent expressions and gestures reveal all her fears, hopes, disappointments, and the wisdom that experience is forcing on her.

But it may be Pirogov's innocent, blissfully grinning performance of the young boy smitten by love which gives things focus. His radiance and freshness are mirrored in the sparse, summery decoration, the baggy, flowing costumes, and the ethereal music which ranges from jazz to the romantic ballads of Alexander Vertinsky and Pyotr Leshchenko.

Fomenko's touch—the proliferation of subtle detail even in sounds and smells—is unmistakable. Some are calling *Tanya-Tanya* a joint production of Fomenko and Prikhodko, while the program lists no director at all. It's a fitting move, because *Tanya-Tanya* is a team effort and a team triumph.

(February 1996)

The Tragedy of Hamlet, Prince of Denmark, Krasnaya Presnya Theater

It has been three years—a long time by the theatrical calendar—since Yury Pogrebnichko's last full-fledged production at his Krasnaya Presnya Theater. That show, a weird and wonderful adaptation of Nikolai Gogol's *The Marriage*, retitled *When I Wrote, I Saw Before Me Only Pushkin*, displayed to near perfection the director's rich imagination and his use of heavy irony and dense visual metaphors.

Whether or not the lull was the result of Pogrebnichko being stricken by a "doubting disease" à là Hamlet is uncertain. But it is a fact that he has re-emerged from his hiatus with a characteristically quirky rendition of Shakespeare's *The Tragedy of Hamlet, Prince of Denmark*.

Pogrebnichko's style marks him no less indisputably than a fingerprint. Dispassionate actors stalk his tiny stage, delivering their lines with such a ponderous aura of importance that the underlying humor of it all crackles in the air like electricity. Their deadpan expressions and lethargic, almost mournful mannerisms seem to carry them off into an isolated, deeply private world of their own.

Yury Pavlov, one of several Hamlets, writing "To be or not to be" on the back wall in Yury Pogrebnichko's production of Shakespeare's *Hamlet* at the Krasnaya Presnya Theater, 1996. Photo: Mikhail Guterman

Hamlet fully maintains those elements of the bizarre, serving up multiple Hamlets, Ophelias and others. Each of Shakespeare's characters is capable at any moment of taking on one or another of the prince's attributes: the ranting intellectual (Andrei Kochetkov), the cool contemporary (Yury Pavlov) or the indifferent killer (Afanasy Trishkin).

When Trishkin's Hamlet murders Polonius (Valery Prokhorov) in Gertrude's chambers it is no mistake. He just walks up to the curtain where Polonius is hiding and plunges his dagger into it.

This is a world of lies and liars, conspiracies and spies where informing and backstabbing are a way of life. No one is surprised to become the victim of another's plot, because everyone knows that he or she is not only capable of, but guilty of the same behavior.

Nadezhda Bakhvalova, who often dresses Pogrebnichko's actors in stylized prison-camp garb, this time emphasized the clone-like monotony of a conspiratorial world by putting everyone in long, loose black over-coats. The women wear metal hoops that protrude from under their coats, providing the only reference to traditional feminine clothing. The minimalist set by Yury Kononenko (who died in December) is dominated by an open trap door-like grave at center stage and the rusty, dented iron panels lining the walls.

Pogrebnichko loves creating visual puns by "illustrating" text. In this case, Hamlet's refusal to be played on as if he were a pipe is already signaled at the outset: The entire cast, like musicians, momentarily take places at music stands which will henceforth be removed and returned frequently.

Shakespeare's play has been heartily transformed. Many key monologues have been edited or reshuffled, while some have disappeared. But, especially in the very strong first act, the new arrangements only give the play a sharper focus. The atmosphere of conniving and scheming—like the fun of theater rooting them out of their hiding places—is so thick you can cut it with a knife.

The second act, though still clinging to the production's strengths as a whole, occasionally buckles under the weight of Pogrebnichko's almost scholarly fascination with intertextual play. Long scenes from Dostoevsky's *Crime and Punishment* and Chekhov's *Three Sisters* shatter the tight focus of the first act, and begin making you feel as if you are in a literature class with quiz to follow.

More to the point are the occasional sound tracks of the late Innokenty Smoktunovsky performing one of the great traditional Hamlets from Grigory Kozintsev's 1964 film. The spectral presence of Smoktunovsky's inspired classicism amid Pogrebnichko's inspired deconstruction reminds us how flexible a truly great play can be.

(*February 1996*)

Khlestakov, **Stanislavsky Drama Theater**

Nobody can accuse Vladimir Mirzoyev of lacking imagination. Like an inventive cook, he doesn't just mix things up, he gives you the works. A wild concoction. Horseradish and cinnamon.

And then he dares you not to like it. As if to say, "Only imbeciles won't like this!"

Khlestakov, Mirzoyev's creative rendition of Nikolai Gogol's *The Inspector General* at the Stanislavsky Theater, is the director's second assault on the classic 19th-century author in less than two years. In June 1994 he marked his return to Moscow after several years in Canada with an energetic, unorthodox version of Gogol's *The Marriage*. That impressive show, featuring two actresses in each female part, irritated traditionalists and delighted appreciative audiences.

In principle *Khlestakov* is much the same, only with lots more of it.

This is no mere story about a slippery Petersburg clerk duping an entire provincial town into thinking he is a high-placed government official. It is a frantic Freudian fantasy on the themes of duplicity, power, brutishness and stupidity, tinged in Oriental motifs.

That's all fine and good, and there are times when this aggressively strange show

Vladimir Mirzoyev's production of *Khlestakov*, an adaptation of Nikolai Gogol's *The Inspector General* at the Stanislavsky Drama Theater, 1996, with (clockwise from top) Vladimir Smirnov, Zhanna Epple, Maxim Sukhanov and Yulia Rutberg. Photo: Alexander Ivanishin

catches fire and sparkles. But just as often it fizzles, smothered by the director's overconfidence that every unexpected trick he pulls is interesting and/or funny.

Standing center stage is Ivan Khlestakov, the low-level clerk whose appearance in the unnamed town with his servant Osip brings down humiliation on the mayor and other local bureaucrats, and sends the mayor's wife and daughter into paroxysms of sexual longing.

But this Khlestakov is unlike any before him. Played as a lump of raw, animal instinct by Maxim Sukhanov, he appears as a kind of whirling dervish, spinning liltingly with the tails of his eastern robe fluttering about him, and leaves on a "magic carpet" pulled by the mysterious, Magus-like Osip (Vladimir Korenev). Khlestakov's bald head, slanted eyes and crude manner suggest the spirit of an invading Genghis Khan.

The mayor (Vladimir Smirnov), Khlestakov's biggest victim, is an obsequious, grinning fool who, even if he does suspect he is being duped, is too spellbound by the visitor's insolence to combat it.

The only prop of note in Pavel Kaplevich's set (based on Dmitry Alexeev's futuristic set from *The Marriage*) is a multipurpose, metal-frame bunk bed. Depending upon the scene, it becomes a prison cell, a baby's crib, a place to lounge aimlessly or a place for making love.

Love, or more properly, sex, is split here into two categories; the physical act, bearing tinges of rape, and the state of unsatisfied arousal. The former is portrayed in Khlestakov's trysts first with a hotel servant (changed to a female from Gogol's male character) and later with a girl (not in Gogol's play) offered as a bribe (both played by Viktoria Tolstoganova).

More effective are Khlestakov's encounters with the mayor's wife Anna (Yulia Rutberg) and his daughter Marya (Zhanna Epple). It is no coincidence that the production's finest moments come with these two actresses flanking the hero as he rattles off a litany of lies about his life in the capital. Anna's cloying, overripe desire is shaded well by Marya's breathless, newly-awakened passion.

Flitting in and out are a trio of "Women Victims" whose purpose is presumably clearer to the director than anyone else.

Mirzoyev lopped off the play's ending, which shows the townspeople learning of Khlestakov's ruse. Instead, all are left in a state of ambiguous, heightened expectation as Khlestakov "flies" off on his carpet. Gogol's famous finale—a dumb scene of the motionless cast staring at the audience—has been moved to the curtain calls.

Khlestakov is alternately disgusting, boring, wonderful or fascinating. But one conclusion is unavoidable: Gogol is a better writer than Mirzoyev is a director. And the closer the latter follows the former, the more intriguing his production looks.

(February 1996)

The Queen of Spades, Vakhtangov Theater

The *Queen of Spades* at the Vakhtangov Theater is unmistakably a Pyotr Fomenko production.

Swirling movement, tense silences, delicate sounds and, perhaps most of all, the sensation of inner freedom—spontaneity—are the masterful director's trademarks. They are what put his stagings of *Guilty Without Guilt* (1993) and *The Magnificent Cuckold* (1994) among Moscow's most celebrated productions of the '90s, and they are all present in his dramatization of Alexander Pushkin's short story about a cautious man who becomes madly obsessed with learning an old countess's secret of winning at cards.

But, here it comes, the "but..."

Despite some fabulous moments of humor, beauty and sensitivity, something holds this show back. The pieces are in place. You can see the torques the director put on the story and the flourishes he added in its telling.

And that's the trouble. Too often you find yourself getting lost in the nuts and bolts of the show's making, while that magic moment when it takes flight and becomes a world of its own never quite happens.

Lyudmila Maksakova, a leading actress at the Vakhtangov, plays the 87 year-old countess and is the primary carrier of the show's comic bent. A famous beauty and a heart-breaker in her youth, the Countess now is a crusty, bewigged old thing whose chief occupation is tyrannizing her young ward, Liza (Marina Yesipenko). But Maksakova's harsh, screechy voice (intended to imitate a deaf old woman?) and her coarse mannerisms are more strained and vulgar than funny.

A subtler countess might have lightened and sharpened the irony of the story, where all the actors partially perform and partially narrate their own parts, although as played here she is more apt to take the wind out of the sails each time things begin building momentum.

Another shortfall is Yevgeny Knyazev's Hermann, the young officer who resolves to learn the countess's unbeatable card combination by going at her through the unsuspecting Liza. Lurking silently in the shadows outside Liza's window to catch her attention, the actor cuts an appropriately mysterious and obsessed figure. But when he sneaks into the countess's bedroom and promises to take on her sins in exchange for the secret, Knyazev has no temperamental reserve to call on and crank things up to a more intense emotional level.

Fomenko envisioned this crucial confrontation as a mock seduction, with the countess dying in Hermann's arms as much from pleasure as from fright. That was the goal, anyway. The reality is a flat scene that illustrates, but does not convince.

More in tune with the director were Yesipenko and especially Yulia Rutberg, who turns in a riveting performance of an added character called Mysterious Ill Will.

Yesipenko has that indispensable actor's sense which allows her to express emotion and have fun with it too. Aflutter with awakening sensual feelings, running and leaping with youthful innocence, her Liza is touching but never simplistic.

Rutberg, severe in a boy-cut blonde wig and a flowing black cape over black tights, is a kind of author's voice and incarnation of Hermann's inner thoughts. In turns she shadows him, echoes him, anticipates his moves and quietly directs him, always creating the sensation of a dark, cutting enigma. She lurks nearby when he dreams that the dead old woman passes on her secret, and she

looks on coldly as he loses his cool, his money and his sanity in the fateful final card game. When all is done, she removes her wig and calmly relaxes—like an actor done with a show, or a devil done with a job.

Stanislav Morozov's revolving, soft gray set accentuates Fomenko's use of movement as it swiftly delivers and carries away the rooms of the countess's home.

Compared to Fomenko's best work, *The Queen of Spades* looks like a rough sketch. But, to be sure, one by a major artist.

(*March 1996*)

An Inspector Calls, Mossoviet Theater

This has been the season of the showcase, that seductive theatrical genre which puts forth a star as the self-contained *raison d'être* for a show and pretty much shapes everything else around him or her.

Often it works, and the success rate this year has probably been even better than average. Productions featuring Vera Vasilyeva (at the Novy Drama and Satire theaters), Yury Yakovlev (the Vakhtangov), Natalya Gundareva (the Mayakovsky) and Alexander Kalyagin and Nikolai Karachentsov (Lenkom) have all been crowd-pleasers even if the critical fallout has ranged from the ecstatic to the cynical.

The latest in the pack is the Mossoviet Theater's *An Inspector Calls*, the mysterious play by J.B. Priestley, starring the classy Georgy Zhzhyonov. This revered actor, whose career couldn't be ruined even by a 15-year stint in the labor camps (1939–1954), is looking as fit, sharp and handsome as ever at 81.

Zhzhyonov is probably best loved for his starring roles in the spy film series, *The Resident's Mistake*, (1968), *The Fate of the Resident* (1970) and *The Return of the Resident* (1982). However, true or not, legend has it that he was already so popular in 1939 that the thieves in prison—notoriously cruel to political prisoners—received their new neighbor with open arms.

An Inspector was directed by Andrei Zhitinkin, a young talent who is fast earning the sobriquet of the Showcase King. It was

Zhitinkin who got the long-time film star Lyudmila Gurchenko to make her stage debut last season in a frightfully garish, but popular production of Edvard Radzinsky's *The Battlefield After Victory Belongs to Marauders* at the Satire Theater, and Zhitinkin was behind Yury Yakovlev's impressive star turn earlier this season in *The Sunshine Boys*.

With Priestley's play, Zhitinkin created a traditional, static production that settles for the relatively easy target of exposing bourgeois hypocrisy rather than driving deeper for an aggressive deconstruction of psychological and moral duplicity.

Zhzhyonov plays an enigmatic figure who appears out of the blue and disappears into a void. Intruding upon a festive evening in the home of an upper middle-class family, he calls himself a police inspector investigating the murder or suicide of a young woman.

All the efforts of the indignant father (Boris Ivanov) and semi-hysterical mother (Nina Drobysheva) to get rid of the unwelcome visitor are in vain. Calmly and persistently, the Inspector pursues his questioning, one by one drawing each member of the family into the field of suspicion.

The girl, it seems, was a waif of doubtful character, who under different pseudonyms crossed paths with everyone present—in all cases suffering unfairly at their hands. Any one of them could have been the catalyst which sent her to her death.

Zhzhyonov plays a sphinx, revealing no emotion, humor or sympathy for anyone, victim or perpetrator. He is, most of all, a presence, a force to be reckoned with. Zhitinkin keeps him almost frozen in a corner of the stage, and from that vantage point his withering eye relentlessly peers through the facades and the self-deceptions of those whom he confronts.

But the revelations hardly end with the Inspector's disclosure of the skeletons in the family's closet. After he departs, his own identity and even existence become the object of heated debate.

Andrei Sharov's heavy, oversized set of a British dining room is dominated by an immense fireplace topped by a huge mirror. From time to time the mirror becomes a window providing Peeping Tom glimpses of people who think they are alone.

Several revivals of *An Inspector Calls* have recently enjoyed big success in the United States and England. The Moscow version is markedly more modest, but it has one draw no other can boast: the charismatic Georgy Zhzhyonov as the Inspector.

(*March 1996*)

The Storm, Chekhov Art Theater

The Chekhov Art Theater's production of Alexander Ostrovsky's *The Storm*, bloodless and tame as it is, can't help but set you thinking: Had there been no Ostrovsky, the Russians would have had to invent him.

Like Shakespeare, more universal perhaps but only barely more protean, Ostrovsky had a genius for creating definitive characters and situations. Unlike the Bard, he focused his keen sights solely on his own people, establishing in 54 plays an astonishing array of evocative and memorable portraits of Russian types.

Excelling in all of his characterizations, he specialized in three: the sensitive, intelligent young woman yearning desperately for freedom; the cruel, willful matron; and the young male upstart, bereft of conscience and blinded by the pursuit of money and status.

The latter type, the forerunner of today's notorious New Russian, is a key reason why Ostrovsky's plays are now being produced by the dozens. But his vision of women—or the woman's lot, if you will—is no less timeless, and he may never have expressed it better than in *The Storm*, one of just a few of his plays to enjoy success beyond the Slavic pale.

The lines are drawn with classical simplicity: Katerina, the beautiful, reflective young wife of a perfectly good, but insufferably weak dullard is unable to fight off temptation when it comes. But while her husband would forgive, Katerina cannot bear the base new reality of her life, reflected in the mean, vindictive behavior of her mother-in-law.

At the Art Theater, designer Valery Levental illustrates Katerina's claustrophobic, dead-end world. Tall, forbidding walls line a country lane, leading to an exit onto the Volga River. The beauty of the Russian countryside, like the image of a church high above the town, is soothing but tantalizingly out-of-reach.

Given a dark, foreboding glow by Damir Ismagilov's lighting, the visuals promise a penetrating glimpse into the catacombs of this cabalistic universe, but the show does not deliver. In the play's "modern redaction" by Vladimir Gurkin and under the direction of Dmitry Brusnikin, the cast only rarely gets behind appearances.

Diana Korzun, a talented young actress who has that priceless combination of tenacity and delicacy, steps so gingerly around the edges of Katerina's complex personality that she never attains either her driving intensity or her cutting despair. There are fleeting exceptions—especially a beautiful scene early on when she spins languorously about the stage wondering "why people don't fly"—but on the whole, Korzun creates a pencil sketch, not a full-color portrait.

As her husband Tikhon, Sergei Shekhovtsov is functional, while Iya Savvina plays the mother-in-law with grim grit. Her tough, unrelenting manner marks her as odious, although one suspects the impact would be stronger were she played with more nuance. For instance, did this old harpy develop out of an idealist like Katerina, or is she now just a jaded hedonist like her daughter Varvara (Marina Brusnikina) will probably be? We never learn, and the show is flatter for that.

As Boris, the youth who briefly becomes Katerina's lover while her husband is away, Sergei Shnyryov is in the right places at the right times, but conspicuously lacks the brakeless arrogance that would make us believe him capable of stealing another man's wife and, more importantly, would justify her going to him.

A cache of folk songs are intended to liven things up, but there is something almost cynical in that, as if the director knew they would squeeze tears from his spectators' eyes if the performance couldn't.

The one triumph in this underachieving show comes from Sofya Pilyavskaya, who was already playing leads at the Art Theater when Stanislavsky himself was still around. Her episodical, "half-mad" old woman, predicting like a seer that Katerina's beauty will ruin her, has all the passion, daring and truth that are the real measure of Ostrovsky.

(April 1996)

The Marriage, Theater na Pokrovke

The Marriage at the Theater na Pokrovke is Moscow's fourth major production of Nikolai Gogol's play—he called it a "completely improbable incident"—in three years. They could hardly be more different.

At the Krasnaya Presnya Theater, Yury Pogrebnichko set the story of a bachelor narrowly escaping marriage to strange, syncopated rhythms, making of it a meditation on Russian claustrophobia and dreams of freedom. At the Hermitage, Mikhail Levitin created a big, blowzy production that was more chaotic nightmare than dream. At the Stanislavsky Theater Vladimir Mirzoyev doubled all the female characters in a Freudian fantasy.

Against this background, Sergei Artsibashev's version at the Theater na Pokrovke may look traditional, but appearances can deceive. That is especially true concerning Artsibashev's aggressively low-key style.

This *Marriage* almost entirely erases the play's usual source of comedy—the belligerent, cat-and-dog conflicts among the characters—finding its humor in tender, thoughtful human portraits. The result is a warm, compassionate show that, like everything Artsibashev does, is fueled by delicate irony.

Also unusual is the casting, Artsibashev taking the rare step of going outside his own troupe to find performers for several key roles. That produced intriguing results, giving the director a broader range of personalities to work with and the actors a chance to try an unaccustomed directorial method.

Benefiting most is Igor Kostolevsky, whose penchant for one-speed, high-volume overacting tends to make his heroes on his home stage at the Mayakovsky Theater look like carbon copies of one another. Here, as

Podkolesin, the man whose idle dreams of married bliss are almost forcibly made real by an overeager friend, Kostolevsky is attractively understated. He is a soft-spoken man entirely satisfied to live in the comfortable if limited world of his own thoughts.

His friend Kochkaryov, often played as a bull-terrier on the loose, is given a warm twist by Mikhail Filippov, also from the Mayakovsky. His is not the customary obsessed brute pushing Podkolesin into an undesired liaison, but an affectionate albeit explosive friend joyously fascinated by the very concept of marriage.

The radical shift in Artsibashev's shading of Gogol's play is readily evident in Kochkaryov's relationship with the matchmaker Fyokla Ivanovna. He is horning in on her territory, of course, and the sparks between them usually fly fast and furious. Here, the pair is all smiles, caresses and kisses, echoing the production's predominant tone: Everyone would like to be happy and no one begrudges their neighbor the same—the problem is that life obeys crueler laws.

As Fyokla, Inna Ulyanova (from the Commonwealth of Taganka Actors) radiates a grandmotherly warmth that embraces and infects everyone, including Podkolesin's three strange but endearing rivals for the heart of Agafya Tikhonovna, the potential bride.

The melancholic undercurrent in this story about shattered dreams of happiness is carried by Yelena Starodub's Agafya. No frivolous husband-seeker, she starts out even more reluctant than Podkolesin and always maintains a certain philosophical skepticism. She is a reminder from the start that the utopia of the others' tender hopes cannot last; when they indeed begin breaking up, we have seen the warnings in her eyes.

Artsibashev, aided by Pavel Gerasimov, gently wrapped the show in pacifying, lullaby-like recorded music and beautiful folk songs performed live by a winking chorus that often takes part in the action unseen by the others.

Designer Oleg Sheintsis inundated the beautiful, inviting set in a jungle of leafy plants and a series of mirrors, one of which can become transparent and allow furtive visions of characters to visit Agafya at her candlelit make-up table.

(*April 1996*)

A Raw Youth, Taganka Theater

The premiere of Yury Lyubimov's latest at the Taganka Theater added to that theater's listings one more of the director's shows that have originated abroad.

Unlike such productions as *Zhivago* and *Medea*—staged abroad with foreign money and Taganka actors—Lyubimov's "new" adaptation of Fyodor Dostoevsky's novel, *A Raw Youth*, is a local revival of a show first staged in 1991 at the Finnish National Theater with Finnish actors.

It is a strange outing—superficial and inconsequential in many ways, and yet, undeniably fresh and engaging.

A Raw Youth, the least-known and least-admired of Dostoevsky's five major novels, is a potboiler about the impressionable Arkady seeking his way in life amidst a squall of obstacles. The illegitimate son of the liberal-minded Versilov, he competes with his father for the affections of the mysterious Katerina Nikolayevna, while getting mixed up with a host of cheats, swindlers and scoundrels.

As is usual for Dostoevsky, there is lots of money offered, demanded, thrown about and refused. In Lyubimov's dramatization, so cryptic that it is tough to follow unless you know the novel, the drama hangs primarily on a damaging letter written by Katerina which Arkady toils to keep out of the wrong hands.

Lyubimov defused the story to a great degree, tempering the characters' passions and blanching their explosive conflicts. It would appear that what interested him most was Dostoevsky's rather atypical attempt at a muted, if not quite happy, ending. When all is said and done, Arkady, as yet unsullied by the real torments of life, still has the simplicity to hope that fights and arguments—"of which nothing comes"—can be set aside.

Lyubimov cast two similar actors (Dmitry Mulyar and Alexander Lyrchikov) in the

Alexander Lyrchikov (right) was one of two actors playing the title role in Yury Lyubimov's dramatization of *A Raw Youth*, the novel by Fyodor Dostoevsky, at the Taganka Theater, 1996. Photo: Mikhail Guterman

role of Arkady, partly to echo the notion that Versilov-the-father is a man split into two personalities, but even more, perhaps, to imply that a new generation is on the rise. The actors' duo precludes perceiving Arkady as just an individual, and suggests by numbers that his is an attitude capable of growing in society.

That is supported in the evocative final chorus, the most striking of the impressionistic music by Edison Denisov. The entire cast lines up across the stage to sing the novel's final words, "It is from raw youths that generations come," pointing comically and insistently at their temples to drive the point home. A motley, four-man revolutionary circle provides comic relief and, as we learn in the epilogue, eventually gets put away in prison.

Lyubimov, never known as an actor's director, drew performances of vastly differing quality from his troupe. Ably anchoring the positive side are Mulyar and Lyrchikov, whose winning sincerity and ingenuousness more than make up for their low-level temperament.

As Versilov, Dalvin Shcherbakov has some keenly penetrating moments, usually in his introspective, one-on-one talks with his son. But when he must go to the well for intense confrontations with his common-law wife (the nondescript Galina Zolotaryova) and Katerina (the believable, if unspirited Anastasia Kolpikova), he comes up nearly empty.

Some of the secondary cast members seem clueless (such as Igor Kechayev playing the unprincipled Prince Seryozha who receives an inheritance intended for Versilov) while Larisa Maslova sends sparks flying in her single episode as Alphonsine, a girl of questionable morals.

Andrey von Schlippe's set (like Denisov's music, imported from the Finnish original) is an attractive, suggestive combination of rapidly moving drapes that instantaneously create walls or make them disappear. Lyubimov's excellent lighting plays with facial spots in darkness and a ribbed curtain of light extending upwards from a row of footlights.

On one hand, *A Raw Youth* is obscurely fragmentary, lacking in the infernal obsessions of Dostoevsky's novel, and marred by uneven acting. But despite all that, it has an appealing, convincing energy to it. For a man whose next birthday will be his 79th, Lyubimov retains a remarkable feeling for youth.

(April 1996)

The Philosophy of the Boudoir, Roman Viktyuk Theater; and *Orchard*, Studio of Individual Directing

The premiere of Roman Viktyuk's adaptation of the memoirs of the Marquis de Sade, *The Philosophy of the Boudoir*, leaves no doubt: The times, they have a-changed.

Viktyuk's titillating, homoerotic shows such as *Lolita, Two for the Seesaw*, and *Slingshot* used to create frantic stampedes of audiences studded with the stars of Moscow's beau monde.

Last week's opener of *Boudoir* at the 950-seat Satirikon maybe drew 800 subdued, anonymous customers. By curtain time, two-and-a-half grilling hours later, they were so numbed into resignation that they almost forgot to clap until a burst of loud music and a quick dousing of the lights squeezed a mild response from them.

Viktyuk's scantily-clad, phallic-outfitted androgynous figures marched around the stage in make-believe transports of arousal, their main purpose being to "teach" a virgin the joys of sex. They did so perfunctorily by furiously drawing ejaculations on a chalkboard, raping the girl, having male orgies in the corner and then apparently killing the girl's mother.

Frequently inundated in heavy sheets of drifting smoke that had the audience choking, this silly exercise in search of de Sade's "magic theater" (!) had no shock value, no erotic charge, and nothing to do with philosophy. The level of theater suggested a censored night-club sex show. With less content.

Boris Yukhananov's production of Chekhov's *The Cherry Orchard*, called *Orchard* at his own Studio of Individual Directing, can get bizarre. Running about seven hours over two days, it is a formless journey ranging far beyond Chekhov's text. The characters, looking like plants, insects or ragged 18th-century courtiers, emerge from an inflatable spaceship and interact with the intensity of a cherry tree seed germinating.

Interesting in conception, it is aggressively self-indulgent in reality. Until now, anyway.

Orchard, which has slowly evolved since first appearing in 1990, was recently joined by an extraordinary group of people with Down's syndrome. They freely move in and out of the action, echoing the primary characters or launching off on their own tangent. In all cases, it has an unbelievably bracing, focusing effect. The Down's actors are intense, serious and controlled—something Yukhananov's own actors seldom are. One tragically inclined man recites poems that seem to be of his own composition and are so powerful they simply stop all other action.

Others include two tender men who tirelessly escort the actors about; a shy but divinely smiling woman with a crooked flute; and a delightfully sly man surreptitiously sneaking about the stage. Their sincerity, ardor and faith in the magic of the theatrical process has a stunning effect, creating the true atmosphere of genuine avant-garde art.

When this production works—as it does when the Down's actors are on stage—it is a stunning, purifying revelation.

(April 1996)

Krapp's Last Tape, Contemporary Play School

Krapp's Last Tape at the Contemporary Play School is rough, tough, riveting theater. And you have to think that Samuel Beckett, the great Irish playwright who wrote the play

Armen Dzhigarkhanyan in Samuel Beckett's *Krapp's Last Tape*, directed by Krikor Azaryan at the Contemporary Play School, 1996. Photo: Mikhail Guterman

and who drove directors nuts making them stage him *exactly as written*, would have agreed.

That doesn't mean this is some comfortable theatrical illustration. And despite the nonsense of Beckett (and now his executor) occasionally going to court to keep directors from getting "too creative," that isn't what the writer was after. He wanted people to make the effort to sink down into the seething, grating dramatic rhythms of his philosophical monologues and dialogues.

In director Krikor Azaryan and actor Armen Dzhigarkhanyan, Beckett's play— about a cranky, 69 year-old man contemplating and reacting to his own taped diary made 30 years ago—has met its ideal match.

Azaryan gives us the bare essentials: the battered old desk dominated by the clunky reel-to-reel tape recorder; the rickety brass bed in the corner; a draped, picture-frame door which catches strange growing and shrinking shadows each time Krapp goes out to dig around in his library of tapes.

As for Dzhigarkhanyan, he puts on a visceral, fearless performance perhaps unmatched by any this season. His total involvement in every move he makes or sound he hears, creates a character of fascinating intensity. His scowl, burning eyes, gravelly grunts and comic hitches as he shakes out the effects of a bad back, all make for vivid, psychologically profound visual images of an old man who finds himself at a stage in life when he is literally alone with his thoughts.

Short, stocky, with a bull-doggish face and a well of power in his breast, Dzhigarkhanyan is a born actor who can turn thoughts into drama. In recent years he has stretched his prodigious talents dangerously thin, taking on increasingly silly roles in what occasionally seems like every Russian movie made in these days of limited cinematic output. His work at the Mayakovsky Theater, where he's been a member since 1969, has borne the tired, familiar stamp of a gifted actor trapped on a treadmill.

That only makes his performance in *Krapp's Last Tape* all the more stunning. It is the work of an artist who has earned the comfort of celebrity, but who appears, at age 60, to have cut loose and gone recklessly searching for risks.

Beckett's play is a graveyard for anyone but the finest. Nearly half of it is passive, with the actor playing Krapp merely listening to the playback of his younger, rather more self-satisfied ruminations.

But Dzhigarkhanyan, whose rumbling, ratchety voice couldn't be more perfect for the recorded segments, shows himself an endlessly imaginative listener. His physical pauses, frozen stares, grimaces, and flashes of disgust or embarrassment with himself, open up a view on a rich, complex internal world.

As the despair of this lonely, hard-crusted man approaching his last days mounts, and as he confronts the lies, illusions, misconceptions and miscalculations of his life, Dzhigarkhanyan raises him to the level of a genuine tragic figure without losing sight of his humanity. His momentary flirtation with the idea of suicide, and his angry, furious rejection of it are a fitting peak to his performance.

Krapp's Last Tape is that rare confluence of gripping drama and brilliant acting. It may not be pretty, but it doesn't get any more real.

(*May 1996*)

Anecdotes, Tabakov Theater

In *Anecdotes* at the Tabakov Theater, Valery Fokin has staged a grim, even cruel show that has them rolling in the aisles. It's that quintessential Russian mix of "laughter through tears" with a farcical, morbid twist.

Fokin went back to a one-act play he originally staged in 1973 at the Sovremennik Theater, Alexander Vampilov's *Twenty Minutes With an Angel*, prefacing it with a dramatization of Dostoevsky's story, "Bobok." Astonishingly, the two works written almost 100 years apart fit like pieces of a puzzle.

"Bobok," written in 1873, is a yarn about a tipsy, two-bit writer who hears the voices of the dead in a cemetery. *Angel*, written in 1962, is a despairing burlesque of moral turpitude in which two drunks and some bystanders persecute a stranger because they think his good intentions are a screen for subterfuge. The people in both pieces are sprouts on the same family tree.

That connection is emphasized in Woldemar Zawodzinski's design. His three-tiered, see-through crypt of act one—filled with bodies "living" and dead—becomes a hollow basement beneath the floor on which the characters of the second act walk. Yefim Udler's bright, narrow spots trained on faces and hands slice through the graveyard gloom of "Bobok," while his open, all-illuminating lighting of "Angel" captures that atmosphere of a cheap, provincial hotel.

As the drooling, red-faced writer in "Bobok," Vladimir Mashkov isn't just a drunk, he's a pickled souse of grand comic proportions. Slurring off wicked condemnations of his times and contemporaries, for a haughty moment he also poses as a statue of Alexander Pushkin. But the dead cow him into silence when they raise their voices.

Fokin's handling of the cavalcade of cadavers is masterful. They begin their chatter frozen motionlessly, eyes closed, muttering about cards and the price of graves before going into a tizzy at the memory of sexual longing. When one decomposing figure murmers that he'd like to "live a bit more," the whole lot bursts into malicious guffaws.

All are set aflutter when the former crook Klinevich (Sergei Bezrukov) almost crawls out of his coffin. They get even more excited—their hands trembling in unison, their twists and turns synchronically choreographed—when he suggests they try "living out their last few months without shame" before totally decomposing.

But there the flabbergasted writer loses contact with the other world.

Dostoevsky's miniature wax museum of not-quite disembodied personalities defined by their puffed-up pride and petty concerns, but also marked by a sympathetic humanity, are reincarnated in Vampilov's hotel dwellers.

Ugarov (Mashkov) and his sidekick Anchugin (Oleg Tabakov) are on the third day of a drinking binge and broke. When Anchugin yells out the window that he needs money, a stranger appears and offers the then-hefty sum of 100 rubles. But such unexplained generosity is more suspect than welcome, so the drunks tie the stranger up until they can figure him out.

With his nerdy haircut, stubby eyebrows, rosy cheeks and fidgety mannerisms, Yevgeny Mironov is an earthly angel of a stranger. Meek, polite and vaguely brushed with the breath of sadness, he only breaks down when his tormentors threaten to put him in an asylum: He wanted to give away the money as penance for neglecting the mother he just buried.

Mashkov and Tabakov ham it up with the shamelessness one suspects the dead were after in "Bobok," although in time their brassy, staggering excess acquires a homespun appeal. Tabakov, reviving the role he played for Fokin 23 years ago, has lost the disarming candor of his youth. But even as he wavers between self-assuredness and self-importance, he has a glib comic touch.

"Bobok" is the prize of this combination, but both "anecdotal" halves are done with neat, brisk and killing humor.

(May 1996)

Much Ado About Nothing, Russian Army Theater

The folks at the Russian Army Theater, like their Chechnya-obsessed bosses in the Defense Department, have had a rough few years. So much so, that you can't help thinking the recent premiere of Shakespeare's *Much Ado About Nothing* was intended as something of a hopeful declaration.

In the fall of 1993, the theater closed its mainstage to let Peter Stein rehearse and perform a grandiose, 8-hour production of *Oresteia*. The idea was to attract worldwide attention and enhance the venue's reputation.

But when the mainstage reopened a year later, things were ready to unravel. Shortly after the premiere of a middling musical prophetically called *On the Hot Spot*, then-principal director Leonid Heifetz was viciously attacked under suspicious circumstances.

The still murky story goes that Heifetz opposed a group whose wish was to seize control of the monstrous Army Theater stage for a disco. When he refused their overtures, it seems, he was beaten up and threatened with death should he try to continue at the playhouse. Heifetz resigned in December 1994, and the Army Theater was plunged into chaos.

Much Ado About Nothing is the theater's first substantial outing in over a year, and it is Boris Morozov's first production since he became the new principal director last summer. You can see that the highly respected Morozov, most recently a staff director at the Maly Theater, wanted to take the bull by the horns.

First, he set out to combat the theater's seriously damaged prestige by tackling Shakespeare's bubbly comedy about the tenacious virtues of love and forgiveness. But he also had another challenge to meet. The immense stage at the Army Theater was built to accommodate real tanks and whole army divisions, and that has made it perhaps Moscow's hardest space to work with. Its cavernous expanses swallow well-intentioned efforts the way sink-holes swallow houses.

Morozov's idea was to have his designer Iosif Sumbatashvili "shrink" the stage with a vast, detailed, operatic set. To a certain extent it worked. The wide-open floor leads into the towering, arched entryways of a forest castle at the back and far sides. The forest itself is painted on hanging drops which gently curve, cornerless, around the stage, giving the illusion that the space is smaller than it is.

The action begins immediately, the actors briskly barging out and launching into energetically delivered dialogues. You can actually feel the intent behind their manners and the visuals surrounding them, as if Morozov had written in surtitles above the stage: "We are going to fill this expanse and turn this place around!"

Well, not quite. With one major exception, the cast members are unable to go beyond merely being attractive in their period costumes and predictable in their expressions of excitement, anger, surprise and merriment.

As the good-natured Don Pedro, the prince of Aragon who has defeated his brother Don John's rebellion attempt and forgiven it, Boris Plotnikov is gallant enough, but so bland as to be quite forgettable. Much the same can be said for three of the four central figures in this play that ends with two marriages, one despite evil designs to wreck it, the other despite the irascible pair's wish to avoid it.

The primary couple of Claudio (Alexei Zakharov) and Hero (Lyudmila Tatarova), homogenized and colorless as milk, strikes no sparks at all. Their overcoming of Don John's plot to separate them—achieved only through an elaborate series of intrigues and deceptions which should bring us to a ringing climax—seems almost unworthy of all the fuss.

As Beatrice, Hero's headstrong cousin who doesn't believe any man deserves her but winds up being tricked into loving the blustery, misogynistic Benedick, Olga Kabo is sprightly and pretty but never gets down into the nitty-gritty of the sexual battle.

There is, however, a saving grace in all of this. Dmitry Nazarov plays a veritable hurricane of a Benedick. An actor of great potential who had floundered underused for years at the Maly Theater, and who defected to the Army Theater with Morozov, he walks out on the airport-sized stage and makes it feel like an intimate enclosure.

Snapping off Shakespeare's sizzling puns and stinging observations with the ease of a lion-tamer cracking his whip, Nazarov has that real actor's flair for wearing his character's skin as if it were his own, while keeping a distance that lets us know he's having a blast doing it. His is a modern Benedick, a chauvinist with a self-effacing charm which suggests all along he knows he's really a blowhard and a pushover.

In *Much Ado About Nothing*, Morozov went for the big-time show to pull his new theater out of big-time troubles. Thanks to a giant-sized performance by Dmitry Nazarov, he achieved a small-scale success.

(May 1996)

Three Sisters, **Lithuanian International "Life" Theater Festival; and** *Macbeth*, **Rustaveli Theater—entries in the Second Chekhov International Theater Festival**

Proving that some things never change, the great Lithuanian director Eimuntas Nekrosius once again fired emotions in Moscow, with most observers vehemently rejecting what they called his "disrespectful, anti-Russian" interpretation of Chekhov's *Three Sisters*, and a vocal minority (count me in) praising his starkly modern, visionary production.

The unusually young, spirited Prozorov sisters had a sharp intelligence, sparkling sexuality and philosophical depth one rarely sees. Olga (Dalia Micheleviciute) was past realistically hoping for satisfaction in love, and she surreptitiously followed her younger sisters, hiding behind furniture and gazing partly in jealousy, partly in fascination at their trysts in the reflections of a hand-held mirror. As Masha, Aldone Bendoriute suddenly broke through the fears and inhibitions imposed on her by her surroundings, hungrily, almost (but not quite) shamelessly throwing herself at Vershinin. Viktoria Kuodite's bright, lean and energetic Irina saw her bubbling optimism crushed, but not her spirit.

Perhaps the most "offensive" moment (and one of those typically vivid scenes in which Nekrosius "illustrates" meaning through visuals) came as Vershinin (Algirdas Latepas) knelt on his head, backside to the audience, to deliver his famous, ultra-Russian, philosophical monologue about how great life may be in "two or three hundred years." Another moment evoking criticism from some was the powerful scene of Tuzenbach (Vladas Bagdonas) eating a long, silent "last supper" before the duel with a sloppy, animal's appetite. He then spun a empty plate on the table and left as the plate continued twirling on its own before finally rattling to a halt.

The finale of the three sisters taking up loose boards left from a deconstructed clock tower and building themselves three new houses where one used to stand, could be perceived as a positive or negative metaphor for what happened to the Soviet Union. Take your pick.

Rather than the usual picture of bloodlust and ambition in *Macbeth*, Robert Sturua staged a story of a young couple's love and runaway sexual passion which are trapped in and destroyed by the churning gears of political intrigues.

Zaza Papuashvili's Macbeth was a tough, street-smart but vaguely uncomprehending young man whose rebellious romanticism had him headed for trouble. It sometimes seemed he was constantly dropping or throwing away knives which stuck in the floor and begged to be picked up again. Like the Idea of murder, they burned him and beckoned to him at the same time.

As his Lady, the ravishing Nino Kasradze both bewildered and incited him with her disarming directness and her unabashed sexuality. Her physical desire for Macbeth—her use of her body and feminine wiles—was the stuff of a true, healthy attraction, but at some fateful, intangible instant, things began breaking up.

When Macbeth raped her against a heat pipe just before going in to assassinate the king, we saw how love was being perverted to a sexual function while the desire for power was transforming into wanton violence. This pair was a kind of Georgian Bonnie and Clyde cut down by their hubris and the cruel laws of natural justice.

At an informal discussion the following day, Sturua explained that his Macbeth and Lady might be "what Romeo and Juliet would have become had they lived—young, loving people who wanted to do good things; but suddenly it grows into something horrible."

As one might expect, Sturua abruptly mixed genres of play and music, imparting to the production's infrastructure a dynamic sense of alternation and movement. Scenes changed quickly from intimacy or conspiracy among a few on the forestage, to elaborate mass activity that encompassed the entire open stage surrounded by Mirian Shvelidze's wall-hugging set. The decomposing exteriors of Caucasian homes stood at the sides while

Nino Kasradze as Lady Macbeth in Shakespeare's *Macbeth*, directed by Robert Sturua, Rustaveli Theater, Tbilisi, Georgia. Performed in Moscow, May 1996. Photo: Alexander Ivanishin

two blank panels at the back variously reflected incandescent blue or green light.

(*Slavic and East-European Journal, Fall 1996*)

The Suicide, The Diary of a Scoundrel, Family Portrait with a Stranger and *Fatherlessness*, Tsvilling Theater

The Tsvilling Theater of Chelyabinsk, headed by artistic director Naum Orlov since 1973, is one of Russia's oldest, most respected provincial houses. This summer it celebrated its 75th anniversary with a tour that took it to St. Petersburg, Sochi and Moscow, where I caught four of its seven traveling shows.

The honors of opening the run went to Orlov's acclaimed 1990 production of Nikolai Erdman's *The Suicide*. Written in the late 1920s, but banned in the Soviet Union until the late 1980s, Erdman's play was then being discovered by theaters all over the country. Most, however, failed to untangle the mysteries of this strange tragifarce which had become an acknowledged classic even though its world premiere took place only in 1969 in Sweden.

Orlov's interpretation sparkled, capturing equally the play's lyrical atmosphere and philosophical underpinnings, while handling the knockabout situations with verve. A Moscow tour in the fall of 1990 won the praise of Muscovites, while a 1994 tour to Germany won Alexander Mezentsev an award there as best actor in a touring production.

But times, sensibilities and expectations have changed dramatically since then, while some of the performers have gotten rather too chummy with their roles. Only a faint echo of the initial success is left now. What once was an introspective, dream-like performance about a weak, depressed but likable man who has lost his way in life, has now become flabby and obvious.

As Semyon Podsekalnikov, the unemployed worker who is pushed toward suicide by a ragtag group of opportunists out to further their own ends, Mezentsev still shines. Wiry, lithe and attractively vulnerable, he is a simpleton with a soul, a fool with a heart. And some of Orlov's visual metaphors—such as Semyon rising into the heavens on the tuba he thinks will save him before dropping painfully back to earth—still ring true. But most everything else has come apart. The play, never an easy one to perform, is no longer served by the busy period detail in Timur Didishvili's set and costumes, which now look clichéd, while most in the cast have slipped into playing zany, predictable comedy.

Erdman's diamond-cut, pun-filled dialogue never lets things fall too low, evoking repeated bursts of laughter, but you can also feel it holding things back. It is a text that is probably written "too perfectly"; if you don't answer its depth with a multi-dimensional approach, it gels awkwardly into a string of silly gags. Except for Mezentsev, the actors have become a team of clowning caricatures muffing the author's ambiguity and wisdom, and steering the show away from its original inspiration.

More characteristic of the theater's current capabilities is Arkady Kats' 1995 production of Alexander Ostrovsky's *The Diary of a Scoundrel*. It is a brisk, fresh show that, while traditional at heart, has an attractive contemporary gloss. Kats severely abridged the play about the young Yegor Glumov making a career through flattery and deception, gaining much in dynamics, and losing some perspective. We get less of Ostrovsky's personalities, but a clearer picture of duplicity and fraud streaking forward like an arrow.

Alexei Martynov puts a recognizably modern spin on his performance of Glumov. He is not the scoundrel mentioned in the traditional English translation of Ostrovsky's title which is closer to something like "In Every Wiseman Hides a Simpleton." This Glumov is appalled by what he has to do to make his mark, but he knows there is no other way. He also isn't much surprised when his scheme unravels.

The striking set by Tatyana Shvets depicts a two-paneled chess board. The actors move about the floor like game pieces, while the panel on the back wall reveals headless "trophies" popping up each time Glumov makes a new conquest. *Diary* has some of the hyper-theatrical histrionics that have grown over *The Suicide* like weeds, but they are offered with a lively wit that usually makes them an asset rather than a liability.

That same kind of fast-and-loose style is also advantageous to Mikhail Filimonov's production of Stepan Lobozyorov's contemporary comedy, *Family Portrait with a Stranger*. Probably the most likable of the quartet of shows I saw, it was also the least ambitious, making a virtue of its modesty.

The extraordinarily popular play (produced in over 50 theaters across Russia in recent years) is disarmingly simple: A man cuts off a potential romance between his sweetheart and a boarder in her household by telling her family that the boarder is nuts, and telling the boarder that her family is crazy. What ensues is a wacky series of incidents involving misunderstood conversations, unintended scuffles, suspected poisonings and a preventive ax attack, all of which naturally convince each side that the other is insane. The characters are simple, naive and sympathetic, and the actors play them with broad, affectionate ingenuousness. As a result, the low-humor situations hit comic bull's-eyes with amazingly high frequency.

Filimonov and designer Oleg Petrov gave the proceedings a heavy folk-oriented feel. The three-dimensional depiction of a snowy, sleepy Russian village floats above the interior of a typical Russian country house, while occasionally the whip-lash action suddenly stops and the actors glide into melancholy folk dances. Other breaks which drive home the play's message that suspicion is a vice involve a pair of house goblins who encourage and comment on the chaos pulling these people apart.

Orlov's production of Anton Chekhov's *Fatherlessness* (a.k.a. *Platonov*) stripped the troupe of its penchant for overplaying, but did little to fill the void with anything else. The direction was purely "traditional Chekhov," the acting was subdued but still theatrical, the characterizations were sufficiently well-defined, but lacking in imagination. Sincere as it was, the performance of this play about a soured school teacher who cracks under the pressure of meeting a

former love, had the feel of a balloon half filled with air. Orlov seated the spectators on three sides of the stage, putting them inside the gates of a country garden (reversing Chekhov's directions of a living room looking into a garden).

Designer Tatyana Selvinskaya created a garden atmosphere simply, placing pieces of flowered carpet (representing flower patches) in semi-circles around the green-carpeted stage and backing that with a bank of multi-colored stained-glass windows looking into the house. In principle attractive, there was something naggingly false in the set which seemed to echo the production as a whole.

(Plays International, October 1996)

A Cube for the President,
Mossoviet Theater

One of the sensations that never flags throughout the Mossoviet Theater's new production of *A Cube for the President*, is that this show is fun. There aren't many belly laughs, there is no singing, no dancing and no fancy costumes. So what makes the performance of this new comedy by Viktor Podlubny so entertaining?

Start with the actors in this breezy political spoof with a philosophical twist. They all have a knack for pigeonholing those typical human quirks that could drive anyone mad, while creating the kind of sympathetic portraits that brings you in firmly on their side.

And then there is Podlubny's play, simply written with a touch of "magic" to brighten things up.

Andrei Ilyin plays a seemingly blank, quietly stubborn but congenial young man who forces his way into the office of the chairman of the state committee on energy. He has an invention to show and he's not about to be turned away.

As the Chairman, Nikolai Prokopovich is brusque and excusably arrogant until he sees what his visitor has brought: a tiny cube containing an inexhaustible supply of electric power. He immediately realizes the implications of the invention and calls in the Minister of Energy (Alexander Pashutin), who calls in a prominent leftist politician (Valentina

Andrei Ilyin and Yevgeny Lazarev in Viktor Podlubny's *A Cube for the President*, directed by Pavel Khomsky at the Mossoviet Theater, 1996. Photo: Mikhail Guterman

Kareva), who calls in the President (Yevgeny Lazarev).

Podlubny's cube, more than just an engine for the plot, is a shrewd dramatic device. You find yourself believing in its power and potential to transform the world, and that faith pervades the atmosphere of the whole performance.

Under the direction of Pavel Khomsky, the cast plays it light and loose, soft-peddling the purposeful incongruities and nearly ignoring the political parallels. It's no coincidence that Khomsky brought the show out as the Russian presidential election campaign reaches its peak before the June 16 vote. But to his credit, he didn't ham-hand the obvious. As a result it's the human element which comes to the fore, not the social satire, and in the end, that even adds an extra pinch of pepper to the satire.

Pashutin is perfect as the minister who is so cocksure and condescending with inferiors, and who grovels like a disoriented puppy when reporting to the president. You can't help but like this guy who thinks he's big stuff, but is nothing more than a figurehead.

Hovering over things from the start is the image of Yevgeny Lazarev's President. His enormous portrait hangs above the desk of the Chairman's secretary (Vera Kanshina),

and when she hurriedly dusts it off before he arrives, she gives it a tender little kiss on the cheek. Indeed, this guy turns out to be a personality-plus president. He is also a puppet of his security agents and a man who knows he has no real power.

All are terrified of what may happen. Forget that the inventor, who created the contraption while sitting in prison, is demanding billions of dollars and a promise that everyone who loses a job will get a new one. The president sees an uncontrollable revolution lurking in this cube, and suggests the inventor just give him a single unit for starters.

Enter Nemo (Anatoly Vasilyev), the top man in the power chain. A shady, but kind-hearted character with worldwide and underworld ties, he is willing to meet the inventor's demands, but to what ends? Not to buy the invention, but to get the young man to destroy his cube. The world is not ready for such a panacea to its problems.

A Cube for the President, set in Enar Stenberg's design of a spacious, nondescript bureaucrat's office, is a casual, compassionate comedy that skillfully plays with topical themes but builds its appeal on the charm of its characters.

(*June 1996*)

PEOPLE, THEATERS
AND EVENTS

PEOPLE, THEATERS AND EVENTS

Problems at the Taganka

Former Soviet Minister of Culture and longtime Taganka Theater actor Nikolai Gubenko arrived at the theater's stage door on April 2 to find a scene he probably didn't expect: a special OMON unit of black berets barring him from entering.

Though he slipped past the troops, Gubenko didn't last long on stage that night. Instead of the planned performance of *Vladimir Vysotsky*, the shocked audience watched as a beleaguered Gubenko gave an impromptu account of the theater's sorry state of affairs.

The incident was only the most public in a string of increasingly ugly episodes in a dramatic showdown for control of the world famous Taganka Theater, the cultural landmark which Arthur Miller once praised for renewing his faith in theater. As always at the Taganka, the drama is filled with controversy, social agitation and politics.

For most of its 28-year history, the Taganka performed a precarious duet with the authorities. Some of its best productions were banned while those that weren't often opened only with the permission of state organs. In 1984, after twenty years of battles and shady backroom deals, Taganka founder Yury Lyubimov was deposed as artistic director, forced out of the country and stripped of his citizenship. He returned to a hero's welcome in 1989.

The April 2 incident with the OMON troops was a stunning reversal in the theater's fortunes: The black berets had been summoned by Lyubimov.

The mixture of political passion and internecine strife created a conflict which Lyubimov called the most "shameless" ever to rock his theater. He has no doubts about the source of the schism.

"The reasons are political," he commented recently before beginning morning rehearsals of the Greek tragedy *Electra*. "This is being done by people who want to destroy the theater. All the [current] government officials are former party members. And don't

forget," he sighed, referring to the man who ran the Taganka from 1987 to 1989, "Gubenko is a former minister."

The rift surfaced in December when it was revealed that, among other things, Lyubimov was seeking to privatize the theater and acquire the right to hire and fire actors. Such practices are common in the West, but they are a radical departure from the system that has long been the norm in Russia. Fearing for their job security, a large group of actors rallied behind Gubenko.

But the developments at the Taganka are more complex than that. On one hand, the theater that found fame and artistic brilliance in courageous political opposition turned out to be a mirror-image of the system it battled for so long. On the other, the Taganka is a purely Russian theater, structured on the basis of a tightly-knit collective that draws its inspiration from a profound sense of family. Lyubimov is sharply criticized for attempting to run the Taganka by phone from his home in Israel, visiting Moscow only rarely. Many contend he no longer understands the problems faced by the members of his "extended family."

The mixture of political passion and internecine strife created a conflict which Lyubimov called the most "shameless" ever to rock his theater.

Actor Alexander Sabinin is one of a handful who have remained neutral. An "old timer" who joined the theater a year after it opened in 1964, he said, "Does one cease being a communist merely by tearing up one's party membership card? Lyubimov says we are freed of communists. But he was a communist for thirty years. When I asked whether he thought Taganka communists were different somehow, ,he didn't understand my question."

Sabinin, though, wants no part of the effort to deprive Lyubimov "of his own theater." At one emotional meeting of actors which Lyubimov initially refused to attend, Sabinin said attacks on the director were so insulting he could not remain silent.

"I said, 'This man is a national treasure. We have to respect him for that.'" When someone acidly asked Sabinin if he was willing to "crawl on his knees and beg" Lyubimov to come to the meeting, he replied he was. Lyubimov reluctantly consented and Sabinin said that a chance for peace arose.

Instead, passions prevailed. When Lyubimov questioned the troupe's fears of layoffs, saying he had never once fired an actor, Gubenko shouted, "You're a liar!" Said Sabinin, "Then everyone jumped on Lyubimov and a free-for-all ensued. Afterwards, I had to apologize to him. He was right in not wanting to come."

A few months later, Lyubimov did fire Gubenko in a move that set the stage for the April 2 clash.

Lyubimov, clearly hurt as well as angered by the events, notes that all the problems plaguing Russian society have been "pulled into the theater from the street." Indeed, as politicians in the Kremlin continue to bash one another over differing attitudes to Russia's political past, this notion arises repeatedly in conversations with members of the conflict's varying factions.

Natalya Kovalyova, a member of the Taganka troupe for 13 years, put it this way: "Kolya [Gubenko] is a strong actor, but he became very involved in politics. Whenever Lyubimov would criticize communists, Kolya took it as a personal affront. I am not personally close to either of them, but the Taganka is Lyubimov's theater." She added that a personality conflict has been ripening between the two for several years.

Said Leonid Filatov, an actor at the Taganka since 1969 who readily admits that Lyubimov is a "genius" while supporting Gubenko, "Lyubimov wants the problem to be political. There is no political problem. People just don't want to leave their home." Filatov emphasized that Gubenko engineered Lyubimov's own sensational return from exile.

The dispute also revolves around the common problem of economics. Many consider the famed Taganka, with its three stages, modern equipment and huge office-space, a potential commercial gold mine.

Kovalyova noted that Gubenko often talked of turning it into an international cultural center. Having relinquished his post of Taganka artistic director and being deprived of his position as Minister of Culture, she suggested he may be looking for a location in which to realize his plan. The idea may have legitimacy. During his time as minister, some western arts figures expressed surprise at Gubenko's interest in money and lack of interest in art.

Lyubimov states it in no uncertain terms, "[Gubenko] wants to seize this valuable piece of property."

Others see Lyubimov as the greedy one. Said Lyudmila Komarovskaya, a founding member of the troupe, "All of this theater's money is going abroad. If Lyubimov would say 'to hell' with money and all his foreign [engagements], we all would welcome him with open arms. But he won't do that."

What does the future hold? Kovalyova said that Lyubimov "is a man who likes to stand his ground" and that Gubenko "appears ready to fight to the end." Sabinin offered a view that encapsulates the conflict's convoluted nature. The Taganka, he said, cannot survive without Lyubimov. But, since he insists on spending most of his time abroad, a strong figure is needed in Moscow to tend to everyday business. When asked who might fulfill that role, he replied, "There is only one. Nikolai Gubenko."

(*April 1992*)

Independent Producers

Depending upon one's point of view, David Smelyansky is either one of a new breed or a throwback to another age. Producers and independent production companies in Russia went out of style about the same time as the tsars, but this lifelong theater lover is determined to see them make a comeback.

Smelyansky is not alone, however. In addition to his Russian Theater Agency, other new indies include the Anton Chekhov Theater, the OK Theater, the Oleg Borisov Enterprise, the All the World International Theater Center and others.

Each of these organizations goes about its business differently. The RTA essentially functions as an umbrella organization that provides support to various directors who have an idea they want to realize. The Oleg Borisov Enterprise, whose most recent premiere, *The Man in a Case*, took place Wednesday, was created as a venue for Borisov himself, one of Russia's finest actors who never quite fit into the structure of a theater with a standing troupe. The Anton Chekhov Theater is the brainchild of director Leonid Trushkin who stages all of the theater's plays himself with actors hired on contract. But all of the enterprises are united by a common goal: to circumvent the expenses and bureaucracy of the repertory theater as it developed in the Soviet Union.

A typical large theater in Moscow, for instance, employs 50 or more actors, many of whom perform seldom if at all. The same theater probably has an unwieldy support staff numbering around 150.

By comparison, Smelyansky's RTA has a staff of four and the Anton Chekhov Theater a staff of five. For an international, dual-language production of *Oresteia* last year, Olga Garibova at All the World also employed a support staff of just five. All of them hire actors exclusively on a show-to-show basis. Said Garibova, "That not only makes us more efficient, it makes us more mobile."

Mobility is something All the World could not exist without. Showing a scope that would impress even a seasoned production company, it has mounted several multinational projects. Using actors from Norway, the United States, Russia and Switzerland, its *Oresteia* premiered in Norway last summer in French. A Russian version was performed last fall in Moscow and English-language performances are planned for Los Angeles in 1994.

Smelyansky, who organized the extremely successful independent production of *The Gamblers—21st Century* in March of this year, also has his eyes set on the world. Among numerous other plans, he hopes to inaugurate an annual theater festival, tentatively entitled the Moscow International Theater Bazaar, that would be modeled on international film festivals.

There is a good reason for his wanting to attract the world's theater leaders to Moscow. He sees it as an opportunity to promote "the richest theater tradition in the world."

Promotion, in the broadest sense, probably explains best what Smelyansky hopes to accomplish at RTA. The crisis gripping the Russian economy has not left the theater world untouched. Many actors, directors and even playwrights have chosen to ply their trades abroad on a long-term basis while others have emigrated altogether. As such, Smelyansky vows he is ready "to do whatever he can" to make creating theater more attractive for homegrown talent.

According to the producer, the "cruel, harsh times" the arts are now experiencing create as many opportunities as problems. So when the respected actor/director Sergei Yursky approached him last year to assist in mounting *The Gamblers*, Smelyansky jumped at the chance. "I had turned down several offers to run traditional repertory theaters," he said, "because it is too easy to get bogged down in petty problems there. Yursky's offer gave me the chance to strike out in a new direction and try to do something in the style of the old, great patrons who laid the foundation of Russian theater."

The collaboration gave rise to RTA which now has several other plays in the preparation stage. Among them are a production of playwright Alexander Galin's new play *Sorry*, starring Inna Churikova and Nikolai Karachentsov under the direction of famed film director Gleb Panfilov, and an adaptation of two Chekhov novellas to be staged by the renowned Kama Ginkas.[1]

Surprisingly perhaps, one problem all the indies seem to have overcome with relative ease so far is financing. Yevgeny Rogov, director of operations for the Anton Chekhov Theater explained that his organization is supported by several businessmen who are kind enough and wise enough to allow director Trushkin total artistic freedom. Garibova noted that foreign sponsors are forthcoming because they are anxious to take advantage of tax breaks while the Russian sponsors she has engaged are happy to

---

[1] The Ginkas project never took place.

receive the foreign exposure her international productions provide.

The biggest problem all the independents face is the lack of a stage they can call their own. Renting halls, which is what they do now, is costly, while building their own is a financial and bureaucratic obstacle that no one is ready to hurdle. Rogov noted that there has been talk among the "competitors" of joining forces to create a centralized independent theater, although nothing serious has come of it.

Concerning the topic of competition, David Smelyansky summed up the attitude of all his colleagues who readily mention one another in their conversations. "I won't be the only one," he said. "And I believe the more of us there are, the better it will be. Many of us may not survive, but theater itself will, of course. Even if the independent system itself doesn't last, it will have a lasting impact by introducing a new atmosphere of freedom for actors and directors."

(*June 1992*)

Opening of the Vysotsky Museum

The stage for the loosely-organized street performance was nestled in between a dilapidated boiler-house with trees sprouting out the roof and a modest old dirty yellow brick apartment building. The crowd of about 1,000 jockeyed for position on an incline covered with abandoned construction materials, nettle-bush and over-sized letter blocks taken from one of the Taganka Theater's most famous plays of the 1960s: *Listen, Mayakovsky!*

The occasion was two-fold and, as it turned out, not lacking in controversy.

Saturday was a holiday, the official opening of "My Hamlet," the first exhibit at the new Vladimir Vysotsky State Museum, located in a single room in the yellow brick building on Nizhne-Tagansky Dead End. It was also a day of mourning, the 12th anniversary of the death of Vysotsky, the Taganka actor and bard whose fantastic popularity throughout Russia can be compared to that of the national poet, Alexander Pushkin.

A clown, invited to help celebrate the holiday, greeted the audience with a big

smile and joyous words of congratulation. An offended spectator who had come to mourn shouted, "You ought to be ashamed! This is a day of mourning!"

For three hours, Vysotsky's friends, family, colleagues and admirers reminisced, sang, danced, joked or mourned the day of Vysotsky's death. But it was difficult to tell who was in charge, the performers or the audience. Most of the performances met with weak applause although few people left before the evening concluded.

There was something attractively inept about this program which included a young actor forgetting the poem he was reciting (he was finally prompted by a woman in the crowd), a scantily-clad hoola-hoop dancer who spent as much time picking up dropped hoops as she did twirling them, a tipsy member of the audience who seized the microphone for a few uncomfortable moments and a couple of journalists pondering whether Vysotsky would have become a people's deputy were he still alive.

A voice rang out of the crowd, "He would have! He would have!" Another voice rang out in response, "No way! No way!" The chorus was picked up by others who shouted, "Who cares? Play some Vysotsky songs!"

Boris Khmelnitsky, the Taganka actor who served as master of ceremonies, admitted that the very idea of a Vysotsky museum struck him as odd. The word "museum," he said, sounds suspiciously like "mausoleum."

But, for all its unkempt strangeness, the evening was worthy of the man it honored. As the film director Gennady Poloka told the crowd, Vysotsky was a brilliant ray of light in the drab 1970s. His songs were loved by everyone from truck drivers to Brezhnev, although their admiration was expressed in vastly different ways.

Excepting a couple obscure singles, Vysotsky was never allowed to release a record in the Soviet Union. Meanwhile, there was hardly a household in the nation that did not own at least one cassette of Vysotsky's songs, recorded at parties or informal gatherings.

Yury Lyubimov, the director at the Taganka Theater, once told of walking with Vysotsky down a provincial Russian town's main street. People flung open their windows and recordings of Vysotsky's gravelly voice floated down on them from every one. Said Lyubimov, "We paraded about town like Spartacus."

In a stonily official age, Vysotsky was an unofficial hero. And there was nothing official about the festivities on Saturday. Several popular performers who were to appear never showed, although that only strengthened the homespun atmosphere. The real stars were the people sitting on newspapers amid the nettle-bush, each who had come for his or her own reasons.

According to Yelena Dmitrieva, the deputy director of the Vysotsky Museum, the idea of opening with the Hamlet exhibit was to unite the personal and professional life of the singer and actor, whose greatest role at the Taganka was his performance of the tormented Danish prince in 1971.

Eventually, the museum plans to take over the entire building located on the quiet dead-end street a stone's throw from the Taganka, but for now it has at its disposal just 24 square meters, a former communal apartment. It is a fitting start for the museum honoring a man who symbolized community more than anyone else of his age.

(*July 1992*)

Daniil Gink

"We have a saying at the Moscow Art Theater school," says Daniil Gink who just completed his studies there in the directing faculty, "The best author is a dead author."

He was commenting on the conservative approach that reigns at that prestigious school. But the remark also hinted at something the articulate, baby-faced twenty-three year-old may not have considered.

Gink is also a playwright, and his first produced play, *Bald/Brunet*, put him in the eye of a storm when it premiered at the Stanislavsky Theater last season. Starring pop-idol Pyotr Mamonov in the lead role, it was a classic case of a new work of art being snubbed by critics and those "in the know," while drawing consistent full houses.

Displaying more good-natured surprise than fury, Gink says he was "furious" when he saw reviews accusing him of having written a second-rate play in the style of the absurd. "Nothing in my play should have caused that response. The director gave it that twist, not me," he adds, referring to Oleg Babitsky, his friend and former classmate who staged the play.

But the conflicting, often competing roles of playwrights, directors, actors and critics are old hat for the young man who grew up in one of Russia's foremost theater families. His father Kama Ginkas—from whom he takes his pen name—is now recognized as one of the country's leading directors, while his mother Genrietta Yanovskaya is the artistic director of the Young Spectator Theater.

It wasn't always like that. Born in Leningrad on April Fool's Day, 1969, Gink says his life began with a "joke": "My parents were poor and in disfavor and I had to sleep in a suitcase."

He spent most of his youth crisscrossing the Russian provinces with his parents who, for most of the '70s and '80s, had to take work where they could find it, usually in such far-flung cities as Alma-Ata, Pskov or Krasnoyarsk. Until recently, both were too nonconformist to be invited to the nation's most influential venues.

Gink never set out to emulate his parents. "I relate to directing more aggressively than dad," he says. "Dad wants to express himself. I want to express the author." Pausing a moment to collect his thoughts, he adds a clarification that gives a glimpse into the impulse that made him start writing his own plays: "I want to be equal to or higher than the author."

As he tells it, Gink first considered pursuing a career in theater when he was eighteen. Having just finished high-school, he found himself in a typical situation for a teenager. He didn't know what he wanted to do. Looking to bide his time, he hired on as a lighting man at the Moscow Art Theater where much of what he saw did not meet with his approval.

"As I watched the productions there," he says, "I realized that I knew what needed to be done to make them work."

That realization brought him to the directing faculty of the Moscow Art Theater school, while it was a similar dissatisfaction with the quality of plays being staged that convinced him to try his hand as a playwright.

"I want to write something I haven't read," he says with his characteristic mix of youthful naiveté and unaffected confidence. "All literature is based on life before or during the Apocalypse. I want to write about the life of saints in paradise. Every generation has its saints. But I don't know how they live, who they are or what they look like."

By his own admission, the first two plays he wrote "didn't work," while his first directorial efforts as an assistant at the Moscow Art Theater and the Tabakov Theater were overruled by artistic directors who didn't understand what he was after. He couldn't find "a place or a play with the air" he needed.

The origins of *Bald/Brunet*, Gink's third play, are the stuff of which legends are made. Gink and Babitsky were strolling down Strastnoi Boulevard when Babitsky said he wanted to do a nostalgic play about "two guys who talk." Two days later, Gink presented Babitsky with a draft of the first half of the first act.

Babitsky was intrigued and Gink set to work in earnest. "I started writing," he says, "and it just took off on its own."

Gink wrote what he considers a "tender, childlike" play about how a "strange person ages and is gradually brought closer to childhood by his dreams." As performed at the Stanislavsky Theater, it is an eccentric and powerful study of a man struggling to overcome his real and imagined limitations.

That tack was heightened by the quirky Mamonov. His elastic facial expressions and puppet-like movements in the role of the Bald Man are charged with a rare electrical energy that clearly has contributed much to the play's popularity. Mamonov, however, plays himself more than the character from Gink's play, increasing speculation that the famous musician-turned-actor "saved" an inexperienced playwright.

Gink holds no grudges. Babitsky, he says, was only doing "what every director should do," and Mamonov only impressed with his "openness and aggressiveness."

"He didn't enter the skin of my character," Gink explains, "he put his own skin on it. But I think that's great. No one could have done it better."

When asked whether the experience has encouraged him to try staging the play himself, Gink responds quickly with a question of his own: "Why try to extract from yourself what you've already extracted once?" Then he softens and adds, "Maybe I'll try staging *Bald/Brunet* in ten years. Who knows?"

He is equally noncommittal about whether he considers himself primarily a writer or a director: "I only know I definitely will write and that I definitely want to direct." Without specifying which medium he has in mind, he concludes, "Most contemporary plays search for harmony in disharmony. What I want is to discover harmony itself."

That's a tall order for a young man just starting out. But it is also the kind of bold ambition that often signals the appearance of a new generation ready to sweep aside the dead wood of the generations which preceded it.

(*October 1992*)

A New Journal for Playwrights

The floor of Alexei Kazantsev's study almost groans under the weight of a small mountain of neatly-stacked, nondescript bundles. As the co-editor-in-chief of the elegant new journal, *Playwright*, he has seen the airy room where he usually writes plays himself take on the look of a mini-warehouse. From here, the thousands of copies will eventually find their way to bookstores, theaters, libraries and individual subscribers around the world.

Kazantsev is convinced that the time is ripe for an "austere, elitist" publication that will mainly print new plays. He perceives it not only as a hedge against what he calls "the dearth of culture" in modern Russian society, but as a stepping stone to its revival. "We want every issue we publish to be a cultural act," he says.

The idea for the journal arose two years ago when many became disillusioned with the plummeting quality of Russia's only other drama periodical, *Contemporary Dramaturgy*. The mild-mannered Kazantsev, who is well known for his outspoken views, put it bluntly: *Contemporary Dramaturgy* became a haven for hack-writers, leading to an "insufficient understanding" among theaters and talented playwrights. The former complained that there were no good new plays, while the latter had no way of bringing their work to the public's attention.

"Russian theater was always known for having an extraordinary feel for the contemporary word," Kazantsev points out. In their prime, the Maly Theater, the Moscow Art Theater, the Meyerhold Theater, the Taganka Theater and the Sovremennik all made their mark producing contemporary works. Today, however, he feels that "the rush to stage nothing but the classics or works on trendy themes" has led to the degradation of theatrical performances.

The first issue of *Playwright* was purposefully conceived to address that state of affairs. It contains eight plays by young, unknown writers. And, in an attempt to create a link with historical traditions, it includes a one-act vaudeville by Savva Mamontov, Russia's first great patron of the arts, as well as a handful of short articles about other major theatrical figures from the past.

According to Kazantsev, the "extremely strong" second issue will make a similar statement that Russia's established playwrights have lost none of their power. It will print new plays by such eminent writers as Lyudmila Petrushevskaya and Lyudmila Razumovskaya.

The list of people taking an active part in publishing the journal speaks highly of its chances for success. In addition to Kazantsev's co-editor, Mikhail Roshchin, one of the most respected playwrights of the "old guard," the editorial board reads like a who's who of Russian drama. Besides Petrushevskaya and Razumovskaya, others lending their expertise are Alexander Volodin, Edvard Radzinsky and Viktor Slavkin.

That hardly means the fledgling undertaking has had an easy go of it. Financing has been haphazard, with grants from private individuals and some organizations (including the Goethe Center), barely covering the costs of the first issue. And while a New York distributor services overseas customers, no efficient system for distribution has been found for potential buyers in the former Soviet Union.

But the unflappable Kazantsev sees only challenges where others see problems. "I like to do things people say can't be done," he says.

(*May 1993*)

More Problems at the Taganka

Accusing Moscow city politicians and former employees of the Taganka Theater of attempting to "seize and close" his theater, the internationally acclaimed director Yury Lyubimov announced at a press conference Tuesday that he was closing the playhouse himself in protest.

The Taganka, once the most daring and popular theater in Russia, will remain closed at least until an arbitration court decides its fate next Tuesday. Court action became necessary after a split developed between Lyubimov and members of his troupe last year.

Like so many other dramas unfolding in Russia today, the case of the Taganka stems in part from the effort to modernize the Soviet behemoth. The plot is complex, the characters flamboyant and the dialogue not always polite.

It all began 18 months ago, when Lyubimov had just returned to Moscow from five years exile abroad. Russia's most famous director because of the political comment in his stagings, he had been deprived of his citizenship in 1984 while staging *Crime and Punishment* in London during a sanctioned trip.

Back home in the new atmosphere of freedom, Lyubimov was given the right to privatize the Taganka at some unspecified future date.

The conflict arose when his antagonist at the theater, Nikolai Gubenko, decided that privatization would threaten jobs. A former Soviet culture minister, Gubenko led a group of actors that broke away from Lyubimov last year to form their own theater, the Commonwealth of Taganka Actors.

In the latest scene—and it was literally a scene—two deputies of the Moscow City Council barged past the guard at the stage door last weekend and forced their way into Lyubimov's office. They came as supporters of Gubenko, who had attempted to hold rehearsals at the theater on Friday and Saturday despite Lyubimov's protests.

It is an ironic turn of history that, at a time of artistic freedom in Russia, Lyubimov once again finds himself fighting for his future and that of his theater.

The Taganka, a red brick building that sits nobly on the square of the same name southeast of the city center, grew famous in the 1960s and '70s as the conscience of the Russian intelligentsia.

Lyubimov took over as director of the theater in 1964. In the ensuing years, Vladimir Vysotsky, the bard beloved of all Russia, performed there in a contemporary adaptation of Shakespeare's *Hamlet*. Lyubimov's staging of *The Master and Margarita*, by Mikhail Bulgakov, galvanized attention around the suppression dating from the Stalin era of the country's most gifted writers.

In the present battle, Gubenko says he is acting in the interest of the theater's actors, who he has repeatedly maintained will be thrown out of work if Lyubimov is given full run of the theater. Lyubimov, on the other hand, insists that the whole argument is a matter of money.

"They want to get as much of the theater's property as possible," he said at the press conference Tuesday.

Lyubimov has stated publicly that the Taganka will cease to exist if the most modern of the theater's three stages is turned over to Gubenko and his supporters, as they demand. Gubenko could not be contacted for comment.

Growing increasingly angry as the 90-minute press conference progressed, Lyubimov called the actions of the deputies "a political act" for which he said they had the backing of such hardline communist sympathizers as Viktor Anpilov.

As he has often done in the past, Lyubimov compared the events dividing his theater to those which are now dividing Russia.

"Look what we have been reduced to," he said through clenched teeth. "As soon as the Communists were deposed, they should have been tried in court. Solzhenitsyn is right not to come here."

The closing of the theater comes just days after the premiere of Lyubimov's staging of *Zhivago*. It has been canceled along with all other productions scheduled through June 29.

A Taganka spokeswoman said that if the decision of the arbitration court is favorable to Lyubimov, canceled performances may be rescheduled.[2]

(June 1993)

Mark Rozovsky

"I have always worked, no matter what," says Mark Rozovsky. "Even when they wouldn't let me."

That no-nonsense attitude is what makes the founder of the Theater u Nikitskikh vorot one of the most productive figures in Moscow theater. His thirty-six year career has seen him develop from a spunky amateur enthusiast into the leader of a theater with an international reputation. What is more, his recent, acclaimed production of *Uncle Vanya* indicates that, at age 56, his best years are still ahead.

But there was a time when even the energetic Rozovsky couldn't have predicted that. The year was 1969 and, instead of celebrating the 12th anniversary of his popular amateur theater, Our Home, he was embroiled in the fight of his life.

"The decree read, 'liquidate the studio, Our Home,'" Rozovsky recalls with a smile.

---

[2] Aside from performances by Alla Demidova's Theater A, the Taganka essentially remained closed until April 1994. At that time, the actors who had remained faithful to Lyubimov held a press conference in which they explained that the theater would perish if it did not reopen. Lyubimov, who declined to come to Moscow for the reopening, did not sanction the move, nor did he oppose it.

"We were accused of anti-Soviet activities. They told us, 'That's how the Czech events began.'"

Deprived of his theater, his name banned in the media, Rozovsky did the only thing he could: He set to work. Mostly, that meant writing plays he never expected to see produced. "To this day, I still pull out old things I thought I could never use," he says.

In 1973, the legendary Leningrad director, Georgy Tovstonogov, extended a hand. He let Rozovsky stage a dramatization of Nikolai Karamzin's 18th-century story, "Poor Liza," on the small stage of his Bolshoi Drama Theater. The success of that project led to a second, this time a dramatization of Leo Tolstoy's story, "Strider," under the title of *The Story of a Horse.*

When it was nearly completed eight months later, Tovstonogov dropped by to watch a dress rehearsal. The next day, with no notice, he moved the production to the main stage and took control of it himself, according to Rozovsky.

"That was the second big blow of my life," says the director. "It was my play, my direction, my music and my set. And he took it all away from me."

The topic remains a sore one. Not only because *The Story of a Horse* went on to garner worldwide fame for Tovstonogov, but because Rozovsky was deeply indebted to the director for protecting him in a time of need. "This man whom I revered let me down," he explains.

Unable to continue in Leningrad, Rozovsky moved on to Riga. There, in 1979, he was struck by the "third blow" of his life. At the invitation of his friend, the novelist, Vasily Aksyonov, he contributed to the uncensored miscellany known as *Metropole.* That samizdat publication, bringing together a host of prominent, "unofficial" writers, caused one of the last "great" literary scandals of the Soviet period. Several participants were forced to emigrate, while the rest were blacklisted or kicked out of the Writers Union.

But this time, as the Soviet system slowly self-destructed, Rozovsky's fortunes began looking up. Oleg Yefremov invited him to mount three productions at the Moscow Art Theater. Even more importantly, in 1983,

Yefremov solved a problem that had dogged Rozovsky for decades. Pulling strings and bending rules, he got the "amateur" Rozovsky a diploma as a "professional director." For the first time in his life, Rozovsky could work as a pro without the intercession of a "name" patron.

With the chance to "start all over," Rozovsky immediately founded the Theater u Nikitskikh vorot. And when Gorbachev came to power in 1985, Rozovsky got lucky "for the first time ever." Taking advantage of relaxed regulations, he set out to expand his theater by raising his own funds.

Using three groups of actors—two touring and one playing Moscow—the theater played a staggering 600 shows per year. Even without a single ruble of outside help, that brought in enough to construct two performance halls in Moscow and create a repertoire of some forty productions. Among them, incidentally, is a revival of *The Story of a Horse.* Three years ago, Rozovsky joined with Trinity College in Hartford, Ct., to found the Summer Theater Institute in Moscow, and Rozovsky's theater frequently tours Europe and the United States.

As the Theater u Nikitskikh vorot celebrates its 10th anniversary, Rozovsky has a chance to look back on a decade of intense activity. Shaking his head, he sighs, "I could never go through that again." Then, peering over the rim of his glasses and grinning enigmatically, he adds, "But, then, who the hell knows?"

(July 1993)

Natalia Shchukina

Mark Zakharov had been working on his production of *The Marriage of Figaro* at the Lenkom Theater for a year and a half when he decided last fall to make some major changes. One of them turned out to be a stroke of genius.

As Natalia Shchukina tells it, Zakharov suggested she take over the lead role of Figaro's scheming sweetheart, Suzanne, because "he wanted to take a risk."

The young actress, 23, had performed some bit parts in movies with the well-known

Natalia Shchukina performing in *The Marriage of Figaro* at the Lenkom Theater. Photo: Mikhail Guterman

directors Eldar Ryazanov and Stanislav Govorukhin, but she was hardly a known quantity. At the time, her only job at the Lenkom was as a cat in the children's production of *The Bremen Musicians*. Still, something prompted Zakharov to take a chance.

When the swirling, action-packed *Figaro* opened in January, it was the effervescent and charismatic Shchukina who turned a fun show into an exhilarating one. Her contagious laughter, sparkling eyes, bubbly voice and graceful, lightning-quick movements radiated that rare kind of energy which infects every other actor on stage and conquers an audience before they even have time to settle into their seats.

Shchukina's triumph was not, however, an overnight success. She had started acting at the tender age of 10 and, from that moment on, her "head was full of nothing but theater." She spent the next seven years under the tutelage of Vyacheslav Spesivtsev, whose Krasnaya Presnya Youth Studio was as famed for its striking, experimental productions in the 1970s and 1980s, as it was notorious for the director's rumored exploitation of his youthful charges.

"It was a very difficult theater," Shchukina says now, although she also recalls it as a "fabulous time."

"I saw the best and the worst sides of theater from an early age," she continues. "I learned to work for nothing except pure personal joy."

The lessons she learned there have come in handy. When she got nothing but rejections the first time she tried to enter a professional acting school, she was undaunted. She kept in shape by spending the next year taking small roles in movies, although she much prefers working on a stage to working in front of a camera. The following year she was admitted to the Shchukin Institute of the Vakhtangov Theater.

The school of hard knocks put her in good stead during work on *Figaro* as well. Zakharov had already mapped out the role of Suzanne with another actress and everything had to be changed to suit Shchukina's very different personality.

"I was insecure because of my age and because I feared there would be a lot of envious eyes looking at me," she says.

Meanwhile, as proof that when it rains, it pours, Shchukina suddenly found herself swamped with work. In addition to being given a part in the Lenkom's production of *A Memorial Prayer*, she was invited to play Sonya in the Et Cetera Theater's inaugural production of *Uncle Vanya*. Rehearsing and performing in four shows simultaneously exhausted her to the point that she became nothing but a "walking body."

The pressure increased further when, just before the premiere of *Figaro*, the Lenkom's lighting man perished tragically in a fire at the theater and Zakharov himself suffered a heart attack.

But the old adage that the show must go on is more than just a catchy phrase. Despite all the tribulations, the first performance of *Figaro* did not merely come off as scheduled. It proved a dazzling showcase for an irresistible young actress who, in a few short months, traveled the distance from risk to star.

(July 1993)

Lyudmila Roshkovan

In her nearly twenty years as the artistic director at the Chelovek Theater-Studio, Lyudmila Roshkovan has experienced everything from the proverbial ecstasy of victory to the inevitable agony of defeat. Under the constant surveillance of the KGB for her underground studio's provocative productions during the 1970s and early 1980s, she was catapulted into the limelight when her theater finally won official recognition six years ago.

"Suddenly, we went from being hounded to being the talk of Moscow," the petite Roshkovan says with an incredulous smile. "I sat here and wondered, 'Is this really possible?'"

It was a far cry from the years when the studio, whose name means "human," hid behind the name of the People's Collective of the Lenin House of Culture, and held clandestine, invitation-only performances in various basements around Moscow. Now, its productions of Slawomir Mrozek's *Emigrants* and Lyudmila Petrushevskaya's *Cinzano*, both directed by Roman Kozak, garnered the troupe international attention at theater festivals and during tours of Europe and North and South America.

But sudden success was also a serious test. Many of the young talents, whom Roshkovan had nurtured since Chelovek's first production in 1974, "changed visibly" when they gained overnight fame. "I find it terrifying how people can transform so quickly," she says. "They all learned quickly to sense the feel of money in their hands."

Instead of enjoying her hard-earned success, Roshkovan could only watch as her theater slowly began falling apart. By 1990, the core of the troupe followed Kozak to the Moscow Art Theater to form the short-lived Fifth Studio. And then came the real blow. As she was stepping out of a car one evening on Mayakovsky Square, she was hit head-on by a drunk driver.

"They scooped me up and put me back together piece by piece," Roshkovan now recalls.

The bones in her pelvis and legs had been pulverized. All 24 ribs had been broken and both lungs were punctured. Later, the doctors told her they had never known anyone to survive such a horrendous trauma.

That may be why she is so philosophical about the professional problems she now faces, as her studio struggles to survive in the new economic climate. "I've got my priorities straight, now," she says with a twinkle in her eye.

Instead of keeping a standing company, Roshkovan now hires actors and technical personnel on a contract basis for each production. More complex is the matter of the two small buildings which Chelovek occupies in the center of Moscow on Skatertny Lane. They are in need of reconstruction. Originally, Roshkovan hoped to outfit them with a pair of performance halls and maybe even construct a theater center. But as inflation spiraled upward, she realized that would be impossible. Instead, she now hopes to find someone to finance the work in exchange for office space.

Meanwhile, Roshkovan quietly continues doing what she has done for two decades. She keeps busy running her theater. Her most recent premiere, a breezy interpretation of Fernando Arrabal's *Orison*, bore the distinct trademark of the studio some say was the most important in the so-called theater-studio movement of the 1970s and 1980s.

When asked what she thinks about her place in Moscow theater history, Roshkovan shrugs her shoulders with disinterest. She even denies there ever was such a trend.

"As always in Russia, that was just an attempt by some to create another mass movement. There was a lot of bad theater around, and we simply wanted to do something professionally and well."

(July 1993)

Yury Lyubimov Interview

Yury Lyubimov is no stranger to controversy. When he took over the Theater of Drama and Comedy on Taganka Square in 1964, he quickly found himself in the eye of a storm. His productions breathed too freely and smacked too plainly of the truth to satisfy the ideologues whose job it was to keep art properly clipped for mass consumption.

Until he was stripped of his Soviet citizenship in 1984, Lyubimov waged one of the most celebrated struggles for artistic autonomy of the Soviet period.

But now that his old nemesis, the Communist Party, has been dethroned, the Taganka is embroiled in yet another vicious battle. This time, the opposition comes from a rebellious group within the theater. Whatever the outcome, one thing is certain: The end of the Soviet era has also marked the end of one of its most prominent cultural landmarks. With or without Lyubimov, the Taganka is a house divided.

Uncharacteristically, the director is looking to the government for support.

"I think the President will take measures to preserve the theater," Lyubimov says. He indicated that Yeltsin has repeatedly voiced support for Lyubimov's side in the present dispute.

Yury Lyubimov's joy upon returning to his office at the Taganka theater on May 10, 1988 proved short lived. At right David Borovsky stands and Nikolai Gubenko sits at desk. Photo: Yury Feklistov

The opposition is led by Nikolai Gubenko, an actor at the Taganka until 1968, when he was fired for skipping the beginning of the season. The two men patched up their differences in 1980, when Lyubimov invited him to star in *Boris Godunov*, a project that was subsequently banned. Shortly before being named the Soviet Minister of Culture in 1989, Gubenko engineered the director's return from exile.

Lyubimov flatly rejects Gubenko's claim that he abandoned the actors who built his reputation. He points out that, since he was reinstated as the Taganka's artistic director in 1989, his productions, old and new, have toured the world to the praise of critics and audiences alike. He also denies that he has tried to stop his opponents from mounting their own productions.

"The mayor gave them their choice of three venues in the center of Moscow," he said, referring to Yury Luzhkov's offer to turn over to Gubenko either the Ukraina, the Kazakhtstan or the Praga cinemas. "But what they want is to destroy the Taganka. And then they'll all cry crocodile tears when I die."

His opponents don't understand that a theater belongs to its director, he says.

"A theater is created by someone and when that person goes, the theater goes with him," Lyubimov explained. "Sure, the physical plant and the people in it carry on under the same name in honor of past glory. But at that point, it becomes something different altogether."

One of the most popular Soviet actors during the late Stalin era, the director is appalled, but not surprised by the recent turn of events. He insists that the forces dividing his theater today are the same ones he battled in the past. Born just two months before the October Revolution in 1917, he characterized the current political situation as "the second October Revolution." And he lashed out at the inability of today's politicians to take effective action.

"They missed their chance when they didn't condemn the Communist Party in court," he said. "They missed their chance when they didn't take immediate advantage of the referendum. They missed their chance when they didn't convict those responsible for the May 1 events."[3]

He sees the current dispute as a litmus test for the future. Belittling the recent decision of a municipal arbitration court to uphold Gubenko's claim to the Taganka's biggest stage, Lyubimov said he hopes to remove the theater from the jurisdiction of the city and put it under the control of the federal authorities. He will appeal the case in an all-Russian arbitration court.

If that action fails, Lyubimov says his days in Moscow are over.

"I have several contracts and offers for productions in the West," he said. "I will not be without work."

(*July 1993*)

Nikolai Gubenko Interview

"The point is this," says Nikolai Gubenko, "Does Russia need you or do you need Russia?"

It was a rhetorical question aimed in absentia at Yury Lyubimov, the director of the Taganka Theater, with whom Gubenko has had a hot-and-cold relationship for nearly 30 years. Things couldn't get much colder than they are today.

Gubenko, who leads a group of rebellious actors that calls itself the Commonwealth of Taganka Actors, has no doubt who is to blame for the schism at the world famous theater. He claims Lyubimov forced the split

by turning his back on the actors who served him for three decades.

"This man," says Gubenko in reference to Lyubimov, "has only one desire: To seize a fat piece, and that's all. He's not interested in artistic work."

Moreover, Gubenko flatly rejects the notion that Lyubimov singlehandedly founded the Taganka.

"He didn't create the Taganka. The Taganka collective created the Taganka. One director without a troupe can't do anything. Theater is the work of an ensemble and this troupe was a unified entity with a common goal," Gubenko explained.

The current row between the two men is not the first, but it is the most rancorous. Gubenko has already won a court case giving him control of the Taganka's largest stage. Meanwhile, Lyubimov has threatened to abandon Russia for good if that decision is not reversed.

Gubenko is not impressed. "He won't go anywhere," he says, "because no one is waiting for him anywhere. Lyubimov is having no success in the West, at least in comparison to what he once had with the Taganka."

Both parties in the 18-month dispute agree on one thing: The bone of contention is the valuable property of the sprawling theatrical complex on Taganka Square. But the conflict has been brewing for a long time.

According to Gubenko, he was the Taganka's leading actor from 1964 to 1968 when Lyubimov dismissed him for missing the opening of the season.

"In 1968, when the highest salary in this theater was 130 rubles, I asked Yury Petrovich [Lyubimov] for permission to earn some money by making a film during the summer. And since the shoot was to end in the fall, I asked him to find replacements to cover for me. He refused. When I reported late, he fired me for violating discipline."

Gubenko was replaced by the bard and actor, Vladimir Vysotsky, whose rough-hewn manner made him a living legend throughout the Soviet Union. When Vysotsky died in 1980, Lyubimov invited Gubenko to take on his old roles again.

But by then, the Soviet authorities had lost patience with the Taganka's provocative

---

[3] 571 people were injured in the 1993 May Day riot, a clash between communist and nationalist protesters and government forces.

style. They banned the productions of *Vladimir Vysotsky* and *Boris Godunov*, both of which starred Gubenko. When Lyubimov was in London in 1984 to receive an award for his staging of *Crime and Punishment* at the Lyric Theater, he was deprived of his Soviet citizenship, leaving the Taganka without a director.

Gubenko questions the received opinion that Lyubimov was the victim in that incident. Claiming the director has no right to compare himself to such exiles as Alexander Solzhenitsyn and Andrei Sakharov, Gubenko says Lyubimov "betrayed his troupe by leaving it one on one with the Brezhnev regime."

"He simply wrote that he wasn't coming back, that's all," said Gubenko.

(The press reported in 1984 that Lyubimov's decision not to return to Moscow was prompted by a veiled threat from a Soviet embassy official. After Lyubimov voiced criticisms of the Soviet leadership in an interview in the London *Times*, the official reportedly told Lyubimov that his "crime was obvious and punishment would follow.")

But most irritating of all, Gubenko says, is Lyubimov's behavior since his return. Gubenko had accepted an offer to lead the Taganka in 1987 on one condition: "That we struggle to return Lyubimov to the theater."

After two years of behind the scenes battles, that goal was achieved.

"We met him with flowers and open arms, and he met us with black berets," Gubenko said, referring to Lyubimov's orders to bar his opponents entrance to the theater.

Gubenko added that he has no intention of seizing total control of the Taganka. He says he only wants a place to work for that part of the company "which can't work with Lyubimov because of the humiliation he has subjected them to."

(*August 1993*)

Exit Yury Lyubimov

Yury Lyubimov, world-renowned director at the Taganka Theater, has gone out slamming the door behind him. Again. He says some disgruntled actors want to seize half his theater. They say the great director has lost touch with Russia.

Door-slamming has been a way of life for the soft-spoken man with a lightning-quick temper since he founded the Taganka in 1964.

But Lyubimov was famous long before he became scandalous. Throughout the 1950s, the handsome and gracious actor sparkled in the roles of positive heroes on stage and screen. He was awarded the Stalin Prize in 1951 for the top male theatrical performance.

When he turned to directing full-time and founded the Taganka, he took his first step toward entering the rarefied ranks of living legends.

For twenty years, Lyubimov's politically daring and artistically inspiring productions delighted the public and frustrated a government that worked overtime to keep art bland and artists tame. Perhaps no other Soviet artist of that era did so much to incur the wrath of the cultural watchdogs, yet had to answer for so little. To a point, of course.

He fought to get nearly every one of his productions past the censor. Naturally, that increased his fame and strengthened his dissident reputation, just as it laid the traps that would one day come back to haunt him. Still, until the hourglass began running out in 1981, only two of his 34 productions had been banned outright. And while scores of major Soviet artists were being silenced through exile or arrest, Lyubimov made the Taganka not only the lightning rod for Moscow intellectuals, but the favorite gathering place of the communist elite.

It is deceptively easy to overemphasize the adversarial nature of the relationship between the old Soviet system and those who found or put themselves in opposition to it. In fact, Yury Lyubimov was not only a child of the Soviet way of life (he was born between the February and October revolutions in 1917), but the art he created was unthinkable without it. Only a man who had seen his beloved grandfather robbed of his property by the Soviet government, and who had been the proud recipient of a Stalin Prize could truly grasp the full range of paradoxes in Soviet life.

For all their backstage bickering and public warfare, Lyubimov needed the communists for inspiration no less than they needed his reputation for legitimacy.

It is rumored that the ties were closer still. None less than Brezhnev and Andropov gave the green light to some of his most daring productions. Where did such contacts come from? No one knows for sure, but from 1940 to 1947, Lyubimov pounded the boards in the NKVD Song and Dance Ensemble. It was founded by Lavrenty Beria to entertain the Red Army troops.

Lyubimov finally lost his citizenship in 1984 for crossing the commissars one too many times. The Taganka has never recovered. Nor has Lyubimov, for that matter.

For five years he wandered the stages of top Western theaters a prodigal son. He was a celebrity, but you could see it in his eyes; without Russia, without his actors, without his theater, it just wasn't right.

The final blow came after his celebrated return to Moscow in 1989. Times and people had changed. The chemistry was gone and not only was the Taganka barely a shadow of its old self, it was at war with itself.

It is an ignominious end for a great director and his theater. But, with the harsh honesty of a typical Lyubimov production, it is probably fitting that the Taganka went the road of most everything Soviet: haggling, bitterness and crippling power struggles.[4]

(*September 1993*)

Peter Stein

Peter Stein doesn't quite understand the attention and he never has.

---

[4] Lyubimov's contract as the artistic director of the Taganka expired on January 1, 1994. The portion of the troupe remaining loyal to him resumed performances of a handful of old productions on the theater's old stage in the spring of that year, still claiming him as their leader. Lyubimov continues to work with them on productions which are often funded by western producers, and programs and marquées at the Taganka bear the statement: "Theater founded by Yury Lyubimov." However, the days when the Taganka was Lyubimov's primary home appear to be over.

The man called "Europe's favorite German director" by the British critic Simon Reade, is revered almost as a demigod in Moscow. It is a "strange" phenomenon that started in the 1970s, he says, and one which must have some "irrational" reason behind it. Even back then, Stein's German colleagues teasingly began calling him "a Russian." But, Stein refused offers to work in Moscow in 1975.

"I said, 'No, come on! I can't work under the Brezhnev situation when you can't say what you want.' You can do theater under slave-like conditions, but I'm not used to it. I was born late enough that I didn't have to learn this kind of behavior under the Nazis in Germany."

But Stein's reputation in Moscow just continued to grow. Triumphant tours to Moscow with his acclaimed Berlin Schaübhne stagings of Anton Chekhov's *Three Sisters* (1990) and *The Cherry Orchard* (1992) prompted many Russian observers to gush—and lament—that the great, lost Russian theatrical traditions had been preserved in the heart of a German.

Following last year's rather rancorous break with the Schaübhne (it refused to go dark for a year to let him rehearse an epic, five-evening *Faust*) Stein is finally in the Russian capital for a project that has been on and off since the mid-1980s. Using Russian actors, he is mounting an ambitious production of Aeschylus's trilogy, *Oresteia*, consisting of the tragedies *Agamemnon* and *The Libation-Bearers*, and the drama, *Eumenides*.

If an old top gun in the former Soviet military complex had had his way, Russia might never have seen the plays.

Gorbachev's Defense Minister Dmitry Yazov, whose duties included the nominal directorship of the Soviet Army Theater, entered Russian theatrical legend when he reportedly nixed the *Oresteia* project with a memorable phrase. "A German," he supposedly said, "will stage a Greek with Russians in my theater over my dead body."

Instead, these days Yazov spends his time waiting for the oft-postponed trial of the 1991 coup plotters to resume, while Stein, 56, is hard at work beneath the cavernous, bomber-dotted sky painted on the ceiling of what is now called the Russian Army Theater. He will eventually hide the tacky ceiling mural with a blank, sky-colored netting, and will place his chorus on a platform in the middle of the audience. But he likes the theater space for its monstrous size. It is one of the reasons why he is in Moscow at all.

Work proposals began pouring in after the advent of perestroika, Stein says, but, since he doesn't speak Russian, he had to choose something he knows well. And he also wanted to do something unusual for the Russians. Since he has "made theater absolutely everywhere that is not apt for it," he decided, first of all, to be creative with space.

"In Moscow," Stein explained, "they are not used to what we do in Western Europe, like playing in exhibition halls or cinema studios or in streets or in a stadium. They have these theaters closed on one side and they do not know the open, in-the-round play."

Then, there is Stein's reputation as one of the finest and purist interpreters of ancient drama. His 1980 production of *Oresteia* at the Schaubühne garnered worldwide attention.

"I'm not only a theater director," Stein continued, "I'm a specialist of the Greek tragedy. The thinking of the ancient Greeks, which is the basis of Western philosophy, is averse to Russian thinking. Greek thinking is able, willing and even keen to look at contradictions, accept them and then find a clear solution. This is not the Russian kind of thinking. I thought, even if I can't speak Russian, I can introduce them to this kind of thinking, feeling, working and acting."

There are still plenty of obstacles to overcome before anyone gets a chance to see anything. And in fact, Yazov may yet have his way.

Referring to the show's scheduled January 29 opener, Stein admits he is "not sure there will be a premiere." There are problems to solve first, he says, not the least of which is money. One of the project's Russian organizers calls it "catastrophically short."

The German government is paying for Stein, his German staff and some of the decoration. But the rest of the production costs—actors' and local technicians' salaries, set preparation, hall rental and the financing of a European tour for the Army Theater in exchange for giving up its main stage for several months—are to be covered by the Munich-based Hahn Productions and the Moscow-based Confederation of International Theater Associations. The Russian side has come up short. Says confederation spokeswoman Ella Levina, "We weren't ready for inflation. We have already spent about $500,000, but we need $200,000 more."

The plan is to recoup expenditures through a world tour of *Oresteia* next year. Dates are set in Scotland, Austria, Germany and Portugal, with negotiations underway for performances in Italy and Belgium. Stein never liked the tour idea—"I just wanted to play in Moscow and basta!" he says—but for the sake of the project, he compromised. As it turned out, it was the first of many compromises.

"I accepted working conditions I have never accepted," he says with a tinge of amazement in his voice. "I'm more or less back to the position of assistant director [I held] 35 years ago. I have never rehearsed so much in my life. Ten hours a day, six days a week. And on the seventh day, I have a lot to do. It's a nightmare."

The difficulties also include coping with the theater's broken heating system—Stein and his actors rehearse in overcoats—and playing along with delays caused by the different expectations of the Russian actors and the German director. Rehearsals, which began October 4 and will run through January, are conducted in German translated into Russian with occasional forays into French or English, both of which Stein speaks fluently. But the problem isn't linguistic, it is cultural.

Many of the actors, trained in the Russian psychological school, don't understand what Stein wants from them. Famed for his meticulous research and fidelity to historical detail, Stein rejects the notion of modernizing or personalizing a work. That is the method which has predominated in Russia throughout the 20th century. Still, Stein tends to brush off misunderstandings with the actors as par for the course.

"These are games," he says nonchalantly. "We must not take actors too seriously."

Looking ahead to the premiere, Stein notes another of this project's many ironies: Recent events have made his production almost too timely for his purist tastes. Russia, he says, is attempting to replace an archaic political system by inventing democracy and a state of justice. With a few of the names and places changed, that is precisely the subject of Aeschylus's trilogy.

Might his *Oresteia* have a tangible effect on events in Russia?

"Absolutely not!" Stein quickly demurs. "Theater never has any effect on anything. It may affect individual spectators when they are in the theater. And when they leave, there may be a greater clarity or confusion in their hearts and minds. If so, that is already a big success."

(November 1993)

Boris Lvov-Anokhin

"I like to joke that I've gone off into an ivory tower," says Boris Lvov-Anokhin in a voice so soft and rhythmic that it mesmerizes. "I've returned to the theater of my youth. When theater for me was a holiday of sheer beauty."

Lvov-Anokhin, 67, really has not changed much since he burst on the scene in the 1950s with several acclaimed stagings. Even then, as in the 1960s, when he rose to stardom by taking over the Stanislavsky Drama Theater and making it one of Moscow's top venues, his calling card was his refined taste and his sense of poetry.

But his lifelong pursuit of theatrical elegance took on the urgency of a mission in 1989 when he became the artistic director at the Novy Drama Theater. His opulent productions of Edmond Rostand's *The Little Eagle* and Christopher Hampton's *Dangerous Liaisons* brought distinct personality to a theater that was no longer new, as its name in Russian indicates, nor even very dramatic. His most recent premiere, *The Aspern Papers*, will surely enhance further the resurgent theater's reputation.

The great British actor Sir Michael Redgrave adapted *The Aspern Papers* in 1959 from Henry James's novella as a showcase for his own prodigious talents. Until now, the enormous success it enjoyed has never been repeated.

In brief, dramatic strokes the play portrays six key moments in the lives of a scheming literary scholar, an ancient woman (the possessor of some documents he desperately seeks) and the woman's niece (who is ripe for his false attentions). They are brought together in an old Italian villa by the memory of the mysterious Henry Aspern, a "great poet" of the early 19th century. He was once the object of the old woman's passion and is now the object of the scholar's research.

"I call it an intellectual detective story or a psychological grotesque," Lvov-Anokhin casually explains as the clock ticks down to curtain time for the first, invitation-only performance. He says the play's rich interplay of "unique romanticism" with flights of irony and paradox, and the "sense of beauty, even demonic magic" attached to the figure of the absent Aspern, provided just the material for him to expand his idea of an "aesthetic theater."

But as Lvov-Anokhin adds new chapters to his 43-year career, the miracle may be that he is still a director at all. The end could easily have come 24 years ago.

Between 1963 and 1969, the man who was instrumental in discovering such talented playwrights as Alexander Volodin, Leonid Zorin and Ion Drutse, presided over the flourishing of the Stanislavsky Drama Theater. There, he created a repertory whose polished artistic vision was spiced with political unconformity. Perhaps most famous were its productions of *Medea* and *Antigone* by the French playwright, Jean Anouilh. So it was no surprise when Lvov-Anokhin announced that his next project would be *Eurydice*, a third Anouilh play.

The new project never came about.

"I was summoned to the Arts Committee," Lvov-Anokhin says, "and they said, 'Your theater is named for Stanislavsky, not for Anouilh. And you are not going to stage any more Anouilh!'"

Only then did the too-daring director begin to understand how much trouble he was in. He tried defending himself by pointing out that the great Alexander Tairov had staged three plays by Eugene O'Neill at the Kamerny Theater in the late 1920's. Why couldn't he do the same?

But his logic was not as foolproof as that of his inquisitors. He was told, "That's right, and there is no Tairov theater any more either."

The all-powerful Arts Committee accused him of an unhealthy interest in a foreign author, not only banning the play, but forcing Lvov-Anokhin to replace his most daring entries with "banal, stereotypical Soviet" productions.

Realizing it was pointless to stay on as the leader of a theater he couldn't lead, Lvov-Anokhin resigned.

The result was ten years of deep depression. Able to work only as a ballet critic—a second profession which has also gained him an enviable reputation—he sought the aid of specialists to turn around what became his "hatred and fear of theater." But he soon learned he had enemies worse than the demons within him.

"I was under the care of several doctors," he explains, "and one day an assistant came to me trembling. She whispered that her boss had been put on my case to prove me psychologically unsound and have me committed to an insane asylum. They were using my depression to put an end to my theatrical career."

It didn't work, however. Lvov-Anokhin's decade of crippling doubt finally ended when the prestigious Maly Theater extended a hand in 1979. There he resurrected his career, creating several of that house's biggest successes of the 1980s. When he was asked to revive the moribund Novy Drama Theater, he seized the opportunity to make up for lost time.

Praising the end of those days when artists were "humiliated endlessly" and listing that as "perhaps the only thing Russia has achieved" in recent years, Lvov-Anokhin says he knows exactly what he wants now: "I want theater to be festive and romantic. I want to tell people that there is more to life than just kiosks on the street. That there is something more eternal."

(*December 1993*)

The Youth Movement

In recent years, dissatisfaction, disagreement and mistrust have been the rule in most every aspect of the theatrical process in Moscow. Playwrights were unhappy with theaters for diving headlong into the classics while theaters were unhappy with playwrights for writing bad, gloomy plays. Critics accused theaters and playwrights alike of churning out so much drivel, while theaters and playwrights were unified in their anger at critics for carping at everything they did.

Things got so bad that everybody finally started looking for a way to break the stalemate. The answer for many was a turn to youth.

Critics were the first to jump on the bandwagon. Fed up with what they perceived to be a tremendous drop in quality in the professional theaters, they turned their attention to a few unusually talented productions at various theatrical institutes. That brought a swift response from the theaters: They tried cashing in on the new fad by including student productions in their repertories. Even a famous movie director (Sergei Solovyov) tried escaping the "other" Russian cultural crisis—in film—by making his theatrical debut with students. Meanwhile, encouraged by the abundant publicity, two graduating classes formed their own professional theaters.

But, as with any fad, there was often more sparkle than gold in the flood of student-oriented productions. This time critics and theaters inadvertently found common ground: They were unified in forgetting that the exciting energy of a student performance looks a lot different when transferred to the professional stage and offered to the public as more than just a learner's exercise.

The first to learn this hard lesson were the members of the 1992 graduating class at the Shchukin Institute. Primarily on the strength of the talented *May 32/City of Mice*, this group succeeded in staying together as a professional theater called the Learned Monkey. (The name is taken from an actors' game made up by Yevgeny Vakhtangov and Mikhail Chekhov.) The problem was that, essentially left alone, the former students were able to do little more than drift apart gradually and quietly. The Shchukin Institute appointed a low-key artistic director (Yury Avsharov), provided some funding and helped them find a location to perform (a stage at a so-called "Palace of Culture"). But efforts to do more than perform some of their student productions were not crowned with success. Eduard Radziukevich, the student who had scripted, scored and directed the haunting *City of Mice*, got almost no support from either his fellow actors or the theater's administration as he tried to stage Daniil Kharms's *Yelizaveta Bam*. It was eventually pushed aside in favor of a very amateurish, all-male production of *Romeo and Juliet* (directed by Anatoly Furmanchuk), the premiere of which came only at the tail end of the 1992–1993 season. It was performed a handful of times and then disappeared. As the 1993–1994 season moved into its second half, the future of the Learned Monkey was unclear. A number of actors had left the troupe, performances were few and far between, audiences were sparse, the critics who once had trumpeted praise were nowhere to be seen and the company's remaining die-hards were talking more about bare survival than growth.

It would appear that the new Fomenko Studio (Masterskaya Fomenko) will have an easier go of it. The students graduated in spring 1993 from the Russian Academy of Theater Arts (RATI, formerly GITIS) and turned professional in the fall. The studio—named after Pyotr Fomenko, the artistic director of both the class and the new theater—has solid financial backing, an active administration and a devoted following. For the moment, at least, it remains the apple of the Moscow critics' eye, and performances (mostly in tiny halls) are well attended. As of the first week in February 1994, it was performing four of its former "exam-productions," was on the verge of premiering its first professional show, and was preparing to revive its fifth student production, Marina Tsvetayeva's *The Adventure*.

The studio's active repertory consisted of Alexander Ostrovsky's *Wolves and Sheep* (directed by Fomenko), Shakespeare's *Twelfth Night* (directed by Yevgeny Kamenkovich), Nikolai Gogol's *The Order of St. Vladimir* and a dramatization of William Faulkner's *The Sound and the Fury* (both directed by Sergei Zhenovach). The new production was to be Kamenkovich's staging of Oscar Wilde's *The Importance of Being Earnest*.

The unprecedented fame garnered by this youthful group started with *The Adventure*. Directed by the Macedonian Ivan Popovski (himself one of the students), it had critics gushing superlatives that are rarely heard in Moscow. The Moscow Critics Association even named it the best production of the 1991–92 season, snubbing all the professional entries in the process. Unquestionably a talented student work, *The Adventure* was performed in a narrow corridor on one of the upper floors of the RATI building. But it was the setting, more than anything else, that gave the performance its sense of innovation. The tiny audience of 40, also crammed into the corridor, saw only fleeting glimpses of the "action" as characters quickly flew down or across the corridor-stage before disappearing into neighboring rooms. As such, the actors seldom had to build or sustain a mood; it was enough for them to strike effective poses and let their youthful energy and Tsvetayeva's verse text do the rest.

Popovski's work, deservedly praised, may have brought him premature fame. When he was contracted to stage Fernand Crommelynck's *The Sculptor of Masks* in autumn 1992 for the Alla Sigalova Independent Company, he quickly learned how fickle critics and artistic directors can be. Sigalova herself removed this very unsuccessful production from her repertory after only a few performances and some unfriendly reviews. In early 1993, Popovski was one of three directors who were fired as quickly as they were hired to help stage the Bogis Agency's production of Alexei Burykin's *Nijinsky*. (The others, incidentally, were Fomenko and Radziukevich.) Popovski's rather inglorious personal experiences in his first forays into professional theater might be seen as metaphors for the problems the Fomenko Studio as a whole may soon face.

While some of the young actors show extraordinary potential, it is clear that many

Pyotr Fomenko during rehearsals of *The Magnificent Cuckold* in 1994. That production solidified his position as Moscow's top director. Photo: Mikhail Guterman

are not ready to be thrust into leading or even secondary roles. Moreover, the play selection that was so crucial to broadening their educational experience can come across as silly in a professional context.

Especially striking in that category is the dreary, four-and-a-half hour dramatization of *The Sound and the Fury*. The young Russians make a game effort to plumb the depths of this wrenching drama about the Compson family, one of the great composite literary images of the decaying American South in the early 20th century. But, despite a stunning performance of the mute Benjy (Yury Stepanov), this one should have been abandoned as a warm memory of lessons well learned. The cultural and generational gaps separating the actors from their characters are downright deadly. It simply is not possible to take twenty-year-olds seriously as they struggle to impersonate such complex characters as Caroline, the bitter, ruthless old matriarch, or Dilsey, the wise and ancient black cook.

The Order of St. Vladimir fares somewhat better, in part because its subject matter is something the students-turned-pros can identify with. Nevertheless, the episodic performance adds up more to a collection of clever sketches than a finished work.

Twelfth Night is simply an excuse to turn loose a stage-full of energetic young people. The problem is that the players are so wrapped up in admiring their own enthusiasm, they seldom get around to drawing the audience into the fun.

It should come as no surprise that the troupe does its best under the guidance of Fomenko himself. The director's light, ironic touch in *Wolves and Sheep*, a wicked comedy about a group of provincials whose only purpose is to cheat each other out of as much as they can, creates a performance so sly and subtle that it almost has an aroma. First and foremost, Fomenko freed the young actors of weighty form and alien content, and encouraged them to just go out and show what they are capable of. Some of them did with a dazzling flair. The Kutepova twins, Ksenia and Polina, are perfectly cast and utterly charming as the dueling principals,

Murzavetskaya and Kupavina. Yury Stepanov, arguably the studio's most mature actor, gives a Siberian-sized, heart-aching performance of Lynyayev, the paunchy, well-meaning judge who is as helpless before the intrigues of his neighbors as before the charms of Murzavetskaya's mysterious relative, Glafira. She is played by Galina Tyunina with the same poisonous grace that this actress gives each of her roles. The remainder of the cast ranges from adequate to the weak.

But the intimate and atmospheric *Wolves and Sheep*, originally staged in 1992, is probably most interesting for another reason altogether. It is clearly a forerunner to Fomenko's spectacular production of *Guilty Without Guilt* at the Vakhtangov Theater in spring 1993. Both make the most of unusual settings in small rooms (the obvious influence of Popovski's production of *The Adventure*), and both recast well-crafted, but somewhat formulaic melodramas by Ostrovsky in a spell-binding atmosphere of intimacy. But *Guilty Without Guilt* was a universally acknowledged masterpiece, many say a turning point in end-of-the-century Russian theater. *Wolves and Sheep* was a clever and endearing performance that showed off some potential talent and gave Fomenko an outlet for some ideas that had captured his imagination at the time.

Whether or not the studio's new production of Wilde will be a step forward remains uncertain. I was allowed to attend a public dress rehearsal a week before the premiere on the condition that I not watch with a critical eye. Since I agreed to try, I can only make the broadest of observations. As with *The Adventure, The Sound and the Fury* (performed in an upstairs room at RATI), and *Wolves and Sheep* (performed in a room in the Yermolova Memorial Museum) the performing space is unorthodox: The stage is the surprisingly tinny, unfashionable runway at the Zaitsev House of Fashion. At the open rehearsal, Dmitry Cholak's wildly imaginative costumes made the biggest impression on the audience, especially since the actors delivered Wilde's stylish patter at such a breakneck speed, they often slid roughly over their lines or forgot them altogether.[5]

Regardless of the outcome of the Fomenko Studio experiment, it has solidified its founder's reputation as the leading director in Moscow today. Suddenly, the former assistant to Yury Lyubimov at the Taganka Theater in the 1960s is hearing people idolize him as a "master," and is watching retrospective showings of his productions on television. The well-deserved critical and popular success of *Guilty Without Guilt* capped it all off, but it was the sustained, one might even say frenzied, publicity surrounding his RATI class that laid the foundation.

Other examples of the student infiltration into the professional world have been less heralded, although their purpose was similar: Directors and theaters were looking to try something new. The dividends (or damages) of hurrying so many young people into the spotlight so early will only become clear with the passage of time. Some are bound to be the actors and directors who will eventually help lead Russian theater out of the Soviet era.

But whatever the case, it is most likely we will now see a decline in the popularity of student work. After all, the unusually high interest in what was transpiring at the schools and institutes was more an emotional rejection of the offerings in the professional theaters than it was an honest appraisal of some talented apprentices. Ultimately, the formation of the Fomenko Studio will probably be seen as the high-water mark in Moscow's youth movement.

(*Spring 1994, Slavic and East European Performance*)

The Class of Expressive Plastic Movement

Gennady Abramov seems to enjoy nothing quite so much as talking about how his fledgling Moscow theater, the Class of Expressive Plastic Movement, confounds the public. And the more people crowd into the tiny, basement room that serves as the theater's auditorium, the more stories he has to tell.

There's the one about the animated group of French producers who supposedly had to be pulled apart when they couldn't agree on the genre of the production they had just seen. Then there's the one about the two Russian directors visiting Moscow from the provinces: They reportedly got into a fist fight back at their hotel when they couldn't agree to what extent the performances of Abramov's actors were Brechtian.

But Abramov's favorite story is about the critics. "Nobody," he says with relish, "has broken as many critics' pens as we have. They all want to write about us, but they don't know how to describe us."

If asked for an explanation, the first thing Abramov does is refer you back to his theater's name. "It is an exact name," he says. "It is both a program and an explanation of what we do."

The Class of Expressive Plastic Movement was founded in 1991 as an affiliate of Anatoly Vasilyev's Moscow laboratory, the School of Dramatic Art.[6] Abramov, 55, is a former ballet dancer with degrees in choreography from the Belorussian Institute of Choreography (1960) and the Russian State Institute of Theater Arts (formerly GITIS, 1976). From 1960 to 1972, he danced more than 36 leading parts in various provincial ballet companies throughout the Soviet Union. More recently, he has choreographed and staged movement for many top theater and film artists, including Nikita Mikhalkov, Maximilian Schell and Johann Kresnik.

Abramov's especially close relationship with Vasilyev goes back to 1976 when the two collaborated on a production of *Hello, Dolly!* in Rostov-on-Don. Subsequently, Abramov choreographed the movement for Vasilyev's renowned stagings of *A Young*

---

[5] See the February 1994 review of the *The Importance of Being Earnest.*

[6] The Class's original fifteen actors were selected from 300 applicants who auditioned in November 1990. Their first public performance took place on January 6, 1991.

Man's Grown-Up Daughter, Cerceau, and *Six Characters in Search of an Author,* and he was a founding member of the School of Dramatic Art.

The idea to create a theater of movement under Vasilyev's roof came during a European tour of *Cerceau.* Abramov and Vasilyev took in a local movement performance that impressed them with its mastery, but they both agreed it could be done better yet. Certainly, another impulse was the creative crisis which has afflicted Vasilyev since the end of the 1980s. Aside from a controversial production of Mikhail Lermontov's *The Masquerade* at the Comédie-Française in 1992, and a production of Dostoevsky's *Uncle's Dream* in Budapest in April 1994, the '90s have not been a productive time for him, at least by any traditional measure. Since *Six Characters* in 1987, he has not completed a single production in Russia.[7] Much of his dissatisfaction has been aimed at what he feels is the degradation of the actor's art in Russia.

As the leader of the new movement class, Abramov's task was to turn a group of novices into a crop of actors who would be as attuned to the physical and demonstrative requirements of performance as to the emotional, intellectual and interpretive aspects. In an interview in January of 1993, just as the Class of Expressive Plastic Movement was gaining its first international attention, Abramov enthusiastically noted the advantageous side of his differences with Vasilyev. "Vasilyev exerts total control," he said, "while I have a theater of actors. By moving towards one another, we will give birth to a third idea."

---

[7] Around 1991, Vasilyev staged some Platonic dialogues that were filmed for, and broadcast on, television. They were occasionally performed, unannounced, as works-in-progress at the School of Dramatic Art. Abramov's 1993 production of *Nota bene,* subtitled "Notes in the Margins for *Joseph and His Brothers,*" was originally intended as an experiment to give Vasilyev ideas for his planned production of Thomas Mann's novel, *Joseph and His Brothers.* Vasilyev did not use any of the elements from *Nota bene* and subsequently abandoned the *Joseph* project.

But as it became increasingly apparent that Vasilyev's experiments were bogging down in a rarefied theater of the spoken word, Abramov and his students found themselves heading in the opposite direction. By early 1994, when his theater had become something of a mecca for anyone interested in avant-garde performance, Abramov admitted that he and Vasilyev were "moving towards a separation."

"I didn't want it," said Abramov, "but after Pina Bausch attended one of our performances, Vasilyev said we had to go. He's probably right. We've grown and we're already so independent that, like grown-up kids, it's time for us to leave the family."

Actually, the arrangement that eventually was worked out leaves Abramov the best of both worlds. The School of Dramatic Art still houses and financially supports his troupe, while Abramov retains total artistic autonomy. He has the right to develop his ideas as he sees fit, and to tour and perform when and where he wishes.

Abramov, ever evasive and ever suggestive, compares his productions to a musical composition. "There is a sort of divertimento-like quality to what we do," he explains. "I consider the divertimento a great discovery. After all, that is what gave rise to the symphony. The divertimento developed into the suite, which developed into the symphony. We are on the level of the divertimento that is on the verge of transforming into a suite. Further along, I hope we will achieve the level of the symphony. However, all of the instruments, all of the bodies, must co-exist independently and freely."

Abramov and his actors collaborate on non-verbal, improvisational performances that combine some elements of dramatic theater, mime and dance, but defy simple categorization. They scorn received notions of plot. They have rejected words, except in rare instances when they are used primarily as sounds that tend to challenge sense rather than make it. If Abramov is to be taken at his word, they have done away with the ideas of direction, scripts, librettos or even planning, except in the most general and technical sense. They evolve

Alexandra Konnikova, Yevgenia Kozlova and Olga Golubeva in Gennady Abramov's production of *They Come and They Go*, Class of Expressive Movement, 1993. Photo: P. Antonov

rather than create their improvisational productions, of which there are now five.

Each piece consists of fifteen to twenty independent episodes in which the language of communication is the highly trained movement of the human body. The often vague themes of the various episodes are unified loosely under the suggestive production titles of *The Persecutor, The Barrier of Isolation, Between Seasons, Nota bene* and *They Come and They Go.*

The ideas for the episodes originate with Abramov, who suggests the basic themes he would like to see his actors explore. But, artistically, the results are the product of the vision, talents, capabilities and daily moods of the individual performers. Aside from the rigorous physical training and exercises which are conducted strictly according to Abramov's own system, the director's main interference is to weed out the episodes he feels are not ready to be shown, and to arrange the order in which the remaining episodes are played.

"I can't demand a single gesture," he says of his preparatory work with his actors. "Even when I make a suggestion, I tell them that I'm only offering an alternative so that they'll offer me back another alternative."

Naturally, that doesn't mean that Abramov sits by idly while his pupils do whatever they want. He is a disciplinarian who locks actors out of rehearsals if they are late by as much as a few seconds. And when he sets a task, he expects to see it carried out to the letter. But he flatly rejects the notion of absolute directorial control. His goal is not to extract a specific result from his actors, but to enable them to express their own creative ideas to the fullest extent. He admits that the power he wields is "enormous," but immediately adds that he applies it in unorthodox ways.

The troupe currently consists of ten actors, the core of which has been with Abramov from the start. Only one had previous professional training as an actor. And while there is a considerable difference in talent and capabilities among the members of the group, each has achieved a remarkable level of technical excellence. In terms of style, some are partial to acrobatics, while others tend to explore the possibilities of emotional communication through abstract movement. Like the dedicated and fiercely loyal teacher that he is, Abramov refuses to evaluate his pupils in judgmental terms.

"We have to understand their improvisations from their point of view, not from ours" he insists. "I don't make them express my visions. I try to draw out their visions, their impressions, their images and their perceptions of movement."

Performances are conducted on a bare, hardwood floor, usually without special lighting and usually with the accompaniment of music that is played on a simple cassette player. The rare, very basic props might include some chairs, a bottle, some scarves or an empty picture frame. Reflecting the youthful concerns of the actors—most are in their early twenties—the motifs of the short, improvisational segments often revolve around the discovery of love or the states of awkwardness, sexual attraction and jealousy. They can be repetitive or even somewhat infantile at times, but the actors' technical execution is always impressive. The best episodes achieve strikingly coherent intellectual or emotional planes.

That is especially true as regards the etudes of Yevgenia Kozlova. Not only does she have an extraordinarily graceful command of her body, she has the remarkable ability to fuse her movements with the thoughts or impulses that guide her. Highly introspective and teasingly enigmatic, she seems to enter another world when on stage, making that transforming experience tangible to her audience. In those rare moments when her attention suddenly fixes on a concrete object—the floor, a window, a spectator—the effect of her transition from one level of consciousness to another is almost startling.

If other of her colleagues, particularly Vladimir Belyaikin and Vasily Yushchenko, create performances of breathtaking agility which skillfully combine elements of the circus and drama, Kozlova invariably finds physical means to evoke the aura of poetry. Her manner is slow and fluid, and her performances are suggestive. They never tell a story or illustrate a situation; they imply the paradoxes and complexities of specific states of mind or being.

So, how does one describe what Gennady Abramov is up to?

He talks about "zones of improvisation in space," "levels of emotionality," "fields of thinking," the "depth of abstraction" and spectators who are "consumers with their own clichés." In short, he isn't about to be pinned down. But he will tell you this: His actors have achieved such freedom, and have developed such physical intuition within the framework of their teacher's system, that they can improvise an entire program to music they have never heard.

"You don't know a theater like that yet," Abramov says with visible satisfaction. "But we can already do that."

(*Summer 1994, Slavic and East European Performance*)

Yelizaveta Nikishchikhina

Well-wishers fumbling with cascading bouquets greeted and jostled each other gaily as they excitedly scurried up and down the backstage halls. The air was definitely laced with the sense that something very unusual had taken place.

Just five minutes before, the curtain had dropped on the premiere of a wildly comic and profoundly moving production of *The Marriage* at the Stanislavsky Theater. For a playhouse with the reputation of being just about Moscow's deadliest, the sight had been almost shocking. The standing-room-only crowd showered the cast with a prolonged, emotional ovation, refusing to let the actors leave the stage.

In the midst of it all, a petite, wiry actress elicited noticeable swells in the cheers each time she tentatively stepped forward and bowed. She looked a bit tired, but mostly she seemed to be in a dazed state of disbelief.

Back in her dressing room afterwards, Yelizaveta Nikishchikhina had already donned her street clothes—a black turtleneck and black jeans—and was receiving a steady stream of visitors. Shrieks and laughter were heard in the corridor, but Liza, as everyone calls her, was thoughtfully subdued as she gave an on-the-spot radio interview.

"It's been twenty years since I had a similar feeling," she said slowly in her rough, gravelly voice. "It's been a very long wait."

Nikishchikhina, 52, was one of Moscow's leading young actresses twenty years ago. She first hit the top in the late 1960s, starring in Boris Lvov-Anokhin's searing interpretation of Jean Anouilh's *Antigone*. But it was her stunning work in the title role of Maxim Gorky's *Vassa Zheleznova*, directed by the young Anatoly Vasilyev, that truly brought her stardom in the mid-1970s.

Then it all collapsed.

In separate incidents typical of the smoldering struggles between artists and the authorities during the Brezhnev era, the highly respected directors of both *Antigone* and *Vassa* were forced to leave the Stanislavsky Theater. That one-two punch effectively plunged the venue—and its actors—into two decades of mediocrity.

For Nikishchikhina there was relatively steady work, but it wasn't much more than that. Her audience never forgot her, but her draw remained the great early roles.

Now, led by Vitaly Lanskoi, the new chief director, the Stanislavsky is again showing signs of life. Nowhere is that more evident than in *The Marriage*, Nikolai Gogol's farcical play about the preparations for a wedding that never happens.

When director Vladimir Mirzoyev told Nikishchikhina this spring that he wanted her in his upcoming production, she thought he had "some old lady" in mind. She was shocked when he offered her the role of the 27 year-old bride-to-be.

She wasn't alone.

A tangible sense of reticence fell over the opening night spectators when Nikishchikhina first appeared as the dreamy, slightly giddy heroine. But as Mirzoyev's unorthodox approach became clearer—every female role is played in doubles by two actresses—the doubts began to fade.

And as Nikishchikhina started gaining confidence, she put a lock-grip on the audience that didn't let up until the show was long over. If it wasn't her most subtle performance ever, it may have been her most electric.

The actress was back in the spotlight. And her fans, who had waited right along with her for this moment, let her know in no uncertain terms. Rolling peals of laughter greeted her every move.

A month later, Nikishchikhina still doesn't trust her renewed success. She talks instead about the 20-year drought when she essentially played "nothing," and of the difficulties of toiling for 36 years in the "theater of socialist realism."

But *The Marriage*, she says, is really about transitions and new beginnings. Maybe that's why it seems like the perfect thing for her to be playing.

(July 1994)

Vasily Bochkaryov

Vasily Bochkaryov is moving energetically in circles around the tiny kitchen of what he calls his bachelor pad, the place where he goes when he needs to work in peace and quiet.

He gestures boldly with his arms, plops down in a chair demonstratively to punctuate what he is saying and then hammers on the wall, laughing, to make sure you got the full impact of his last point.

Even if you didn't see this man's imposing performance of Boris Godunov in this season's sweeping production of *Tsar Boris* at the Maly Theater, you couldn't possibly doubt that he is an actor. If you have seen *Tsar Boris*, or any other of Bochkaryov's powerful roles for that matter, you begin to understand the source of the incredible intensity he brings to the stage.

Bochkaryov, 52, has been around. And all of it, the good and the bad, has been filed away for future use. As he puts it, besides "leaving the child in you to the very grave," an actor's duty is to know himself.

Thirty years of professional acting has taught him plenty.

He has worked with several of Russia's top directors, among them, Andrei Goncharov, Boris Lvov-Anokhin and Anatoly Vasilyev.

He has been caught in political traps, such as when he quit the Stanislavsky Theater in 1979 to protest the firing of Lvov-Anokhin on "ideological" grounds. As recently as 1990, he was even completely out of work: The Maly, his professional home since 1979, closed down every show he was working in that year.

Through it all, Bochkaryov's philosophy has remained simple. He compares himself to a working man, and his profession to manual labor.

"I get a role and I work on it like a peasant who plants a seed," he says. "I till, and I till, and I till. Whatever you did last year is gone. And you don't know what lies ahead."

But bring the conversation around to Boris, and the expressive Bochkaryov hesitates. Not because he's avoiding something, but because even he is in awe of the character he plays, and he wants to make himself clear.

"I do not play Boris, and we are not trying to recreate him in our show," Bochkaryov says. "We are creating a myth. This was an extremely complex man and no one really knows who he was."

Godunov, whose short reign initiated the Time of Troubles in the early 17th century, was indeed an enigma. Russia's first "liberal" leader, he sought to open the country to western influence, but was soon felled by the persistent legend he had murdered the last tsar's son to win the throne.

The Maly's production of A. K. Tolstoy's play essentially accepts that legend as truth.

When Bochkaryov was cast in the role, the first thing he did was make a pilgrimage to the tsar's grave. There he "begged forgiveness" of Godunov for "using his name to create a myth." He still spends much of the day in church before every performance.

For the actor, the theme of repentance and mercy is the point of the show. And the central moment in his performance is when the doomed Boris begs absolution for his crime.

"That image of Boris on his knees is what is most important for our time," says Bochkaryov. "It applies to every Russian. We weren't there when the last tsar was murdered, but our ancestors were. And their tacit guilt is alive in us."

Bochkaryov's sense of personal responsibility—to history as well as his job—is what gives his characters such impact and makes them so believable. He is blessed with that vague but indispensable actor's ability to assume the essence of another while always remaining himself.

His powers of transformation even affect his physical appearance. Of average height in real life, Vasily Bochkaryov looks a giant on stage. Even when on his knees.

(*July 1994*)

Natalia Vdovina

When Natalia Vdovina was still a girl dreaming of becoming an actress, she thought actresses just starred in popular plays and basked in the adulation of the public.

"I was very mistaken," adds the soft-spoken young woman who stars in one of the season's biggest hits, Pyotr Fomenko's production of *The Magnificent Cuckold* at the Satirikon Theater, and—in addition to becoming a favorite with the public—was the recipient of this year's Crystal Turandot award for best acting debut.

What she didn't know then, but knows quite well now, thank you, was how much blood gets shed and how much luck it takes to get that far.

Flashing a charming, reticent smile, Vdovina, 25, tells of nearly getting kicked out of theater school ("I just wasn't mature enough"); of spending her first two years as a professional actress on maternity leave ("Having a baby is what gave me the life experience I needed"); and of spending the next two years playing walk-ons and bit parts in productions of fairy tales.

In short, when she finally got her big break—an offer to play a lead for Moscow's top current director—the rather shy, thoughtful native of Simferopol was ready. She had to be, for parts don't come much more complex than Stella in Fernand Crommelynck's gripping play about love, passion and the terrible consequences of violating human trust.

Stella is a young bride driven into wanton promiscuity by a husband so jealous and so in awe of her beauty, that he is convinced she

Natalia Vdovina, as Stella, in *The Magnificent Cuckold* at the Satirikon. Photo: Mikhail Guterman

must have a lover, and stops at nothing to find out who he is. Vdovina is breathtaking as the ill-fated heroine, allowing her to pass from the joyous, carefree early scenes to the psychologically wrenching finale without ever losing her incorruptible, wholesome delicacy.

Rehearsals lasted a long nine months ("It was like giving birth all over again"), the last three of which the actors essentially worked without days off, "literally living in the theater day and night." There, the young actress finally abandoned her simplistic childhood impressions of the acting profession.

"It was bloody work for everyone," says Vdovina, who went through periods of such severe doubt that she even suggested getting her a back-up in case she didn't have what it takes. But she was pulled along by experience—at first the experience of Fomenko and her co-star, Konstantin Raikin, and then by her own tenacity and growing belief in herself.

"Even Raikin had problems," she says of the Satirikon's artistic director, leading actor and son of Arkady Raikin, the legendary Soviet comic actor. "And when I saw him struggling with them, I realized I didn't have the right to give up. I used to think talent is something you either have or you don't. But Konstantin Arkadyevich showed me that's not true. You have to work to bring talent out."

And what about Fomenko?

"Fomenko is incredible. He doesn't put any pressure on you, and he is always positive and encouraging. If you do something that even hints at what he's driving at, he smothers you in praise."

The irony of Vdovina's story about the myths of an actress's life is that it looks as if her future may come out resembling her childhood dreams. She is already slated to play that pearl of all female roles, Juliet in a production of *Romeo and Juliet* slated to open at the Satirikon next spring.

Not bad for a young woman who once stood on the brink of getting expelled from theater school because she seemed unfit to be an actress.

(July 1994)

Yelena Gremina

When Yelena Gremina heard last winter that opera diva Galina Vishnevskaya would be starring in her new play, she was astonished.

"I couldn't have been more surprised if someone had told me the Statue of Liberty was going to play the lead," jokes the writer whose play, *Behind the Mirror*, was a huge popular success when staged last season at the Chekhov Art Theater with Vishnevskaya playing Catherine the Great.

"I adore Vishnevskaya," Gremina continued with girlish amazement. "I consider her a model of womanhood and beauty. A symbol of splendor. Here was this woman who was making history when I was a kid, and then I find out she's going to be starring in my play."

In addition to delighting Gremina, 38, Vishnevskaya's acceptance of the offer to play Catherine suddenly shined the glare of publicity on the playwright. Not all of it was positive. Many in Moscow's stable of perennially dour critics turned up their noses at Gremina and Vishnevskaya both for creating what they carped was just one more "commercial" show.

But if the critics missed the point, failing to appreciate the irony, tenderness and unobtrusive wisdom of Gremina's story about Catherine's tragic love affair with a man half her age, audiences were more perceptive.

Before shows, crowds gathered on the street outside the theater, clamoring to buy the rare extra ticket. Inside, the house was buoyed by a genuinely festive air. Similar scenes were recently played out during the show's mid-summer tour of Omsk, and things likely won't change when *Behind the Mirror* resumes in Moscow in October.

Gremina was caught off-guard by the success of the play, the fifth of six she has written since 1984. Until its premiere in February, she was what she herself ironically calls "famous among select circles."

It is a situation she says all contemporary playwrights know well.

"We are well-known among the literary directors at theaters and the editors at journals who publish us. Someone, somewhere is always said to be producing our plays, although nothing ever comes of it. The prestige of writing plays in Russia is very low."

Wheel of Fortune, Gremina's third and favorite play, is a case in point. Highly praised by those who know it, it has only been produced at two tiny studios. Since it was written in 1989, numerous major theaters throughout Russia have rehearsed it, including the Mossoviet Theater in Moscow. All to no avail.

Shrugging her shoulders and flashing her typical quick wit, she quips, "I don't know what happened to it. Probably the same thing that happens to youth and money."

The spell was finally broken by Vyacheslav Dolgachyov, a young director to whom Gremina owes a "tremendous amount." While others mouthed praise, made promises and did nothing, Dolgachyov produced results. He directed two Gremina plays last season: *The Case of Cornet O*, performed as *Russian Eclipse* at the Pushkin Theater, and *Behind the Mirror*.

The success of the latter caused it to be picked up quickly by three other Moscow theaters, creating the extraordinary situation of one play being performed simultaneously in four different productions.

But popularity is not likely to change Gremina, whose name is actually a pseudonym based on her father's name and her mother's maiden name of Mindadze. She lives in an apartment that may pack more literary talent per square meter than any in Moscow, but she didn't want any breaks she didn't earn.

Her father Anatoly Grebnev, and her brother Alexander Mindadze, are two of Russia's most respected screenwriters. Meanwhile, her husband, Mikhail Ugarov, is a playwright for whom a bright future is also predicted.

Even Gremina's son by a previous marriage, Alexander, has just entered the Gorky Literary Institute. Like his mom, he's not telling anyone who his relatives are. Because, like his mom, if he makes it big, he wants to do it on his own.

(August 1994)

Kama Ginkas

One of the highlights of the first half of the 1994–1995 Moscow season was the "return" of Kama Ginkas. His production of the enigmatically-titled *K.I. from "Crime,"* based on the character of Katerina Ivanovna Marmeladova from Dostoevsky's *Crime and Punishment*, was not merely his first show in Moscow since 1991. It is now the only one of the numerous productions he has done in Moscow over the last decade which is being performed. Due to problems with changing casts and the insurmountable difficulties of introducing new actors into old shows, every one of his other shows had gradually dropped out of various theaters' repertories by 1993. *K.I. from "Crime"* was also notable for being Ginkas's third consecutive production of Dostoevsky for Moscow's Young Spectator Theater, making it clear that his attraction to the great novelist is anything but passing.[8]

Ginkas began building a reputation as a gifted director shortly after graduating from Georgy Tovstonogov's directing course at the Leningrad State Institute of Theater, Music and Cinema in 1968, but it was only in the mid-1980s that he achieved broad recognition. After more than a decade working in the provinces and staging now-legendary shows in his apartment in Leningrad where no one would hire him—the most famous being *Pushkin and Natalie*, a one-actor show starring Ginkas's longtime favorite actor Viktor Gvozditsky—he finally got an invitation to direct in Moscow. His first production in the capital was of Sergei Kokovkin's *Five Corners* in 1981 at the Mossoviet Theater. Then followed his acclaimed interpretation of Nina Pavlova's *The Club Car* at the Moscow Art Theater in 1982, Ibsen's *Hedda Gabler* at the Mossoviet Theater in 1984, and Alexander Galin's *The*

---

[8] After this article was written, Ginkas staged Vladimir Kobekin's opera for three based on Dostoevsky's *The Idiot* for a festival of Russian music in Locum, Germany. It played there and in Ludwigsburg in August 1995.

Toastmaster at the old Art Theater affiliate on Moskvin Street in 1986.

But Ginkas only acquired something resembling a professional home with the perestroika-inspired appointment of his wife Genrietta Yanovskaya to the position of artistic director at the Young Spectator Theater in 1986. There he seemed to find fitting surroundings in which to tackle Dostoevsky, the author who would occupy the greater part of his thoughts for some time to come.[9]

Returning to an old Leningrad "apartment project" that he never could complete, Ginkas staged his own dramatization of *Notes from Underground* in 1988. It was an intense, jarring production which some accused of lacking taste, but which many more, this observer included, found to be extremely powerful. (Viktor Gvozditsky's rancorous underground man drooled saliva and spat food, while Irina Yuryevich's angelic Sonya appeared stark naked from her bed in Act II.) In 1990 Ginkas mounted an innovative production of scenes from *Crime and Punishment* at the Lilla Theater, a Swedish-language venue in Helsinki, Finland, which he then recreated in mirror-image in 1991 at the Young Spectator Theater under the title of *We Play "Crime."* In Helsinki, the cast was joined by Irina Yuryevich, who performed the part of Sonya in Russian. In Moscow, Ginkas brought the star of the Helsinki show, Marcus Grott, to play Raskolnikov in Swedish, while the rest of the cast, all Russian actors, performed in Russian. The result was an extraordinary display of penetrating theatrical devices that, among other things, challenged the traditional, primary role of language as a means of communication. In 1993 Ginkas returned to Helsinki, where he teaches at the Swedish Theater

Academy, to stage his own dramatization of *The Idiot*. Finally, with *K.I. from "Crime,"* he returned again to *Crime and Punishment*, creating a one-actress show based on a dramatization written by his son Daniil Gink, the author of the 1991 hit play, *Bald/Brunet*.

In a conversation held shortly before the premiere of *K.I.* on November 1, 1994, Ginkas said his fascination with Dostoevsky centers around the writer's profound understanding of the inviolability of the individual. "What I, and not only I, see in his genius," he said, "is that Dostoevsky diagnosed the major ills of the 20th century. The idea of socialist prosperity is unnatural. You can't make everyone equal. People don't want equality, they want to be different. If I can't be prettier than you, then I'll be uglier. If I can't be smarter, then I'll be dumber."

For Ginkas it all boils down to a matter of people having the freedom to express themselves. "A person can be good or bad," he said, turning to a vocabulary clearly connected with Dostoevsky, "but if you don't let him develop, you begin getting what I call 'epileptic seizures.' And when a person is in a state like that, he is capable of killing you. He starts thinking, 'what can I do to be different?' If he's a great poet, he writes poetry. If he can't, then he might kill, or blow up a mausoleum."

According to Ginkas, Dostoevsky had a rare insight into the herd instinct that determines so much of human behavior. "We need to have our herd distinguish itself in some way," Ginkas said. "Russians will do it one way and Americans will do it another, but if you don't allow groups, peoples or nations to express themselves, it means driving them to 'epileptic seizures.' That is why Dostoevsky was pathologically against revolution. Not for political reasons, but because he understood the problem on a genetic level. He knew that no matter what prohibitions people or civilizations may create, people will still be moved to make their mark by whatever means they have available to them."

And, frequently, the means are violent and destructive. To a certain extent, Ginkas sees the Bolshevik Revolution as an example of frustrated people striving to leave their mark by "defiling and burning."

---

[9] Ginkas has also shown an abiding interest in Anton Chekhov, staging *Theater of The Watchman Nikita*, a dramatization of *Ward No. 6* at the Lilla Theater, Helsinki, in 1988, *Life is Beautiful*, a dramatization of two Chekhov stories at the Lilla in 1995 and *The Seagull* at the Swedish Theater Academy of Helsinki in 1996. He made an earlier attempt to stage *The Lady with a Dog* in Turkey in 1993, but left it unfinished due to artistic differences with the theater.

How does Ginkas, a Lithuanian Jew, respond to the sticky question of Dostoevsky's anti-Semitism? Philosophically and with a sense of humor.

"You can be a genius and still have pimples," he said, "but that doesn't change the more important things. Dostoevsky didn't hate only Jews, he hated Poles and Europeans in general." Calling the writer's refusal to accept Poles, Germans and Jews a response on a "physiological," rather than a "global level," Ginkas explained that it was less a matter of racism or nationalism than a matter of rejecting Western rationalism. "For Dostoevsky," Ginkas continued, "logic and ideology were terribly dangerous. And he pitted against them the childlike qualities of ingenuousness. Rationalism is always complex and impressive, and even the greatest evil is very attractive. That is the source of Dostoevsky's 'fear and hatred' of Jews and Europeans, whom he perceived as being too rational."

That is also at the crux of what attracted Ginkas to the story of Katerina Ivanovna, who, he says, comprises the most difficult female role in world literature. Calling Dostoevsky an "impulsive constructivist," Ginkas pointed out the symmetrical qualities of *Crime and Punishment*, wherein a character with the irrepressible life force of Katerina stands diametrically opposed to that of Raskolnikov. Ginkas explains: "Napoleon and Hitler had almost nothing human in them, because they excluded others; they didn't put themselves in others' places. Similarly, Raskolnikov thinks he has to get rid of the human elements in him, because they make him funny and weak. He wants to cut out his conscience like you would an appendix, although he can't quite do it. Unlike Raskolnikov, Katerina Ivanovna is five-hundred percent human. She's unpleasant, she's petty, she's even malicious and cruel, but she is alive! And she is totally natural, which makes her funny and charming at the same time. Even as she is dying and has no hopes of recovering, her natural impulse is to go on living at full speed. Her most important task in life is simply 'to be,' and she is instinctively aware that the goal of life, with all of its horrors, is the very fact and process of life."

Like *We Play "Crime," K.I. from "Crime"* is performed for a small audience of just over fifty. It begins in a foyer on the third floor of the Young Spectator Theater before moving into a blinding white rehearsal room adapted for use as a performing space. Suggesting that "you need to give people air," Ginkas pointed out that his last three Dostoevsky productions have all been done in white. He described Sergei Barkhin's set for *The Idiot* as "brilliant and fantastic," with 3,000 white roses and snow gently falling on stage as sparklers burn all around. *K.I.* is significantly less ornate with its sole large props being a long banquet table that seats part of the audience, and a ladder which descends to take Katerina away in the finale, but it runs a risk that none of the other Dostoevsky productions has: With its action taking place during Katerina Ivanovna's memorial dinner for her late husband, the actress and her three children (Oksana Mysina plus Olga, Anna and Oleg Rayev) interact with the spectators as though they were the invited guests, including the respected Raskolnikov and Katerina's hated landlady, Amalia Ivanovna.

"This creates difficulties," Ginkas says matter-of-factly. "The actress's partner is the audience, and a lot in this production depends on the partner."

Perhaps Ginkas's greatest triumph was to bypass Dostoevsky's sentimentality, melodrama and agony, mining instead the author's intellectual, emotional and, frequently, comic power. Spectators at performances of *K.I.* are often involuntarily coerced into laughing uproariously at scenes that are anything but funny, leaving them wide open to be hit full-force by the tragedy of Katerina Ivanovna's predicament. The widow sits down next to spectators; shows them a tiny picture of her husband or a dried flower she keeps as a memento; ties a mourning band on someone's arm; drifts off quietly into a world of her own; explodes in anger at the woman chosen to be Amalia Ivanovna; or huddles in a friendly, confidential chat with the man selected as Raskolnikov. It is invariably done without aggression and without pathos, allowing the qualities that Ginkas is driving at to shine through undistorted.

For all its pushing and pulling of the emotions, *K.I.* is a profoundly cathartic production, one that genuinely transforms pain into joy. A few critics have seen in that vague hints at some religious revelation, but, in fact, this show is more open-ended than that. More to the point is that, while *K.I.* is relentlessly challenging, it is a soaring celebration of that which will not be extinguished, be it some aspect of theater or be it some element of life.

"What I am trying to stage," said Ginkas, "is the desperate effort to live life fully to the very last second of life. I want people to be in ecstasy over Katerina Ivanovna. I want them to say, 'This is one fabulous woman!' She may be out of her mind, but you can't play neurosis. On the contrary, she has nerves of steel even if her head is totally turned around. She is convinced that you live in her world, while you keep thinking she must be nuts."

While Ginkas's use of the children caused a small minority of observers to raise questions about bad taste—Katerina beats them, sends her son Kolya begging among the spectators and then strips them all to their underwear in the finale before she dies—in fact, this is one of the production's more powerful elements. Never exploitative and never maudlin, the image of the children is laced with a tough veracity that draws no conclusions and makes no judgments.

At the age of six weeks Ginkas himself was placed by the Nazis in a Jewish ghetto in his hometown of Kaunas. Of the thousands of people interred with him, he was one of just six to emerge alive. And when watching Katerina's children silently respond to every humiliation and every warm word with the same kind of blank stoicism and inner fortitude, it is difficult not to sense the vague aura of an experience that still exists within the director himself.

Ginkas was probably drawn to directing by what Yanovskaya has called his "egotistical meticulousness."[10] When asked what a director does, he replied: "Ginkas would say Ginkas is trying to record what is going on between people. An artist 'sees' in color and form, and a writer 'sees' in language, but a director's eye is not just an eye—it is more. A director sees multiplicities and sees everything in terms of action. He must have the ability to see everything at once: rhythm, color, meaning, sound, movement, humor and tragedy, and the falseness, superficiality and inadequacies of the human experience. You may suffer very sincerely while I talk about my childhood and yet, at the same time, your shoe is pinching your foot and causing you great discomfort. That's natural and that's the kind of thing I see and give form."

K.I. from "Crime" would appear to be a summing up for Ginkas. It echoes *Pushkin and Natalie* in that it is essentially a one-actor show where the audience plays a crucial role; it could justifiably be called the "sister" to *We Play "Crime"* in that it is the flip-side, female half of Ginkas's two treatments of *Crime and Punishment*; and, finally, it has a history similar to *Notes from Underground* in that both were conceived in Ginkas's Leningrad apartment long ago, but only brought to the stage at the Young Spectator Theater many years later.

"I tried to create a play based on these scenes 20 year ago," Ginkas explained. "But I couldn't do it. I have done lots of dramatizations, but this one just wouldn't work. Then, at my request, Danya [Gink] found a way to overcome the difficulties. I think he created a stunning play. That may not be apparent to a reader, but I think the spectator will see it in performance."

As usual, the director's eye did not fail him.

(*Summer 1995, Slavic and East European Performance*)

Andrei Zhitinkin

Andrei Zhitinkin looks like somebody who's looking to shake things up.

With his pair of glasses hanging around his neck on an old-fashioned chain, his unusual, "drapery" style of dress, and his pointedly refined manner, Andrei Zhitinkin, 35, is a director with style.

---

[10] Genrietta Yanovskaya, "My s nim davno ne razgovarivali," *Moskovsky nablyudatel'*, 5–6 (1992): 30.

Andrei Zhitinkin matched popular success with critical acclaim with his production of Alexei Arbuzov's *My Poor Marat* at the Mossoviet Theater in 1995. Photo: Mikhail Guterman

He may not always be the critics' favorite, but this is a man who knows how to grab attention.

Look at the shows that have formed Zhitinkin's rather florid reputation. In 1991 there was Albert Camus's *Caligula* with a full-frontal male nude scene. In 1994 there was *Dead Man's Bluff*, a play by the émigré writer Mikhail Volokhov that was rife with obscenities and ended in cannibalism.

And then, in May of this year, there was Alexei Arbuzov's *My Poor Marat*. An enormous favorite in Soviet times (it played over 3,200 times between 1965 and 1969), *Marat* tells of three teenagers, two boys and a girl, who help each other survive the cold, hunger and death of the siege of Leningrad.

Zhitinkin not only gave it a twist that would have been unthinkable not long ago, he gave it a depth it may never have had.

"Arbuzov was a man of the regime," says the director, "but he was also quite clever. And he was a man with his oddities. I think he encoded a story that we brought out in our production."

What he brought out was an entirely unorthodox view of the relationships among the three heroes. In the past the story was always played as a contest between two nice boys for the girl's hand and heart. Zhitinkin blew off tradition, clearly suggesting that the boy-girl pairings sputter so long because there's a serious boy-boy thing going on that must be solved first.

"I don't care what sign love carries if it's real," says Zhitinkin when asked about the homosexual thrust of his production. "For me there are no taboos in art. I want to provoke the spectator into taking a new approach. I want to destroy fear."

The taboos against, and fear of, homosexuality have proved tenacious in Russian theater as in Russian life at large.

Roman Viktyuk drew back the curtain on the topic in the late 1980s with an all-male version of Jean Genet's *The Maids*. He has since followed with numerous suggestive homoerotic productions. However, with one exception—Nikolai Kolyada's *Slingshot* in 1994—Viktyuk has avoided addressing the subject head-on, preferring instead to hint repeatedly and heavily at an unnamed love.

But Viktyuk's continuing reticence has robbed his work of whatever power it once had. By refusing to face openly what is clearly his real theme, he has undermined his reputation as an innovator, essentially becoming a victim of the fear he once challenged.

That makes Zhitinkin's respectful, unflinching treatment of the topic all the more striking. It has the feel of truth, honesty and courage.

And indeed, it took courage to shake up the sexual chemistry in one of the canonical Soviet plays about World War II. Having dedicated his production to the 50th anniversary of V-E Day, Zhitinkin risked incurring the wrath of veterans whose memories of their youth and the war are nearly sacred.

"It was a dangerous move," admits Zhitinkin. "The veterans might have said, 'this isn't true.'"

Instead, they appreciated the unusual interpretation of Arbuzov's play, responding to its intensity, its sense that life on the brink of death is full of huge, maybe even shocking surprises.

"Every survivor of the war had his own mystery or played his own Freudian game," the director noted. "On one hand, there was a war to be fought; on the other, life had to be lived. Many of the veterans who saw my show said, 'We truly lived for the present. We had to love today because we knew we may not be able to tomorrow.'"

It was a time, Zhitinkin continued, when love was both spontaneous and calculated. People fell into relationships quickly, for fear it may be the last time, while women, he added, purposefully got pregnant so as not to squander the chance.

What made Zhitinkin's interpretation so effective was its ambiguity. He did not merely stage a homosexual story, he created a tender, universal and tolerant world in which everything is possible.

"I hate the hypocrisy of society," concludes Zhitinkin. "I want to liberate the spectator so that he is free to feel."

(July 1995)

Producers Update

When David Smelyansky's Russian Theater Agency changed its name last year, it was no mere cosmetic alteration.

The RTA had been a pioneer in post-Soviet, non-government theater financing and production, and so when it quietly became the Russian State Theater Agency, it was an unmistakable sign that something had dimmed the bright future once predicted for independent producers.

The rise of so-called "producer" or "commercial" shows was one of the first key trends of post-Soviet theater, almost immediately causing speculation that the familiar repertory system was on the verge of extinction. Many openly stated that the time had passed when theaters could indulge in the luxury of maintaining costly repertories of up to 30 shows—each of which often played only one or two days a month.

The producers, as enthusiasts said at the time, would revive the hallowed, pre-revolutionary traditions of patronage, and they would streamline the way theater is made in Russia. Theater institutes began adding management and producing courses to their curriculums.

With some of the big houses carrying payrolls of over 200 people, financing in an era of tight money was a problem. The state, while pouring significant amounts of money into culture by western standards, could not keep the pace set under the Soviet system. And, with the notion of corporate sponsorship still vague, if not obscure in 1991 and '92, there was a natural tendency to think that the new producers were carrying the future of theater in their wallet pockets.

Moreover, as the thinking went, the quality of productions would jump. If the best actors, directors and designers would be gravitating to the money, they would be doing the best shows.

It hasn't happened that way. Although there are now approximately 10 independent agencies or production companies and over 60 private theaters registered in Moscow, only a handful are actually turning out shows of any note or with any regularity.

The clearest sign of the slow-down was the RTA's retreat last winter to the protection of the state.

Smelyansky had started raising money for projects in 1991, creating the RTA in 1992. It was responsible for several high-profile shows over the next few years. But gradually the agency's activity slowed, with several projects falling through, including a grandiose English-language production of a Chekhov play that was to be directed by the well-known film director, Andrei Konchalovsky.

Smelyansky's most recent project in November 1994, this time under the aegis of the Russian State Theater Agency, was a joint production with the Australia Council for the Arts of *Lou*, a play by the Australian playwright David George. Starring the Soviet-era film star Yelena Koreneva, who spent the 1980s in the United States, it was supposed to follow its Moscow run with an English-language tour of the West. But the show closed after just 6 performances and the tour never materialized.

Smelyansky's agency continues to be active in the provinces, but the impact once expected from it has never been realized.

The only other organization capable of matching the RTA's visibility and quality has been the Bogis Theater Agency, founded in 1993. Beginning its activities with a highly publicized and extremely popular production of *Nijinsky* starring the top actors Oleg Menshikov and Alexander Feklistov, Bogis has taken careful and prudent steps ever since, creating just one show per year.

The agency is the brainchild of Galina Bogolyubova, whose several decades working on the Moscow theater scene have given her the experience and contacts needed to start a risky new business from scratch. But what has separated her from the rest of the pack is an uncanny eye for talent, a gift for organization, and a shrewd feel for how far she can go out on a limb without falling off. Each of Bogis's productions has been mounted with exquisite good taste and impeccable organization.

Last year the agency repeated its inaugural success with a much-acclaimed one-actor production of *Bashmachkin*, starring

Feklistov, while this season it proved it has the vision to work with newcomers.

The new show, entitled *Immersion*, featured a first-time playwright, a novice director and starred two young actors. A pleasant if somewhat cloying outing, it took its share of lumps from the critics. But what its detractors overlooked was that it was a calculated move to support young, inexperienced talent. Whatever the modest show's failures, Bogolyubova proved again that she is a woman of courage and daring.

If it happens, Bogolyubova's next project will be her biggest yet. Planned for spring 1996, it should bring the renowned Lithuanian director Eimuntas Nekrosius to Moscow to stage *Hamlet*. True, rumors have surfaced that he has begun having second thoughts, but if anyone can keep the temperamental director interested it is probably Bogolyubova. In any case, she recently told this observer that she is prepared "do anything" to keep Nekrosius happy, and she is not one to waste words.[11]

But Bogis has been the exception to the rule. Other production companies, such as the All the World Theater Agency and Moscow Salon, surface very irregularly and for very short periods.

Meanwhile, the private theaters have proved incapable of creating a quality product. The Roman Viktyuk Theater coasted for a few years on the celebrity status of its founder, but its most recent show, *Love with an Idiot*, bombed in May, closing after just two performances.[12] Such once-publicized theaters as Alla Demidova's Theater A, Alla Sigalova's Independent Company, and the OK Theater have disappeared from sight.[13]

---

[11] The Nekrosius *Hamlet* project fell through.
[12] It was revived with a changed cast in the fall of 1995, but that made the show no better.
[13] All three of these theaters reappeared briefly at the end of the 1995/96 season: Theater A with a one-time performance of Heiner Müller's *Medea* done jointly with the Attis Theater from Greece; Sigalova with two performances of her excellent new adaptation of Anatoly Mariengof's novel, *Cynics*; and the OK Theater with a handful of revivals of old shows.

The Anton Chekhov Theater, the first to gather actors for specific shows on a contract basis, has lost its early sheen. Never a favorite with critics, it did create a loyal following by serving up stars. But the absence of any broadly recognizable names in its latest show, *Subway*, is an indication that the venue's best days may be over.

Then there is the case of the Et Cetera Theater, founded by the popular actor Alexander Kalyagin. After two years of struggling artistically and financially, the Et Cetera recently went the way of the Russian Theater Agency: It became a municipal theater, leaving behind the bothersome freedom of existing independently of government.

(July 1995)

The Old Guard

Adrian Hall, the artistic director of the Trinity Repertory Theater in Providence, Rhode Island, decided last year he could no longer handle the theater he had brought to national recognition. So he resigned.

Two years ago, when Germany's Peter Stein had a falling-out with the administration at the Berlin Schaubühne, where he was the artistic director, he resigned.

The changing of the guard in theaters the world over is much the same. Nothing lasts forever and when it's time to go, you go. It's a natural process that injects new blood into a theater's system and is often a way for talented directors to escape creative ruts.

Not so in Moscow, where—as it has been done in the Kremlin from time immemorial—the guard seems to change only by death or deposing.

That may not automatically be bad, but in these volatile, post-Soviet days, most of this city's key theaters continue to plod along as they have for decades. All have their occasional hits and their loyal followings, but none are at the cutting edge of the theatrical art. And that is a come down, since each of them, at one time or another in the past, has been a trendsetter.

In a word, there is plenty going on in Moscow theater, but little of it is to be found at the big-name playhouses.

The dean of the directors is Valentin Pluchek, who, at 86, has run the Satire Theater since 1957. Next in line is Andrei Goncharov, 77, the top man at the Mayakovsky Theater since 1967. Thanks largely to troupes full of popular actors, neither venue has trouble selling tickets, but artistically both are treading water. And with the two captains running tight ships, there seems to be no limit to how long they can keep drifting in calm seas.

On the other hand, rancorous power struggles in recent times almost become a way of life at some theaters, although usually it was much ado about nothing. The most publicized case was the tussle at the Bolshoi Theater where Yury Grigorovich was finally ousted after years of talk and rumors, but Moscow's drama theaters have been no less dramatic.

Coups or uprisings swept away elderly leaders at the Vakhtangov and the Maly theaters in the late 1980s, while the replacements, Mikhail Ulyanov, 68, and Yury Solomin, 60, respectively, did little to change their theaters' profiles. A row at the Yermolova in 1989 has left that once-proud house crippled and divided to the present day. The noisiest tussles occurred at the Moscow Art Theater and the Taganka Theater.

In 1987 the prestigious Art Theater shocked the public when its troupe voted to split in two. Some remained in the historic, art nouveau building on Kamergersky Lane with Oleg Yefremov, taking the name of the Chekhov Art Theater. The rest followed the popular actress Tatyana Doronina to a newly-built location on Tverskoi Boulevard, retaining the original name of the Gorky Art Theater.

Doronina, now 62, sports a resumé fit for a Politburo member, holding the posts of managing, chief and artistic director. Never having been anything but an actress when she became an administrator, she has done little to distinguish her theater aside from occasionally supporting nationalist political groups.

Yefremov, 68, was once the knight in shining white armor called to save an aging theater. Now, in poor health largely because of a drinking habit no one mentions in more than a whisper, he holds that most familiar of old Soviet reputations: praised and honored in public, ridiculed in private.

It is a shocking and ignominious turn-around.

A man whose courage and sincerity few would question, Yefremov was one of the finest actors to emerge in the 1950s. He was also the mastermind behind the Sovremennik Theater, which from the late '50s through the 1960s was a national icon and a fantastically popular phenomenon. Its youthful, up-beat, probing shows captured the spirit of the Thaw generation.

It was at the peak of his powers, in 1970, that Yefremov was appointed to head the Moscow Art Theater and inject some youth into the 72 year-old institution. But it didn't work. The once-innovative playhouse founded in 1898 by Konstantin Stanislavsky and Vladimir Nemirovich-Danchenko was hopelessly trapped in the mire of trying to live up to its past. When the break-up came in 1987, the stakes were more for power than artistic integrity.

This May, a pair of young directors, Roman Kozak and Dmitry Brusnikin, were named Yefremov's assistants with augmented powers, but more than create real change, the move mostly will fuel talk about successors. Although as the Art Theater makes grandiose plans to celebrate its 100th anniversary in 1998, it seems certain that Yefremov will be at the helm when it limps into its second century.

The Taganka wars have followed their own scenario, but the results have been just as fruitless. With world-renowned director and founder Yury Lyubimov, 78, spending so much time abroad, many in his troupe despaired of being left without work. So they rallied around Nikolai Gubenko, 54, a Taganka actor who served briefly as the Taganka's artistic director before Lyubimov returned from exile in 1988. Gubenko promised to keep and create jobs and, after a bitter court battle with Lyubimov, won control of half of the Taganka in 1993.

The reality has been more sobering than the promises. In two years, Gubenko's Commonwealth of Taganka Actors has produced three productions of dubious artistic value, all of which flopped at the box office.

Meanwhile, Lyubimov's troupe continues to stagnate. His recent production of *Medea*, the first he has done with the Taganka in two years, has only played a few times in Greece, and most of his actors remain idle. Some recent independent projects carried out by youngsters in the troupe have shown promise, but it remains to be seen whether that is a real sign of rejuvenation for the Taganka.

(*July 1995*)

The Pacesetters

Moscow in the 1920s was known as a theatrical mecca. The words were originally uttered by Anatoly Lunacharsky, the first Soviet education commissar, but he was not just limbering up his penchant for phrase-making.

With the Moscow Art Theater, the Meyerhold Theater and Alexander Tairov's Kamerny Theater attracting global attention, Moscow could rightfully brag of being the seat of theatrical innovation. That kind of leadership flagged over the ensuing years, although Moscow has almost always had one or two pacesetting venues, the kind of place that sums up the state of the art, and to which people could look to catch a glimpse of the future.

In 1995 there is no such theater, nor has there been for some time. Whether that is a sign of the tumultuous, fragmented times, or whether it is a sign of the de-officialization which has pluralized the face of post-Soviet Russian culture, it is a fact that no single Moscow theater today is a standard bearer.

That doesn't mean, however, that nothing of interest is going on. In fact, Moscow is full of new theatrical ideas and experiments. You just have to know where to find them.

The most consistent house in town these days is the Mossoviet. Under the quiet leadership of artistic director Pavel Khomsky, 70, it has worked out an effective policy of mixing showy, undemanding crowd-pleasers on its mainstage—often staged by Khomsky himself—with an impressive array of unusual shows on its small, fourth-floor stage "beneath the roof"—usually mounted by one among the theater's stable of young directors.

In recent years, this space has rendered a string of critically-acclaimed, well-attended shows, the most recent being this season's provocative revival of Alexei Arbuzov's *My Poor Marat*.

Furthermore, the Mossoviet has a group of talented young actors coming up through the ranks, suggesting that its future is bright indeed.

The fastest rising reputation probably belongs to the Satirikon, a theater that has existed in one form or another since 1939. Until 1987 it was run as a miniature and vaudeville house by the legendary satirical actor, Arkady Raikin. When he died in 1987, he was succeeded as artistic director by his son, Konstantin, who had already made his name as a dramatic actor, and who since has proven an able administrator.

Konstantin Raikin's first shrewd move was to tamper with success, rejecting his father's trademark genre of comic skits in favor of traditional drama. That produced some notable results over the next few years, but few could have predicted the sharp upturn that would occur in 1994.

That is when Raikin, now 45, turned to Pyotr Fomenko, whom many call Moscow's best director, inviting him to stage Fernand Crommelynck's *The Magnificent Cuckold* at the Satirikon. The result, with Raikin playing the lead, was a stunning show that gained world-wide recognition.

Rather than rest on his laurels, Raikin next brought in another top director, Valery Fokin, to stage what would become one of this year's top shows: a dramatization of Franz Kafka's *The Metamorphosis*, again starring Raikin. Like *The Magnificent Cuckold* before it, *Metamorphosis* took the Crystal Turandot award for best show, giving the Satirikon back-to-back triumphs.

At the award ceremonies, the grinning, gap-toothed Raikin joked that he has gotten used to winning and that he would be perfectly happy were the Satirikon to become the perennial best show recipient. With the kind of track record he is establishing, it would seem foolish to bet against him.

The Hermitage, another house with a strong reputation, is structured fully in the mold of the theaters which have historically been Moscow's most influential. A so-called "author's" theater, its every manifestation bears the distinct stamp of its heart, soul and mastermind, the artistic director Mikhail Levitin, 49.

Since taking over in 1988, Levitin—who is also a Booker Prize-nominated novelist—has run an eclectic, uneven and occasionally spectacular theater. His unchanging style is a modern, theatrical interpretation of the unorthodox, Oberiu literary movement from the 1920s, often popularly described as a Russian version of the absurdist movement, and he freely applies it to material ranging from Molière to Lewis Carrol.

His most perfected works—still running in repertory—have been productions of Yury Olesha's *The Beggar, or the Death of Zand* (1986), and *An Evening in a Madhouse* (1989), based on the writings of several authors, while this season's *Goodbye, Deadmen!* was an impressive and typically uncommon interpretation of *Maria*, a forgotten, unfinished play by the short-story master Isaac Babel. But whatever the show, there is always at the Hermitage a lively, intriguing air of iconoclasm and irreverence.

There are several directors whose presence on a marquée is an almost certain guarantee of quality, beginning with the previously-mentioned Pyotr Fomenko and Valery Fokin. Joining them on a single plane of excellence and accomplishment is Kama Ginkas, who usually works out of the Young Spectator Theater. Ginkas in recent years has worked more in Europe than in Moscow, although his probing, challenging production of *K.I. from "Crime"* this season won him heaps of praise, as well as the best director Crystal Turandot.

Among the younger, 30 to 40 year-old generation, several names undeniably speak of vision and individuality, even if their product can be irregular. They include Sergei Artsibashev, whose own Theater na Pokrovke has produced a series of fascinating reworkings of Russian classics, and Sergei Zhenovach, whose slow, meticulous productions at the Malaya Bronnaya Theater have been controversial but noteworthy. Every bit their equal are Alexei Levinsky, who has quietly given a distinct personality

to the Yermolova International Theater Center since taking over as its acting principal director a few years ago, and Vladimir Mashkov, probably best known as Russia's top movie star.[14] However, Mashkov's work as a director for the Tabakov Theater (including this season's sensational *Death-Defying Act*) has shown him to be a man of multiple talents.

Whether or not Moscow is on the verge of becoming a world-wide theatrical mecca again is uncertain. But let there be no doubt: its tradition of innovation and quality is alive and well.

(July 1995)

The Small-Stage Boom

It was a sign of the early post-Soviet period. Currency exchange windows started popping up in the entryways to theaters like paparazzi at Cannes.

And the Lenkom Theater, long one of the city's leaders in fashion, was at the avant-garde of the movement. But before anybody else had the chance to do them one better, the Lenkom took the next step. It closed down its state-of-the-art small stage and rented it out to a night club.

But that was then, as the song goes, and this is now.

These days a theater without a small stage—or at least a show or two performed in a rehearsal room, a foyer or a stairwell—is hardly fit to be called a theater at all. And this time around, it's not just fashion that's pulling the train, it's the call of the future.

The change—perhaps the most clearly defined to hit Moscow theater since a tidal wave of blackly pessimistic, often downright offensive productions surged forth in the late 1980s—has been coming for some time. Many of the best shows over the last few seasons have made excellent use of intimate

---

[14] In a controversial shakeup at the Yermolova International Theater Center shortly after this article was written, Levinsky was "demoted" to staff director. Late in the 1995/96 season several experimental works he had done at the Yermolova Center were moved to the Krasnaya Presnya Theater.

spaces, but nothing can compare with what happened in the season just ended.

Virtually every one of the top productions in the 1994/95 season was performed either on a small stage or in a small, unorthodox location adapted for performance.

An abridged list of the shows which experimented with space is telling of the variety that could be found. *K.I. from "Crime"* at the Young Spectator Theater started in a foyer and ended in a rehearsal room. *The Metamorphosis* at the Satirikon played in a specially constructed, expanding box. *Ivanov's Family* at the Pushkin Theater was performed in a circle around the audience which was seated on the stage itself. *Waiting for Hamlet* at the Taganka used the venue's foyer and numerous staircases. *One Night* at the National Youth Theater was staged in a basement beneath the theater's main stage.

The number of productions taking place on traditional small stages was equally impressive. The Stanislavsky, the Mossoviet, the Yermolova, the Yermolova International Theater Center, the Tabakov Theater and the Taganka all produced at least one, and in some cases several, quality small-stage shows.

Characteristic of the new trend was the Novy Drama Theater's year-end premiere of *A Heroic Comedy*. Director Boris Lvov-Anokhin, who is known for his opulent, historically-veracious, grand-scale productions, surprised everyone by going miniature with a slimmed-down, modern-dress interpretation of a play set in the Napoleonic era.

Fittingly, the season began auspiciously with Vladimir Mashkov's sensational production of *The Death-Defying Act* for the Tabakov Theater.

It was the kind of magnificent spectacle that, with its stunning light effects and thrilling magic acts, might have seemed ideal for a large stage and a 1000-seat hall. In fact, Mashkov told this observer during the winter that he had wanted to work on a big stage, but money restraints had held him back.

That, however, only proves that accident is often the best catalyst for the new. The reality is that the confines of the small stage were one of the key elements that raised *The Death-Defying Act* out of the pack of good shows and put it into the elite class of innovators. It was the very combination of spectacle and intimacy that kept the audiences sitting breathless on the edges of their seats.

The "intimization" of theater is no fluke. Aside from being a shrewd response to runaway inflation, it is a natural and aggressively creative development.

In a society that has been rocked with a decade of mind-bending and often frightening changes, it provides the direct human contact which has always been theater's calling card. You don't need opera glasses in a 100-seat hall—with the bare eye you see the wrinkles on the actors' laughing faces and their tears when they cry. That intimacy creates an almost magical attraction in a social climate which is defined by crass indifference and rampant depersonalization.

That is essentially what Alexei Borodin had in mind when recently discussing his production of *One Night*, a play about the siege of Leningrad. Referring grimly to the war in Chechnya and the bloody hostage incident in Budyonnovsk, Borodin said, "I staged *One Night* in a space below the stage. But there's another space even further down that I may use yet. I have the feeling that pretty soon we're going to be staging shows in sub-basements and playing ourselves."

But the trend is not just financial or social, it is an artistic choice.

Yury Yeryomin, the artistic director at the Pushkin Theater, one of the city's weakest in recent times, has taken some bold steps to turn around his fortunes. He closed this season with two new shows that seat the audience directly on the stage, then announced that he is taking a year's sabbatical. The purpose? To put the finishing touches on a newly-constructed, 80-seat hall which is scheduled to open with fanfare sometime in 1996.

Said Yeryomin, "You won't hear anything from me for at least a year. And when we open the new stage, it will immediately have three shows in repertory: a Greek tragedy, a Russian classic and a modern play."

Not everyone has greeted these developments enthusiastically. When the Crystal

Turandot awards were handed out in May, the prize for best play was presented by Mark Zakharov, the opinionated artistic director of the Lenkom Theater. Zakharov praised the winner for writing a "big play for the big stage," taking an unmistakable pot shot at all the shows being staged these days in "corridors and elevators."

But the response to Zakharov's skepticism followed immediately. In the course of the next hour, small-stage shows swept all the major production awards: best show, best director and best designer.

Indeed, with perestroika fading into history and the 21st century coming ever closer, Moscow theater is looking bolder, healthier and more innovative all the time.

(August 1995)

Playwrights

In early spring it looked like a ringing declaration about the resurgence of Russian playwriting would be in order by the end of the season. The Fomenko Studio's production of *Tanya-Tanya*, a brilliant new play by Olga Mukhina, seemed to have crystallized a trend in the making: after a long drought, modern writing was again making it to the stage.

It was a happy sign, since the plight of the contemporary playwright, bruised, battered, regaled, rejected, ignored and forgotten for the whole post-Soviet period, has been an unenviable one.

But a funny thing happened during the home stretch of the season. Several announced productions of new plays never happened and there were few surprises to fill in the gaps.

The numbers are only approximate, since it is impossible to catch all the shows that play rarely or in out-of-the-way places, and it is often difficult to define the difference between an original play and a dramatization. But even by including free adaptations in the list, the number of new plays produced this season (about 19) exceeded last year's output (about 15) by only a small margin.

That is a step up, of course, and it is the highest number of new plays to be done in any Moscow season in the post-Soviet period. But it also indicates that the corner has not yet been turned; new dramatic writing is still struggling to attract attention.

There have been attempts to address the problem, with an informal playwriting laboratory opening up this season at the Chekhov Art Theater, and Andrei Goncharov having the students of his class at the Russian Academy of Theater Arts devote themselves entirely to new plays this year. But it is still too early for such efforts to show results.

While the contemporary Russian playwright has been a stranger in his own house, a lot of very famous, very dead playwrights have been getting staged by the dozens.

A rough count reveals a whopping 28 productions of plays by Alexander Ostrovsky currently running in Moscow. Anton Chekhov, with 15 productions, is followed by Nikolai Gogol (12) and Molière (10) in the city's necrophilic playwright popularity contest. Chekhov, incidentally, only wrote four major plays, while Gogol only wrote two full-length works.

Fyodor Dostoevsky, who never wrote a play in his life and died in 1881, is right up there with the lot: There are 14 dramatizations of his stories and novels presently in repertory throughout town.

Productions of two new works by Nikolai Kolyada characterized the way the new play situation sounded better than it really was. *Persian Lilac*, essentially created as a commercial tour/export show, played in Moscow just three or four times, while the opener of *We're Riding, Riding, Riding* has been pushed back several times at the Sovremennik Theater. It is now tentatively scheduled to open July 4 when the vast majority of Moscow's audience will be gone on summer vacation.

Kolyada, more popular with audiences than with critics, has been the top playwright of the decade. A native of Yekaterinburg, he is one of the first Russians to touch on the themes of homosexuality in such plays as *Slingshot* and, to a lesser degree, *The Oginski Polonaise*. In December 1994 his hometown hosted a festival featuring 10 productions of his plays from all over Russia and Germany. A half-dozen of his titles are currently on in Moscow.

It was a checkered crop of writers who did see their creations come to life this season.

Viktor Rozov, in the 46th year of his career, had his first premiere in recent memory with *Hoffmann* at the Chekhov Art Theater. Sergei Kokovkin (*Mrs. Lev* at the Contemporary Play School) and Alexander Galin (*Czech Photography* at the Lenkom) continued their relatively regular appearances on the boards of the city's playhouses.

Then there was the breakthrough of several respected writers who for some time couldn't seem to buy a production in Moscow. Maria Arbatova's *A Trial Interview on the Theme of Freedom* opened at the Theater na Pokrovke, while Alexei Slapovsky's *In the Bermuda Expanses* was mounted at the Pushkin Theater. Stepan Lobozyorov's comedy, *Family Portrait With a Stranger*, which has been staged at over 50 theaters throughout Russia, finally made its Moscow debut this season at the Mossoviet Theater under the title of *Birthday with Crutches.*

None of the productions of these plays was especially noteworthy, leaving Mukhina's *Tanya-Tanya* as the clear standard-bearer of the season. The Mossoviet Theater has just unveiled Viktor Podlubny's timely and entertaining *A Cube for the President*, and ahead is the Sovremennik's *We're Riding, Riding, Riding*. But coming so close to season's end, they can't generate the publicity that *Tanya-Tanya* did.

Like Mukhina, a few young writers in recent years have succeeded in pushing through the mossy tangles of anonymity. Daniil Gink (*Bald/Brunet*, 1991), Alexei Burykin (*Nijinsky*, 1993), Yelena Gremina (*Behind the Mirror*, 1994) and Oleg Antonov (*The Death-Defying Act*, 1994) had major hits. But it hasn't been enough to get conservative directors to take chances on other unknowns with any frequency. After the acclaimed 1995 premiere of Nadezhda Ptushkina's *By the Light of Others' Candles*, nearly half a dozen theaters announced productions of her plays for this season. Not one came about.

Vladimir Sorokin, the author of experimental plays, has had his *Dismorphomania*, a psycho-ward *Hamlet* parody, staged at the Alexei Levinsky Studio, while the émigré writer Mikhail Volokhov has had two plays staged independently. But, as with Sorokin's play, the actual performances of Volokhov's *Dead Man's Bluff* (a grisly, gay-oriented play set in a morgue) and *The Great Comforter* (a treatment of AIDS and homosexuality in an émigré menage-a-trois) can be counted on two hands.

A small army of writers, by all outward appearances, simply don't exist. Mikhail Ugarov, Ksenia Dragunskaya, Vladimir Malyagin, Olga Mikhailova, Alexander Zheleztsov and Alexander Seplyarsky, to name a few, have been staged throughout Russia, translated, published and performed abroad, and won awards. With rare exception, they are ignored in the Russian capital.

Simultaneous to the premiere of *Tanya-Tanya*, some playwrights with a sense of history and humor initiated the so-called Treplev Lectures. The idea of Yelena Gremina, this informal exercise was named after the failed, suicidal playwright in Chekhov's masterpiece, *The Seagull.*

The point was to "celebrate" the first production of *The Seagull* bombing 100 years ago. It was both an act of revenge against a writer whose plays have a lock on the city's stages, and an expression of confidence: If a play everybody once thought was so bad turned out to be so good, then there must be reason to hope for the writers of today.

(June 1996)

Boris Yukhananov

Boris Yukhananov is nothing if not a fount of ideas.

Yes, he is an avant-garde theater director, an experimental video filmmaker and one of the most influential and colorful figures in Russian underground performance art of the last ten years. But even a short talk with this pensive artist with a mesmerizing voice leaves no doubt: There probably aren't enough genres and different kinds of art to satisfy his hunger for dreaming up, playing with and realizing ideas.

Maybe that is why Yukhananov once almost seriously proposed carrying out a series of "theatrical terrorist acts," wherein his actors would burst into performances at other theaters and play out their own scenes before making quick exits.

It may also be why he was so intrigued when two years ago a psychologist friend suggested he try working with some people with Down syndrome. He jumped at the chance, and the result has been a series of new ventures at his Studio of Individual Directing.

In addition to adding the Down syndrome actors to his unorthodox seven-hour, two-day production of *Orchard*, an interpretation of Anton Chekhov's *The Cherry Orchard*, he has initiated a project called *Down People, or the Hunt for Golden Birds*. It involves a theatrical production called *Craig*, based on dialogues written by the turn-of-the-century English director Gordon Craig, and a video film called *Down People Comment on the World.*

Yukhananov has been "amazed" by his Down syndrome actors. "Their internal personality is developed much more highly than ours," he says, "and they fantasize much more quickly than we do. I teach them nothing. I simply try to enter into contact with them, keeping their gestures, live reactions and improvisations."

All of it is just one more facet of what Yukhananov calls his "research" of directing, an art form which he points out is still very young, having come into being only in the 20th century.

"I study directing and its possibilities," he says. "I'm interested in the concept of it, what it entails before it breaks up into the directing of a video, a film or a piece of theater. You can't put your finger on what the director does."

Yukhananov, 39, began his career ten years ago with an undertaking whose wit, imagination and scope set the tone for everything that has come since. With a few like-minded colleagues, he created what he calls the "first underground theater in the Soviet Union" or the "first wave of post-Soviet underground." He named it the Theater Theater.

"We did that at a time when everything was doubling," he says, referring to the forces that were about to begin breaking every-

thing from state structures to prominent Moscow theaters in two.

But merely reflecting social trends in his art was not enough. He also wanted, by his own admission, to do nothing less than "remove" the competitive, occasionally even hostile relationship that has existed between Moscow and Leningrad/St. Petersburg for nearly 250 years. The idea was to set up a two-city theater that, through development and interaction, would bring the two capitals closer together.

The Theater Theater appropriately debuted on April 1, 1986, with a street performance of Molière's *The Misanthrope* on the Arbat. It later continued its progression in Leningrad in an imaginative show called *Mon Repos*. Starring the Leningrad actor Nikita Mikhailovsky, whose apartment was Yukhananov's Leningrad base, it was performed in and around an abandoned building. According to legend, the great Russian philosopher Pyotr Chaadayev was held there in the 1830s by the tsarist police and forcibly "treated" for "insanity."

"The spectators," explains Yukhananov, "gathered on the street and were led by a silent guide past outdoor scenes. Then they would enter the building and the guide would turn on his flashlight, illuminating various other scenes for them."

Ultimately, they would reach a tower on the top floor with two windows. From the obstructed view of one window, it seemed to them that Mikhailovsky, who would soon die of leukemia, leaped off a roof to his death reciting the poetry of Joseph Brodsky. When the observers were led to the other window, they could see him on the street waving goodbye. At that point, the guide would turn off his flashlight and leave them to find their own way out.

"That's when the real horror theater started," says Yukhananov with a good-natured laugh.

All ended on a conciliatory note as the confused spectators were treated to drinks and snacks when they finally reached the street.

Mon Repos, like *The Misanthrope*, was only played a handful of times and failed in its task to erase the latent

Moscow–Leningrad animosities. But for Yukhananov, the most important thing is the concept, the idea, the attempt.

That does not mean that he is a mere dreamer. While his name remains best known only in elite circles, he has avoided the fate of many artists from his generation who made an early splash and then either disappeared or got stuck in a rut.

"This is not amateurism," Yukhananov says firmly about his work at the Studio of Individual Directing. "We had to rethink the method of actively existing in the contemporary world."

He rejected the idea of emigration ("which only leads to stagnation") and scorned the notion of dissidence ("which everybody could see exhausted itself in the 1970s").

"I saw in 1989 that I had to come up with another approach," he says. "I wanted to survive."

The Studio—based in, supported by, but independent of Anatoly Vasilyev's famous School of Dramatic Art—is involved in a multitude of activities, from the Good Films Agency, which shows experimental video films at the Cinema Museum, to ambitious theatrical undertakings, such as the work with Down syndrome actors.

Yukhananov has twice taken his troupe to England, most recently in September to the prestigious Edinburgh Festival, and he is on the verge of striking a deal to make an hour-long film of *Orchard* for German television.

Orchard remains the keystone of all the Studio's endeavors, which in one way or another, are aimed at creating or at least discovering modern myths and mythological systems. Having gone through five incarnations since it was first created in 1990, Yukhananov purposefully keeps it changing to keep it alive.

"If it doesn't change," he says, "it will die."

(July 1996)

Sergei Artsibashev

Sergei Artsibashev thinks his directing career may actually have begun taking shape in his native village in the far north of the Sverdlovsk oblast when he was thirteen years old.

He was a soccer fanatic and his dream was to put together a local powerhouse that would take him all the way to the finals of the Leather Ball Tournament in Moscow. With that in mind, he organized a whole league of eight teams in "a town with only eight streets."

"I had all the thugs in town playing for me. I'd just go up to them and say, 'you're playing on this team,' and they'd quietly come along."

"The adults were jealous," Artsibashev adds with sparks of pride still flashing through a grin these 32 years later. "My field was just like in the Olympics and they all wanted to come play on it."

But even if Artsibashev's team never quite made it to Moscow, he had already proved one thing: He was a great organizer. "And what is directing if not a matter of organization?" he asks. "A director gets lots of people to bend their will in the service of a single idea."

As Artsibashev has repeatedly shown, that is something he does well. So well, in fact, he was awarded a State Prize in June for achievements in staging the Russian classics. His productions of Anton Chekhov (*Three Sisters*), Ivan Turgenev (*A Month in the Country*), Alexander Ostrovsky (*Talents and Admirers*) and Nikolai Gogol (*The Inspector General* and *The Marriage*) had already brought him international acclaim. Now they have won him Russia's highest cultural prize and given him the recognition that is often hardest won at home.

"It doesn't mean a whole lot for me personally," Artsibashev says of the prize, "I've still got to go out and prove myself again with every new production. But it is a nice thing for my theater."

His theater, the Theater na Pokrovke, will observe its fifth birthday at about the same time that Artsibashev celebrates his own 45th this September. In that half-decade, the director has gone from the proverbial "future talent" to one of the top names in Moscow's middle generation of directors.

It may be a contradiction in terms, but the Theater na Pokrovke and its artistic director have had a quiet, almost uneventful rise to stardom. He doesn't throw splashy, publicity-laden premieres. Like the reserved, often elusive productions he creates, the soft-spoken, close-cropped man is far more apt to be subtle in conversation than sensational. While most of his shows have traveled all over Europe, getting information about when they play in Moscow has not always been easy. Artsibashev himself handles the scheduling, and sometimes he just doesn't make up his mind until the last minute.

The near-anonymity which surrounded the Theater na Pokrovke until recently had other sources too. For almost four years, despite its name, it wasn't even located on Pokrovka Street, but was tucked away on the second floor of an obscure building behind a muddy courtyard on Olkhovskaya Street, a typical backstreet if ever there was one.

The reason was simple: The construction of the small, but elegant theater which finally opened in the spring of 1995 on the corner of Pokrovka and the Garden Ring took more time and money than had been planned for. But the State Prize looks like it might be the sign that the rough road is ending.

Artsibashev began his life in the professional theater at the top, taking a roller coaster ride down before heading back up again. In 1980 he joined the world-renowned Taganka Theater as a staff director under Yury Lyubimov.

"I got there at the peak, when Vladimir Vysotsky was still there," says Artsibashev of the popular actor and songwriter who died at the age of 42 in 1980. "And then I was there for the most tragic period, the departure of Lyubimov and the stagnation that followed."

Speaking of the Taganka's split into two warring factions in 1992, Artsibashev says "that was just the echo" of what transpired there in the '80s.

In 1989, as Lyubimov was returning from the West, Artsibashev struck out on his own, taking over a little troupe called the Moscow Theater of Comedy. But it wasn't long be-

fore he realized he was after something else and, taking about a third of the actors from that company, he regrouped and founded the Theater na Pokrovke.

Although Artsibashev "had never staged a single classic play" before, the credo of his new theater right from the start was to dig into the riches of the past. Was it, as it has been for many directors in the post-Soviet period, a calculated escape from contemporary life?

"Absolutely not," Artsibashev responds quickly. "It's just that I had become so saturated reading the works of the Golden Age for so long, I couldn't wait to get at them. Those writers have a breadth, a scope to them, while modern writers have a more narrow view."

In fact, during the first years at the Theater na Pokrovke, Artsibashev also ran a playwriting laboratory designed to develop young writers. Of the twelve plays he worked on over two years, he says "about four decent shows came of it."

"But then I realized that the writers didn't need it," he continues. "They just wanted the result and praise. I wanted them to work with actors and learn the process."

He hasn't rejected contemporary drama entirely, as is witnessed by his staging of Maria Arbatova's *A Trial Interview on the Theme of Freedom* last fall. But more to the point was his far more successful interpretation of Gogol's *The Marriage*, which opened in April and showed off beautifully his special brand of tenderness and understatement which invariably gives 19th-century writers a new, unexpected sheen.

And now that he has gotten his own theater on a firm setting, Artsibashev has tackled a new challenge, accepting Yevgeny Kolobov's invitation to stage the Tchaikovsky/Pushkin opera, *Eugene Onegin*, for the Novaya Opera Theater. According to the schedule, it should open in October.

As rehearsals progress this summer, Artsibashev admits to feeling a little like a fish out of water working with opera singers. But it doesn't bother him.

"They know the laws of singing," he says, "but I know the laws of human nature.

Whenever they tell me they can't do something, I just say, 'Yes you can. Do it'."

(*July 1996*)

Olga Mukhina

People keep telling Olga Mukhina that her plays can't be staged. Some say she doesn't even write plays at all, although they don't seem able to define exactly what it is that she writes.

Who would have guessed it judging by her play, *Tanya-Tanya*? It created a minor sensation when it opened in February at the Fomenko Studio, signaling the appearance of a major new playwriting talent. Since then there have been productions in St. Petersburg and Chelyabinsk, and there is talk of a possible Paris production. *Tanya-Tanya* has already been translated into French, and the Fomenko Studio version has toured to festivals in Poland and Germany.

Not bad for a playwright so many can't seem to figure out.

But over the last few years, Mukhina, 26, has worked out her own response to the skeptics.

"My second play, *Alexander August*, is my favorite," she says. "It's a very pretty play about the countryside which I can't seem to get around to finishing. When I showed it around, nobody liked it. But finally I found one person who did and I decided to believe that opinion. Now, if somebody likes what I write, I listen to them. If they don't, I don't pay any attention."

Mukhina originally wanted to write for the movies. But her experiences there anticipated the reactions she soon would be getting as a playwright. Four years in a row, she took the entrance exams at the cinema institute, and four years in a row she failed with flying colors.

"They didn't understand what I was up to," she says about the test compositions she wrote in hopes of being admitted to the institute's screenwriting division.

While trying to get into the cinema institute, Mukhina whiled away her time working as a courier, then as a secretary for various scientific journals.

Finally, she changed gears, thanks in part perhaps, to the influence of her mother Tanya, a geologist who has been an avid theater fan all her life, and who lent her name to her daughter's most successful play.

"Suddenly, I just wrote a dialogue between a 'he' and a 'she,' and it was very easy," Mukhina says of her first dramatic work which she titled *The Sorrowful Dances of Ksaveria Kalutsky*. She submitted it to Yuliu Edlis, a well-known playwright of the Soviet period who teaches at the Gorky Literary Institute. He was impressed and admitted Mukhina to his course.

But if Edlis liked that first play, his reactions to his student's subsequent works have been more equivocal. "He thinks my other plays aren't plays," says Mukhina with a shrug of her shoulders and a little laugh.

Tanya-Tanya, Mukhina's fourth play, second to be published and first to be staged, is a strangely wonderful, densely atmospheric piece that observes the emotional entanglements of three men and three women one soft summer. A highly poetic work in spirit, in structure it betrays the author's early attraction to film.

The action jumps around freely from episode to episode, and there is no linear plot development from any traditional beginning to any conventional end. As in a Chekhov play, everyone is hopelessly in love with someone, while as in a Fellini movie, the very air seems to be under a magic spell. Champagne flows, kisses are stolen left and right, hopes and desires are excited, and at least a couple of characters are said to "fly away."

That is just one of the stage directions which appears to have earned Mukhina her dubious reputation as an unstageable playwright. Elsewhere in *Tanya-Tanya* she writes: "Maybe they kiss. Maybe something else seems to happen. Maybe everything comes out just the opposite maybe."

As if that wasn't enough to drive traditionalists mad, Mukhina has another unorthodox "habit." She sprinkles her texts with pictures and considers them as important as the words.

"I see the pictures as I write," she says. "Maybe I'll run across something at someone's house, or maybe I'll see something in a magazine. I'm always so happy when I find something, because they have a big effect on me."

They also caused her grief when the journal *Contemporary Dramaturgy* prepared her third play, *The Love of Karlovna*, for publication in 1994. The editors cut out all her pictures and "cleaned up" her peculiar use of punctuation and capital letters.

"They fought me over every letter and comma," she says. "I corrected the proofs, but when it came out they had ignored all my corrections. I was very upset and they told me I have a terrible character."

Nowadays when she hears that someone has been reading that published version, she winces and hurriedly offers to supply a "good copy, with pictures."

She was luckier with *Tanya-Tanya*, which attracted a huge amount of attention when it was first read publicly in the summer of 1995 at the annual playwriting seminar in the Moscow suburb of Lyubimovka. The play was quickly picked up by the more progressive journal, *Playwright*, where the editors were so attentive to Mukhina's style that they even inadvertently introduced some confusion about her name.

A close friend had prepared the typescript on his computer—with pictures, missing periods and occasional sentences in all caps—for submission to the journal. Without thinking, he wrote the name "Olya Mukhina" on the title page, using the diminutive form of "Olga." The editors conscientiously printed exactly what the author submitted, thus making for the childlike form of her name that is published over the play.

Mukhina says she hasn't been overwhelmed with attention since the premiere of *Tanya-Tanya*, but she still is having trouble getting to work on her newest idea, which has a tentative title of *YoU*. As an editor and scriptwriter for the popular television musical program, *At Ksyusha's*, almost all her time is spent on the set or in the studio, editing footage, writing texts or coordinating shoots.

"I need a month to write a play," she says. "It's a kind of meditation process." So she is

taking August off and is heading for the peace and quiet of the country. If all goes well, she should have a new play written especially for the Fomenko Studio when the new season opens in the fall.

(July 1996)

Armen Dzhigarkhanyan

It has been a year to remember for Armen Dzhigarkhanyan. Even for an actor who has seen plenty in an illustrious career that began way back in 1955 at the Russian Drama Theater in Yerevan.

Over the last 18 months, Dzhigarkhanyan quit the All-Russian State Institute of Cinema, where he had taught acting for years; took a "sabbatical" that is increasingly looking like a permanent escape route from the Mayakovsky Theater, his professional home for 26 years; and founded a new theater called the Theater D.

If anything, those moves have only made one of Russia's busiest—and best—actors busier still.

Even in these days of minimal cinematic output in Russia, Dzhigarkhanyan, 60, continues to land a staggering number of roles in films, usually shooting several simultaneously. Right now, for good measure, he is also squeezing in a 26-episode t.v. series called *The Kings of the Russian Private Eyes.*

In theater, his one-man show of Samuel Beckett's *Krapp's Last Tape* at the Contemporary Play School was one of the top events of the 1995–96 season.

Dzhigarkhanyan was stunning in the uncompromising role of the crusty, uncouth old man at death's door. With his remarkably expressive face that looks as if it were cut from a mountain crag, and his rumbling, edgy voice that could stop Alexander Lebed in his tracks, he was ideal for the character that spends his time making tapes of caustic, unguarded thoughts and listening back to them.

That doesn't mean his performance pleased everyone, of course. One woman shortly after the spring premiere stood up in the middle of the show and, as she marched out, shouted at anyone who cared to listen, "Shame on this actor! Shame on this theater!"

Dzhigarkhanyan, a fearless performer of intense psychological precision, says those are the moments when an actor is tested, "when you find out if you really know that person you are playing."

The show is taxing, but obviously rewarding for him. "I get tired," he says in his no-nonsense, but almost gallantly polite manner. "I sweat, and I come to the show experiencing anxiety, but I feel comfortable in it."

But of all the projects he has going right now, Dzhigarkhanyan's "passion" is looking after the young actors of the Theater D. What made such a busy man take on the immense task of creating a new theater?

There is lurking in the answer to that question a shadowy scandal and a lesson in loyalty and responsibility. Dzhigarkhanyan touches on the subject with tact, saying only that "there were some tough minutes at the cinema institute, so I wanted to stick by my kids."

What happened was that the actor fell from favor as a teacher with the administration at VGIK, the State Institute of Cinema. They reportedly called him in to ax him, and—as the story now circulates—he walked out without a word before they could do it.

He told his students to finish their education and he wouldn't abandon them. Theater D was the result.

You get inklings of the source for the conflict at VGIK when Dzhigarkhanyan talks about teaching acting. They seemed to think the actor was too busy with other things; he thought they didn't have what it takes to recognize and cultivate talent.

"There used to be a program," he says of the institute, "now it's just a conveyer belt that promotes mediocrity."

As if responding to an unvoiced question, he continues, "Of course I'm busy. Any master, if he is a real master, is busy. But what you need in creative work is the right atmosphere, a climate in which kids become actors, not just learn how and where to stand."

He compares a good teacher to a good director who "creates an aura, a magnetic field in which you stop knowing yourself."

When Dzhigarkhanyan's class graduated without him in the summer of 1995, he says "nobody was there to help them" and he didn't want them to get lost in what he calls the "cruel world of the theater and cinema."

"It's a jungle, really," he adds.

Dzhigarkhanyan should know. After working 11 years in Yerevan, he was brought to the Lenin Komsomol Theater in Moscow in 1966 by Anatoly Efros, one of the great directors of the 1960s and '70s. But just six months later, Efros was removed as one "unfit" to run a theater bearing Lenin's name, and the playhouse (which later became known as the Lenkom) entered a decline.

In 1969, Dzhigarkhanyan accepted Andrei Goncharov's invitation to join the Mayakovsky Theater. There he became a star playing the leads in such popular and critically acclaimed productions as Tennessee Williams' *A Streetcar Named Desire* (1970), Mikhail Bulgakov's *Flight* (1978), and Edvard Radzinsky's *Conversations with Socrates* (1975) and *Theater in the Time of Nero and Seneca* (1985).

But there were also often gaps of several years between new roles at the Mayakovsky, the late 1980s and early '90s being especially skimpy. You can't help but wonder whether that didn't influence Dzhigarkhanyan's decision to found a new theater. For now, all he will say about his leave of absence is, "I still have not quit the Mayakovsky. Doctors say that after age 60 you should make no abrupt movements."

Dzhigarkhanyan has taken an unhurried approach in forming the Theater D.

He spent most of the 1995–96 season running bureaucratic gauntlets to get the troupe a place to call home. They will eventually take over the old Litva movie theater near Moscow University, although for the next year or two while that location is being rebuilt, they will rent a small, 120-seat hall near the Novodevichy Monastery.[15]

---

[15] In a real estate dispute common in the 1990s the Theater D lost the Litva movie theater to a business concern. The former Progress movie theater was later given to Dzhigarkhanyan by city authorities.

To keep pressure off his former students, Dzhigarkhanyan had his staff director Valery Sarkisov bring along several of the shows he had staged in the past for his own Sarkisov Theater Group. Theater D actually debuted quietly this spring with those productions featuring veteran actors from various Moscow theaters.

Meanwhile the ex-students rehearsed portions of Alexander Pushkin's *Little Tragedies* under Sarkisov, with Dzhigarkhanyan himself taking the role of Salieri in *Mozart and Salieri*. If things go as planned, the show will open in September or October.

Dzhigarkhanyan is looking like the man who could be everything: a loyal teacher, an artist at the peak of his powers, and, not least of all, someone just plain having fun. Not a bad place to be for an actor in his fifth decade of working in the "jungle."

(August 1996)

INDEX